DECEIVING HITLER

DOUBLE CROSS AND DECEPTION IN WORLD WAR II

OSPREY
PUBLISHING

DEDICATION

For my father

DECEIVING HITLER

DOUBLE CROSS AND DECEPTION IN WORLD WAR II

TERRY CROWDY

First published in Great Britain in 2008 by Osprey Publishing,
Midland House, West Way, Botley, Oxford OX2 0PH, United Kingdom.

443 Park Avenue South, New York, NY 10016, USA.

Email: info@ospreypublishing.com

Many of the photos in this book come from the Imperial War Museum's huge collections, which cover
all aspects of conflict involving Britain and the Commonwealth since the start of the twentieth century.
These rich resources are available online to search, browse and buy at www.iwmcollections.org.uk.
In addition to Collections Online, you can visit the Visitor Rooms where you can explore over 8 million
photographs, thousands of hours of moving images, the largest sound archive of its kind in the world,
thousands of diaries and letters written by people in wartime, and a huge reference library. To make
an appointment, call (020) 7416 5320, or email mail@iwm.org.uk.

A CIP catalogue record for this book is available from the British Library.

ISBN-13: 978 1 84603 135 9

Page layout and cover design by Myriam Bell Design, France

Index by Alison Worthington

Maps by The Peter Bull Art Studio

Typeset in Perpetua

Originated by PDQ Digital Media Imaging, UK

Printed in China through Bookbuilders

08 09 10 11 12   10 9 8 7 6 5 4 3 2 1

For a catalogue of all books published by Osprey please contact:

NORTH AMERICA

Osprey Direct, c/o Random House Distribution Center
400 Hahn Road, Westminster, MD 21157, USA

E-mail: info@ospreydirect.com

ALL OTHER REGIONS

Osprey Direct UK, P.O. Box 140, Wellingborough, Northants, NN8 2FA, UK

E-mail: info@ospreydirect.co.uk

www.ospreypublishing.com

Front cover: Vauxhall Heritage Archive

Back cover: National Archives

Small Images: National Archives and Imperial War Museum (see photo section for further details)

CONTENTS

ACKNOWLEDGEMENTS

I would like to thank the staff at the National Archives, Kew; the Imperial War Museum, London; the British Library, London; and a special mention for Caroline Herbert at the Churchill Archives Centre, Churchill College, Cambridge. Many thanks for the helpful advice of Richard Stokes, Felix Sefton Delmer, Nigel West, and the late Lieutenant Colonel T. A. Robertson and his family for kindly supplying his photograph. At Osprey I would like to thank Anita Baker, Ruth Sheppard and Venetia Bridges for helping me to realize this project. Last, but by no means least, none of this would have been possible without the kind consideration and eternal patience of my wife, Sarah.

PREFACE

The deceiver by stratagem leaves it to the person himself whom he is deceiving to commit the errors of understanding which at last, flowing into one result, suddenly change the nature of things in his eyes.[1] (von Clausewitz)

WRITING OVER 400 YEARS BEFORE Caesar attempted to invade the British Isles, the legendary ancient Chinese general Sun Tzu pronounced, 'All warfare is based on deception.' Aside from the days of chivalry, when rival heralds would agree a fixed time and place for battle to commence, or when officers invited their opponents to fire first, commanders have often resorted to ruses and devious stratagems to mislead and stupefy their opponents.

During World War II the military deception practised by the Western Allies was so sophisticated it is unlikely to be repeated on the same scale again. Principally a British creation, at the crucial part of the war, when the Allies began the liberation of France, entire German divisions were held back from the fighting or delayed in their arrival because Hitler and his generals had been duped into deploying them elsewhere.

To summarize, the cornerstone of this success was security. In the 1940s Britain was an island with a watchful and vigilant public on high alert. It was not an environment conducive to German spies. Worse still, from the German point of view, the Germans' chief spy in Britain at the beginning of the war was also working for the British. Through information provided by this agent British code-breakers were able to break the German secret service's codes, which allowed them to be forewarned when new spies were despatched.

Where the British were incredibly smart – or perhaps devious would be a better word – was in the way that they used the captured agents. Despite a general clamouring to have captured spies executed, wherever possible the spies were kept active and given controlled information to pass back to their masters. This practice was also employed by the British security services in the Middle East with equal success. Before long, there grew a need for organizations that could vet the information passed back by the spies. This was to ensure that nothing operationally vital was accidentally leaked, and to ensure a consistent approach to German intelligence questionnaires.

This led to the establishment of a system of global deception, ensuring the coordination of misinformation provided to the German intelligence services. From Kabul to Lisbon, and Nairobi to Reykjavik, the German intelligence stations were fed a picture entirely of the Allies' making, all of which was digested, sent to Berlin and placed before Hitler and his staff. As Nazi High Command pondered and deliberated, the progress of these bogus reports was monitored at the British code-breaking establishment at Bletchley Park. By reading the German intelligence services' secret traffic, the deception planners were able to tweak the performances of their best channels. It allowed them to play on the fears of the German High Command, or to endorse the delusions Hitler most wanted to believe.

Of course, there were a number of means by which to deceive the enemy other than through double agents. The first and most obvious was by physical means – by the use of camouflage to hide what could be seen, or to make it appear to be something else. This included the creation of dummy installations, vehicles and even ships, which might confuse enemy reconnaissance. There was also the possibility of deceiving one's opponent by emitting false signals traffic, which the enemy 'Y Service' (radio intercept service) would intercept. In much the same way that the ancients would count the campfires of an enemy army, by World War II one could count the number of radios on the air, and, by the urgency of their operation and movement, forecast intentions without necessarily being able to understand the language used. Thus we find dedicated teams of radio operators driving round deserts and the fields of south-east England, reproducing the noise and chatter of colossal phantom armies, which double agents had already led the Nazi hierarchy to believe existed.

The third means of deceiving the enemy was the use of psychological warfare, through what came to be known as 'Black propaganda'. The British conducted a masterly campaign, planting rumours and gossip among the German soldiery and command and even setting up radio stations and newspapers purporting to be the work of the Germans themselves. These factors combined to form a symphony of lies, delivered and orchestrated by the highest and most secret branches of the Allied command structure, ones that few people knew of and even fewer appreciated or understood.

True enough, no one doubts that the liberation of Europe was a result of the fighting men at the sharp end of the conflict. Deception was by no means a guarantor of success, and many cover plans failed to work, went unnoticed, or were completely ignored by the German military and High Command. In many cases, Allied commanders were distrustful of their purpose and suspicious of the practitioners, seeing them as diverting resources away from the real task at hand. However, even in those cases where deception plans gave no tangible benefit, neither did they do any harm.

It is no coincidence that for the Western Allies the biggest turning points in the war against Hitler – El Alamein, the *Torch* landings in North Africa, the invasions of Sicily and Normandy – were all backed by elaborate and well-executed cover plans, which were promoted by the double agents. This is not to say that these operations would have failed without them, but victory would almost certainly have come at a much higher price: perhaps even too high a price.

On a personal note, I was introduced to this subject by my father, who did important work during the 1980s in helping to document Kent's World War II invasion and anti-aircraft defences. Although principally interested in ack-ack, my father came across an interesting story about how a decoy for Chatham naval base was built on the marshes near the Isle of Sheppey. A man who had worked at the site during the war explained that at night they would use lighting effects to simulate doors opening and closing, and other breaches of the blackout instructions. The Germans would see these pinpricks of light and deduce they were over their target. Once the bombs started to rain down, the operator would ignite large tanks of oil and other flammable material. Water would be sprayed onto the fires to create large plumes of steam, and give German pilots the impression that firemen were trying to extinguish the blaze. Adding to my fascination with this ruse, my father then told me about a double agent called *Garbo* who tricked the Germans into thinking the D-Day invasion was due to arrive at Calais rather than Normandy. After several years of research I know that this story was just the tip of the iceberg. I have remained fascinated by this subject ever since, and hope this work will help introduce others to the world of double cross and deception during World War II.

Much of the secret material relating to this subject has now been declassified by the British Security Service, but it must be remembered that this was not a story that the authorities wanted told. Not realizing that Soviet spies like Kim Philby had long since betrayed the secret of Britain's wartime deceptive apparatuses, the story of double cross, deception and code-breaking remained a closely guarded secret after the war. The memoirs of Churchill, Eisenhower and Montgomery all allude to certain stratagems employed to hoodwink the Nazis, but with conflict against the Soviets a real possibility, they did not want to reveal their most secretive tricks of the trade.

Until the dam began to burst in the 1970s, only a handful of deception operations trickled into the public consciousness. One of the most well-known operations was told in the film *The Man Who Never Was* (1956) based on the book by Ewen Montagu, one of the real planners behind Operation *Mincemeat*, the planting of bogus information on a corpse left adrift off Spain. Another ruse, albeit told with great artistic licence, led to the making of *I Was Monty's Double* (1958), a film starring M. E. Clifton James, who reprised his real wartime role for the cameras. The first inkling that double agents might have been used came with *The Eddie Chapman Story* (1953). The actual spy involved, Eddie Chapman, came out with his own version of events – *The Real Eddie Chapman Story* (1966) – which found its way onto movie screens as *Triple Cross* in the same year.

The sense that something big was waiting to come out was increased by the arrival of *The Counterfeit Spy* (1971), by journalist and ex-Black propagandist Denis Sefton Delmer. This ostensibly introduced the world to the career of the double agent *Garbo*, whom Delmer gave the codename *Cato*. In 1972 the former MI5 officer and Oxford don J. C. Masterman circumvented officialdom by releasing his book *The Double-Cross System* in America. This account was originally written as an official report at the end of the war. In it Masterman detailed the extent to which the British 'Twenty Committee' controlled Nazi espionage and double crossed their controllers. The report also made mention of one of the Twenty Committee's biggest 'customers', the London Controlling Section, the organization responsible for global deception policy.

In 1974 the Yugoslav Dusko Popov released his highly readable memoirs, *Spy/Counterspy*. Although certain names were changed, and certain situations somewhat enhanced to fit Popov's billing as 'the real James Bond', they fleshed out Masterman's story. However, many of Masterman's former colleagues saw his publication as a betrayal of trust and they retained their silence. The most partisan champion of 'the deceivers' was David Mure, a former member of the A Force deception organization in the Middle East. Mure was scathing of Masterman and highly prejudiced against what he called the 'private armies' of the security services and others. Despite this bias, which with the hindsight of several decades does appear unfortunate, Mure's book *Master of Deception* (1980) is useful. Partly based on the unpublished memoirs of Dudley Clarke, the commander of A Force, it contains a foreword by Noël Wild, Clarke's one time deputy and also head of deception on Eisenhower's staff at the time of the Normandy invasions. Mure's work is complemented by the excellent work *Trojan Horses* by Martin Young and

Robbie Stamp. This contained numerous important accounts given by those actively involved in deception, including David Strangeways, the implementer of the D-Day deceptions.

Over the course of a decade, more and more information came to light about the secret war – much unearthed by the trailblazing author Nigel West and, more officially, through the publication of Professor Hinsley's multi-volume official history, *British Intelligence in the Second World War* (1979–90). The fourth volume of this work is particularly useful and is complemented by Michael Howard's volume *Strategic Deception in the Second World War*, publication of which was much delayed by the Thatcher government. More recently, since the turn of the millennium, interest in deception and the double cross system has continued to grow. The most important publication in this period came from Thaddeus Holt in *The Deceivers* (2004). This weighty tome sets out, really for the first time, the American angle on deception, and is absolutely essential from that point of view.

In terms of information on double agents, we have benefited from the declassification of a number of Security Service documents, in particular the Guy Liddell diaries. Although occasionally 'weeded' for information still considered too sensitive for our knowledge, the minutes from Twenty Committee meetings and the dossiers of individual double agents are also available. Many of these have been consulted for this work and give a great level of detail and wonderful colour to the agents' stories.

Following the release of this information, it is time to revisit the story of the double agents and their controllers in detail and to show how, through the formation of the Twenty Committee in 1941, the British double cross system expanded, was copied in other theatres, and ultimately became the most profitable means by which Allied deception planners could sell their lies to German Intelligence. Without the availability of double agents like *Garbo*, *Tricycle*, *Tate* and *Brutus*, it is unlikely the deceivers would have attained anything like as much success as they did. In return, without dedicated organizations providing the double agents with material to feed back to their controllers, none of the named cases would have survived very long without their duplicity being discovered. For that reason, the value of the double agents must be reasserted and their activities set in the proper context.

Although the arts of deception and double cross were practised by other nations during the war, the aim of this book in covering the origins of the double cross, the deception agencies and how they developed from deterring the German invasion of England to protecting the Allies' eventual return to the Continent, means that there is a focus on activities in Britain and by the British during the war. In keeping with the informal atmosphere of the wartime secret services, names, once introduced, are given informally without accompanying rank. Also in keeping with the style of the day, the terms MI6 or SIS refer to the British Secret Intelligence Service and are used interchangeably throughout for colour and accuracy.

PROLOGUE

ON 24 SEPTEMBER 1942 A top-level secret meeting took place in London. Among those present were the Directors of Intelligence of the British Army, Royal Navy and Royal Air Force. The guardian of the Enigma secret and head of the British Secret Intelligence Service (SIS) was also present, along with the head of the Security Service's B Division, who was responsible for counter-espionage in the United Kingdom. Sitting before them was an immaculately dressed colonel in his mid-forties. Known simply as the Controlling Officer, Johnny Bevan had been charged with masterminding a global deception policy with the aim of hoodwinking the Axis into wasting their resources and manpower by whatever means came his way. Like his predecessor in the post, the Controlling Officer had some inkling that the secret services had some special means of feeding information to the German intelligence service, the Abwehr.

However, where his predecessor had been kept in the dark about the true nature of this 'special means', Bevan was about to be told. Like the breaking of the Enigma code, it was one of the greatest secrets of the war. As he listened, first to the head of the SIS and then to Guy Liddell, the head of B Division, it became clear that the Allies had a major advantage over the Germans in this war. In addition to being able to read the secret codes of the Abwehr and other enemy organizations, the Security Service, MI5, firmly believed it controlled the only active German spy rings then operating in the United Kingdom. If Bevan wanted to dupe the German intelligence services, there was a pool of well-established double agents on hand to carry out his bidding.

How this had come about, and why Germany's spies were now working for the British, was quite a story. As Bevan quietly took this information in, Liddell explained to him how everything had begun with an agent he called *Snow*.

1

SNOW

ACCORDING TO HIS security file, Arthur George Owens was a shifty-looking, short, bony-faced, Welshman.[1] Born in 1899, Owens had emigrated from the United Kingdom and become a naturalized Canadian, only to return to Britain in 1933. On paper he lived in Hampstead with a wife and son, but in truth Owens was a bit of a rolling stone, with a taste for Scotch and a string of infidelities to his name. By trade he was part electrical engineer, part travelling salesman. Always on the move, often left short of cash by his vices, Owens' descent into the world of espionage was both predictable and necessary.

On returning to the United Kingdom from Canada Owens obtained a post with a company that had contracts with the Admiralty. Through business he travelled to Belgium, Holland, and occasionally Germany. After these trips abroad, Owens would often pass technical information back to the Admiralty. In 1936 Owens decided to profit from this arrangement and asked for payment in return for future reports. With the authorities in agreement, Owens was passed from his usual contacts in the Naval Intelligence Division (NID) to Britain's Secret Intelligence Service (MI6) and given the codename *Snow*.[2]

It was not a happy union.

When Owens was introduced to his case officer, Lieutenant Colonel Edward Peal, something in their chemistry collided. In his dealings with Peal, Owens developed a very real hatred of the English and came to think of himself as a Welsh Nationalist. In revenge for centuries of abuse against his homeland, Owens determined to pull one over the old foe and, towards the end of 1936, he developed ambitions of becoming a German spy.

Considering his contacts, Owens thought he would be highly attractive to the German secret service. In addition to his work for the Admiralty, he made regular trips to restricted RAF stations and had friends – also Welsh Nationalists – working in secure locations such as the Short Brothers works at Rochester in Kent.

On the pretext of picking up German girlfriends for weekend flings, he started attending a social club for German ex-patriots on Cleveland Terrace, Bayswater.[3] The club was managed by Peter Brunner, who was the London representative of Captain Hans Dierks, an Abwehr officer stationed in Hamburg. Owens befriended Brunner, telling him about his trips to Hamburg and Cologne and his love of the country, and, of course, the local *Mädchen* (local women). The only regret the Welshman expressed was that he often spent his evenings abroad sitting in dreary hotel rooms companionless and bored out of his skull. To alleviate this, he asked Brunner if he could put him in touch with some friends of his to keep him company when working abroad.

Brunner took the hint, and before long told Owens that he knew an engineer called Konrad Pieper who would be eager to meet him next time he travelled to Brussels. Convinced that Pieper would turn out to be an Abwehr recruiter, Owens checked into the Metropole Hotel in the Belgian capital. He met Pieper and was rather cryptically informed that he might like to go to Hamburg and contact his firm, A.G. Hellermann, and to speak with a certain Herr Müller about making a business deal.

In the world of espionage using such double speak was standard fare. Everyone stuck to elaborate cover stories, because they never knew who was listening or if they were being set up as the victim in a 'sting'. What if Owens was a 'plant' by the British secret service? What if there had been a terrible misunderstanding by Brunner and all Owens wanted was a drinking buddy after all?

Owens travelled to Hamburg and met with Müller, in fact an alias of Brunner's controller, Hans Dierks. Owens volunteered his services and, despite some misgivings that the Welshman was too good to be true and might well be a British secret service plant, Dierks accepted him into his nest. At first Dierks kept Owens at arm's length, never meeting him on his home turf of Hamburg, but always abroad. However, after socializing with Owens, Dierks came to respect the Welshman's seemingly absolute hatred of the English race – a hatred born of rivalries that people not of the British Isles might find surprisingly intense.

The one problem Dierks had with Owens was his information on naval matters – the Abwehr man's primary concern – was not up to scratch. Owens was far more useful as a source on the RAF, so Dierks passed his case over to a colleague in the summer of 1937.

The new contact introduced himself as Dr Rantzau, the managing director of the import-export Reinhold & Company. He was in fact Captain Nikolaus Ritter, Leiter of I.Luft, Hamburg, that is to say Chief of Air Intelligence in the Abwehr's Section I (espionage department). Ritter was in his early forties and had learned his English in a ten-year stint in New York where he had worked in the textile industry. When a slump had put an end to his business, Ritter was scooped up by the Abwehr and – despite an almost complete lack of technical training – was put in charge of air intelligence matters relating to Britain and America.[4]

The 'Doctor' took Owens out for dinner at the luxurious Vier Jahreszeiten Hotel and then went onto the Münchener Kindl for a drink. It was here that Ritter made his approach to Owens, offering him cash in return for intelligence. Pleading that he was short of cash for various 'domestic' reasons, Owens accepted the German offer and was thereafter codenamed *Johnny*.[5]

All the while Owens had been ingratiating himself with the Abwehr, he continued to meet his MI6 case officer. Either from intuition, or from a reciprocal dislike of the Welshman, Peal became suspicious of Owens and asked Scotland Yard's 'Special Branch' to monitor him. Intercepting the Welshman's mail, in September 1936 Special Branch came across an innocuous letter to 'Dr Rantzau' asking for a meeting in Cologne. What attracted the censor's attention was the address given for this Rantzau – PO Box 629 in Hamburg's Central Post Office. This was a known Abwehr pick up address.[6]

When Owens next went abroad, Peal had him tailed by British agents. They followed him and gained proof that he was meeting with the Abwehr. In turn, it appears Owens must have noticed the tail, or had a well-developed sixth sense for sniffing out trouble. On his return to the United Kingdom he was scheduled to be brought in for questioning, but before this could happen, Owens went to Peal and confessed to being in contact with the German secret service. This was quite an admission, but Owens was ever so slightly economical with the truth.

He told Peal that he had approached a German engineer named Pieper from whom he had been buying secrets. Unfortunately the material provided was not of sufficient quality to be of much use to him, so Owens soon found himself unable to pay Pieper's expenses. When he told the German of this, Pieper invited Owens to make money by working for the Abwehr. Owens had wrestled with his conscience, but ultimately decided to go along with Pieper in order to best serve the British secret service.

Of course, Peal – rightly – did not believe any of this, and told Owens he was going to turn him over to be prosecuted. Bold as brass, Owens defied Peal to do this, threatening to expose his contacts with the British secret service in his trial. To avert publicity, Peal allowed Owens to escape with a formal caution and continued to allow him to come and go as he pleased. Behind the scenes, the MI6 man ensured that all the Welshman's mail was intercepted.

Owens went back to Hamburg and met with Ritter without revealing his brush with the authorities. Ritter began organizing training sessions for Owens on his visits, including a course on using wireless transmitters. Other than that, Ritter treated Owens to nights out in Hamburg's infamous red light district – the Reeperbahn.

Here Owens explored his fascination with the seedier side of German life under Hitler. His favourite nightspot was the Valhalla Klub. In the club every table had a telephone. If you liked the look of someone on another table you simply called them up and invited them over for a drink. It wasn't long before Owens had a particular favourite among the girls who frequented the club, to whom he frequently poured out his heart and soul over his favourite tipple.

In the background, the Abwehr was watching Owens like a hawk. To prevent there being any risk to security, after one of Owens' visits the pretty blonde was arrested by Abwehr officers and told to leave town in a hurry. She was replaced by the blonde-haired 'Ingrid' – a trusted Abwehr agent. When Owens next went to the club, Ingrid was sitting on the next table and telephoned the Welshman. Owens replied and from that point on Ingrid became his regular Hamburg girlfriend.[7]

Meanwhile, Owens continued to report to MI6 and somewhat boastingly revealed that he had been appointed the top German agent in England and had been promised a radio transmitter by the Germans.[8] In the build-up to war he claimed to have raised a network of 15 sub-agents or informers. Although the British thought this list was purely notional, it is clear that Owens was somehow getting information from at least 35 different sources.

At the Abwehr's request he also tried to contact the British Union of Fascists (BUF), planning to bring four secret transmitters into the country to transmit Black propaganda in the event of war. This idea soon died a death after the members he contacted made it quite clear that although they might be sympathetic to a fascist government's policies, they would never betray their own country in wartime.

In January 1939 the Abwehr stepped up its preparations for the coming war. Owens had been receiving radio training in Ritter's Hamburg apartment and although *Johnny* was not much of a radio operator – spending most of his time singing Welsh folk songs for the amusement of his operators – towards the end of the month, Ritter sent a wireless transmitter in a diplomatic pouch to the German embassy in London. The transmitter was concealed inside a harmless-looking suitcase and deposited at the cloakroom in London's Victoria train station. The receipt for this piece of left luggage was posted to Owens.

On 7 February, the Welshman retrieved the radio and took it to Special Branch for them to look over. They in turn gave it to MI6, who dismantled it and then could not work out how to put the thing back together again. Farcically, MI5 had to be called in and their specialists had a go. The MI5 men did manage to fix the set and then handed it back to Owens who, puzzled at why the British had not wanted to hang on to the set themselves, went and hid it at the Kingston home of his mistress, Lily Funnell.

Over the coming months Europe began to slide towards the abyss of war. Having given up the Sudetenland to Germany in October 1938, Czechoslovakia ceased to exist when Hitler ordered the occupation of Bohemia and Moravia in March 1939. That same month Hitler denounced an earlier non-aggression pact between Germany and Poland. Reading the writing on the wall, Britain and France – shamed out of appeasement by the fall of Czechoslovakia – pledged their support for Poland if it was attacked.

August 1939 would be the last month of peace in Europe for almost six years. As the Germans secretly negotiated to keep the Soviet Union out of the war, they also drew up their plans to attack Poland. Knowing that Britain had threatened to intervene and that war between the two countries might soon be upon them, Owens was called to Hamburg on 11 August for one last meeting – or '*treff*', as meetings between agents and their German case officers were known.

Earlier in 1939 Owens had left his wife and moved in with Lily Funnell. According to Owens' German paymaster, Ritter, 'Lily was blonde like *Johnny*'s wife, but that was the only thing they had in common. While his wife was small, calm and affected, Lily was large and robust, a whole head taller and a number of years younger than *Johnny*, merry, intelligent and with a great deal of natural sex appeal. *Johnny* was obviously in love with her.'[9] On this last peacetime meeting, Owens took Lily and a friend of his, Alexander Myner, whom he thought had potential as an Abwehr recruit. On 18 August, while the party was away, Owens' long-suffering wife called in at Scotland Yard and reported that her husband had tried to recruit their son and various friends as German spies. This let the cat out of the bag with the authorities, and would have been the end of the case had Owens been apprehended on his return to England. Fortunately, as it turned out, when Owens returned on 23 August the port authorities missed him and he was not detained.

On the same day that Owens returned to the United Kingdom, the Molotov–Ribbentrop Pact was signed in Moscow between Nazi Germany and the Soviet Union. This non-aggression pact, with a secret clause to partition Poland, paved the way for Hitler to attack. On 1 September the German Army broke through the borders into Poland and on 3 September British Prime Minister Neville Chamberlain announced that Britain had declared war on Germany. Thus began the second great European war of the 20th century.

XX

With the outbreak of war all German and Austrian nationals in the United Kingdom were required to report to their nearest police station. In September 1939 there were 71,600 enemy aliens registered and in addition to this number MI5 had identified almost 400 other suspects it wanted to intern at the commencement of hostilities. To sift the good from the bad, the suspects were processed by special one-man tribunals and put into three categories: A, B and C. Those marked Category A were to be detained immediately; B were subject to certain travel restrictions and were not allowed to travel more than short distances without a permit; while the majority of individuals were labelled category 'C' and were left at liberty.[10]

In 1914 such a measure had crippled the German espionage ring in Britain. On the first day of the war – in fact at dawn on the day Britain declared war – a fledgling MI5 had arrested every German spy in Britain, leaving the Kaiser's armies blind and allowing the British Expeditionary Force (BEF) to cross the English Channel unnoticed. However, in 1939 the dragnet failed to deliver the same results and a handful of spies were left at large.

Principal among these was Arthur Owens. Having arrived back in the United Kingdom, Owens had begun radio transmissions to Germany in the early hours of 28 August. Owens was still puzzled as to why the authorities had given him his transmitter back. Had they done so hoping he would incriminate himself by using it? When sending out his initial messages, Owens was curious to see if he was intercepted. He wasn't – but he did not know that. He believed the authorities were just setting a trap for him – giving him enough rope to hang himself with.

Therefore, again hedging his bets, on 4 September Owens telephoned his contact at Special Branch, Detective Inspector Gagen, and asked for a meeting at Waterloo train station. At their rendezvous the inspector served a detention order on Owens under Emergency Regulation 18(b) and took him into custody.[11] From his cell in Wandsworth Prison, Owens asked to see his MI6 case officer, Edward Peal, and also a MI5 officer who had followed his case over the years, Thomas Argyll Robertson.

Known by colleagues informally as Tommy, or more commonly 'TAR' after his initials, Robertson had joined MI5 in 1933. A graduate of Sandhurst, his recruitment was perhaps typical of the service: he was friendly with the son of the head of MI5, Vernon Kell. In 1939 Robertson was head of a sub-section of MI5's B Division, the branch responsible for counter-espionage. His own sub-section, B1, was concerned chiefly with German espionage.

By all accounts Robertson was a very personable fellow, non-judgemental with a natural ability to read people and situations. He was extremely handsome and was most often seen in a military uniform, by preference in the tartan trousers worn by the Seaforth Highlanders – the regiment he had served in before joining the Security Service.[12] One often told story that perhaps best demonstrates his manner is how, a few years before the war, he got a communist mole, John King, drunk at the Bunch of Grapes pub in the Brompton Road, Knightsbridge. When the suspected communist passed out from drink, Robertson took the keys to his safe from him, broke into his office and seized a number of incriminating papers.[13]

In contrast to his relationship with Peal, Owens appeared to get on quite well with Robertson, and so the Welshman offered him a deal. In return for his liberty, Owens would reveal the location of his hidden transmitter, thus enabling the British to use it to broadcast misinformation to the Abwehr. Robertson agreed and Owens revealed that his radio was hidden in the home of his mistress in Kingston.

Owens' motivation at this stage is worth considering for a moment. Was he, as MI5 believed, a double agent, playing for both sides but mainly siding with the British, or was Owens in fact a triple agent? By this we mean he was primarily a German agent, but one who had gone to the British and convinced them he was working for them (thus a double agent), but who had done so only in order to carry on working for the Germans under the very nose of MI5. It may have even been the case that he was not working to any grand scheme, but was an opportunist who would shift allegiances as and where necessary in order to secure his liberty and his next pay day. This last hypothesis may be closest to the truth.[14] But regardless of the reasons behind it, the transmitter was brought to Owens' cell in Wandsworth and set up for broadcast to Germany. For MI5 it was to prove a pivotal moment in the course of World War II.[15]

XX

Before describing the first message broadcast to the Germans, one should be aware of a certain fact concerning Morse code. To the trained ear, as Morse code is transmitted, the style in which it is tapped out can be as distinctive as a person's handwriting. It would be certain that whoever taught Owens how to use the radio set would also be able to identify Owens' hand as it tapped out the message. The British were aware of this, but they did not want Owens sending the messages himself. They instead recruited a prison warder who mimicked Owens' Morse style.[16]

From his cell in Wandsworth Owens dictated the following cryptic message to be broadcast to Germany:

MUST MEET IN HOLLAND AT ONCE. BRING WEATHER CODE. RADIO TOWN AND HOTEL WALES READY.

When Robertson asked for an explanation of this cryptic message, Owens told him that his primary mission was to transmit meteorological information vital for the use of the German Air Force and Navy. Now that war had been declared, he needed a shortened version of the code, which would allow him to spend less time on air and reduce the risk of his transmissions being picked up by British listening devices. Owens had also been asked to recruit sub-agents from the Welsh Nationalist Party. Owens needed to travel to Europe in order to meet Ritter and obtain funds and further instructions. Robertson accepted this explanation, and when Ritter replied, suggesting Brussels as the venue of their next meeting, the MI5 officer allowed Owens to go free.

On 15 September 1939 the Welshman crossed the Channel to Rotterdam and went on to Antwerp, where he met Dr Ritter in an Abwehr safe house. At the meeting Owens told Ritter that he had recruited a promising Welshman named Gwilym Williams, a former Swansea police inspector and an ardent Welsh Nationalist. Ritter appeared keen and asked *Johnny* to bring Williams over to the Continent on 21 October for industrial sabotage training.

At this meeting in Antwerp, Owens introduced Williams to Ritter along with someone called the 'Commander' and Major Brasser of Air Intelligence. The real identity of the 'Commander' was Kapitänleutnant Witzke, head of the Hamburg Abwehr's Section II – sabotage department. He took Williams under his wing and interviewed him.

At 6ft 2in (1.88m), Williams was an imposing figure. He explained that he was an activist in the Welsh National movement who had retired from the police force that January. He had served in the artillery during World

War I and claimed to be an explosives expert. He was also – remarkably for a man who was illiterate when he left school – a keen linguist, proficient in 17 languages or dialects. He told the Commander he was ready for action as soon as they could smuggle in equipment to him. The Commander indicated that this should not be a problem, as Belgian smugglers would be employed for the mission. Williams was gladly accepted into the fold and assigned the serial number A.3551. As a mark of his importance to Ritter he was given his own separate cover address in Brussels through which he could contact his controllers.[17]

In the excitement of his recruitment, Williams had omitted to mention one important fact. Through his gift for languages, he had also worked as a court interpreter and had come into contact with MI5. Working for the British Security Service under the codename *GW*, the former policeman was in fact a British spy!

Matters were to get worse for the Germans. Having decided that Williams was going to be used as a saboteur, they planned to use Owens as a messenger to their existing contacts in the United Kingdom. This was exactly what MI5's Tommy Robertson had hoped they would do.

Ritter also gave Owens £470 in banknotes and four detonators concealed in a block of wood.[18] His instructions were to bank the money and await instructions about recruiting more agents. He was also offered £50,000 if he could find someone who would pilot one of the RAF's latest aircraft back to Germany – clearly an attempt to obtain the Supermarine Spitfire fighter, which had come into service in 1938.

Owens was also asked to get in touch with another agent still operating in the Liverpool area called Eschborn, codenamed A.3527. He was given a message to pass on to Eschborn from Captain Dierks, which was contained in some microphotographs hidden behind a postage stamp on a letter.

Owens was also instructed about receiving payments. At the railway station on the way to Antwerp a man introduced himself to Owens as Ritter's secretary and was joined by a woman. No names were given. The couple told *Snow* he was going to be paid by a woman who lived near Bournemouth. The woman would either hand him the cash or put it through his letter-box. She might meet him in the street in Kingston and would probably be wearing a fur.

Sure enough, when Owens returned to England, Robertson revealed that two envelopes, each containing £20, had arrived for him. Although Robertson suspected that these had been posted by a foreign diplomat resident in London, without any scruple Owens told Robertson all about the female agent U.3529 in Bournemouth.

Searches were made in the sorting offices of Bournemouth and Southampton for envelopes similar to the ones addressed to Owens, but the German agent appeared to cover her tracks well, using post boxes in a variety of locations.

In the end it was the last batch of four £5 notes that led MI5 to the German paymaster. Tommy Robertson, his assistant Richmond Stopford, Owens and his mistress Lily – who had also been served a detention order – sat down together and looked at the banknotes. On the back of the notes was written 'S&Co', which Lily Funnell deduced meant the Selfridges department store on Oxford Street. In 1939 a £5 note was a significant amount of money and so Stopford went to the store to see if any of the cashiers could remember handling the notes.[19]

As luck would have it, one of the cashiers at Selfridges could clearly remember that an elderly foreign lady had come into the store and asked to exchange five single £1 notes for a £5 note. Not only had the lady made this unusual request, she had placed an order at the store and the cashier remembered making a note of her name and address. The tip was followed up and by the end of November it led them to a woman living in Bournemouth named Mrs Mathilde Krafft. She had avoided being picked up because she had married an Englishman and had become a naturalized British citizen in 1924. When Krafft went visiting a steamship company, MI5 had two girls from Selfridges identify her as the lady that had changed the £5 notes.[20]

At first the authorities did not arrest her, but put her under surveillance in order that she might lead them to other spies. In due course her intercepted mail revealed that she was corresponding with an Editha Dargle in Copenhagen, a city known to be used by the Abwehr as a forward base. MI5 called in MI6 and asked them to investigate Dargle. Unfortunately MI6 went to the Danish police, who bungled the operation by confronting Dargle directly about Krafft. Dargle denied everything, and sent a letter to Krafft warning her not to use this address again.[21] With no further use for her, Krafft, alias *Claudius*, was interned at Holloway Prison. She was not released until 1944.[22]

In addition to selling out Krafft, Owens handed Robertson the microphotographs intended for Abwehr agent Eschborn. When developed, they revealed a miniaturized questionnaire of intelligence queries, which Eschborn was meant to complete. Tommy Robertson decided to send Owens to meet Agent A.3527 as ordered, telling him not to mention anything about his work for MI5 and to see what happened. Owens made contact with the man and then passed his address on to MI5.

After Owens' visit, Robertson paid the German spy a call. Eschborn turned out to be one of three brothers recruited by the Abwehr in Cologne the previous year (1938). Eschborn was a Manchester businessman of German–English parentage but entirely sympathetic to the British cause. Suspecting this, the Germans coerced him and one of his younger brothers into working for them by threatening reprisals against the third brother who remained in Germany. What made him so valuable to the Abwehr was his expertise in microphotography. It was hoped that he could photograph and reduce the reports of other agents working in Britain to help get them back to Germany undetected.[23]

Interestingly enough, following a different enquiry into German activity, Eschborn had already been brought in for questioning by MI5 at the beginning of the war. However, despite having virtually confessed that he was a spy, he had been left at large.[24] This time Robertson enrolled Eschborn as a very willing double agent, dubbing him *Charlie*. Robertson decided not to tell *Charlie* about the *Snow* case, hoping that he and Owens would each check up on one another's bonafides. *Charlie*'s brother, Agent 3528, was also at large in the United Kingdom. When he was brought in for questioning he turned out to be far less trustworthy. He was classified Category A and detained for the duration.

It is important to note that Owens' cooperative spirit towards MI5 at this stage did not mark something of a turnaround in his loyalties. Owens was coldly trading information to MI5 solely to keep his liberty. If other German spies were captured – well, too bad for them. Owens was making a tidy profit out of his illicit trade and nothing could be allowed to get in the way of that.

Not only had Owens sold out the Abwehr's three last remaining independent spies in the United Kingdom, he was to cause untold damage to the Abwehr's cypher security. While Owens was gallivanting off on his missions, he had been given a code by the Germans. This was passed to the trusty prison warder operating his wireless set, who began to get a feel for the hand of the German radio operator in Hamburg. The warder then began to distinguish between the operator dealing with Owens and those dealing with other communications. From the clues provided by the operation of Owens' radio set the British intercept organization, the Radio Security Service (RSS) based at Hanslope Park near Bletchley was able to make a number of important breakthroughs in the whereabouts of German spies and the codes they were using. The chief among these was traffic between the Abwehr's Hamburg station and a ship called the *Theseus* in the North Sea.

ABWEHR STATIONS AND AREAS OF INFLUENCE

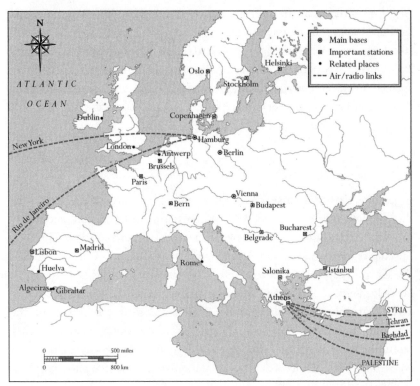

Posing as the Swedish ship *Hese*, the Nazi vessel was working off the Norwegian coast, transmitting weather reports and making contact with agents in Holland, Belgium, Luxembourg and France. In April 1940, there was also traffic detected between it and a transmitter somewhere in Eire.[25]

The Abwehr relied on two principal types of codes. Agents in the field like Owens enciphered their own messages by hand; however, messages from Hamburg relayed to Abwehr HQ at 76/78 Tirpitzufer, Berlin, were enciphered by machine – this was the so-called Enigma traffic.

The codes provided by the Abwehr for Owens' use were passed to the Government Code and Cypher School (GC&CS) at Bletchley Park. There they were attacked by a group under veteran code breaker Oliver Strachley until the first decrypts were issued on 14 April 1940. From that point on, any German spy working in the United Kingdom was liable to be intercepted by RSS and have their messages read by Strachley's group. The intelligence derived from this source – known as ISOS (Intelligence Section, Oliver Strachley) – could then be passed to the Security Service to help track down the spy.

Later, a separate group under Bletchley's Dillwyn Knox attacked the Abwehr's Enigma traffic between the various Abwehr outstations and Berlin. On several occasions Knox's group – which was codenamed ISK (Intelligence Service Knox) – was able to follow a message sent to Hamburg and then on to Berlin. By comparing the original message sent to Hamburg against the one arriving in Berlin, ISK was helped in its quest to understand the operation of the German cipher machine, allowing the first ISK transcript to be released on Christmas Day 1941.[26]

XX

In January 1940 the Abwehr recruited a new agent in Britain – or at least they thought they did. In fact MI5 had beaten them to it again, and a new double agent was added to the books of the British Security Service. This time the culprit was Bernie Kiener. A student born in Britain to a German mother, Kiener had grown up in Germany then returned to England in 1938. There he lodged with a German, who was in Britain as the representative of a Hamburg chemical firm. Günter Schutz was in fact representing the Hamburg branch of the Abwehr, and was involved in what he called 'commercial intelligence' – in other words industrial espionage. During his weekend breaks, Schutz would go up and down the country photographing various industrial sites, often accompanied by Kiener.

A week before the war broke out Schutz mysteriously packed his bags and quit England for pastures new. Kiener heard nothing more from his former flatmate until January 1940 when he received a letter from Schutz, inviting him to the Continent where he had a little proposition for him. Suspecting that Schutz's proposal would involve recruiting him as a spy, Kiener went to the police and explained everything to them. The police put him in touch with MI5 who asked Kiener to go to Antwerp and see what Schutz actually wanted. Kiener agreed and found himself recruited into the Abwehr with orders to report on developments in aviation, air defence and air raid damage using high-quality secret ink. Further instructions would be sent to him in microphotographs hidden in the punctuation marks of official letters from a Belgian firm by which he was supposedly engaged.

Kiener returned to the United Kingdom and dutifully reported back to MI5. He was engaged by Tommy Robertson as a double agent and given the codename *Rainbow*. In April *Rainbow* was called back to the Continent again, and this time was given new emergency cover addresses in Switzerland and

Yugoslavia. Clearly something was about to happen that would rule Antwerp out of the equation as a safe meeting point for spies.[27]

The advice given to *Rainbow* confirmed similar warnings given to *Snow*. In February of that year the Welshman had been warned not to be on the Continent in April. MI5 took this to mean that something was going to happen that would affect Holland and Belgium's neutrality – as these were Owens' cover addresses on the Continent. In order to force the Germans' hand, MI5 instructed Owens to insist on meeting Ritter in Brussels on 6 April.

The meeting took place as agreed and removed any doubt that something big was about to occur. At the meeting Ritter asked Owens to procure for him another recruit to be trained in sabotage. There was, however, one small problem. Ritter hinted at a coming offensive and said that there would be no more *treffs* in Holland or Belgium. Owens suggested neutral Lisbon, but Ritter had other ideas. He suggested that the ever-resourceful Owens should get his hands on a boat and make arrangements to meet him in future out on the North Sea.

Owens returned to London and passed on the news. Robertson authorized the sea meeting to go ahead and managed to procure the trawler *Barbados* from the Fisheries Board. The sabotage recruit was another stooge out of MI5's stable. Codenamed *Biscuit*, Sam McCarthy was a conman with a long history of drug smuggling and petty larceny. He had worked for MI5 for some time as an informant and was viewed by the Security Service as being quite honest in his dealings with them. *Biscuit* was introduced to Owens in such a way that the Welshman had no idea he was an MI5 plant – something that led to an almighty mess.[28]

On 19 May 1940 the trawler left Grimsby and headed out for the agreed rendezvous point just south of the Dogger Bank fishing area of the North Sea. What occurred onboard the ship is still uncertain, but according to *Biscuit* Owens got drunk and told him he really was a German spy and had been fooling the British all the time. *Biscuit* also got the impression that Owens knew he was a plant by MI5 and that made him panic.

On the evening of 21 May, two days before the rendezvous with Ritter was to take place, a German seaplane circled the trawler and flashed the agreed recognition signal. *Biscuit* saw this and was mortified. How on earth could the aircraft be two days ahead of schedule unless Owens had double crossed MI5?

In his mind the rules had changed. If Owens knew he was a British agent, he might hand him over to the Nazis to increase his own standing with them. Faced with the potential of torture and execution, *Biscuit* made an executive decision. He locked a hung-over Owens in his cabin and ordered the skipper of the boat to douse the lights and head back to Grimsby.

In the debriefing that followed, Owens had some very fast talking to do. He claimed that he had no idea that *Biscuit* was a plant and that he believed him to be a genuine German spy. Therefore he had played along with this idea, telling *Biscuit* that he was a real German spy too in order to protect himself. *Biscuit* on the other hand was entirely convinced that Owens was a German spy.

Had *Snow* triple-crossed MI5?

This option became increasingly likely as Owens was found in possession of certain documents that had not been given to him by his case officer. This really did call for some explaining by the Welshman. Again, Owens said he had procured some extra information on the side in order to convince *Biscuit* he was a genuine spy.[29]

With the case seemingly blown, a submarine was sent out to the rendezvous point on 23 May. If Ritter appeared in a submarine, the British crew were to sink it; if a trawler appeared, they were to board it and try and capture Ritter. Unfortunately it was foggy and no one showed up.[30]

In order to try and salvage something out of this mess, and to keep the radio channel to Hamburg alive, MI5 decided to give Owens the benefit of the doubt. The Welshman told Ritter that he had been at the agreed meeting point, but there had been too much fog – that at least was true. This was accepted by Ritter, who suggested meeting in Lisbon.

MI5 decided to send *Biscuit* alone to Lisbon to meet Ritter. Clearly they did not think the *Snow–Biscuit* double-act was ever going to work again. Arriving in the Portuguese capital posing as a wine importer, *Biscuit* gave a much changed account of the trawler fiasco, defending Owens, whom the Germans accused of being inefficient, and blaming the heavy fog for the failure. The Germans swallowed the story and got on with indoctrinating *Biscuit* into the ways of a spy. He was given an intelligence questionnaire, a radio set and $3,000 in cash. In return, *Biscuit* handed over his identity card and a traveller ration book. These had been doctored by MI5 to include a certain flaw which would be noticeable to the eye of a trained policeman, should the Germans use *Biscuit*'s documents as a specimen for other spies. According to MI5's Joan Miller, the flaw was that ID cards were folded by hand but through these doctored documents the Germans were led to believe they were machine-folded.[31] The Germans jumped at the bait, copied the flaw and thus sealed the fate of many of their future spies.

In the meantime Owens had to restore trust with Robertson and explain where he had got hold of the unauthorized documents he was intending to give to Ritter. Again Owens dropped others in the soup in order to protect himself.

The information had been provided by a London restaurateur named William Rolph, a former MI5 officer during World War I. Owens had secretly recruited Rolph before his last *treff* with Ritter. Robertson and Stopford interviewed Rolph, who admitted his treachery but pleaded that he would cooperate fully. Robertson was not sure what to do about Rolph. If he arrested the spy and the Germans learned of this, they might think Owens was also blown. Alas, the question became academic when Rolph stuck his head inside the gas oven in his Dover Street flat. Rather than a verdict of suicide, which the Abwehr might find suspicious, MI5 had the coroner record that Rolph had died of a heart attack.[32]

Snow had just had another close call ... but he was beginning to run out of lives.

XX

Increasing the tension at that time, dramatic events had been occurring as a backdrop to the botched trawler mission. The so-called Phoney War finally came to an end when Germany invaded Denmark and Norway on 9 April 1940 – three days after Owens had last met Ritter in Brussels. On 10 May the British government collapsed after a no-confidence vote and Prime Minister Neville Chamberlain was replaced by Winston Churchill. Before Churchill had a chance to get his feet under the desk, that same day Germany invaded Luxembourg, Holland and Belgium. The German forces outflanked the Maginot Line and began a drive to the Channel coast, cutting the British Army off from the rest of France on 20 May – the day before *Biscuit* ordered the trawler to turn around.

On 24 May Hitler ordered his panzers to halt outside the port of Dunkirk and allowed the Luftwaffe the glory of annihilating the British and their allies. Quite why Hitler stayed his hand has often been the subject of speculation. Some have pointed out that his panzers had driven so far and so quickly, they needed a breathing space to allow support troops to catch up with them. Perhaps it was the boasting of Luftwaffe head, Hermann Göring, who convinced Hitler to let his aircraft finish the British off. Others have said that Hitler deliberately held back so as not to humiliate the British, with whom he hoped to negotiate a peace settlement once Europe was his.

Regardless of the reason, the pause allowed more than 330,000 British, French and Allied troops to be rescued.

This small success in the face of so much gloom lifted spirits in the United Kingdom temporarily. Churchill had to remind the country on 4 June that 'wars are not won by evacuations'. After Dunkirk the German offensive pressed on to Paris, which was occupied on 14 June. The rest of France fell 11 days later on 25 June – it was humiliated and dismembered by the victorious Nazi leader.

The loss of France marked perhaps the lowest point in the war for British morale. American journalist Mollie Panter-Downes reported the reaction to the news in the *New Yorker* describing London as 'quiet as a village'.[33]

Better informed than most on the developing crisis was Guy Liddell, of MI5's B Division. On the evening of 22 May he dictated a diary entry to his secretary Margot Huggins that the news was 'so bad it made me feel physically sick'. In the period between the opening of the German offensive and the fall of France his diary entries – once one of the most closely guarded secrets in the MI5 archive – reveal that MI5 was in utter confusion and turmoil. With thousands of refugees landing in Britain from France and elsewhere, the internment of Italians after Mussolini belatedly declared war on 10 June, and the continued internment of British fascists and right-wing sympathizers, MI5 was swamped with work. Things were not made easier by suspected 'Fifth Column' activities being reported by thousands of jumpy citizens. Everything – suspected parachutists, mysterious messages chalked onto telegraph poles, strange shapes appearing in the countryside to guide German bombers – was reported, almost all of which proved unfounded on investigation.

The jitters quickly spread to the Cabinet, who perceived that Britain's secret services were in need of a big shake-up. On 10 June 1940 Churchill forced Sir Vernon Kell, the Director General and founder of MI5, into retirement. He was replaced nominally by the Head of B Division, Brigadier Jasper Harker, until Churchill appointed Sir David Petrie to the post in March 1941. In the meantime effective control of MI5 was given to the somewhat 'abrasive' former Cabinet minister Lord Swinton, the chairman of the Home Defence (Security) Executive. This had been formed primarily as a control measure against suspected 'Fifth Columnist' activity and was composed of representatives from the Home Office, the Commander-in-Chief Home Forces, MI5 and MI6.

In the shake-up Guy Liddell was promoted to head of B Division, becoming responsible for investigating espionage and counter-espionage and for running the double agents. Born in 1892, Liddell was a veteran of the Great War and winner of the Military Cross. At the end of the war he joined Special Branch and concentrated on anti-communist subversion. In 1931 he moved to MI5's B Branch under Harker, where he became the acknowledged expert in Soviet and Nazi subversion.

An intensely private man, he was described by one MI5 employee, Joan Miller, as being one of the 'grey men' about the office. Miller remembered that he only ever seemed interested in music and was an accomplished cellist, having studied the instrument in Germany. She wondered if his manner was an act to put people off guard. Liddell apparently once told MI6 officer Kim Philby, 'I was born in an Irish fog and sometimes I think I have never emerged from it.' Philby was not taken in by this nebulous nonsense. He recorded that Liddell had a 'deceptively ruminative manner' and that 'from behind the façade of laziness his subtle and reflective mind played over a storehouse of photographic memories'. Such views of course may have been clouded by the passage of time and events. However Liddell may have come across to others, it is certainly true that in his promotion he became one of the most important figures in the secret war against the Nazis.[34]

2

THE INVASION SPIES

FROM THE OUTBREAK OF EUROPEAN war in September 1939, when Germany attacked Poland, Hitler had gone on to conquer Denmark, Norway, Luxembourg, Holland and Belgium. On 25 June 1940 France surrendered, allowing itself to be partitioned, retaining only the southern portion of the country, which was governed by a puppet government. With the United States still maintaining its neutrality and the Soviet Union actively in league with Hitler over Poland, by July 1940 Britain stood truly alone with its empire against the bloated Nazi Reich.

The question on everyone's lips was, when would the invasion of Britain begin? If the British had transported over 300,000 men across the Channel at Dunkirk under attack from the Luftwaffe, what was to stop the Germans moving a similar number of men across under the eyes of the RAF? British troops had left all their equipment in France, and the fledgling Home Guard was preparing to contest the landing of German parachutists armed with little more than kitchen knives and hastily improvised spears ... or at least that was the common view of the situation around the world.

On 16 July Hitler had issued a directive to prepare for the invasion of the British Isles, which was to be codenamed *Seelöwe* (*Sealion*). On the evening of 19 July 1940, American CBS journalist William L. Shirer attended a session of the German Reichstag, during which Hitler gave a speech. In Shirer's opinion it was one of the Führer's finest – a dramatic final peace offer to the British people. It concluded:

> In this hour I feel it to be my duty before my own conscience to appeal once more to reason and common sense in Great Britain as much as elsewhere. I consider myself in a position to make this appeal since I am not the vanquished begging favours, but the victor speaking in the name of reason. *I can see no reason why this war must go on.*[1]

Shirer left the session and drove to the radio studio in Berlin from where he planned to report the speech in his broadcast back to the United States.

While he was driving to the studio, in London another journalist was preparing to make a broadcast, this time on the BBC German Service. Denis

Sefton Delmer was a journalist for the British *Daily Express* newspaper. Born to an Australian father in Berlin, Delmer had grown up in the German capital and had unique understanding of the German character and mentality. Working for the *Daily Express*, Delmer was the first British journalist to interview Hitler and was also acquainted with the likes of Göring, Goebbels and Himmler, having charted their rise to power through the 1930s.

As the war broke out, Delmer moved to Paris and then, as France began to fall, moved with the French government to Bordeaux. From there he managed to get on a liner bound for Britain. Looking for a job, the 36-year-old Delmer considered that he was too unfit for active service but might make himself useful in the secret service, in view of his background in Germany and his understanding of the German language and people. However, the very credentials that made him suitable for such a post led many to wonder if he was not a Nazi stooge himself and so the secret services kept their distance. Instead he was invited to work on the BBC's German broadcasts by Duff Cooper, the Minister of Information. His first broadcast was scheduled for the evening of Friday 19 July.

It thus became Delmer's first duty to respond to Hitler's triumphant Reichstag speech. This was a daunting prospect. Delmer had never spoken on the radio before, but he had a good idea how to put Hitler's nose out of joint – which was the agreed intention of the broadcast. Delmer sat before the microphone and, using his best deferential German, addressed the German nation:

> Herr Hitler, you have on occasion in the past consulted me as to the mood of the British public. So permit me to render your Excellency this little service once again tonight. Let me tell you what we here in Britain think of this appeal of yours to what you are pleased to call our reason and common sense. *Herr Führer* and *Reichskanzler*, we hurl it right back at you, right in your evil-smelling teeth ...[2]

In Berlin various Nazi officers and officials were listening to the BBC broadcast intently. When they heard what Delmer said, Shirer recorded how their expressions drooped and that they could not believe their ears. One of the Germans shouted at Shirer in disbelief 'To turn down peace now? They're crazy.'

Delmer's speech caused quite a stir in Britain too, especially among the pacifists. The Socialist MP for Ipswich, Richard Stokes, was outraged at Delmer's broadcast, asking how an answer to Hitler could be made so quickly and without consultation with the Prime Minister. To Delmer's rescue came the Minister of Information, Duff Cooper, who told Parliament that Delmer had the Cabinet's full backing. If he did, it was only with hindsight, for as Churchill noted in his history of World War II, the rejection of Hitler's offer was given by the BBC 'without any prompting from His Majesty's Government'.[3]

XX

The rejection of a peace offer was bad news for Hitler and his generals. By preference they would rather have done a deal with Britain in the summer of 1940 – one that would no doubt have allowed them, in the fullness of time, to take stock of their victories, re-arm and, above all, build a navy capable of matching Britain on the high seas.

In the back of their minds, those called upon to draw up the invasion plans knew that the United Kingdom's position in 1940 was perhaps not as perilous as at first it seemed. Certainly, if the Germans had been able to get across the Channel, land in large enough numbers and find a means of bringing over their tanks, they might have had a chance of establishing themselves. But Churchill was determined to contest every brick and blade of grass. On 14 July he made a radio broadcast designed as much for the ears of German planners as for his own population:

> Should the invader come to Britain, there will be no placid lying down of the people in submission before him, as we have seen, alas, in other countries. We shall defend every village, every town, and every city. The vast mass of London itself, fought street by street, could easily devour an entire hostile army; and we would rather see London laid in ruins and ashes than that it should be tamely and abjectly enslaved.[4]

Undoubtedly the biggest problem facing the Germans was the Channel. The fall of France had been so swift that there had not been the time or the foresight to consider how to mount an invasion across the English Channel. If one considers the planning and resources that went into the Allied cross-Channel invasion in 1944, it is evident that the Nazis in 1940 could not match that commitment of resources.

Although it is possible to see across the Channel to France on a clear day, this famous narrow stretch of water had protected Britain for nearly a thousand years. It is a violent passage. Momentary calm soon gives way to perilous storm as the waters of the Atlantic and North Sea vie with each other for possession of the narrow Strait of Dover.

The ensuing Battle of Britain is famous for its aerial combat, but it should not be forgotten that the British had a 10:1 advantage in ships – the German Navy having been roughly handled during the invasion of Norway. If the Germans thought they could protect their invasion barges by laying a protective screen of sea mines, they were to be disappointed – the British had far more mine-sweepers than the Germans had mine-layers. In any case, in the struggle of life and death that the invasion would provoke, the Royal Navy would simply have sent its ships through the minefields one behind the other. Even if they lost a few destroyers in the process, enough warships would break into the lanes left clear for the invasion barges, where they would have run amok. The barges the Germans were proposing to use were designed for plodding up and down the Rhine, not crossing the open water of the Channel. The Royal Navy would not even have needed to open fire – the wake from its passing ships would have been enough to flood the German vessels and send them to the bottom of the sea.

As for the threat from the Luftwaffe, a swerving warship moving at full speed would be a hard target to hit from the air, in particular if the German pilot was also trying to dodge an oncoming Spitfire. At Dunkirk, those ships hit by German bombs were stationary, picking up soldiers. A battle in the Channel would not present the same opportunities.

The British also had the advantage of the radar network and of the fact that the RAF would be working most closely to its own bases. In the battle for France, the RAF had suffered badly from having to fly fairly long distances to engage the Germans. In fact by knocking France out of the war, Germany had done the RAF a big favour: now it could concentrate on home defence.

Perhaps equally crucially, the intelligence war now swayed heavily in Britain's favour. Like Caesar 2,000 years before him, Hitler's men could see the British Isles from France, but had little idea what was going on there and what was preparing to meet them on the invasion beaches.

The rapid success of the German Army had also left the Abwehr with a problem. At the beginning of May their forward bases for operations against the United Kingdom had been in cities like Copenhagen, Antwerp and Brussels – all of which had been overrun by the Blitzkrieg. Now – and unexpectedly – the Abwehr's supremo Admiral Canaris was told to prepare the way for the invasion by forming a brand new network of spies in the British Isles no later than 15 September. That left less than two months to recruit, train and infiltrate agents across the Channel – agents without whom the invading army would be largely blind.[5]

Canaris put Ritter in charge of Operation *Lena* – what became known as the Abwehr Spy Offensive in Great Britain. Rather than providing the day-to-day intelligence being reported by the likes of *Snow*'s Welsh network, the *Lena* spies were to be trained as forward scouts for the invasion troops, locating potential invasion beaches and landing sites for parachutists and gliders. They were then to make contact with the invading forces and act as guides through the countryside.

Ritter set quite a narrow limit on the type of people suitable for this mission. They were to be aged between 20 and 30, in good physical health and possessed of some technical knowledge. The man chosen as talent scout for the mission was Dr Praetorius. Nicknamed the 'Pied Piper,' he trawled his net over the occupied territories looking for suitable candidates among hothead Nazi stooges and disaffected young men who could be blackmailed or otherwise cajoled into undertaking what would be a perilous mission.

The first team recruited consisted of four men: Karl Meier, a German by birth who had been raised in Holland and had been recruited through the Nazi Party earlier in 1940; Charles van den Kieboom, a Dutch YMC receptionist, and Kieboom's friend, Stoerd Pons, a former Dutch Army ambulance driver – both of whom were recruited after being threatened with being sent to a concentration camp for currency offences; and finally Jose Rudolf Waldberg, who had joined the Abwehr in 1937 and was a veteran of espionage missions against France.[6]

These four men were sent to Brussels where they were given a crash course in Morse, radio transmission, cryptology and techniques to help them recognize the various army units, vehicles, emplacements and aircraft they would encounter over the Channel. Of the four, only Meier received any in-depth training, with instruction on British Army structures and what sort of information might reveal the location of individual battalions and so on.

In late August the four men were taken to Boulogne on the Channel coast. On 2 September they were taken for lunch at a restaurant at Le Touquet and given their final instructions by Captain Jules Boeckel. They each had various missions. Waldberg was to report on the divisions and brigades on the south coast, on fortifications and on artillery emplacements, both coastal and anti-aircraft. The other three were given more general tasks, reporting on civilian morale and the RAF.

As they were loaded onto a trawler with their luggage, the four men must have had some sense of foreboding. Waldberg could not speak a word of English and Pons and Kieboom could only understand it when it was spoken very slowly. Only Meier was anywhere near proficient.[7]

As they chugged out of Boulogne harbour they were joined by two mine-sweepers that would act as an escort. Seven miles from the Kent coast the spies split into two groups. The first pair off the trawler was Waldberg and Meier, who climbed into a dinghy and began paddling their way toward Dungeness. After continuing north in the trawler for 20 minutes, Pons and Kieboom climbed onto another dinghy and set off for the coast.

Even before the first pair reached the shore they were in trouble. Waldberg and Meier noticed a British patrol boat coming uncomfortably close and so they dropped some of their belongings overboard – including their cipher wheels, papers and maps. When they reached the shore they scrambled over the pebbles and set their dinghy free to go out with the receding tide. Their food supplies were hidden in a disused lifeboat washed up after the Dunkirk evacuation and the radio transmitter was buried in the sand. The two agents then took a few hours' sleep against the wall of a nearby house.

When it was light enough the radio transmitter was retrieved and then hidden in a ditch covered with shrub. Meier decided he was thirsty, and, as he was the one who could speak English, he set off on the road to nearby Lydd and stopped at the first pub he came to. He saw a sign outside the pub advertising champagne cider, and, thinking this sounded very refreshing, went in and ordered himself one.

Genuine residents of England would have known that the selling of alcohol in pubs was restricted to certain hours – it was one of the most basic pieces of common knowledge about the country. So when Meier walked into the Rising Sun pub at 9.30am and ordered a drink, the landlady, Mabel Cole, was both surprised and suspicious. She politely told Meier that she was unable to serve him a drink and that he would have to come back later. Meier also asked for cigarettes, so Mrs Cole directed him to a store across the road. As the German spy turned to leave, he smacked his head on and broke the light fitting hanging from the typically low bar ceiling. As Meier wandered off in search of a smoke, Mrs Cole sent a warning message to her husband, who owned the butcher's just up the road.

When Meier returned to the pub he encountered an air raid warden who had arrived in his absence. Without thinking the warden's sudden appearance was in any way a cause for alarm, Meier decided to strike up a conversation. After making small talk for a while, Meier decided that his new friend would be a useful source of information and so began quizzing the warden about the number of British troops in the area. In return, the warden asked to see

Meier's ID card. He became flustered and admitted that he did not have such a document as he was a refugee. He then dropped his partner Waldberg in it too, when he told the warden: '*We* arrived last night.'[8]

Meier was taken to the local police station and handed over to Sergeant Tye. The police sergeant took Meier's particulars and spent the next three hours grilling him about his story. In the end Meier confessed he was a spy and told the police where they could find Waldberg.

In the meantime Waldberg had spent the whole day and evening waiting for his friend to return. At 8.30pm he decided to send out the first of two reports using an emergency code, rather stupidly – as it turned out – incriminating himself by signing off with his real name:

ARRIVED SAFELY DOCUMENT DESTROYED ENGLISH PATROL TWO HUNDRED METRES FROM COAST BEACH WITH BROWN NETS AND RAILWAY SLEEPERS AT A DISTANCE OF FIFTY METRES NO MINES FEW SOLDIERS UNFINISHED BLOCK HOUSE NEW ROAD WALDBERG

Then, as the manhunt for him was in full swing, he asked the Germans whether he should continue or not – telling them to send planes 3km north of his landing site:

MEIER PRISONER ENGLISH POLICE SEARCHING FOR ME AM CORNERED SITUATION DIFFICULT I CAN RESIST THIRST UNTIL SATURDAY IF I AM TO RESIST SEND AEROPLANES WEDNESDAY EVENING ELEVEN O'CLOCK THREE KM NORTH OF ARRIVAL LONG LIVE GERMANY WALDBERG.

Early on the morning of 4 September, Waldberg began to transcribe a third message in his notebook. It read:

THIS IS EXACT POSITION YESTERDAY EVENING SIX O'CLOCK THREE MESSERSCHMITT FIRED MACHINE GUNS IN MY DIRECTION THREE HUNDRED METRES SOUTH WATER RESERVOIR PAINTED RED MEIER PRISONER[9]

Before he had a chance to send the message, Waldberg was discovered and taken in for questioning along with his radio and the incriminating evidence in his notebook.

Meanwhile Pons and Kieboom had not fared much better. They had arrived a few miles up the coast, near to Dymchurch. They carried their belongings up onto the shore and were attempting to cross the coastal road and get into the fields beyond when a car with two British officers pulled up. Kieboom was spotted and challenged. As he was arrested a search of the area began, in which Pons too was challenged and arrested. Their wireless transmitter was also located and taken in as evidence. The pair were taken into custody along with Waldberg and Meier. Although Kieboom was able to flush his secret ink, codebooks and maps down the toilet, all four were doomed by two pieces of evidence: the first was Waldberg's notebook and the second was their UK ID passes. These passes had been forged by the Abwehr using information planted on them by MI5 using the *Snow* network.[10]

The four spies were reunited at Seabrooke police station and then sent on to MI5's secret new interrogation centre at Latchmere House, near Ham Common in West London. Codenamed Camp 020, this interrogation centre had been set up to house British subversives and dangerous enemy aliens who could not be classed as prisoners of war (POWs). The commandant of 020 was Lieutenant Colonel Robin Stephens. In his Ghurkha Rifles uniform, he came across as a fearsome-looking man, described as 'alarming' by one and by another as 'a monocled Prussian type ... who punctuated his questions by slapping his riding boots with a swagger stick'.[11] Although he may have shared many similarities with a stereotypical Teutonic officer, Stephens was no Gestapo thug. Although wildly xenophobic and with a particular loathing of the 'Hun' he was well travelled, had dabbled in journalism and fancied himself as a bit of an amateur psychologist. The commandant of Camp 020 had set a simple objective for his interrogation officers: 'Truth in the shortest possible time.'[12]

On arrival the prisoner was stripped naked, searched and then handed a flannel prison uniform. He or she was then escorted to a cell and left with no contact with anyone, before being taken out, given a preliminary interview to establish his or her particulars – name, nationality, address, physical characteristics, etc – and photographed. The first photograph would be a typical mug-shot in prison clothes; the second would show the prisoner in civilian clothing. The idea behind this was that the second photograph could be circulated without having to reveal that the subject was in custody.

As quickly as possible the suspect was interviewed. Stephens considered the first interview at 020 the most vital part of the breaking process. The idea was to create the atmosphere of a court martial – the man's life was at stake after all. The prisoner was marched in and left standing at attention throughout the process. Politeness was refrained from, while the luxuries of a chair and cigarettes were to be denied. Stephens encouraged his officers to be bitter and uncompromising towards the prisoners – male or female, there was no room for chivalry – but on no account should be a prisoner be assaulted. The prisoner was only to speak when spoken to, and had to answer the question posed and nothing else. The target was to get the prisoner to incriminate himself by making a written confession. Using that document as a base, the interrogators would probe for inconsistencies in the confession. When a new fact was established, a second statement would be taken and so on.[13]

When the four invasion spies arrived at 020 Stephens called his officers together to discuss tactics. Although the group was already partially broken, it was necessary to find out all its secrets – in particular information on Abwehr officers and any information that might reveal the German invasion plans. They decided to start their inquiry on the man perceived to be weakest among the group – Waldberg.

Persistent and detailed interrogation against Waldberg produced enough information to be used against his three comrades. Meier and Pons complained about the lack of preparation given to them by the Abwehr. Kieboom on the other hand put his hope in salvation by the imminent arrival of German soldiers on British shores – something all four men had been told would happen soon after their landing. Eventually Kieboom revealed that Waldberg was a pre-war Abwehr agent and that he was the ringleader of the group. As the questioning continued, it was revealed that Waldberg had another secret mission that had not been divulged to the other three. After landing he was to seize a motorboat and return to Boulogne to make his report and collect one of the instructors from Brussels, known to him as Werner. They were then both going to return to the Dungeness area and continue their mission together.

Instead they were now all locked up and faced with the death penalty. On 7 September Kieboom was instructed to send a radio message to Germany. He radioed that Pons had been shot and the rest of the party had gone into hiding.

XX

A day after the arrival of the four spies in Camp 020, they were joined by another suspect who had been captured on 6 September in Northamptonshire. This time the man had been parachuted in, which marked an alarming escalation in the Abwehr's attack on the British Isles. This would be the first of two parachutists to arrive that month, both of whom would have a significant role to play in the secret war between MI5 and the Abwehr.

Along with the four Brussels spies, Abwehr talent scout Dr Praetorius had recruited two Scandinavians who were both ardent supporters of the Nazi 'New Order': the Swede Gösta Caroli and the Dane Wulf Schmidt.[14] A mechanic by trade, Caroli was 27 years old and had a German mother. He had visited England several times before the war and had been a resident there as late as December 1939, working as a journalist. Schmidt, on the other hand, was from a part of Denmark that had been German until the end of World War I. His parents were both therefore German by birth and thence lay his loyalties to the Reich. He was a year younger than Caroli and very bright, having served briefly in the Danish Army before making trips abroad to Argentina and Cameroon. On his travels he had learned English quite well, which made him exactly the type of recruit Ritter was looking for.

Despite time constraints, the two men were given training far in advance of that provided to the Brussels team. The two men were told about the inherent risks of the trade they had volunteered for, and that once they were in England, they were on their own. They checked into Abwehr lodgings in Hamburg – a place known as the Klopstock, run by a Fräulein Friede. Here they were put through their paces by Captain Boeckel, taught Morse code, aircraft recognition and meteorology, and given demonstrations in recognizing the size of anti-aircraft guns and the basic operation of airfields. At the end of this training they were driven out towards Cologne to test their radios – Caroli finding more success than Schmidt – and then sent off to Brussels to await a favourable opportunity to be parachuted into Britain. While waiting for this opportunity, Ritter took his agents out for what might be their last chance to paint the town red.

Ritter noted that Caroli had started getting a little too attached to a girl he had picked up. Ritter had the girl locked up for a few days and took his prize agents on to the bright lights of occupied Paris for a good time instead. In the French capital Ritter and his two agents were housed in the Hotel Lutetia – the Abwehr's chosen headquarters in the occupied city. After the agents had spent the day practising their radio transmissions from the roof of the hotel, by night Ritter let them loose on the city. Due to the fantastically exorbitant exchange rate set by the Nazis after the fall of France, men on the Nazi payroll found Paris a cheap night out. As yet, in August 1940, none of the hardships of occupation had set in, and in certain areas the arrival of so many German 'tourists' was not exactly unwelcome. The two spies therefore capped their Paris tour with visits to the Sphinx, an extravagant bordello that was doing a roaring trade with the conquerors. On from Paris, Ritter took his men back to Brussels for a final briefing.

At this point the two spies were separated. On the night of 1 September, Caroli climbed into a specially converted bomber used for spy missions. The aircraft was painted black, without any markings, and stripped of its bomb release mechanisms to reduce weight and increase speed to a maximum. The pilot, Oberleutnant Karl Gartenfeld, took them from an airfield at Rennes and flew low across the English Channel. Unfortunately as the aircraft reached Britain it was caught in the glare of a spotlight and Gartenfeld aborted the mission, turned back towards the mainland of Europe, and landed in Brussels.

On the night of 5–6 September a second attempt was made. Taking off from Brussels, Gartenfeld crossed low over the water, and, passing the English coast, climbed sharply up to 20,000ft. When the bomber was over Northamptonshire around 1.30am, it quickly lost altitude and Caroli jumped from 5,000ft.

Before the mission, Gartenfeld had advised Caroli to put any heavy equipment on a separate parachute and push that out first. Concerned that he might become separated from his equipment, Caroli instead strapped the radio transmitter to his chest. When he jumped out of the aircraft into the dark sky night he plummeted like a rock.

Carrying the extra weight, Caroli reached the ground somewhat more quickly than expected. On impact the strap on the radio snapped and smacked him on the chin, knocking him unconscious. Five hours later he came to. Still groggy, he gathered up his parachute and equipment, dragging the whole lot into a nearby ditch in which he promptly went to sleep. It was in this position that he was discovered around 5.30pm by a farm hand returning from work in the fields who noticed his shoes protruding from a hedge.

The farm hand reported his discovery to the farmer, who was also a member of the Local Defence Volunteers (LDV) and before long a small posse gathered and went to investigate. They found Caroli, who was now awake. Sitting with his parachute, there was not very much he could do but come clean. He told the startled onlookers in excellent English that he was Swedish and had come from Hamburg the night before. He then showed them his German automatic pistol and his wallet packed with banknotes. The LDV man took Caroli to his farmhouse and called his superior, Sergeant Smart, his landlord Lord Northampton, and Superintendent Frost of the local police force, who took Caroli to Northampton.

Among Caroli's possessions were his Swedish passport and a genuine UK Alien Registration Certificate dated from May 1939. Because Caroli was a neutral citizen and because he had been living with friends in the Birmingham area the previous year, his captors did not know what to do with the parachutist. There had been a lot of spy scare stories in the press, and the country was awash with legitimate refugees of all nationalities. It was not until 7 September that MI5 were involved in the case.

This was particularly annoying as the Security Service had been forewarned about the arrival of the parachutist by *Snow*. Guy Liddell had noted this in his diary as early as 27 August, revealing somewhat ironically that MI5 was trying to find a suitable landing spot where the parachutist would not be killed and not be discovered by the LDV. In their secret communications with *Snow* the Germans had proposed finding a suitably remote safe house from where this spy and other agents could be accommodated. Warning had been sent out to the MI5's Regional Security Liaison Officers (RSLOs) to expect the agent's arrival, but clearly there had been a breakdown in communication with the local police, who should have handed Caroli over immediately.

From the point of view of expanding the network of double agents, MI5 set itself three criteria in selecting potential recruits. Firstly the German agent would have to be captured almost immediately on landing, before he had a chance to communicate with Germany. This ruled out using the Brussels spies, as Waldberg had radioed that Meier had been arrested. Almost as importantly, the spy's capture had to be unobserved by the general public. If word got out that a German spy had landed and was captured, the ensuing rumours and press articles might find their way to Germany and the deception would be blown. Again, this probably ruled out the Brussels team, because Meier had been in a pub and had talked to a number of people. Thirdly, the spy had to agree to be 'turned' – and this was no easy matter in many cases, especially with Caroli.[15]

The Swede was handed over to give an initial statement to MI5's veteran interrogator, Colonel Hinchley-Cooke, who had handled early interrogations with *Snow* in the pre-war years. Caroli could hardly protest his innocence. He had been found in civilian clothes with a parachute, a wireless transmitter, £200 in notes, maps of the local area, a compass, and a loaded automatic. He also had a British ID card that MI5 knew was faked, because it too was a copy of the one the *Snow* network had provided to the Germans in Lisbon. Caroli told Hinchley-Cooke he was a Swede of German origin and that he had intended to land somewhere near Birmingham. On landing he believed he was somewhere near Stratford on Avon – he had in fact landed about 50 miles off target. After giving the statement Caroli was sent to Latchmere House for a rendezvous with 'Tin-Eye' Stephens.[16]

Caroli was evidently a full-blown Nazi fanatic at the start of the interview process and appeared to care little if he was shot for espionage. His interrogators were determined to fire questions at him before he had time to get his bearings and entrench himself behind a plausible cover story. The first line of questioning was to establish a link with the four spies who had landed in Kent days before him. Other than being part of a general programme to put spies into Britain, Caroli declared he had no knowledge of these spies.

However, before long he had given his interrogators the names of various Abwehr officers he had dealt with and claimed – falsely, as it turned out – that he had been recruited by the Abwehr only two months before. He had been chosen, he revealed, because he had worked in England before the war as a journalist for the Swedish press agency. His mission was to report on Oxford, Northampton and Birmingham, and in particular assess the bomb damage to Birmingham.

The interrogators continued in their attempts to tease information out of Caroli, who let slip that another agent using the alias *Leonhart* was expected to arrive in the next few days. (This of course was Caroli's training partner Wulf Schmidt.) However, because the man was his personal friend, and because he, Caroli, was a dedicated Nazi, he would not disclose anything that might bring the man to harm.

This piece of information gave the interrogators everything they needed to exert leverage on the Swede. They offered him a deal – a once-only deal that was never to be offered to anyone else again. Testing whether Caroli was as dedicated a friend as he made out, the interrogators promised that when his friend was caught – and caught he would be – they would spare him from the gallows, if – and only if – Caroli agreed to cooperate. The bargain was not exactly legal, and neither was it very ethical, but it was extremely effective. The Abwehr had clearly made a huge mistake in allowing personal friendship to develop between two different spies in the field. It was a basic mistake in espionage and would cost them dear in the years to come. Caroli did not fear the firing squad for himself, but he saw that his friend's life was in his hands. If he failed to cooperate and his friend was captured, he would be killed and that was too big a burden for Caroli's conscience to take with him to the grave.

Caroli relented and revealed that his friend would be dropped somewhere in the region of the Fens. He also divulged that they had agreed to meet up outside the Black Boy Inn in Nottingham on 20 September. He offered his interrogators a description of his friend, which was quickly forwarded to MI5 and then passed on to police forces across the country.

Having punctured Caroli's armour, the interrogators now changed tack and tried to recruit Caroli as a double agent. He was initially reluctant to comply, but the interrogators went some way to persuade him that he had been given a rough deal by the Germans. If anyone was his enemy, it was not the British who were holding out a lifeline to him, but the Germans who had sent him ill equipped and poorly prepared for such a hazardous mission. Caroli began to see some sense in this and on 9 September, two days after arriving at 020, he was handed over to MI5 to begin his new life as the double agent *Summer*.

While waiting for the arrival of Schmidt, no time was lost getting *Summer* on the air and double crossing his former employers. In his interrogation *Summer* had revealed his code and his radio instructions. He was taken from Camp 020 and his equipment set up in a field on the estate of the Chief Constable of Buckinghamshire, near Aylesbury. Each end of the aerial was put up on long sticks protruding out of a pig sty. For two nights in a row *Summer* lay on his belly and began tapping out his call sign. On both occasions he was unsuccessful.

However, with *Summer* was a radio ham minder, who was placed with him to ensure that he stuck to the vetted script when tapping out the Morse message. The minder suggested setting the radio equipment up at nearby Aylesbury police station, where the aerial could be erected higher and would be less obstructed.

This advice turned out to be sound and before long *Summer* was on the air. On 12 September he radioed Hamburg and told his controllers he had been experiencing considerable difficulties and had injured himself on landing. On 14 September – the day the invasion had been expected – *Summer* reported that he was hiding in the vicinity of Oxford, but because of the bad weather he was going to try and find shelter posing as a refugee.

In an extraordinary development, Hamburg vetoed this course of action. Instead they radioed *Snow* and instructed him to mount a rescue mission for the Swede. In turn *Snow* suggested High Wycombe station as the rendezvous, which would take place on 16 September. Of course, the whole rescue mission was a stunt planned by MI5. *Snow* reported that sub-agent *Biscuit* made the rendezvous and collected the Swede as planned. In fact the meeting did take place, but there were MI5 minders making sure that *Summer* didn't make a run for it. They were also waiting to see if the Germans sent anyone else along to monitor the meeting. No one else was observed.

Summer was then notionally taken to a safe house in London. In reality he was in a secure MI5 holding centre under guard. *Snow* radioed the Germans that unfortunately the Swede had fallen ill while exposed to the elements and that he would need some rest before commencing further operations. In the meantime *Snow*'s contact would get the Swede's papers properly in order. Hamburg radioed back its sincere thanks to the little Welshman for his timely intervention and his continued service to Germany. They had no idea what was really going on.

XX

The arrival of this first batch of spies had proved slightly baffling to the British. On 8 September, the day after *Summer* had been handed over to MI5, Guy Liddell had a meeting with Kenneth Strong from Military Intelligence who had just interviewed the prisoners.

Strong admitted he was puzzled as to why the Germans appeared to have given the agents details of their plan of attack. There was a possibility that the Germans had sent the spies over deliberately ill prepared to deceive the British, but information received from other secret sources and from aerial reconnaissance reinforced what the spies had claimed – namely that the invasion would be a simple dash across the Channel into Kent and Sussex, not a move against weakly defended Ireland as some had suggested. That said, Kenneth Strong could not comprehend the idea that the famously efficient Germans could have sent agents to England with such poor preparation and so little idea of what to do when they arrived.[17]

To shed some light on this, a few days later, Liddell's deputy, Dick White, explained to Liddell that the evidence indicated the Germans had not attempted to build up any espionage service in the United Kingdom until after the fall of Holland and Belgium. If this was the case – and we now know that it was – White said it would explain the 'slip-shod' performance of the German spies to date.

This run of bad luck continued for the Nazis on the night of 19–20 September. Gartenfeld took off in his blacked-out bomber with the spy Wulf Schmidt on board. At 3,500ft, the parachutist jumped out of the plane over the Cambridgeshire countryside near Willingham. As he jumped he hit his wrist and shattered his watch. He also got caught up in some telegraph wires and when he finally untangled himself and dropped to the ground he twisted his ankle.

Next morning Schmidt hid his equipment and, dressed in a smart blue suit, made his way into nearby Willingham. Although his English was excellent, it was accented, and, along with his sudden appearance in such a rural setting, it was not long before people became suspicious. After he had bought a new watch and a copy of *The Times* and had breakfast in a café, he was stopped by a member of the LDV. He was arrested and found to be in possession of £132, $160, a Danish passport and a fake British ID card in the name of Williams. Again the information on the ID card was incriminating, as it had been designed after the one provided by the *Snow* network.

The parachutist was whisked off to Latchmere House for interrogation, which was carried out not by Camp 020 officers, but by three Military Intelligence officers from the War Office. The reason for this was that the Director of Military Intelligence (DMI), Major General F. C. Beaumont-Nesbitt, had argued that now the United Kingdom was in the zone of operations – i.e. the invasion was expected any day – the military should be given first chance to extract anything in the nature of urgent operational intelligence from parachutists.[18]

The vital first interrogation on 21 September did not really progress very far as Schmidt came across as a hard case and was uncooperative in the extreme. While the interrogators broke for lunch, Schmidt was sent back to his cell. However, one of the interrogators, Colonel Alexander Scotland from MI9 – the section of the War Office then responsible for interrogating German POWs – followed the prisoner back to the cell and assaulted him. A scuffle ensued during which Schmidt landed a punch of his own. The fight was stopped only when one of the MI5 men, Malcolm Frost, turned up on the scene and saw Scotland punching the prisoner in the jaw. Frost quickly intervened and got Scotland out of the cell. Stephens was furious that Scotland had assaulted the prisoner and got the War Office team out of the camp immediately, handing the case over to his own staff.

The Schmidt case was of paramount importance to MI5 and nothing could be allowed to jeopardize Schmidt's rapid transition into double cross work. It must be remembered Schmidt was supposed to meet *Summer* in Nottingham. If the rendezvous did not take place as planned, the Germans would want to know why. If *Summer* was blown, because of the 'rescue' mission staged by *Snow*, the Welshman's network would also be blown. In short, MI5 would be back to square one.

The interrogation carried on into the afternoon. The Nazi Dane stuck to his cover story, that he was a refugee who had got into trouble with

Germans at home. He had crossed the North Sea on a yacht with brown sails and then on a motorboat. Arriving near Hartlepool, he had spent three months travelling through the country sleeping rough. How then, asked his inquisitors, had he done his laundry and where did he last have his hair cut? He had obviously washed recently as he was very well groomed when he was picked up. That level of grooming would have been hard to maintain for three months living rough.

With Schmidt's confidence undermined by the persistent questioning about such mundane concerns, the 020 team played their trump card – the information provided by *Summer*. Going over his story again, the interrogators dropped in to the conversation that they knew all about his meeting at the Black Boy Inn with Caroli. Yes, they knew all about it because his friend the Swede had betrayed the whole mission to them. As a *coup de grâce*, they told Schmidt about the description of him the Swede had given. Schmidt could not believe it and called his betrayer 'a swine'.

This revelation changed everything. Out came a torrent of information about his recruitment, training, whom he knew in the Abwehr, what agents he had met in Brussels and the nature of his secret mission. The interrogation team lapped it up and then they changed tack beautifully. They told Schmidt it was not his friend's fault he had been betrayed, but the Abwehr officers that had trained them and sent them on such a desperate mission. That night Stevens telephoned Guy Liddell and told him the good news – Schmidt had agreed to show them where he had hidden his wireless transmitter set and equipment.[19]

Just as it seemed that they had won Schmidt over, disaster almost struck. Next morning Colonel Scotland turned up for a second day of interrogation, armed with a syringe which he claimed was filled with a truth serum drug.[20] Clearly Colonel Scotland thought he had unfinished business with the German spy. He was commandant of MI9's infamous secret Combined Services Detailed Interrogation Centre (CSDIC) at 6–8 Kensington Palace Gardens, London, known as 'The Cage'. Physical and mental abuse were routine there under Scotland's leadership and it was the site of various alleged war crimes until its closure in 1948.[21]

With Scotland's bullying tactics, any chance of converting Schmidt into a double agent would be wasted. Stephens met Scotland and told him in no uncertain terms that, following the previous day's altercation, the prisoner was in no fit state for interrogation. In reality there was nothing wrong with Schmidt, but Tin-Eye, despite his imposing manner and his hard views on the treatment of spies, had a strict rule about violence towards prisoners.

Not only was violence against a prisoner cowardly, it was counter-productive. A man being beaten would tell his tormentor anything he wanted to hear. Stephens was only interested in the truth – and real truth was rarely beaten from a spy.

Guy Liddell was informed about Scotland's treatment of the prisoner. Like Stephens, Liddell strongly disapproved of such 'Gestapo techniques' and thought that violence was immoral and counter-productive. He was swiftly in contact with the DMI and told him that Scotland and the War Office team were no longer welcome at 020. From that point on the Schmidt case was handled by 020 officers exclusively.

Schmidt was driven up to Cambridgeshire with an armed escort to recover his two-way transmitter and codebook. Although they were successful in finding the hiding place, there was a small problem. No one had told the local RSLO that they were coming up to retrieve it. Since Schmidt's arrival, the local police and LDV had been scouring the area trying to find the parachutist's belongings. Eventually they came across some people who reported seeing a mysterious group arrive by car and dig up what looked like a radio transmitter. Of course the police were alarmed as to who these mysterious individuals might be. When they made enquiries and realized they were in fact MI5 the Cambridge police were more angry than relieved and caused quite a stink. Liddell apologized, putting the oversight down to over-excitement.[22]

The radio was set up on the second floor of Latchmere House and Schmidt was allowed to make contact, advising Hamburg about his twisted ankle. To prevent German direction finders from pinpointing Schmidt's location at Ham, he was passed over to MI5 to work as a double agent. Tommy Robertson took the Dane under his wing and gave him the codename *Tate* – after the music hall comedian Harry Tate, whom Robertson thought he resembled. He was assigned Russell Leigh as his case officer and lodged with *Summer* at an MI5 safe house at Hinxton Grange, a farm estate house in Cambridgeshire, not far from RAF Duxford.

While *Tate* was being set up, a third parachutist arrived near Wellingborough on the evening of 3 October. The agent was Kurt Karl Goose, a member of the Brandenburg Regiment – an Abwehr-sponsored commando unit of ex-pat foreign language speakers trained for sabotage missions. Goose had been a geology student in the USA but had returned to Germany at the beginning of the war to volunteer. After completing his infantry training he was attached to the Abwehr in Brussels, where he underwent three weeks' intensive training in espionage and radio transmission.

Brandenburgers had a policy of always wearing their German uniform beneath their disguise. In Goose's case he had no intention of being shot as a spy, and so he decided to uphold this policy and jump into the United Kingdom wearing his uniform and carrying his pay book.

Goose's mission was to cover the north-west of England, between Bedford and Liverpool, and including the towns of Leicester, Birmingham and Coventry. He was given no support, not told of any other agents and left to develop his own itinerary. His only definite mission was to report meteorological data, civilian morale and the location of road blocks. He was told to remain in Britain until the invasion took place and then to rejoin the German Army when he could. Unfortunately for him, while completing his training he had met with another agent, who presented him with a pistol. That agent was *Tate*. Now working for the British, *Tate* told his interrogators to look out for Goose.

Goose landed safely and hid in a hedgerow to see if his landing had gone unnoticed. In the morning he cut up his parachute and buried it, then walked to a nearby barn where he stored his equipment. He changed out of his uniform into civilian clothes and that was as far as his mission went. He was caught by a local farmer who turned him over to the police. The next day he was taken to Camp 020 for interrogation and quickly agreed to work for the British. He claimed he had no intention of spying, but was trying to get back to America, all of which sounded plausible until he was caught trying to bribe a warder to smuggle a letter to the German embassy in Dublin. Nevertheless, Goose was turned over to MI5 and received the rather predictable codename *Gander*.[23]

3

BURNING LIES

B EHIND THE SCENES THROUGH the summer of 1940, the recruitment of the enemy spies had caused no end of difficulty to MI5's internal organization. Since mid-July the day-to-day running of the double agents had gone from Liddell's B Division to a new body called the Wireless, or W Branch. In theory this body was set up to search for all possible enemy channels of wireless communication in the United Kingdom — including double agents — and contained representatives from MI5, MI6 and other interested parties — namely the RSS (Radio Security Service).[1]

W Branch was run by Malcolm Frost, who was seconded to MI5 from the BBC where he had built up an extensive knowledge of German foreign broadcasting. In May 1940 Frost had put forward the theory that coded messages to Fifth Column subversives in the United Kingdom were being broadcast by the German propaganda service — the NBBS (New British Broadcasting Station). Unfortunately his appointment came as a mixed blessing. Although W Branch was supposed to be an independent division in its own right, in practice it was guilty of duplicating the workload of Liddell's B Division and to some degree subordinated itself to that body.

In relation to double agents like *Snow*, W Branch had been providing mostly true information to the spies, including accurate meteorological reports in order to protect their bonafides. The biggest sponsor of information for *Snow* had actually been Air Commodore Boyle, the Air Force Director of Intelligence, who had taken it upon himself to provide MI5 with a lot of truthful information. But now, with a German invasion expected imminently, information would have to come from across the board if they were not to jeopardize future operations. The information would also have to be vetted at a high level. For instance, should the agents be encouraging the Germans to invade, or should they be trying to delay proceedings?

Such were the topics when Liddell held a meeting with the DMI on 10 September. The DMI was in favour of encouraging the Germans to come over, but when the matter was referred to the Chiefs of Staff Committee (the most senior military decision-making body below Churchill's War Cabinet in 1940 and composed of the three service chiefs) it was decided to deter the Germans by letting them have the truth about the strength of Britain's defences, which were getting considerably stronger by the day.

During their meeting another subject arose, namely that of obtaining suitable information for the double agents to transmit. Until then the likes of *Snow* had been fed scraps from the various service intelligence chiefs on an unofficial basis, but as the demand for information grew, something more substantial would have be worked out.

Speaking with Liddell, Captain Felix Cowgill, the head of MI6's Section V (the department responsible for counter-espionage outside the limits of the British Empire) expressed dissatisfaction with this arrangement. He said that the heads of service intelligence were on the one hand too important to provide the sort of low-level information – or chickenfeed as he called it – that the double agents required; but on the other hand were not important enough to make decisions on the high-level information that might be needed to be passed to the enemy.

At the same time information was not provided quickly enough – in the espionage game, the usefulness of the double agent required speedy decisions. Cowgill stated that every time someone asked for a piece of information, he was referred elsewhere and the delay became considerable. Privately Liddell sympathized with Cowgill's point of view, but admitted in his diary that they were stuck with the present scheme for the foreseeable future at least.

On 16 September, the day after heavy German daylight air raids, Liddell started to make arrangements for a body that would oversee the running of *Snow* and the other double agents. His idea was to form a small committee to meet in future to deal with their traffic. It would consist of Malcolm Frost (MI5), Dick White (MI5), Jack Curry (MI5 – counter-subversion), Tommy Robertson (MI5), Felix Cowgill (SIS) and himself. Although this idea would eventually grow into something more substantial, at the time MI5 was under a lot of pressure from the government, which was looking to reorganize the service, and from the demands for quick action to keep the existing double agents active.

Meetings therefore continued on an informal basis. On 23 September Liddell called such a meeting in his office, inviting Valentine Vivian (SIS), Cowgill, Frost, White and Robertson to discuss the cases of the various double agents they had acquired. It was decided that because *Summer* had been provided with the papers of a sailor, they might be able to build a scenario where *Summer* met another seaman who would allow him to travel to Lisbon. They were also very anxious to get *Tate* working, but were concerned about his frame of mind after Colonel Scotland's assault.

Liddell suggested using *Tate* or one of the other agents as a deliberate double cross agent. In other words they would have him send information so obviously false that the Germans would guess he had been captured and was not transmitting freely. This would make the traffic from the other double agents more believable and enhance their standing with the Abwehr. No firm decision was taken on this, but all agreed that it was important to get *Tate* on the air as quickly as possible.[2]

More progress in organizing a lasting system for providing information to the double agents was made on 30 September. Liddell attended a meeting in the DMI's office along with Victor Cavendish-Bentinck, the chairman of the Joint Intelligence Committee (JIC). The subject of the meeting was the establishment of the W Committee – a secret body that would be responsible for the dissemination of false information to the enemy using the double agents.

This was exactly the sort of body Liddell had been lobbying for and one which had the support of Admiral John Godfrey, the Director of Naval Intelligence (DNI). Godfrey wanted this new organization to be informal and to avoid setting any rigid charters or directives. As for sanctioning the information provided, it was suggested that each of the three service directors could consult with their respective Chief of Staff, telling them vaguely that they had a means of delivering misinformation to the enemy, but it would mean having to give some true pieces of information in the bargain. To prevent the Chiefs of Staff from becoming too curious, they were to be told that it was all very hush-hush and the less they knew about it, the better it would probably be for them.[3]

The DMI was also keen on such a body. He explained how anxious he was to centralize the dissemination of rumours and false information and to take stock of the 'channels' through which such information could be distributed. These 'channels' were means of getting information to Germany indirectly – for example through foreign journalists and diplomats in London, through British embassies in neutral countries and through secret agents working abroad. As the DMI saw it, the double agents being run by MI5 had great potential as channels for deception purposes.

Liddell said that as far as B Division was concerned, the priority was keeping the double agents in the game and that meant getting quick answers to the questionnaires or enquiries that the enemy was sending over. In order not to compromise planning and security, Liddell explained that it was important for MI5 to know the actual truth and, secondly, how much of this truth could safely be put over to the enemy. Once this was known the double agents could be sent out to see how much information they could glean themselves – and if necessary they could then be censored.

This was an important part of running the double cross agents. Wherever possible, the agents had actually to live the life of a spy. This was especially important if the agents were ever sent to meet their German controllers in neutral countries like Portugal. Having actually carried out a reconnaissance in person, the agent would be able to stand up to cross-examination far more convincingly than if he had not visited the factory or town in question, or made the journey by train or bus from A to B. It was the sort of attention to detail that the Abwehr's *Lena* spies had sadly lacked.

Liddell reiterated that they were in the business of sending true information over to the Germans, but he did not mind using the occasional half-truth that another government department was trying to put over. Indeed, some of the rumours being circulated by agencies such as SIS and the Ministry of Economic Warfare (MEW) were cropping up in the questionnaires coming back from the Germans. Unless they knew what the rumours were, the agents might end up contradicting the information another department was keen on pushing.

It was suggested that the correct place to pool all rumours and false information was the ISSB – the Inter-Services Security Branch. This organization was an off-shoot of JIC and was made up of representatives from the three services, MI5 and MI6. In addition to general security issues relating to military operations (including registering code words, mail censorship, supervision of neutral journalists, leaks to the press, sealing of camps, stopping leave, the security of ports and airfields, the movement of troops etc) the ISSB was also responsible for 'cover planning' – in other words putting out false information to act as cover for military operations.[4] The DMI advised Liddell that they should submit their questionnaires to the secretary of ISSB, who would provide answers that would not contradict that body's deception operations.

Liddell was concerned that enquiries might take too long to be answered by this route, but the DMI's response was that he could always go directly to the individual Directors of Intelligence. In the meantime the W Committee would meet fortnightly to discuss the rumour policy.[5]

XX

Rumour became an important weapon in dissuading the Germans from invading. It was bad enough for the average German soldier that he was going to be dragged across the English Channel in a Rhine barge at a few knots, as the Royal Navy and RAF threw everything they had at him.[6] If he believed that terrible secret weapons awaited him on the other side of the Channel then his reluctance to make the trip would grow yet stronger.

In July 1940 JIC had put out a paper entitled 'Action designed to disconcert the Enemy in relation to the Invasion of the United Kingdom'. The idea was to circulate rumours which, it was hoped, might put off the German invasion.[7] They were not always plausible – in fact some were ridiculous. One of the more outlandish rumours put about in the late summer of 1940 was that the British government had imported 200 man-eating sharks from Australia and had set them loose in the Channel to eat downed German pilots.[8] This particular rumour was attacked by the *Daily Mail* as ridiculous – as indeed it was – but others were far more plausible.

Through their channels, the British claimed that they had prepared for German paratroopers by stringing high-tension wires along the telegraph poles that would kill them if they became entangled. They said that powerful mines had been disguised to look like harmless post boxes, and that specially constructed armoured vehicles were ready to be driven into German gliders as they landed. Another rumour said that, fearing the welcome they would receive, 200 parachute troops had refused to volunteer for the invasion and had been shot in a German town for cowardice.

One rumour in particular really did take hold and spread like wildfire across the Continent. It was completely false, but again surrounded by enough truth and plausibility to make it believable – the key to any successful piece of deception.

The rumour was started by Major John Baker White, an officer working on Black propaganda for the DMI. It consisted of just eight very carefully chosen words:[9]

'The British can set the sea on fire.'

With echoes of Sir Francis Drake's fire ships, which were sent against the Spanish Armada, Baker White's rumour came about after a visit to beach defences on the Kent coast. He was initially horrified by the defences waiting to repel Hitler's victorious armies. The entire area was defended by a single under-strength rifle company with two Bren guns and a machine gun hidden in a cave. The company was part of a battalion covering an area that should have been protected by six times that number, and was supported by some obsolete French World War I-vintage artillery with 20 rounds per gun.

However, at St Margaret's Bay he was shown a new device that worked on the same principle as the artificial rainmakers used by market gardeners. An oil tank positioned some way off the beach fed a series of pipes running under the beach. Inside the tank was a combination of petrol, fuel oil and creosote. On activation the flammable mix was sent down the pipes and sprayed up over the beach in a fine mist, which was then ignited. The resulting inferno would completely engulf the beach in fire, destroying anything or anyone with which it came into contact.

Although the device would be short lived and was susceptible to damage by a preliminary bombardment, an idea began to ferment in Baker White's mind. What if the German soldiers across the Channel could be made to believe the British had developed a new weapon that would set the sea on fire if the Germans tried to invade? Imagine the fear of soldiers in the invasion barges as they approached the British coast, knowing full well that at any moment the waves would erupt into a veritable sea of flame.

Before releasing the rumour, Baker White made enquiries about the feasibility of the scheme. Fearing that German chemical warfare specialists would issue a denial, exposing the scheme as pure fantasy, Baker White approached British scientists with the scheme and asked if it was possible to set the sea on fire. The experts replied that it was possible but it would be an extravagantly expensive weapon to employ; but that wasn't Baker White's problem. From the Grand Hotel in Stockholm, to the Café Bavaria in Geneva, to the Ritz in Madrid, in Lisbon, Cairo, Istanbul, Ankara and New York, the rumour mill was fed a diet of burning sea stories.

It was several weeks before there was any comeback. Then a German pilot was shot down over Charing in Kent. Under interrogation at the Air Intelligence interrogation centre, Trent Park, Cockfosters, he revealed that the Luftwaffe knew all about the British 'burning sea defences'. Three days later another German pilot was shot down and gave the same information, although he was from a different airfield from the first.

After that, for the next fortnight the rumour began appearing all over the place. It was given credence by a real stroke of luck for the British. The RAF had been trying to bomb the German invasion barges with incendiary bombs. During one of these missions the RAF caught a battalion of German troops carrying out embarkation practice on the barges in Calais. With the use of incendiaries, there were of course many men who received burn injuries. Of these the most serious had to be sent to hospitals in Paris for treatment.

Already the fledgling French underground movement had heard about the burning sea tactic and within hours of the arrival of the burns victims from Calais, the rumour was in full swing. It was reported that the Germans had tried to invade Britain and that the sea had been set alight. The rumour spread throughout occupied Europe that there were trains loaded with the burnt corpses of German soldiers and hospitals full of severely burned Germans, after a failed attempt to invade.

With black humour, Frenchmen would unnerve the Germans they encountered in the cafés and restaurants, pretending to warm their hands on them as if they were burning. In Brussels a shop exhibited men's bathing suits labelled 'for Channel swimming'.[10]

A second stroke of luck came when a German flak boat was captured off the French coast. In addition to the crew of the ship, ten German soldiers were taken prisoner. They had been put on the ship to serve the anti-aircraft guns and had been taken from a random assortment of German units. Realizing there might be a potential propaganda coup in the offing, a German language broadcast from London declared that the men had been brought to Dover unhurt having been plucked from the sea. Their names and rank numbers were read out and the announcement closed with the words: 'We know nothing of the fate of their comrades' – read out with Wagnerian funeral music in the background.

Rather than deny this rumour, the German High Command caused further jitters among its troops by looking into fire-proofing its barges. A trial was carried out at Fécamp in Normandy, when a barge was lined with asbestos sheets and steered into a pool of burning petrol. The boat survived but all on board were horribly burned to death. To make matters worse, some of the charred remains of these victims fell into the water and were washed up along the French coast.

In fact the rumour did so well that it even got back to Britain, having been planted on Germans in neutral Dublin. One of the rumours was that German soldiers had been brought ashore at Harwich, Dover and Newhaven with their hands and faces covered in bandages. It was said that smoke had been seen over Sandwich Bay and that the bodies of hideously charred German soldiers had been buried in the sand dunes.

Prime Minister Winston Churchill remembered the rumours, recording that during August 1940 the corpses of about 40 German soldiers were washed up along the British coast between the Isle of Wight and Cornwall. Churchill explained that these men had drowned when their ships had been sunk, either from bombing or in bad weather. However, when the rumour went about that these men had been part of an attempted invasion which had been stopped by the burning sea, Churchill remarked that no steps were taken to contradict these claims.[11]

Perhaps the most devilish piece of psychological propaganda relating to the sea on fire rumour came from Dennis Sefton Delmer, the journalist who had so upset the Germans with his negative and insulting reply to Hitler's peace offer. In one of his German broadcasts he gave a spoof English lesson to the would-be invaders, giving them some phrases he thought they might find useful during the Channel crossing. Asking the Germans to repeat the phrases parrot fashion, Delmer read the words:

Das Boot sinkt	the boat is sinking
Das Wasser ist kalt	the water is cold.
Sehr kalt	very cold.

He then moved onto conjugating a useful verb:

Ich brenne	I burn
Du brennst	you burn
Er brennt	he burns
Wir brennen	we burn
Ihr brennt	you burn
Sie brennen	they burn

Bringing it all together he came up with the phrase: '*Der SS Sturmführer brennt auch ganz schön*' – 'The SS Captain is also burning quite nicely.' Outrageous stuff, but it all added perfectly to the grand scheme.[12]

XX

It wasn't just radio that played a part in the effort to deceive the Nazis – the British film industry quickly found itself at the heart of a top-secret deception campaign.

Following the bombing of Guernica by the German Condor Legion in 1938 during the Spanish Civil War, it was believed that a new European war would see the terror bombing of cities. The British decided that an intricate system of decoys should be established to simulate airfields, aircraft, busy factories and even entire cities, all in order to make the Germans dump their bombs harmlessly into open fields.

The man chosen to head the decoy campaign was a former chief engineer to the Air Force in India and Director of Work and Buildings at the Air Ministry. Colonel John Turner was brought out of retirement in September 1939 to head a department so secret it did not even have a name – it was known simply as Colonel Turner's department (CTD).[13]

Turner's first duty was to oversee the building of dummy aircraft. Before his arrival work had been farmed out to a number of film studios including Warner Brothers, Gaumont British Films and Alexander Korda's London Film Company at Denham. There was an obvious parallel between building studio sets and decoys – the purpose of both was to trick a viewer through a lens, either a movie goer, or a German airman looking through his bomb-aiming sight or reconnaissance camera.

After viewing the early attempts of cinema prop makers to simulate cheap and convincing dummy aircraft, Turner was most impressed with the work of Sound City Films at Shepperton Studios. Sound City was owned by the Scottish businessman Norman Loudon. With a slump in movie work, Loudon had planned to build a theme park called Sound City Zoo and Wonderland, which was scheduled to open in 1940. Unfortunately the war put paid to this project and the studios were crying out for work. The contracts from Turner proved something of a life-line.

The first priority for Turner was to build dummy airfields known as K sites. Expecting to be bombed, the major RAF fields had already dispersed some of their strength to satellite stations, often no more than large open fields. What Turner did was identify an area of flat ground, 5–6 miles from the real airfield in the expected direction of attack, and scatter a number of the decoy aircraft around the place. To these were added areas resembling fuel and ammunition dumps, shelters for ground crew and machine-gun nests, which the decoy staff were trained to use. The sites were topped off with a wind sock and smudge fires (smoke-producing fires to indicate wind direction) just like a real satellite station.

To make the station even more convincing, the decoy crew were required to turn each aircraft at least 90 degrees each day so it appeared in different locations if reconnaissance photos from different dates were compared. They also had to make tracks to simulate where the aircraft had taxied and taken off. In some cases extra credence was given to the sites by having real aircraft land on the dummy sites. The idea of this was that any German spies operating in the area would see some traffic at the base. Where RAF planes were not available, trainer aircraft were used.

Once the German bomber offensive began after Dunkirk, Turner was pleased to see that a number of his sites were attacked. Although more real sites were attacked, every German bomb that was dropped into an empty field was a minor victory in itself. As the number of craters began to mount, Turner issued orders that crater damage had to be repaired, just as it would be at a real airbase.

Because the bulk of the attacks was being made against real airfields, Turner had some of his dummy aircraft sent to them to act as decoys. While the real aircraft were hidden on the edge of the airbase, often alongside the edge of trees, the dummies were placed in the dispersal areas to tempt strafing and bombing runs by the Germans away from the real planes.

Another consideration for the airfields was that of damage. If the Germans erroneously believed they had actually bombed an airfield, then their photo-reconnaissance planes flying over the site would expect to see craters. In order to satisfy these demands, Turner's department developed dummy craters created from a large piece of canvas sheeting, painted in such a way to look like bomb damage. There were two kinds: one for sunny days, with deep shadows, and another for cloudy days, with faint shadows.[14] These craters were placed onto runways and were rotated periodically through the day to ensure the shading in them matched the position of the sun.

The effect was real enough to fool not just German reconnaissance planes, but more than a few RAF pilots returning from missions. They needed careful persuasion to land on the seemingly pock-marked runway.

In addition to airfields, the Air Ministry decided it needed to protect the factories building aircraft, so the K site programme was extended to include some factories. The decoy factories were built to protect Shorts at Rochester, de Havilland at Hatfield, Boulton & Paul at Wolverhampton and the Bristol Aircraft Company works at Filton. In addition, two wireless stations at Leighton Buzzard and Dagnall were provided with decoy sites. Loudon designed these sites as full-scale replicas of the original plants. They had vehicles in the car parks and dummy aircraft parked nearby as if awaiting despatch from the assembly line to the airfield.

In addition to K sites, Turner built a number of night decoys. These consisted of electric lamps set out to resemble runway lights and a powerful headlight lamp on a swivel, which resembled the lights of an aircraft taxiing in the dark. The advantage of these Q sites was that unlike the K sites, which had to be built on flat, open, uncultivated ground, these could be built anywhere. The usual technique was to mount the lamps onto poles so that agricultural work could carry on in the fields around them. As a German aircraft approached in the evening, the lights would be quickly, but not completely, doused. The German pilot would think that it was a real airfield with poor blackout discipline and bomb it. Fortunately for Turner, the Luftwaffe had instructed its pilots to go after light sources when selecting targeting opportunities.

The down side of Q sites was that sometimes RAF planes tried to land on them having seen the runway lights. Because the Q sites were often built on arable land, landing on them had the potential for disaster. Turner suggested that the lights should be blinked or shut down completely, but problems persisted. In the end a series of nine red lights was placed running across the dummy runway to form a 'T' shape. Once RAF pilots were briefed to look out for this mark, the accident rate plummeted.[15]

As the Germans switched more and more to night bombing from September, so the number of Q sites rose. By the first week of November 1940, it had increased from around 50 to 100 sites.

Turner also noticed that the Germans were using a lot of incendiary bombs. For his Q sites to appear realistic when bombed, he realized that he would have to start fires. The new Q-Fire, or QF, sites started out as a simple arrangement of placing tins of creosote below roofing felt. The fires were ignited and as the roofing felt eventually collapsed, the fire would shoot up into the air. To further enhance this illusion, the QF site operators would simulate the walls of houses by erecting asbestos sheets to contain the fire beneath the roof felt. From the point of view of a German pilot, this would look like the roof of a building collapsing and a sudden rush of combustible materials catching fire below.

The lighting of the sites had to be carefully timed. The idea was that the first wave of bombers would go off and bomb their target. The next wave of bombers would be looking for the fires of the first wave. If the decoys were lit too late, the pilots would notice their sudden appearance and ignore them. To make it work, the target was responsible for deciding when its decoy should be lit and a telephone line was installed to the bunker from where the QF site was controlled.

Over the winter of 1940–41 the decoy network was again expanded to include fire decoys for major cities. The principle was an expansion of the QF sites. However, rather than simulating building fires, the new sites used a series of flammable baskets, strung out in a line, which, when ignited, would look like a 'stick' of incendiary bombs dropped by German pathfinders. The idea was that ensuing bombers would see the decoy fires and drop their bombs harmlessly. These new sites became known by the codename *Starfish*. From simple arrangements of burning baskets, they came to include complex pieces of plant, where water would be sprayed into a burning liquid fuel – the result being a huge fiery explosion whooshing up into the night skies, easily visible from the air.

4

THE SYSTEM

ALTHOUGH THE IMMEDIATE THREAT OF invasion appeared to have passed as the autumn of 1940 approached, the change in season did not bring about an end to the arrival of enemy spies. In fact, as the Germans switched their tactics from invasion to air bombardment and U-boat blockade, it became even more imperative for them to have spies working in the United Kingdom. Although aerial reconnaissance might reveal something of the damage being caused by air raids, the effect of bombing and blockade on civilian morale could be accurately gauged only by people on the ground. Other than sympathetic staff working in neutral foreign embassies, notably the Japanese and Spanish legations, the only other means of gauging this information was from spies.

On 30 September there was report of another landing, this time on the east coast of Scotland. Two suspects – a man and a woman – turned up at Portgordon railway station shortly after 3am, dripping wet. As a precaution against invasion, all railway station signs had been removed, and the two strangers were forced to admit to the stationmaster that they had no idea where they were. The stationmaster sold them two tickets to Forres and then reported them to the local police station.

The two suspects were taken in and questioned. They gave their identities as Vera Erichsen, a Dane, and Franziskus de Deeker, a Belgian. They claimed to have travelled up from London on a visit, but then quickly retracted this, saying they were refugees from the Nazis who had sailed from Bergen in a fishing boat 12 days before. The police were not impressed and searched the couple's baggage. In Deeker's bag they found a two-way radio set, a loaded revolver, a cipher disk and a list of locations that included RAF bases.

A short while later an inflatable dinghy was found on the shore. It appeared to be the type used by the Luftwaffe, indicating that it might have been carried by a seaplane and was large enough for four passengers. A manhunt began for the other spies.

At 6pm a porter at Waverley station, Edinburgh, contacted the police saying that a man with a wallet stuffed with banknotes had deposited a suitcase that was wet and had sand and seaweed on it. The man said he had come from Aberdeen and would be back later that day to pick up the case.

The police put the station under surveillance and when the man returned and offered his luggage ticket, the police pounced. In the struggle the man tried to pull a Mauser pistol from his pocket but was overpowered.

A search revealed a Swiss passport in the name of Werner Heinrich Waelti, £195 cash, maps of the east coast, a compass, codebooks, a cipher disk, graph paper and a wireless transmitter. Waelti feigned surprise at the find – the police did not.

The three suspected agents were quickly transferred to Camp 020. Interrogations proved complex and tiresome and there appeared little opportunity to use the spies for double cross work. Through information given by *Tate* and *Summer*, the group were definitely linked to the Rantzau (Ritter) stable. Vera Erichsen claimed she had been married to Dierks, the first Abwehr controller of *Snow*. In reality it appears the two were lovers after Dierks walked out on his wife – in any case their romance had recently been ended by Dierks' death in a road accident.

While the interrogations were taking place, there was an intervention from 10 Downing Street regarding the handling of spies. On 7 October Lord Swinton asked why none of the captured spies had been brought to trial and shot. Liddell explained to Swinton that his understanding was that MI5 had been given a free hand to grant the life of a captured spy in return for information. Swinton took exception to this omnipotent attitude and instructed that no one was to be offered their life without his express authority. This put Liddell's nose out of joint. He rather snottily recorded in his diary that he was not sure what rank Swinton held, but that he appeared to think he was head of both MI5 and MI6. Liddell should have remembered that, with the Prime Minister's backing, Swinton technically was just that.

But in the circumstances, Swinton's attitude is perhaps understandable. As 1940 was drawing to a close, any sign of British success against the Germans was good news. Therefore on 24 October the four Brussels spies – Meier, Waldberg, Pons and Kieboom – were sent from Camp 020 to stand trial for espionage under the Treachery Act at the Old Bailey. Somewhat unexpectedly, Pons was found not guilty after he argued that he had been coerced into becoming a spy. There was a certain irony in the fact that Pons, who had earlier been reported as being shot, was the only one of the group not to receive a death sentence.

While Pons was interned for the rest of the war and handed over to the Dutch authorities at the end, Meier, Waldberg and Kieboom were executed at Pentonville Prison. First to the gallows were Waldberg and Meier on

10 December. Kieboom appealed against his sentence, but then changed his mind. He followed his comrades to the gallows seven days later.

The case of the Brussels spies was fed to the press, although no mention was made of Pons, and only the three condemned men were exposed. Photographers were even allowed to snap the spies' equipment to increase publicity and demonstrate to the population at large, albeit somewhat ghoulishly, that the security services were doing their job.

XX

About the time of these executions, a long-anticipated Yugoslavian double agent arrived in London as a guest of both MI5 and MI6. Dusko Popov was one of the more flamboyant characters at work in the secret services of any nation during World War II, and with a reputation enhanced by his colourful memoirs, he is often credited as being one part of the inspiration for the fictional spy James Bond. Popov was a business lawyer, and unlike most spies, who are often attracted into the profession by money, he was already rich and lived a playboy lifestyle of fast cars, casinos and glamorous women.

He had first been sounded out by the Abwehr in February 1940. A friend from Popov's university days, Johann 'Johnny' Jebsen was at best a lukewarm Nazi who had joined the Abwehr in order to avoid being drafted as cannon fodder into the army. He asked Popov to prepare a report for him on French politicians who were likely to collaborate when the Nazis conquered France. Popov complied, but also engineered a discreet meeting with the First Secretary of the British embassy at an official reception. Taking the official to one side, Popov explained the Abwehr's approach and handed over a copy of the report he had given to Jebsen. The British official quietly told Popov to keep him informed if there were any more approaches in the future.

Later in the summer, in mid-July, a more formal approach was made to recruit Popov. France had fallen and everywhere the Germans were behaving smugly, predicting the fall of England any time soon. What the Germans were looking for was someone who could mix with the upper strata of British society, report on possible opposition to Churchill and identify people who might be willing to negotiate with Germany. Popov asked for a short time to consider and went back to the British embassy for advice.

He was told to contact a man named Spiradis at the British Passport Control office. Popov went along and met the man, who was in fact an SIS agent. The agent – Spiradis was his cover name – told Popov to accept the German offer and advised him to set up a legitimate business reason to travel from neutral Yugoslavia to Britain. He then instructed Popov to tell his Abwehr contacts that he was friendly with a Yugoslav diplomat in London who was short of cash. Of course the man did not exist, but he would be a notional source of intelligence that would no doubt be fed to Popov by the British secret services.

When Popov explained this to the Germans, they were naturally suspicious and asked Popov to reveal the diplomat's name. Popov refused to do so at the present time and his standing was high enough because of his earlier report for Jebsen not to push him too hard on the matter. They handed him a phial of secret ink and an intelligence questionnaire, both of which Popov passed on to his MI6 contact.

Unknown to Popov, the Abwehr had put a tail on him and very soon Jebsen had a list of every movement he made over many weeks. Although the majority of addresses visited were those of his girlfriends, Jebsen noted that Popov had been a frequent visitor to the Passport Control office. Popov tried to explain this away by saying it was for his visa, but Jebsen told him it was common knowledge that the British secret service always based their agents in these offices abroad.

Popov was crestfallen. He had blown his cover as a double agent before he had even started his mission. Curiously, though, Jebsen was still willing to keep him on. Popov was unsure to what extent Jebsen was anti-Nazi, but his friend was so desperate to maintain his position in the Abwehr and avoid service at the front that he was prepared to tolerate Popov's flirtation with the British. The only problem was that the existing report could not be doctored as long as the informant – one of Popov's domestic servants – was left alive. Popov made the necessary arrangements with a gang of hoodlums he found in a local bar. One night he sent the servant out on an errand and the hoodlums did the rest.

The only trouble now was the need for Popov to receive a signal from Berlin to begin his journey to Britain via Italy and Portugal. Again, Popov went to his British contact for help. The MI6 agent arranged for a bogus letter to be sent from the fictitious London-based diplomat friend to Popov asking for him to come to London in person and to bring money with him. Popov told the Germans his friend must have gathered important intelligence and so they sped him on his way to Lisbon.

In the Portuguese capital Popov was met by the head of the Abwehr in Lisbon, Major von Karsthoff. While waiting for a flight to Britain, Popov became genuinely close to von Karsthoff, who personally took him through his training. He was taught about codes and mail drops and given a Leica camera and instructions to use it. The Abwehr man gave Popov a sound piece of espionage advice, telling him to have a girl pose in the picture when he was taking photos of installations. When not training he whiled away his hours like so many transient foreigners, blowing money in the casino.

Eventually on 20 December Popov managed to get a seat on board a KLM flight to Britain. To avoid the Luftwaffe, KLM flew a route that went out into the Atlantic and then came in towards Britain from the west. As the plane approached the British coast, wooden panels were placed over the portholes to prevent spies seeing anything of the island's defences.

At Bristol's Felton Airport Popov was met by MI5's top chauffeur, the racing driver Jock Horsfall. When something or someone needed to get from A to B in a hurry, Jock Horsfall was the man for the job. As the car sped off, Popov thought he was going faster than the aircraft he had just climbed out of.

Around ten miles from London the driver began to slow down and allow Popov to witness London in the Blitz. In the distance the Yugoslav could see mushroom clouds shooting up into the sky, marking the detonation of Nazi bombs. Horsfall sped up, travelling straight into the heart of the burning British capital.

Popov was dropped off at the Savoy Hotel, where he was amazed to see a crowd of people utterly indifferent to the bombing. Out of the group of people milling around, Tommy Robertson came and introduced himself to Popov. As he was taken to the Savoy bar Popov thought Robertson looked like something out of a Hollywood movie – a typical 'English dashing type'. Over a sandwich and a beer Robertson explained that they would get down to business in the morning, but he just wanted to have a chat first and get acquainted.

Later, Popov went to his room, but could not resist looking out of the window to watch the drama in the skies to the east of him. For a couple of hours he listened to the pounding anti-aircraft fire and the whistling of falling bombs and awful crump as they landed. The Yugoslav found the whole experience slightly disconcerting. Everyone seemed to be getting on with life as if it were normal to be under attack, making small talk and polite conversation while bombs rained down outside. That night he became utterly convinced the British were going to win the war.

In the morning, his introduction to the secret world of double cross began. Technically Popov, or *Skoot* as he was first codenamed, was the property of MI6 because he was recruited abroad. However, now that he had moved to the United Kingdom the natural place for him to fit into the pantheon of secret agents was among the double agents of MI5. In fact Popov would have a foot in both camps, because it was intended for him to travel back to Lisbon – thus he would be working overseas, which was MI6 territory.

Although Popov had been well treated since his arrival, he came to realize that the Savoy was, at this stage, not much more than a comfortable prison. True, he had been spared the rigours of Camp 020, but his interrogation at the hotel was in-depth and intense. Popov was interviewed by, one after the other, MI5, MI6, Naval Intelligence, Air Force Intelligence and Cavendish-Bentinck, the chairman of JIC.

Slowly, as his case was trawled over, suspicions towards him began to lessen. On Christmas Day 1940 Robertson took Popov out for a traditional festive lunch. They met at the exclusive Quaglinos restaurant and then went off to spend the afternoon playing billiards at the Landsdowne Club in Berkeley Square. Having worked up an appetite at the Landsdowne, Popov and Robertson returned to the Savoy for dinner. By now well lubricated with champagne, they joined a couple and went off to the Suivi nightclub to dance towards the morning. Needless to say, both returned to the Savoy in the early hours somewhat the worse for wear but in excellent spirits.

Popov next found himself invited to London's oldest gentleman's club – White's, in St James's Street. Here he was introduced to Stewart Menzies, the head of SIS, who did much of his work there. Menzies was informally known as 'C' for chief, but more properly 'CSS', Chief of Secret Service. The SIS chief invited Popov to spend New Year's Eve with him at his brother's home out in Surrey. It was not really the sort of invitation Popov could refuse.

A bachelor, Menzies often used his brother's house as a venue for social gatherings, in which business would invariably come to be mixed with pleasure. Arriving at the house, Popov was introduced to the other guests including Friedl Gartner, whom Popov would later describe as 'the most glamorous creature' he had clapped eyes on since his arrival in Britain.

Ms Gartner was an interesting prospect for the Yugoslav spy. Her elder sister had come from Austria to London in 1937 and had worked at the London Casino posing in an enormous sea shell, clad in a flesh-coloured body stocking. Following the unification of Germany and Austria in 1938, Friedl arrived in Britain and was registered at the German embassy as a Nazi sympathizer. In fact she had little time for the Nazis and instead worked for MI5, penetrating and reporting on right-wing high society.[1]

Popov had to be literally prised away from Gartner by Menzies, who took the Yugoslavian into a study where they sat in armchairs by the fire. After the joviality of the last week, Popov now found himself under the intense glare of Menzies' intuitive character assessment of him. Drawing on a tobacco pipe, with a whisky and soda at his side, Menzies dissected Popov's ego, concluding: 'You have the makings of a very good spy, except you don't like to obey orders. You had better learn or you will be a very dead spy.' With this advice ringing in his ears, on 2 January Popov took a flight back to Lisbon to meet up with von Karsthoff.

The British had provided *Skoot* with a number of answers to the complex questionnaire he had brought with him. He had been required to obtain samples of ration cards and ID cards, and supply details of the location of food depots, the morale of the working classes, the measures in place against parachutists and the organizations responsible for investigating and countering Fifth Column activities. He was to provide a detailed order of battle for the British Army, the details of coastal and anti-aircraft defences, and information on aircraft construction, the reserves of raw materials, damage to shipping by mines or torpedoes and where goods from the United States were being unloaded. He was also told to get in touch with a number of members of the House of Lords who were believed to favour a negotiated settlement with Germany and the entourage of Admiral Sir John Tovey, Commander-in-Chief Home Fleet. Such a level of detail was beyond MI5's scope and Popov was given only sketchy details, for which he was admonished by the Germans and told to do better the next time.[2]

XX

Popov's arrival in London coincided with a key moment in MI5's development. In order to accommodate the growing number of double agents in the MI5 stable, a system for managing them and the flow of traffic they required was at last close to being finalized.

A month before Popov's arrival, on 18 November 1940, Liddell had attended a meeting of the W Committee – the body responsible for providing operational intelligence for the spies to report to Germany. He set out some constructive proposals for running what he called 'our XX system' – 'XX' representing a 'double cross'. In his mind the three main objectives were:

1. to keep our agents sufficiently well fed with accurate information so as not to lose the confidence of the enemy,
2. to control as many of the enemy's agents in this country as we can in order to make them feel that the ground is covered and they need not send any more whose arrival we might not be aware of and,
3. by careful study of the questionnaires, to mislead the enemy on a big scale at the appropriate moment.[3]

For this purpose, Liddell argued that the seniority of the members on the W Committee was such that they needed to delegate the day-to-day control of the double cross system to a sub-committee on which all the services were represented, along with the various branches of Home Security. A similar proposal had been put forward by Godfrey, the DNI. The weight of traffic required was taking up too much of the service chiefs' time. Godfrey wanted a subordinate body set up called the W Section, which would deal with the business of collecting, handling and disseminating false information. This proposal met broad agreement and so, over the coming weeks, positive steps were taken to have this new W Section created.

The function of the new section was to discuss the questions set to the agents, and act as a clearing-house for double agent information and as a liaison centre for the various departments concerned. Shortly before its inaugural meeting it was aptly named the Twenty Committee – the Latin numeral for twenty being 'XX'. This body would meet weekly and would report to the W Committee, which would be henceforth known as the W Board and only meet when required to make the most important decisions. At first this would still be on a fairly regular basis, but as the sub-committee found its feet the former's meetings became less frequent.

The chairman of the Twenty Committee was selected by the Director General of the Security Service from among the increasing numbers of 'amateurs' looking to join the war effort. John Cecil Masterman was a tutor of modern history at Christ Church, Oxford. A few months short of 50 when he was assigned to MI5, Masterman had sat out World War I interned in Germany, where he had been a student. A keen sportsman, in his earlier days Masterman had represented England at cricket and hockey and played cricket for the Marylebone Cricket Club. He had also successfully dabbled in writing crime novels.

He was assigned to MI5 on 2 December after being interviewed by the DMI. Liddell was immediately thrilled at the news and recorded Masterman had 'a very good brain' and that he looked forward to his putting forward some very good suggestions regarding the planning of double cross work. Masterman, on the other hand, was initially disappointed with the news and could see only problems in working for the Security Service, but his attitude soon changed and he was pleasantly surprised by the nature of his work and his new colleagues.[4]

Of these new colleagues, Masterman was already on intimate terms with Dick White. Liddell's deputy had once been one of Masterman's students at Christ Church and it was Masterman who had nominated White as a potential MI5 recruit in 1935.[5] White was MI5's first graduate recruit. He had arrived at a time when the main threat to Britain was perceived to be the Soviets and the Communist Party of Great Britain. At the time he arrived there were only 29 officers, most of whom were from the Indian police force, or, for various reasons, former soldiers.

Perceiving that the Nazis might be more of a threat, White's first task before being accepted fully into the MI5 fold was to visit Germany, not as a spy, but simply to immerse himself in the Third Reich, learning as much about Hitler's regime as possible, allowing him to gain an insight into German thinking. If war with Germany did materialize, such knowledge would prove invaluable to an intelligence officer. As part of his mission, he had attended the 1936 Berlin Olympics and had witnessed Hitler's discomfort at Jesse Owens' four gold medal wins. White could not believe how far the Germans had been taken in by Hitler simply because he provided them with jobs.[6]

Masterman was full of praise for White, crediting him with having the idea of the double cross set up.[7] According to Masterman, 'in the early days' White had written a memorandum pointing out that it was more profitable to turn spies round than to have them shot.[8] He had come to this conclusion in 1939 after visiting Paris on his way home from a second spell living in Germany. In the French capital, White met with his opposite numbers in the French Deuxième Bureau intelligence service and was shown how they had been attempting to persuade captured German agents to send false information back to their German controllers. Returning to Britain, White wanted to take the idea further and so approached Vernon Kell, who explained how he had tried to use double agents for deception purposes in World War I. Encouraged to find out more, White returned to France in October 1940 and met with the Deuxième Bureau for a second time to discuss using *agents doubles*.[9]

This French influence on the early origins of the XX system is further confirmed by Masterman. In his report on the wartime double cross system, he revealed that on 5 May 1939 a member of the Deuxième Bureau had given a lecture to MI6 officers on the value of double cross agents.[10] Although the Oxford don states that the British were already alive to such possibilities, it is perhaps not amiss to credit the French secret service with having some influence on what occurred in Britain. It is interesting that under the Vichy regime the Deuxième Bureau was one of the hotbeds of active resistance and, when working as part of the Free French under de Gaulle, ran double agents of its own for deception purposes; more of which later.

Masterman was also immediately taken with his direct chief, Tommy Robertson. Although 'Tar' was not an intellectual type, in Masterman's opinion, he found in him 'a born leader', possessing 'extraordinary flair' for his secretive profession. After the war, a critic of Masterman, David Mure, argued that it should have been Robertson who chaired the Twenty Committee. Mure was opposed to so-called amateurs being brought into service and believed that Robertson, who had a military background before joining MI5, should have been given the job.

In his 1980 book *Master of Deception*, Mure put this argument to Robertson and published the former MI5 man's reply. In Robertson's opinion, Masterman was a 'first-class choice' for the role of chairman as he had a knowledge of German and an understanding of the German character from the time he was interned at Ruhleben in World War I. More importantly, Masterman had a wide range of friends in the academic world and in sport and was in a position to approach almost any Ministry at the highest level if need be, because he happened to know someone (an old pupil) there. Robertson concluded that his lack of military training was no handicap, because he was surrounded by military personnel on the Committee, which was after all, primarily an 'intelligence body'.[11]

In the reorganization, Robertson was placed at the head of B Division's section B1a, which was exclusively concerned with the actual day-to-day management of the agents and the administration that went into keeping them. They had to organize not only the agents' real lives, but also the 'notional' lives that the Germans believed they were living. For this an agent would need a case officer, guards and a wireless operator. He would also need to be lodged securely and given a housekeeper to take care of his daily needs. Occasionally case officers would have to procure female companionship for their charges – anything to keep the case alive.

In order to discuss the cases, usually each day at noon Dick White would chair a meeting of all the B1a case officers.[12] The object would be for everyone to draw information together and for guidance to be issued. If a problem arose, or a major decision had to be taken on the cases, this would then be brought up at the weekly meeting of the Twenty Committee.

Moving into the New Year, with the new administrative and decision-making structures in place, the first meeting of the Twenty Committee was called for 3pm on 2 January 1941 in the hospital block at Wormwood Scrubs. From the fifth meeting onwards, they were every Thursday afternoon at 3.30pm in MI5's offices at 58 St James's Street, Mayfair. Present at the first meeting were representatives from the War Office (MI11), General

Headquarters (GHQ), the Home Forces, the Home Defence Executive (HDE), Air Ministry Intelligence, NID, MI6, Colonel Turner's deception department and of course, MI5, represented by Robertson, Masterman and Flight Lieutenant Charles Cholmondeley, who acted as secretary.

Despite his rank of captain, taking a look at the 'brass' around him, Masterman later admitted he found it embarrassing to announce that he had orders to take the chair and preside over the meeting. He was relieved when all the members agreed and noted that the committee benefited from an absence of 'red tape' and a certain informality, so much so that it was known as the 'Twenty Club' by its members.[13]

As chairman, Masterman explained that his role was to 'harmonize the interests and demands of different services and different departments – or, to put it shortly, to make the machine work'.[14] His first decision was that at every meeting tea and a bun should be provided for every member. Although this may appear a seemingly insignificant decision, it was nevertheless important as it created a congenial atmosphere that promoted cooperation. If the project was to work, cooperation would be the key and there was no room for egos and prima donnas – everyone would have to contribute openly. Masterman believed that in ration-hit Britain the provision of such small luxuries contributed to a 100 per cent attendance rate at the Twenty Committee's eventual 226 weekly meetings.

There is an amusing anecdote from the first meeting told by the representative of the DNI, Lieutenant Commander Ewen Montagu. Fearing that Montagu would be outranked and marginalized by higher-ranking Army and Air Force representatives, Admiral Godfrey had sent along a chaperone in the guise of Commander Halahan RN – Montagu's boss. It was not being outranked that concerned Montagu, however; it was the fact that his younger brother Ivor was a member of the Communist Party and he was concerned that MI5 might run a check on his background and mistake their identities.[15]

After the meeting he confided in Masterman over a cup of tea. He admitted having little faith in MI5's record keeping and thought that the two brothers might be confused. The Oxford don told him not to worry, and that he would not dream of checking up on someone vetted by the DNI. However, a week later, at the second meeting, Masterman went up to Montagu and, implying that a check had been made, asked: 'How is the table tennis going?' Masterman was left red-faced when Montagu's lack of faith in MI5's filing system proved itself justified. It was Ivor, not Ewen, Montagu who was a noted table tennis player.[16]

The main thrust of the first meeting was Masterman's decision to present a memorandum that echoed the concerns given by Liddell at the first meeting of the W Committee in relation to MI5's running of the double agents (see Appendix A). Masterman revealed to the assembled members that a stable of double agents had been secretly built up by MI5, but, unless everyone was willing to support it by providing traffic, it would be very difficult to keep the double agents in operation for much longer. However, if the services could provide this information there was the potential for a very useful instrument. Through the double agents MI5 would be able to keep abreast of what the Germans were planning. If, for instance, they were asking their agents for information on foodstuffs, it was because they were leaning toward a blockade; if, however, they were looking for landing beaches, it would indicate that an invasion was back on the cards.

By controlling German espionage, they could control the flow of information back to Germany and, by studying the questionnaires sent to the agents from Germany, make an assessment of what the Germans already knew, and what they were keen to find out. Incidentally to this they would also be diverting money from the German secret service into British coffers. The radio traffic to and from the agents would help the cryptographers break German ciphers. Lastly – and in the still dark days of early 1941 this must have appeared a very distant prospect – there was the possibility of deceiving the Germans about British intentions operationally. If the credibility of the double agents could be built up through the provision of mostly true and accurate information, one day they might be able to drop a large-scale deception on the Germans at a critical moment. If that meant losing the agent, it was a sacrifice the secret service would not hesitate to make. The committee members agreed to this document as a policy statement and referred a series of questions to the W Board relating to questions set by the German secret service to the controlled agents.[17]

The W Board met on 8 January to discuss the meeting of the Twenty Committee. This body now comprised the three Directors of Intelligence, Stewart Menzies, Guy Liddell and Ewen Montagu who acted as secretary. Its chairman was the new DMI, General Davidson, who had taken up the post on 16 December after Beaumont-Nesbitt was sacked, apparently for being perceived as too weak.[18]

During this inaugural meeting, the DNI expressed his keenness for the use of double agents and took the line that the fewer people who knew about the double agent system the better. He considered that knowledge of the double cross system should be limited to MI5, MI6 and the three Directors of Intelligence – otherwise it might become the 'plaything' of higher authorities. He was critical, therefore, and objected to the participation of the HDE, the Home Forces, and Turner's deception organization in the Twenty Committee.

The DNI had a point, but at the same time, information given by the double agents might lead to attacks by the Germans, so it was important that the civilian agencies and Home Defence people had some inkling of what might come. In fact, at the Twenty Committee meeting the HDE representative had stated that some civil authorities, including the Ministry of Supply and the Ministry of Home Security, would expect to be consulted if air raids were diverted from one place to another. Davidson smoothed things over with the DNI, who eventually came round to the majority view that these departments merited their representation.

Next came Liddell's turn to present the questions set for approval by the Twenty Committee. The three Directors of Intelligence said they would accept responsibility for answering these questions, but that in cases of major policy they might have to consult with the Chiefs of Staff before giving final authorization.

In the first instance, their general advice was that information passed by the double agents regarding air raid damage and public morale should be more or less accurate, but it should provide no information on the comparative effect on morale by the bombing of rich and poor areas, something in which the Germans appeared very interested. Wherever possible the double agents were to ensure bomb damage was spread as evenly as possible and that no particular area should be singled out as more deserving of German bombing than any other. The agents were also to discourage German invasion by emphasizing the strength of Britain's invasion defences.[19]

At the second meeting of the Twenty Committee on 9 January, Sir Findlater Stewart, the senior civil servant on the HDE, questioned whether the findings of the Wireless Board ought to be implemented without referring to the relevant civil authorities. It was his opinion that there might well be repercussions for ministers who were responsible to Parliament. For example, the information passed by the double agents might have an influence on the German bombing policy on industrial and civilian targets. Although Stewart accepted the need for secrecy, he believed that someone appointed by the Prime Minister should give approval before information was passed to Germany. His recommendation was to approach Sir John Anderson, the Lord President of the Council, a former Home Secretary, who had been responsible for air raid precautions.

This approach was agreed at the second meeting of the W Board on 10 February. Eight days later Stewart met the Lord President and explained the XX system. The proposition raised all sorts of implications. The key difficulty was having someone officially act on behalf of the various Cabinet ministers without consulting them first. This could give rise to any number of problems where a minister might be held accountable for something he knew nothing about. An important member of Churchill's Cabinet himself, the Lord President told Stewart that neither he nor the Prime Minister could offer any official seal of approval, but they did back him unofficially to act as an adviser to the W Board on behalf of all the civilian ministries. From that point on, Findlater Stewart attended every meeting of the W Board.[20]

On the afternoon of 10 February, Lord Swinton paid Liddell a visit to enquire about the activities of the Twenty Committee. Liddell had Dick White and Masterman give him an appraisal of the situation with which he, thankfully, appeared quite satisfied.

Liddell used his visit to raise the matter of what he called the 'incurables' – those detainees that were not fit for XX work, or who had been blown. His argument was that purely from an intelligence point of view they should stop 'bumping off' captured enemy agents. Liddell argued he wanted to keep the agents alive to retain them as 'reference books' since one never knew when they might turn out to be useful or might need to be interrogated again. Swinton told him to present a case for the matter, although personally he did not hold out much hope for it as the Prime Minister was eager for trials and, if necessary, executions. Swinton fudged the issue somewhat by sending out a memorandum in March saying it was the Prime Minister's policy that in all suitable cases spies should be brought to trial, unless that course conflicted in 'any serious manner with the interests of intelligence'. With hindsight the bloodletting was probably necessary. If no German agents had been brought to trial and executed, surely the Germans would have grown suspicious.[21]

The fate of the agents led to another issue. Liddell wanted a home for the 'incurables' a mile or two away from Latchmere House, which Tin-Eye Stevens could run as an annexe to Camp 020. Swinton agreed in principle to this and a reserve camp was built at Huntercombe, designated Camp 020R.

This second camp was of double importance since Latchmere House was twice struck by bombs in the winter of 1940–41 and Commandant Stephens was asking for a second camp where he could relocate in an emergency. In the first attack on 29 November, an aerial mine hit the roof and caused enormous material damage. The secret listening devices wired into the cells were knocked out of action and the officers' mess was destroyed, along with their offices and living quarters. In January 1941 a second raider came out of the clouds and dropped a stick of four bombs on the camp. According to Stephens a sentry had a miraculous escape when a bomb exploded 2ft (0.6m) from his sentry box. The only damage sustained was the loss of the man's cap badge, which earned him a ticking off from his regimental sergeant major, who thought he was improperly dressed! Above all Stephens was suspicious about the second attack. Did the Germans know about Camp 020 and its inmates? As Stephens remarked, 'a reccurring accident ceases to be an accident'.[22]

The last consideration that needed to be addressed in formalizing the XX system concerned the promulgation of secret decrypts from Bletchley Park. Before meeting Swinton, Liddell had visited Camp 020 and had dinner with Stephens on 3 February. One of the topics in their wide-ranging discussion touched on the importance of making decrypts of Abwehr hand ciphers (ISOS) relating to XX cases available to the interrogators at Camp 020.

The decrypts coming out of Bletchley Park were classified as information covertly derived from a foreign source. In that case the correct body to handle such material was MI6. In November 1939 MI6 had been dealt a paralysing, if not fatal, blow by the German secret service in what was known as the Venlo incident. Two MI6 officers working in Holland, Captain Sigismund Payne Best and Major Richard Stevens, were kidnapped by a Nazi snatch squad on the Dutch–German border, having gone to meet what they thought was a group of disaffected German officers preparing to overthrow Hitler. From the interrogation of the two officers in Berlin, the Germans were able to mop up the bulk of SIS's operations in Europe just on the eve of their spring offensives. The only real prestige SIS had left after this debacle was its control over the flow of secret information derived from Bletchley – and it was something it guarded with the utmost jealousy.

Material derived from the ISOS was passed to MI6's Section V (Counter-intelligence) under Felix Cowgill. In theory he should have passed the relevant information on to MI5, but, such was the desire for secrecy, it appeared that Cowgill was at best being uncooperative, or at worst deliberately withholding information that could have been put to good use in the war effort. Liddell raised the matter of ISOS with Cowgill and was told that Tin-Eye would be provided with the gist of the messages, but that even this edited information was not to be shown to the officer carrying out the interrogation in case he inadvertently let the code-breaking secret slip.[23]

5

SNOW FALLS

IN HIS CELEBRATED RECORD OF the Twenty Committee's work, *The Double-Cross System*, Masterman famously boasted that 'we actively ran and controlled the German espionage system in this country.'[1] Sure enough, in total, by the end of the European war in May 1945, some 100 cases had passed through the hands of B1a. To the best of our knowledge, from 1940 onwards there were only four German spies who avoided capture, interrogation and the choice between working for MI5 or execution.

The first of these was an unfortunate fellow who avoided capture by landing in the middle of the Manchester Ship Canal near the Mersey estuary on the night of 7 September 1940 and was drowned.[2] The second was Dutchman Engelbertus Fukken, alias Willem ter Braak. This spy successfully landed by parachute dangerously close to Bletchley Park on or around 4 November 1940. He put his radio set into the cloakroom at Cambridge railway station and found lodgings in the area, living for some time without arousing suspicion. The fact that he had been living less than 50 yards from the local RSLO office in Cambridge without detection and that his landlady had not reported the Dutchman to the police was worrying to say the least. From what the investigators could work out, the spy had run out of money and, with the details of his ration book at last queried, had gone off and shot himself to avoid being exposed. His body was discovered in an air raid shelter 36 hours later.

The next two agents were perhaps more successful and their existence has only recently been revealed by document releases. Albert Meems successfully moved in and out of Britain without being detected. A Dutch-born German livestock trader of apparent toad-like appearance, Meems first arrived in the United Kingdom on 31 October 1939, a few weeks after the outbreak of war, and stayed for a week at the Grafton Hotel on Tottenham Court Road, central London. He entered Kent in 1940, where a fellow livestock trader reported him after becoming suspicious, since the livestock trade with Holland had ceased. The agent only came to MI5's attention in 1944 when his existence was betrayed by a captured Abwehr agent named Emil Genue.[3]

The other was Wilhelm Moerz. Reputed to work for the Gestapo, Moerz was reported being seen getting into a taxi in London's Regent

Street on 25 May 1940. Moerz was known to the authorities from earlier espionage assignments in Czechoslovakia and was a feared operative. For a time MI5 feared that Moerz had come to Britain to take control of German espionage in the United Kingdom, but this proved unfounded. After this incident, additional sightings cropped up all over the country but none led to an arrest, or even a positive identification.

These examples go to show that MI5 was not infallible, and that in the early days at least, there were holes in the net. For the first three years of the war, the whole double cross operation was still touch and go. In fact the organization was very lucky to survive the course of 1941, as it was swiftly hit by a number of major setbacks and the unexpected closing down of a number of the most prominent cases.

The first of these crises came in January, with what was in hindsight a comical escape bid by *Summer*. It will be remembered that *Summer* arrived in Britain as a committed Nazi. Sometime over the Christmas period he appears to have become depressed and suffered pangs of guilt about the duplicitous course his career he had taken. About 2.30pm on Monday 13 January, *Summer* crept up on his minder who was playing a game of double solitaire to pass the time. The double agent pulled a piece of rope across the minder's neck and tried to garrotte him. A struggle ensued in which *Summer* proved himself the stronger man. The minder, a man named Paulton, blacked out momentarily, allowing the Swede to put ropes around his arms and ankles.

The spy apologized to Paulton for his rough treatment of him and said that although he knew he would swing for doing it, he could not go on with his double life any more and was making a bid for freedom. He searched Paulton's pockets and took some money, cigarettes and his identity card. He also picked up his own identity card and the seaman's papers that MI5 had sorted out for him. Going into the kitchen he took some tinned food, including sardines, pilchards, pears, pineapples and a lump of cold beef.

After a short time, Paulton managed to cut himself free of the ropes as *Summer* had carelessly left a penknife on a nearby table. He crept into the study and telephoned MI5 HQ for help. While waiting for the call to be connected, Paulton saw *Summer* go past the window pushing a motorcycle. The spy seemed to be having trouble carrying a canvas canoe he had picked up. At first *Summer* tried to sling the canoe across his back, but then managed somehow to tie it to the side of the motorcycle before tentatively driving off at a slow speed in the direction of the Wash. Paulton made a note of the motorcycle's registration number (CXP 654) and reported it to Robertson's deputy, John Marriott, who answered his call.[4]

With the police armed with the registration number and alerted to be on the look-out for a man riding a motorcycle with a canoe attached to the side of it, *Summer*'s escape bid was doomed to fail. In fact, the police did not have even to catch the spy – he gave himself up after repeatedly crashing the motorcycle because of the canoe. It was a very lucky break for MI5.

From the Germans' point of view, *Summer*'s sudden disappearance from the airwaves was explained in the following terms. The Germans knew that *Summer* had *Biscuit*'s address for use in an emergency. Therefore *Biscuit* reported to *Snow* that *Summer* had written to him saying that he believed he was under surveillance by the police and had used his seaman's papers to make a run for it. *Snow* contacted the Germans, saying that *Summer* had made a bid to get back to Europe. He also reported that his wireless set had been left in the cloakroom at Cambridge railway station. The Germans appeared to swallow the story and later ordered *Biscuit* to go and pick the transmitter up – which is exactly what MI5 had hoped they would request and thus allowed them to give the radio to another double cross agent.

In reality *Summer* was bundled off to the safety of Camp 020 for interrogation. After his second round of questioning, *Summer* slit his wrists with a razor blade in his cell. His guard found him in a pool of blood and summoned a doctor. His life saved, *Summer* revealed some hitherto unknown information. He had not been recently recruited by the Nazis as he had first made out. In fact, during his stay in Britain before the war he had been in contact with the Abwehr since October 1938 and had passed on many secrets.

In light of his escape bid, his fragile state of mind and the revelation that he had withheld information from his first interrogation, *Summer* could never be trusted again and his case was ended. The winding up of the *Summer* case had been a sobering lesson to all concerned. As well as the flow of traffic, Robertson and his team would have to keep an eye on the psychology of the agents. In future a single case officer would be assigned to each agent, in order to watch their every move, constantly monitoring their state of mind. As one MI5 employee later commented, life for an ordinary agent in wartime is strenuous enough; for a double agent, the unremitting duplicity meant there was a real chance the agent would fall into a schizophrenic state.[5]

XX

The next major case to fall was the founding agent of the XX system – *Snow*. Although much attention had been showered on the new arrival *Tate*, the *Snow* network remained the most important double cross outfit at the beginning of 1941. After attempts to tempt *Snow*'s controller Nikolaus Ritter (alias Dr Rantzau) to visit the spy in Northern Ireland, in January 1941 *Snow* at last agreed to a meeting with Ritter in Lisbon, Portugal. On this new venture *Snow* decided to take along a 'side-kick' he had discovered, someone he described as being an ex-RAF technician.

The man in question was an ex-con named Walter Dicketts. A former air intelligence officer from World War I, Dicketts had been cashiered for dishonesty and had since served several jail sentences for financial fraud. Dicketts met the 'little man' – as he referred to *Snow* – in a south London pub called the Marlborough on 16 March 1940. *Snow* was going by the name of Thomas Wilson. He and Dicketts got into a conversation about foreign travel, with *Snow* telling him he 'looked like a man who had travelled'. After an evening of plying Dicketts with drink, *Snow* invited him back to his flat for a game of darts. Dicketts agreed and stayed at *Snow*'s apartment until the early hours of the morning.[6]

Snow asked Dicketts what he did for a living, to which he admitted doing very little indeed. *Snow* confided in Dicketts that he had a lot of spare cash as he was in the diamond game and was making a killing. Sensing an opportunity, Dicketts asked *Snow* if he would be interested in financing a scheme he had thought up. He said he had come up with an idea to make squeezable mustard containers that were similar to toothpaste tubes. Dicketts had clearly not done his market research, as the market leader in mustard – Coleman's – already had such a product on the shelves. Unaware of this, *Snow* told him that he and his financial backers might consider financing the idea and asked to meet Dicketts again at the Marlborough.

Of course, Snow had no intention of financing mustard containers; he was simply grooming Dicketts as a potential spy. For his part Dicketts was also playing a game of his own. He was quite sure the little Welshman was a German agent and saw an opportunity to get his old job in the Air Ministry back by exposing him as a spy. Over the next few weeks he met *Snow* again, and secretly followed him to one of his regular meetings with Tommy Robertson. Noticing the clandestine nature of this rendezvous, Dicketts also began trailing Robertson, believing that he too was a German spy. Armed with this belief, Dicketts went to his former employers and expected to get his old job back with the evidence he had accrued. Instead he was put in touch with MI5 and was properly introduced to Robertson who recruited him to 'the family'.

Robertson gave Dicketts the codename *Celery* and bailed him out with £3 to pay his rent.[7] In return for an income, *Celery* begged Robertson for security-related work. From Robertson's point of view the best use for *Celery* was for checking what *Snow* was really up to. The 'little man' was still very much a loose cannon in Robertson's eyes and the MI5 officer was very disturbed to hear that *Snow* had indiscreetly told *Celery* how he was the top man in the British and German secret services. This statement earned the Welshman a dressing-down from Robertson.[8]

With this nonsense behind them, Robertson planned *Snow*'s Lisbon trip and invited *Celery* to go with him. The former RAF man was naturally concerned and before agreeing to go sought reassurances from Robertson that his family would be looked after if he were killed. In preparation, *Celery* was briefed about the sort of information he should be expected to know as an RAF mechanic and was sent on several undercover 'espionage' missions to British factories to see what he could find out for himself. Robertson confided in *Celery* that he would travel to Lisbon by ship via Gibraltar on board the *Cressado*, while *Snow* would fly ahead, arriving a few days before. Once in the Portuguese capital *Celery*'s mission was twofold: to check on the loyalty of *Snow* and to penetrate the Abwehr as far as possible and get into Germany.

Nothing was heard from either agent until the end of March. Both agents arrived back in Britain on 27 March and were immediately taken in for debriefing by MI5. As with the previous trawler incident, the accounts of the mission varied wildly. *Snow* was carrying a large sum of money and explosives concealed in shaving soap, a flashlight, a fountain pen and a pencil. According to *Snow*, he had arrived in Lisbon and was met by a man called Duarte outside a hotel. He followed him to a car, got in and was driven to an apartment where he met Ritter. In *Snow*'s story, the German immediately confronted him and told the Welshman he knew he was in touch with British intelligence. *Snow* matter-of-factly admitted this, replying: 'That's perfectly true. I've been trying for two and a half months to get over to see you about it.'

Robertson could not believe it. Why had the Welshman admitted everything to the Germans without trying to bluff his way out? *Snow* told Robertson that he believed the Doctor was always well informed and that if he had hesitated before answering the accusation, it would have blown the game completely. Realizing that Robertson was having trouble believing him, *Snow* asked if he thought he was trying to double cross him. Robertson hurt *Snow*'s feelings when he replied 'It wouldn't surprise me.'

What Robertson could not understand was if *Snow* had told the Germans he was working for the British, why on earth had Ritter given him £10,000 and the explosives? More to the point, why hadn't the German arrested *Snow* and confronted *Celery* as also being in the pay of the British secret service?

Over and over again, Robertson and, afterwards, John Marriott, went over the story. *Snow* said he told Ritter that the British secret service had walked in on him the previous December. If that was the case, Robertson found it incredible that Ritter did not go all out to try to get descriptions of his opposite numbers, interrogation techniques and so on.

Every time it appeared that a fact had been established, *Snow* would frustratingly contradict himself. Throughout the interviews *Snow* would blame others for his predicament. At one point he even accused *Celery* of being a dope fiend who had taken the barbiturate Veronal before the flight home because he was scared of flying. Such was the confusion surrounding *Snow*'s version of events that Marriott admitted on 3 April, 'I am more than ever convinced that *Snow*'s is a case not for the Security Service but for a brain specialist.' He concluded that *Snow* was lying and had probably not told Ritter anything like what he was claiming.

Meanwhile *Celery* came up with a very different take on things. During his initial debriefing on 28 March, *Celery* appeared very nervous and was astonished when told that *Snow* had been carrying explosives with him. According to *Celery* he had arrived a few days after *Snow*. He first met Ritter, or Dr Jantzen as he was called in Lisbon, in a bar with *Snow*, who had been drinking heavily. Ritter poured half a tumbler of whisky for the British agent and their introduction began. *Celery* had been led to believe that the German was a hard drinker who enjoyed hearing dirty stories. In fact he described Ritter as 'a high pressure salesman of the American type – a clever man and an extremely lucid and convincing talker.'

Ritter suggested that *Celery* ought to go to Germany where he could be questioned in more detail about his information on the RAF. At the sound of this *Snow*'s eyes lit up and he asked if he could go too. Ritter told the Welshman it was hard to get tickets, so for now only *Celery* would be able to go. At this news *Snow* became somewhat dejected and became privately very envious of the attention being shown to his sub-agent by the Germans. He then proceeded to drink himself silly and was in no fit state for anything. *Celery* described *Snow* as almost paralytic from booze every time he saw him.

What started to puzzle *Celery*'s British interrogators hearing this story was the absence of any mention that *Snow* had been blown as working for the British. Nothing was said to *Celery*, who said that *Snow* gave him no particular instructions about going to Germany, except that he did once ask if he wanted to back out of going at the last minute. Although he had offered this way out, he did not give any special reasons why *Celery* might want to take it.

Celery went on to describe how he travelled to Stuttgart, Berlin, Hamburg, back to Berlin and then finally to Madrid before returning to Lisbon. He was gone for 3½ weeks and most of that time was spent in Hamburg, where he was very closely and sometimes aggressively interrogated. Although *Celery* had visited a lot of factories and installations prior to the mission, his German interrogators were not really impressed with the quality of information he provided. *Celery* mitigated these shortcomings by telling the Germans that *Snow* had not actually given him any instructions on what sort of things to look out for. They seemed quite satisfied with this explanation and showered hospitality on him, allowing *Celery* to walk round Hamburg quite freely.

From his time there *Celery* told his British interrogators that the bomb damage was minimal, that there was plenty of food in German restaurants – he had even kept some menus – and that civilian morale was good. In his time in Berlin *Celery* stayed at Hotel Adlon with his Abwehr minder, Georg Sessler, to whom he became quite close and whom he suspected might want to defect. *Celery* was taken to Berlin's train stations to see the lack of bomb damage on them. He was also taken to meet someone described as the assistant of the Information Minister, Dr Goebbels. There he was given some books and gramophone records – parodies of popular British songs – to take back to the United Kingdom and circulate.

When *Celery* eventually returned to Lisbon, *Snow* was beside himself with joy. As far as *Celery* could make out, in his absence *Snow* had spent his whole time getting drunk and was in an awful state. The Welshman had been ill and was being nursed by a Portuguese girl at whom he literally threw money, although *Celery* did not believe there was anything untoward in their relationship. *Snow* had also got himself entangled in a complicated domestic affair, acting as a mediator between a man called Patrick Nolan and his wife, who was contemplating running away with a Frenchman named Olivier Regnault. When *Celery* met the Frenchman, Regnault told him *Snow* had gone out of his mind with drink. Apparently he had worried himself senseless in *Celery*'s absence and his friends thought he was having a nervous breakdown. Regnault called it 'Lisbon fever'.

Lisbon during World War II was described by one visitor as being like Cannes or Monte Carlo during the thirties.[9] With so much suffering going on in the world, the bright lights of Lisbon and the Estoril Casino harked back to happier times. In their last days in the Portuguese capital, *Celery* and *Snow* went to a nightclub and stayed up until 6am with some German girls, one named Sophie and the other Ruth Hutte – a recent arrival from Tangiers where she had been doing a speciality act at Casino Cabaret. Another girl called Lotti Schade turned up at the club, and gave *Celery* her address in Berlin and a photo, telling him to look her up some time.[10] Of course *Celery* and *Snow* knew the girls were German agents – honey traps sent to keep watch on them.

In his time abroad, *Celery* had picked up quite a lot of information on the German secret service. He described how they worked very long hours and that about 50 per cent of them were regular drug users. Apparently they would take cocaine in the morning as a pick-me-up to get through the stresses of the day and then Veronal at night to knock them out and ensure a heavy sleep. When *Celery* asked about the health effects of doing this, he heard the old story given by addicts that it was they who controlled the drug – not the other way round.

Over dinners and conversations, *Celery* gained huge amounts of anecdotal evidence about German invasion preparations, plans and their confidence that it would go ahead at a time of Hitler's choosing. The people he spoke to were convinced that the Royal Navy would be neutralized by mine-laying U-boats and fast patrol boats, and that the RAF bombers could not hit a barn door if they tried. They were totally taken in by Nazi propaganda and unwilling to listen to any argument that conflicted with their innate sense of superiority.

Celery also fulfilled the other part of his mission, by checking up on *Snow*'s standing with the Germans. *Celery* reported that the 'Doctor' was genuinely fond of *Snow* and was planning to use him as a contact point when the Germans finally got round to invading the British Isles. *Celery* reported Ritter as saying: '[*Snow*] is a fool in many ways. He drinks too much and he lives on his nerves but I am prepared to go on trusting him because I have known him for more than four years and he has never, to my knowledge, let me down.'

When *Celery* had probed Ritter, asking if the information *Snow* had provided had been very good, the German replied: said: 'No, [*Snow*] has not given me very much but I think he is going to be very useful to us in other ways.' *Celery* asked what these other ways might be. 'Don't ask too many questions,' cautioned Ritter, 'but [*Snow*] is a very clever chemist. In fact in some ways he is brilliant ... I am very fond of [him] but he is a goddam lazy son of a bitch and he won't get going unless someone gives him a good kick in the pants ... [*Snow*] spends a hell of a lot of money but we don't mind. We have plenty of it here.' *Celery*'s own opinion of *Snow* was less charitable: 'I think he is a maniac and lives in an atmosphere of mystery.'

On 1 April Robertson decided that *Celery* should be told that *Snow* had given the game away to Ritter before his arrival in Lisbon. Masterman told

Celery that *Snow* claimed to have betrayed them to the Germans and explained that this piece of information had been withheld from *Celery* by MI5 for obvious reasons. *Celery* took the news calmly and, after some reflection, said that he thought *Snow* was lying and did not believe he had told Ritter anything of the kind. *Celery* explained that *Snow* had not mentioned a word about this to him and that he would on no account have gone to Germany if he had known. Masterman told *Celery* that they believed *Snow* had told Ritter, and *Snow* had not warned him on Ritter's say so. Pressing home the point, Masterman told *Celery* he believed that *Snow* had allowed him to travel to Germany knowing full well it would result in a death sentence. Taking in the full enormity of the revelation, *Celery* said he would like to confront *Snow* about this face to face.

The following day, 2 April, there was a lengthy interview between both men. In the exchange of words between them, almost nothing could be agreed upon. Witness this exchange relating to *Snow* telling *Celery* about the £10,000 he brought home:

Snow: I told you that the first time I met you.
Celery: You never mentioned the thing.
Snow: By God, I'm certain of that.
Celery: It was when I came back [from Germany] that you mentioned the second £5,000.
Snow: I'm not selling – to Christ you're a liar – to cover yourself as much as you ...
Celery: I've nothing to cover myself on at all.
Snow: You're a bloody liar.
Celery: Why do you bluff?
Snow: I'm not bluffing. You know bloody well I'm not bluffing.
Celery: I know perfectly well that you are bluffing.
Snow: You know I'm not.
Celery: Or else giving you the benefit of your mentality, your memory is very short.
Snow: So you think I'm crazy like you tell me these people think I'm mental?
Celery: You said to me that you were very simple ...

And on and on it went.

With *Snow* and *Celery* contradicting one another, the matter was referred to a meeting of the W Committee on the morning of 5 April at which Robertson and Masterman were also present. Masterman set out what he believed the various facts might be.

The first was that *Snow* had not betrayed them to the Germans, but had concocted this story to enable him to retire without fatally damaging his standing in either camp. On the other hand his story might have been true, in which case Ritter was keeping him on for some unknown reason. Lastly it might have been the case that *Snow* was a rogue and that the Germans had known he had links with the British all along, but believed his first loyalty was to Germany.

There was also confusion over *Celery*. Masterman wondered if he had really been to Germany or not. Some of the information about ships in Hamburg did not bear up to scrutiny when checked by Ewen Montagu and there was some concern over the lack of bomb damage *Celery* reported seeing in Berlin and Hamburg. With this in mind, Masterman speculated that *Celery* might now be working for the Germans.

It must be remembered that at this time the likes of Robertson and Masterman were not entirely sure of the extent to which they controlled German espionage in the United Kingdom. Although they suspected they controlled the majority of it, at least all the active agents, their confidence had been shaken on 1 April by the discovery of ter Braak's corpse in a Cambridge air raid shelter. If one spy had eluded them, how many more were out there?

In an attempt to solve the case, Masterman met *Celery* on 10 April for an interview. The agent had been allowed a short holiday during which he had come up with a scheme of hiring a boat to get over to the German-occupied Channel Islands. He clearly wanted to continue his double agent mission and gave Masterman the impression that he was loyal and had been visibly upset about the doubts cast on him. In his debrief, Masterman said that although *Celery* had an excellent memory, the conversations he had with him were of such length and complexity he found it difficult to believe *Celery* could repeat a story of such length without introducing errors and contradictions unless the story was substantially true. Masterman concluded that although *Celery* was dangerously impressed by German efficiency he had in the main behaved with loyalty and done his best for the British cause. Robertson generally agreed with Masterman and although he suspected that *Celery* might have gone some way towards becoming a proper German agent said: 'whatever faults he may have had in the past, he has done a brave deed by going into Germany in wartime.' In a little twist, after the war Sessler revealed that *Celery* had told him he was a British agent.

Later that day, Guy Liddell called a meeting with Dick White, Robertson, Masterman and Marriott and had a long discussion about the case.[11] They agreed the only safe option was to assume that Ritter knew as much about the network of controlled agents as *Snow* or *Celery* did. On this assumption, *Snow* was of no further use. *Celery* would be mothballed until more light could be cast on the subject, perhaps through *Tate*.

There was one question they wanted answered before closing the file completely. Why had Ritter given *Snow* £10,000 and the explosives? *Snow* had claimed that although he told Ritter he was working for the British, he had said that his network in Wales was intact and not under control. Masterman speculated that Ritter might have believed this and was retaining *Snow* for use as a paymaster or for use in the event of an invasion. He might also study the traffic that *Snow* was sending over under duress and from that work out what information the British regarded as unimportant or important. Masterman also speculated that the German might have retained *Snow* even though he was suspicious of him, in order to maintain his own prestige in the Abwehr. Whatever the reason, it was clear Ritter wanted to keep the *Snow* network running, and for that very reason it had to be closed down.

Robertson and Masterman met *Snow* and told him the news. All they wanted him to do was to radio Germany and ask for advice on what to do with his equipment. *Snow*'s response was quite bizarre. He asked the two MI5 officers if there was anything useful he could do for Britain. His patience in the Welshman expended, Robertson turned the question back on *Snow* and asked him the same. What did *he* think he could do?

The Welshman seemed at a loss to understand why he could not continue on as normal. It was as if he could not grasp the seriousness of his apparent disclosure to Ritter. Masterman told *Snow* that he could not carry on because his cover was blown and that he had betrayed *Celery*, endangering his life by not warning him. As *Snow* wriggled his way around an answer he contradicted himself after almost every sentence. This is an excerpt from the interview:

Robertson: Well now, I am coming on to a second point now. We have been through your statements, as I said before, very carefully. We have been through *Celery*'s statements very carefully, and we are unanimous in our opinion that you did not tell *Celery* that the game was blown before he went into Germany.

Snow: Well, I did tell him before he went into Germany.

Robertson: Well, that is our opinion, and that being the case, you definitely sent a man on a most dangerous mission.

Snow: That's a lie.

Robertson: You sent him knowingly, I maintain, to put the worst construction on it, to his death probably.

Snow: I did not. I did nothing of the kind …

Robertson: But I gathered that this exchange of confidences between [*Celery*] and you took place, according to you, before you went to the meeting?

Snow: What confidences do you mean?

Robertson: Informing him that the game was up.

Snow: I believe I told him in the room.

Robertson: In which room?

Snow: But I know I told him in front of the Doctor, definitely. In the room there.

Masterman: Doesn't it seem to you that it was a very treacherous act, to say the least of it, not to tell him before he got to the Doctor?

Snow: I am positive that I told him before he went to the Doctor.

Masterman: Positive you told him before he went to the Doctor?

Snow: Yes ... [etc]

The day after this meeting *Snow* was informed that a radio signal was to be sent to Hamburg saying that his nerves had collapsed and that he was giving up secret service work. In the message he would ask what to do with his transmitter and explosives. The reason given for the Committee closing down the case was that they believed *Celery*'s story and that *Snow* was guilty of treachery by not warning *Celery*. Despite the best attempts by his son to have him released, *Snow* was interned for the rest of the war, first at Stafford Jail from where he tried to escape with a Dutch fascist called Dirk Boon, then at Dartmoor Prison and finally on the Isle of Man.[12]

XX

It is worth pausing for a moment at this point and lingering longer on the Lisbon meeting. What if *Snow* had told the truth and Ritter now suspected he was working for the British? There is a very different 'German' perspective on the events that shows how lucky MI5 really was. In 1958 a book was published called *They Spied on England* by Scottish writer Charles Wighton, in collaboration with the investigative journalist Günter Peis. It was advertised as being based on the war diaries of General Lahousen, head of Abwehr Section II (Sabotage). It drew on a number of interviews with Abwehr officers that were conducted mostly by Peis, and was apparently vetted by MI5 before release. What is most important about this version is that it claims to be the real story that Lahousen and others withheld from MI5 when interrogated at the end of the war. Lahousen told his fellow Austrian, Peis, that the contents of his war diary were to be withheld until Austria and Germany were restored as sovereign states at the end of Allied occupation. This occurred in May 1955, by which time Lahousen was dead and beyond cross-examination.

This version of the story concerning agent *Johnny* correctly names him as Arthur Owens, a Welsh Nationalist. It says that before the war there were several attempts made to contact members of the Welsh Nationalist Party and other extremists. One of these missions was undertaken by Hans Heinrich Kuenemann, who posed as the managing director of a German engineering firm with a branch in Cardiff. Other missions were carried out by Professor Friedrich Schoberth, a visiting lecturer at Cardiff University; Franz Richter, the manager of a factory in Barry; and the German consul in Liverpool, Dr Walter Reinhard. In their book Wighton and Peis assumed that one or more of them had got to Owens before they successfully left the United Kingdom in the weeks and days before war broke out in 1939.[13]

They then explain how Owens began frequenting the German club in Bayswater and how he managed to make contact with the Abwehr in Brussels during the spring of 1937, all of which fits with the account given by MI5. Where their account starts to differ is with the arrival of Owens in Lisbon in June 1940 around the time of the Dunkirk evacuation. Even here the story more or less holds up if one assumes that Wighton and Peis confused Owens with his sub-agent Sam Macarthy (*Biscuit*) who did go to Lisbon around that time, after the trawler rendezvous.

Where the account gets interesting is with the arrival of 'Doctor Randzau' [sic] on the scene. Wighton and Peis explain how the Doctor had been in charge of Owens for some time, how the Welshman had taken his girlfriend Lily to meet him and how they had been treated as personal friends by the Doctor and his wife in Hamburg – all of which fits with previous accounts. However, what is new is how the Doctor travelled to Lisbon posing as a diplomatic courier, flying from Stuttgart to Barcelona, and from then on travelling overland to Portugal.

On this voyage the Doctor began to harbour doubts about his favourite Welshman. How on earth was a seemingly insignificant travelling salesman able to get clearance for a trip abroad to Portugal? The more he thought about it, the more concerned he became. Back before the war had started, the Doctor had apparently given Owens a little piece of advice. He had told the Welshman that if he ever got into trouble for his illegal activities he ought to go to MI5 and come clean. By doing so there was at least a chance he would save his own neck. Had the little Welshman gone to MI5 as he had suggested? Was the Doctor being double crossed? Ritter was determined to find out in the Portuguese capital.[14]

Reaching Lisbon the Doctor made contact with one of his agents, a Spaniard known as the 'Don'. In early 1940 neutral Lisbon was a hive of refugees and spies. Every major espionage agency in the world had its tentacles in the Portuguese capital, and for this reason Ritter had to be very careful by whom and with whom he was seen. With his growing suspicion over the Welshman an additional factor, 'Randzau' did not want to meet him in public – which is where the Don came in.

Before setting out for Lisbon, Owens had been told to watch out for a man with a sharp nose drinking on the terrace of a prominent café. Owens was told to carry a copy of *The Times* under his arm and to introduce himself with the words: 'Jack told me to say he was asking for you.' With these formalities completed, the Don took *Snow* to meet his Abwehr controller. Although the chronology is out of sequence, with the account giving this conversation as having occurred in June 1940, it bears such striking similarities to the secret interviews conducted with *Snow* and *Celery* that it cannot be discounted as evidence, albeit anecdotal.

The day after Owens' arrival in Lisbon, 'Randzau' confronted him and asked him to explain how on earth he had got permission to travel and, more importantly, whether he had taken the advice about working for the British if caught. Owens replied to this second query 'not directly'. He told the Doctor that he had applied for an export permit to sell electrical equipment to Portugal. He then described how he was interviewed by a captain he believed was with the 'Field Security Police'. The captain appeared sceptical about the story and asked about his previous business links on the Continent, in particular in Germany. Owens claimed to have told the captain that he had done business with a German export-import firm in Hamburg. According to Owens' story, the following day a colonel put him through an intense interrogation, which he had survived. The British had then agreed to his export permit because they were desperate to maintain as much trade with neutral countries as possible. This account appeared to placate 'Randzau' and the two men got down to business.

If this is the German version of events, possibly given by Ritter to Peis in an interview in the 1950s, it is interesting to note that there was a confrontation and an accusation, but that Owens did not reveal he worked for the British, only that he had been interrogated by them quite hard. That version of events would fit in with MI5's belief that Owens was probably lying when he claimed to have told Ritter everything.

The Wighton/Peis account goes on to explain how Owens told the Doctor he had recruited a technician from the RAF called Jack Brown

(*Celery*). Owens said he could bring Brown to Lisbon at a later date, in perhaps two to three months. Again there is a discrepancy with the chronology, with the subsequent meeting supposedly happening in October 1940. Taking into account lapses in memory after almost 15 years from the events to the time Wighton and Peis were making their enquiries, and the non-disclosure of the MI5 files which would have given them a firm underpinning to the chronology of the *Snow* case, the mix-up is perhaps understandable. What is certain is that there are too many similarities with the British records for the account to be a complete fabrication.

As with the MI5 interrogation accounts, the Wighton/Peis version has Owens arrive 48 hours before 'Brown' (*Celery*). Brown then arrived by boat, as was the case. In this new Lisbon account, Ritter quickly came to the conclusion that Owens was in a state of near-hysteria and concluded that the pressure of being a spy was getting to him. He privately decided that it would soon be time to dispose of Owens.

In the meantime Owens told him that his brother-in-law was a foreman in a munitions factory and asked the Doctor for some explosives to pass on to him. Ritter passed Owens on to Dr Rudolfs who worked in Lahousen's sabotage section in Lisbon. It was Rudolfs who gave Owens the fuses disguised as fountain pens – photographs of which exist in the *Snow* files in Britain's National Archive.

Brown arrived in Lisbon and was introduced to the Doctor, who wondered if the new arrival's limp handshake indicated a weak personality or a distaste for dealing with Germans. The Abwehr man in fact noticed that Brown's eyes were very hard and penetrating, which immediately gave Ritter the impression that he was dealing with a far more complex character than Owens. Brown explained that he had been flung out of the RAF and was desperately short of money. He required £250 a month and for the sum of £2,000 was willing to undergo a thorough examination at the hands of German technical experts to prove how much he knew. Ritter replied that he was not really qualified to interrogate Brown on technical matters and asked if he was prepared to go to Germany. To bring technical experts to Portugal would, he explained, draw too much attention to their activities. If Brown agreed to go, Ritter gave him his word of honour that he would be allowed to return to Lisbon whenever he wished.

At this point in the conversation, Owens butted in and told his compatriot 'That's wonderful. Accept the Doctor's word. Let's go, Jack.' Owens naturally assumed he would be able to tag along, but the Abwehr officer would not allow it. Ritter was worried that the little Welshman was too keen to go to Germany and that, once there, he might not ever agree to go back to England again.

There is now another important component that is missing from the story told to MI5. In this account, after Brown agreed to go to Germany, Ritter flew off ahead of him, telling Brown that he would send an escort to pick him up in a few days. Within a week Brown was picked up and taken to Hamburg by the Abwehr's Dr Sessler. The British interrogation reports give the impression that Ritter remained in Portugal during *Celery*'s visit to Germany. On the contrary, in this account, Ritter entertained Jack Brown during his stay.

While he was in Hamburg Brown was treated well, although his movements were constantly monitored by the Gestapo. Brown gave no indication that he was a double agent. In fact he did nothing at all, went nowhere, did not try to contact anyone and did not probe his contacts for any sensitive information. The only thing that really made Ritter suspicious was a signet ring Brown wore, which Frau Ritter pointed out during a dinner with the ex-RAF man. Brown opened the ring and it contained a picture of a beautiful woman. Frau Ritter asked Brown if the woman was his wife? Brown laughingly replied 'Not yet.'

Ritter went off and made a telephone call to Abwehr headquarters. A short while later a man arrived and joined the party. At this point, at a discreet signal from her husband, Frau Ritter made her apologies and left. When the next round of drinks arrived, a sleeping pill was dropped into Brown's whisky. Brown knocked back the drink and quickly passed out under the effects of the drug. In the meantime Ritter sent his ring off to be photographed. Within two hours, the ring was back on Brown's finger, as he woke up in the bar feeling groggy, apologizing to his companions for having fallen asleep. Ritter laughed it off and told him the Scotch in Germany must be stronger than in London.

Next morning Ritter had the photographs of the ring examined. The German scientists did see some numbers and letters, which they said might be the address in a neutral capital used as a post box by the Russian secret service, which made them suspect he was a Soviet agent trying to get out of England. At this point Abwehr chief Admiral Canaris began to take a personal interest in the case and quizzed Ritter about the trustworthiness of the new agent. Canaris wondered if Brown should be kept in Germany as a precaution, but Ritter told his chief that he had chivalrously given a promise he could return to Portugal and did not want to break his word. Canaris was not about to make Ritter do this, and so Brown was allowed back to Portugal. Ritter was adamant that *Celery* was a communist spy who went AWOL on the way back to Portugal in Madrid and contacted the Spanish underground before travelling to Russia.[15] As for Owens waiting in Lisbon, he had broken down completely under the watchful eye of the Don. He pleaded to be allowed to go to Germany, but the Don had been told under no circumstances to allow this to happen. He was sent back to Britain and was classed as having outlived his usefulness and denied future help.

The Wighton and Peis account was expanded by the Pulitzer prize-winning author Ladislas Farago in his 1971 book *The Game of the Foxes*. When writing his account of the *Snow* case, Farago had the earlier work of Wighton and Peis and literally thousands of captured microfilms from the Abwehr's wartime archives he had discovered in the United States. Most importantly, he met Ritter and discussed the war years with him and was shown a draft of the memoirs Ritter was writing.

This story agrees that there was a confrontation between Ritter and Owens after the German became suspicious of how the Welshman got clearance to travel to Lisbon. Owens told Ritter he had found it almost impossible to find a way to Portugal, so he had gone to the secret service and volunteered his services to them, simply in order to make the trip to Lisbon. He also told Ritter that the British were suspicious at first, but that he tried to allay their fears by saying he wanted to do something for the war effort but was too old to be a soldier. A secret service captain interviewed him and said he knew he had been working for the Nazis, but if Owens told him everything he would be prepared to help. Owens said he told the captain about everything, including his relationship with Ritter. The captain was then alleged to have asked him if he would be able to arrange a meeting with Ritter in Casablanca. Owens told the captain that he could arrange a meeting in Lisbon or Madrid, which is how he had managed to get the permission to travel. The Welshman then proceeded to show Ritter some material that he described as rubbish – what the British secret service had planted on him – before revealing some bona fide material, including a sample of a new alloy being used in the manufacture of shells. In the Farago account, Ritter reacted to this revelation with the words: 'A fine story' and gave 'a sardonic grin'. Owens pleaded with the German, asking if he had ever let him down in the past.

What appears most likely is that Owens told Ritter he was working for the British secret service, but lied by saying he was still a loyal German agent. Ritter appears to have accepted this and thus believed that *Celery* was genuinely recruited by Owens. However, because of the revelation that the British secret service were on to Owens, and believing him burnt out by the strains of secret service work, Ritter decided that *Johnny*'s days were numbered.

This version of events is certainly endorsed by Ritter's memoirs. At the end of the war he was picked up by the United States Air Force. They passed him over to the British, but not before telling him 'Don't tell the Limeys what you've told us'. He was passed on to MI5 for interrogation. The trouble was that the British to a certain extent tiptoed around the interrogation because they did not want to reveal to Ritter that they had controlled his agents. For his part, Ritter did not volunteer as much information as he could have because he genuinely feared being tried for war crimes.

As for Owens' admission that he was working for the British secret service, Ritter took the news with a pinch of salt. *Johnny* had worked for him for two years and had always been truthful, and Ritter admitted that he liked the little fellow. In his memoirs he described hearing the news and what his reaction was:[16]

> But now everything suddenly had an unpleasant taste. If I put myself into the position of my English opponents, then I could not quite actually imagine them letting *Johnny* travel alone to Lisbon. Nevertheless, it would soon show up whether the little one was betraying me or my British colleagues. I smiled somewhat ironically and said: 'That's a great story!'

Ritter has a point here. If the British were suspicious of Owens, they could have had him travel with *Celery* acting as a minder. The fact that *Celery* travelled separately was an indication that *Celery* was not a British secret service minder, but a genuine spy whom Owens had recruited. In any case, Ritter decided to trust the Welshman for the time being.

Fortunately for the British, Ritter was not around long enough to discover Owens' duplicity. Even before *Snow* and *Celery* left Portugal, Ritter was summoned by Admiral Canaris from Lisbon and met him on 20 March. Ritter was informed he was to be reassigned for special duties in Africa under General Rommel. All of his cases were passed over to Jules Boeckel.[17]

At the end of this mission in September 1941, Ritter was travelling back to Lisbon via Rome. As he was preparing to take a military flight to Portugal, he received a telephone call from Berlin. It was from the chief of Abwehr I, Hans Piekenbrock, who read him the headline of the *New York Times* dated 20 September 1941:[18]

'GERMAN SPY RING BROKEN'

In addition to his work against Britain, Ritter had looked after business in the United States. A major German spy ring headed by South African-born Frederick Duquesne was betrayed by William Sebold, who was a double agent working for the FBI (Federal Bureau of Investigation). Sebold had been recruited by Ritter, whose name was printed in the *New York Times* article, along with his alias in the United States – Dr Rankin. This disclosure was the end of Ritter's secret war and he was reassigned to active service.

When, years later, Ritter was told that his little *Johnny* was a double agent named *Snow*, he didn't believe it. When the *Snow* story first came out it was still years, decades in fact, before the MI5 records were released. Because of this there were some inaccuracies, and these were seized upon by Ritter, who ended his memoirs declaring that *Johnny* had remained loyal to him and that it was the British who had been deceived. He went as far as to call him 'a master spy'.[19] Although Ritter wrote that he had lost contact with *Johnny*, he drew great satisfaction from news that the Welshman was living in Ireland with Lily and their children.

6

THE 'DICKY' PERIOD

ON THE NIGHT OF 7–8 April 1941, a German seaplane deposited Tor
Glad and John Moe into a dinghy off the Banffshire coast in Scotland. The
two spies were Norwegian, although Moe had British citizenship through his
mother, and spoke English with a Lancashire accent having spent holidays with
his grandparents in Ashton-under-Lyne. Both men had no intention of working
for the Germans and had decided to give themselves up on arrival in Britain.

Landing near Crovie, on the Moray Firth, in the early hours, the two
agents went to a nearby fisherman's cottage and bashed on the door with the
butt of a pistol. When the occupant eventually answered he was surprised to
see two armed men at the doorway. When Moe told him they had just been
landed by a German aircraft, the fisherman slammed the door shut in their
face and telephoned the police. The two men went off on bicycles and
eventually flagged down the police car that had been sent to investigate the
fisherman's call. The two men immediately offered themselves into custody,
claiming they had been landed as German spies.

At Banff police station they were treated well enough, offered cups of tea
and before long became the object of curiosity among a number of local
visitors. When the local chief constable arrived he contacted someone in
Aberdeen and was told to put the spies into isolation – too late, as it turned out.

By 6pm a security officer, Major Peter Perfect, arrived from Edinburgh
and took control of the situation. He was annoyed at the chief constable for
having allowed the two men to speak to so many locals, and demanded a list
of names of everyone who had visited them. In turn all these people were
tracked down and had the frighteners put on them – *they had definitely not
met any German spies that afternoon.*

The security officer sat the two Norwegians down and began a preliminary
interrogation. They told him they had been recruited by the Abwehr in Oslo
and had undergone the training specifically to get the opportunity to travel to
Britain, where they could join the Allies. They outlined their mission, and
showed Major Perfect their equipment, including a set of detonators concealed
inside a hairbrush.[1]

Despite spending a night in a cell, the two Norwegians were still treated
hospitably on their trip south to London the next day. That is, until they

arrived at Camp 020 in the back of an army truck. As the tarpaulin cover opened, a captain screamed at them: 'Get down, you bloody spies!' John Moe began explaining that they were not really spies, but was met with a barrage of abuse by the seemingly hysterical captain: 'Shut up, you bastards! Nazi pigs.' At this point the two Norwegians began to realize that perhaps everything was not going to work out as smoothly as they had anticipated.[2]

The two men were taken to separate cells and submitted to the full works. First up for Moe was a visit to Dr Harold Dearden, the camp's often-maligned resident psychiatrist. After a physical examination, Moe was examined by a dentist who searched his mouth for items hidden in dentures, including suicide pills. Following the examinations, he was taken to face Commandant Stephens for the first time.

Moe describes walking into a huge dining room with a table at one end. Behind the green baize-covered table was seated a group of men whose faces were obscured by the light of two large windows behind them. To the side he noticed his radio set had been brought into the room. It suddenly dawned on Moe that this was a court martial and he was about to be tried for espionage. His discomfort increased when he asked the panel of seated men if they wanted him to show them how to work the radio. One of the panel, probably Stephens, yelled at Moe: 'Come here! And in future only speak when you are spoken to.'[3]

Eventually Moe managed to establish his identity through his grandfather, a colonel in the 9th Manchester Regiment. The panel checked this information and appeared to relax somewhat. A chair was brought for 'Mr Moe', who proceeded to tell the panel everything he knew about the Abwehr in Oslo. Next up for a grilling was Tor Glad. What neither Moe nor Glad had any inkling of was that their arrival was not unexpected, but had been revealed by ISOS.[4] What the panel at 020 was doing was checking their version of events against the information provided by the Bletchley decrypts.

Whereas Moe appeared to be genuine, the panel were suspicious that Glad had worked for Nazi censorship in Norway. Although some suspicion remained against Glad, the two Norwegians were handed over to B1a and taken out for dinner.

Moe recalled meeting a group of civilians in plus-fours, checked socks and tweed jackets with leather trim who introduced themselves as Charles, Jock and Bill. They were then joined by a Danish-speaking man who could understand Norwegian and were taken out for dinner at a restaurant called L'Ecu, near Piccadilly. After a full meal, followed by drinks and cigars, the two Norwegians were taken by tube to Earls Court, where MI5 kept a safe house in Argyll Mansions.

All the while the Norwegians were being entertained they were also being interrogated by the secretary of the Twenty Committee, Charles Cholmondeley, and ferried around by Jock Horsfall. On 10 April, the day after their night out in Piccadilly, Liddell recorded his verdict on the new arrivals. His concern was that Moe appeared 'under the thumb' of Glad, who had joined the Germans very soon after the invasion of Norway. Although Glad said he had helped a lot of his countrymen to join up with the Norwegian forces, Liddell was not sure about him.[5]

By the end of April the two agents were very much set up. They had been unkindly codenamed *Mutt* and *Jeff* after the cartoon characters whom they were thought to resemble. Like the cartoon duo, Moe (*Mutt*) was short and stout, while Glad (*Jeff*) was tall and lanky. They were installed in a safe house at 35 Crespigny Road, Hendon, and assigned Christopher Harmer as their case officer. Living next door with his wife and son was radio expert 'Ted' Poulton who would supervise their transmissions.

Although *Mutt* appeared to be completely genuine, suspicion over *Jeff* continued. In attempt to loosen his tongue, one of the pair's minders took *Jeff* out on a pub crawl. It was a disastrous move. While *Jeff* could hold his drink, his minder Philip Rea entirely lost control of himself and started telling the Norwegian all about daredevil exploits he had performed for MI6. In the end *Jeff* had to carry Rea back to Crespigny Road. He was very quickly transferred out of MI5.

The end for *Jeff* came when, bored at the relative inactivity, he broke his curfew by spending the night with a nurse called Joan. He then upset the authorities by trying to sell his brand new Leica camera to a local photographic shop. This version of the German camera was new and unavailable in Britain and so the shopkeeper became suspicious and reported the matter to the police. On 16 August *Jeff* was taken by Harmer to John Marriott, who informed the Norwegian that he was unreliable and could not be used. However, because of the secrets he knew, he had to be interned for the duration of the war. From that point on, *Jeff*'s messages would be sent by an MI5 substitute.

XX

Since arriving in the United Kingdom and coming under British control, *Tate* had been operating from Barnet under the alias Harry Williamson. So impressed were the Germans with the quality of his traffic that six weeks into his mission Nikolaus Ritter nominated him for the Iron Cross First Class.[6] His British employers were equally happy with him and *Tate* enjoyed quite a degree of personal freedom. For a spell he lived at Robertson's home, with his wife Joan and their young daughter.

MI5 feared that if Ritter believed *Snow* was working under British control, then he would have to accept that *Tate* was also controlled. With this in mind, and obviously not realizing that Ritter was no longer in Portugal running the agents in England, MI5 decided to test *Tate*'s position with the Abwehr by urgently requesting more funds. By judging how much effort the Germans put into supplying this money, and by looking at the amount of money offered, they hoped to gain some appreciation of the agent's standing with the enemy.

On 10 April Liddell recorded that *Tate* had made an urgent request for cash. *Tate* had a certain way with words and his broadcasts were often peppered with expletives. His message to Hamburg went along the lines of a demand that unless they paid him £4,000 they could 'go fuck themselves'.[7] A week later Liddell recorded that the Germans had suggested dropping money from an aircraft and then sending a larger amount of money later on, care of the Post Office at Watford. Encouraged by this news, Liddell made arrangements with the Air Ministry not to shoot down the German plane. However, the Abwehr changed its mind and informed *Tate* they were arranging for someone to parachute in with the money. Furthermore, *Tate* would know this agent from his time in Hamburg.

The arrival of this new agent was also foretold by another captured agent called Josef Jakobs, who had arrived in Britain by parachute on the night of 31 January. As he landed, Jakobs broke his ankle and spent the night in agony caught up in his parachute and unable to move. The pain was so unbearable that in the morning he pulled out his pistol and began firing into the air to attract attention. He did not have too long to wait before being picked up, and after an initial interview at Camp 020, Jakobs was taken to hospital and allowed to recover from his injury before further attempts were made to interrogate him. Although the spell in hospital had revived his spirits and he proved a tough nut to crack, on 29 April 1941 Jakobs revealed the description of a man who might be expected to arrive in the near future.

In the early hours of 13 May, agent Karel Richter parachuted into England from a plane piloted by Gartenfeld. After burying his equipment and going into hiding for three days, Richter walked into the town of Colney and approached PC Scott in the High Street. Richter told the policeman he was feeling unwell and asked to be taken to the nearest hospital. Instead, Richter found himself in the local police station where he was searched and a sum of £500 and $1,400 was found on him. The local superintendent had previously been warned by MI5 to be on the look-out for anyone carrying large sums of money, so Richter was immediately suspected of being a spy. The fact that his identification papers had been based on the *Snow* blueprint sealed his fate.

Under questioning, Richter claimed he was a Sudeten Czech; he had landed in a boat ten miles west of Cromer on the previous night and was on his way to London, where he was due to meet someone outside the barber's shop of the Regent Palace Hotel. He claimed not to know who this person was but he had been told to hand over £450. Richter told the police that he was formerly in a concentration camp and accepted the mission for a chance to escape to America. A plausible story, perhaps, but MI5 had heard that sort of thing before.

Richter was sent off to Camp 020, where he proved a difficult subject. Much to the annoyance of his interrogators he gloated over them, telling them that very soon the Germans would invade and it would soon be him sitting on the other side of the interrogation table. His spirits were dampened somewhat when the information about him provided by Jakobs was revealed. Then, after much careful grooming, Jakobs was brought into the interrogation room to confront Richter.

After this unexpected rendezvous, chinks began to appear in Richter's armour. It still required 17 hours of interrogation before the German agent revealed where his parachute and equipment had been hidden. Accompanied by Commandant Stephens and other camp officers, Richter was taken back to the place where he had hidden the equipment near Hatfield.

Further interrogation revealed that Richter had been recruited by Jules Boeckel who had had him trained in air intelligence and radio transmission. He was then handed over to Hauptmann Praetorius who completed his instruction. The most alarming revelation to come from Richter regarded his mission. Initially he said that he had to give some money and a quartz radio crystal to another German agent at the Regent Palace Hotel. After this he was to make meteorological reports and provide details of the electrical grid system in England. However, as the interrogation progressed, Richter revealed his primary mission was to check up on the reliability of *Tate*. Richter explained some of the recent messages sent by *Tate* had caused the Germans to become suspicious that he was either under control or had been substituted by another person, which was in fact the case. Praetorius had apparently described *Tate* to Richter as 'our master pearl' before adding: 'If he is false, then the whole string is false.' Richter then went on to explain that once he had met *Tate* he had to make every effort to obtain a boat and return to Germany in order to report back in person.

This was alarming news to say the least. Tommy Robertson later described it as 'a dicky period in our career which we were never anxious to be looked at too closely'.[8] Clearly Richter could not be allowed to return to Germany and therefore his usefulness as a double agent was very limited, as the Germans would press him to report on *Tate*.

Meanwhile, *Tate* had been on the air complaining that his money had still not showed up. He sent the German another of his short, but violent tirades, this time not even bothering to encode it, but sending the message *en clair*: 'I shit on Germany and its whole fucking secret service.'[9] This cajoling appeared to work, and it was not long before the Germans suggested a new plan. *Tate* was told to take a No.11 bus from Victoria Station at 4pm. On board the bus would be a Japanese man carrying a copy of *The Times* and a book in his left hand. At the first stop *Tate* and the Japanese would get off the bus and wait for the next No.11 to come along. *Tate* was to sit next to the Japanese and ask him if there was any news in the paper. The Japanese man would hand *Tate* the newspaper, which would contain the money.

Agreeing to the plan, *Tate* pointed out that the No.11 no longer had a terminus at Victoria and suggested using a No.16 instead. Robertson decided that some undercover Special Branch officers should put the Japanese courier under observation to establish his identity and see where he went.

After a few missed opportunities, the plan went ahead on 29 May. The scheme almost failed when the bus was stopped by a policeman at a crossroads. Believing this was the first stop, *Tate* and the courier jumped off the bus, which then drove off without them. Realizing their mistake, the pair were then unable to get onto the following bus, which was not held up at the crossroads. Eventually the pair got onto the fourth bus to come by, all of which messed up the Special Branch officers waiting up the road. Luckily another Special Branch officer – a champion cyclist – was following the bus on his bicycle. He saw what had gone wrong and so cycled off ahead to warn everyone further up the road. The exchange went ahead as planned and *Tate* walked away £200 the richer. He later radioed Hamburg and informed them he would be off the air for several days as he was going to get drunk. The Japanese courier was photographed and followed back to the Japanese embassy by two Special Branch women. He turned out to be Lieutenant Commander Mitinory Yosii, one of the assistant naval attachés.

Despite getting the money, *Tate* needed a means of regular income. Even at 1941 prices, £200 was not going to last an active spy without any other income too long in the field. The answer to the problem was aptly codenamed Plan *Midas*.

This plan was the brainchild of Dusko Popov, the double agent brought to London just before Christmas. The Yugoslavian playboy had been kept quite busy, making several trips to Lisbon. Furthering his career as a German spy, Popov had carried out several reconnaissance missions with his Scottish case officer, William Luke – whom Popov knew by the alias Bill Mathews. The Yugoslav merited special considerations because he was not a radio agent – he would actually have to report back to the Germans what he had seen under cross-examination. Therefore he was actually taken out by his case officer to visit the sites in question. However, once they arrived close to a site, Popov was left in a local pub while the case officer went and took the photographs on behalf of the agent. Once developed, these photos would be shown to him, often with bits blacked out, revealing what he was meant to have seen. The trouble was that if the Yugoslav actually saw the sites himself, the Germans might be able to coax more out of him than the British wished them to know. This was especially true when he was sent to spy out some of Colonel Turner's decoy sites. If Popov saw that a Q site was actually nothing more than a series of lights on top of poles, there was always the danger this might leak out.

He had also spent considerable energy promoting a deception scheme devised by Ewen Montagu, codenamed Plan *IV*. Montagu proposed Popov be given a nominal source for passing naval intelligence to the Germans. The source would be a Jewish barrister who had become an officer in naval intelligence and was desperate to ingratiate himself with the Nazis in return for preferential treatment when the invasion came. He gave Popov the cover story that this officer could get his hands on a chart showing the location of sea mines. In return he wanted a letter from the Germans saying that if he was captured he was to be handed over to the Abwehr, not the Gestapo. Popov had his reservations and said he would need a name for this offer to work. Montagu offered his own name, saying that it cropped up on enough Jewish charity committees and the Germans could also check it on the law list. Popov accepted and from that moment on Montagu became Germany's most important source on secret naval intelligence. It was only at the end of the war that he considered the potential repercussions of being fingered in captured Nazi documents as an agent![10] Unfortunately although the scheme was well thought out, Popov had trouble selling it to his employers. Even when Popov announced that Montagu was prepared to hand the mine chart over in person at the Shelbourne Hotel in Dublin, the Germans – unusually, it must be said – still would not take the bait.[11]

Popov had much more success when he reported the recruitment of two sub-agents in London to keep things ticking over while he was away.

Both agents were of course nominated by MI5. The first was Dickie Metcalfe, codenamed *Balloon*. Metcalfe was introduced to Popov as a disgraced army officer who had been forced to resign after financial irregularities. With a taste for fast living, Metcalfe was in desperate need of cash and had a grudge against the British government. In fact Metcalfe had resigned his commission in 1935 without any disgrace attached to his name at all.

The second agent was Friedl Gartner, the Austrian socialite Popov had met at the home of Stewart Menzies' brother. Popov and Gartner had been romantically linked since his return from Lisbon. She was given the codename *Gelatine*, which was apparently a corruption of 'jolly little thing'.[12] Her forte was supplying political information to the Germans she was supposed to have picked up from society gossip. The information was in fact all provided to her by their case officer, Bill Luke. All Gartner did was phrase the information in her own style and then have it written in secret ink.

Because he was now head of a network of three agents, MI5 codenamed Popov *Tricycle*, the name by which he is most famously known. Alas, the popular myth that he was called *Tricycle* because he enjoyed three-in-the-bed romps is unfounded.

In Friedl's case, she did not require the Germans to pay her as an agent because she was nominally a supporter of their cause. For *Balloon* this was totally different. He was a mercenary and needed payment in return for the information he provided. *Tricycle*'s German employers asked him to take cash from Lisbon to pay *Balloon*, but *Tricycle* declined this, pointing out that he would be searched and the numbers on any banknotes would be recorded. If the money was handed over to *Balloon* and he was subsequently caught, the British secret service would be able to trace *Tricycle* by the numbers of the banknotes. Instead *Tricycle* suggested a much more complex means – one that already had the backing of the Twenty Committee. If von Karsthoff also agreed to this, it meant that MI5 would effectively become the paymaster of the German espionage system in Britain.

Plan *Midas* was quite complex. Devised by Popov and Tommy Robertson, it centred on a wealthy London theatrical agent named Eric Glass who agreed to cooperate with MI5, even though he had no idea what this cooperation entailed. Mr Glass, so the cover story went, was entirely convinced that Britain was going to lose the war and, to protect his interests, wanted secretly to move his money out of Britain. To achieve this he was willing to pay over the odds on the exchange rate and was prepared to pay 10 per cent commission to anyone that would facilitate the deal.

Tricycle travelled to Lisbon on 28 June. In his first meeting with von Karsthoff, *Tricycle* mentioned the theatrical agent's plight. As expected, von Karsthoff immediately took the bait, thinking this would be the perfect way to pay the agents in Britain and make a little bit of money for himself on the side. It took several weeks for authorization from Berlin to proceed, but finally the deal was done. Less the 10 per cent commission, which was shared equally between von Karstshoff and *Tricycle*, the sum of $40,000 was paid into a New York bank account in the theatrical agent's name by the Abwehr. In return, the theatrical agent in London would pay the same sum to a person in Britain of the Abwehr's choosing.

Where the plan nearly blew up in MI5's face was when *Tricycle* was asked the name of the theatrical agent and his address. He mistakenly gave Glass's name as Eric Sand, at 15 Haymarket, just off Piccadilly. When *Tricycle* returned to Britain and reported in, the mistake was quickly realized. The name plaque in Mr Glass's office was changed to read 'Mr Sand', Glass was told to answer all his calls as Mr Sand and an MI5 receptionist was temporarily installed in the building. Dick White was furious about *Tricycle*'s mistake, rightly pointing out that if the Germans checked up on this 'Mr Sand' they would quickly find out he did not really exist.[13]

It was now a question of waiting to see who turned up to collect the payment from 'Mr Sand'. In the end, it was *Tate* who received the instruction to go to Piccadilly and collect the money. He reported collecting £18,000 cash from the theatrical agent in his next transmission to Germany.

Clearly *Tate* was still trusted by the Germans, otherwise they would not have chosen him to make such a large pick up. In an almost comical twist, by solving one problem, B1a had now created an even bigger headache for themselves. Although relieved that *Tate* appeared to be back in the Germans' good books, they realized that with £18,000 burning a hole in his pocket, the Germans would now expect *Tate* to be able to go anywhere and buy information and make reports like never before. Solving that problem would take a little more thought.

In the meantime, the *Tricycle* case took an unexpected turn that effectively put him out of action until the end of 1942. Having instigated Plan *Midas*, the Yugoslavian was sent by the Abwehr to the United States in order to form a spy ring there. This mission was to cause untold trouble, as *Tricycle*'s case was passed firstly from MI5 to MI6, and then to the American FBI. It was hoped that FBI boss J. Edgar Hoover would see the advantage of using *Tricycle* to set up and run a German espionage network that the United States could control much the same way MI5 had done in Britain. Unfortunately this was not to be so.

One of the most controversial aspects of *Tricycle*'s mission related to a questionnaire he was given by the Germans. A sizeable portion of this questionnaire was dedicated to information on the naval base at Pearl Harbor. According to Popov's post-war memoirs his contact in the Abwehr, 'Johnny' Jebsen, had left him quite clear that Japan was planning an attack on Pearl Harbor, probably using the British torpedo attack on the Italian fleet at Taranto as its model. Furthermore, due to the limitations of Japan's strategic oil reserves, this attack would have to be launched before the end of 1941. In his account of the double cross system, Masterman appears to confirm this, indicating that Popov was sent to give the questionnaire to the Americans in person to make the argument more persuasive.

Arriving in New York City in August 1941, *Tricycle* was passed over to the FBI, who greeted the agent like a treacherous enemy pariah. Rather than allow *Tricycle*'s contact with the Abwehr to pass through the British, the FBI was uncooperative in the extreme. Hoover fell out with *Tricycle*, believing that the Yugoslav was immoral and that the only possible use for him was to catch spies and earn headlines for his organization. More crucially, according to Popov's memoirs, nothing was done about the Pearl Harbor questionnaire except to 'bury it', with disastrous results.[14]

Tricycle's cover in the United States was to report the views of British propaganda by Yugoslavs living in the United States. From the Abwehr's point of view, *Tricycle* was to use his playboy lifestyle to ingratiate himself with the current movers and shakers in American society. To this end, *Tricycle* rented an exclusive penthouse on Park Avenue, bought an expensive car, took skiing holidays at Sun Valley and had a long-running affair with the French-born Hollywood actress Simone Simon, all of which infuriated the apparently puritanical Hoover.

In November 1941 *Tricycle* was ordered to Rio de Janeiro to meet the Abwehr representative there. He was asked to set up a radio link with Brazil and given a large sum of money. This radio link was operated by the FBI, who refused to allow *Tricycle* to have any say in what information was sent over to the Abwehr. This was potentially disastrous, as when, or if, *Tricycle* ever did return to Lisbon, he would have no idea about the information he was supposed to have collected.

Towards the end of the year, Twenty Committee member Ewen Montagu was sent out to America to see how the case was developing. On his return from America he gave a report on *Tricycle* to the Twenty Committee on 26 February 1942. His report on the agent's handling in America was not good reading. In short, *Tricycle* was depressed. Since arriving in America he had done very little except his mission to Rio and living out his playboy lifestyle. Montagu pointed out that the only FBI officers with previous experience of double cross cases were senior members of their service who were now unavailable to run cases of this nature. The juniors in charge of the case knew little or nothing of the technique and, to make matters worse, Montagu speculated that there might be upwards of six counter-espionage services in the United States, none of whom appeared to be cooperating. His gloomy conclusion was to try to get *Tricycle* out of the United States and into Canada as soon as possible.

There was more trouble to come with *Tricycle*, this time on the other side of the Atlantic. Although *Tricycle* had no idea what the FBI were sending the Germans, the British secret service was intercepting the Abwehr's opinion of it through ISOS. When MI5 enquired about this ISOS material, the SIS refused to pass on any of the secret material relating to *Tricycle*, citing the three-mile limit of Empire protocol, and pointing out that *Tricycle* was the property of SIS as long as he remained beyond that limit.

Eventually, in May 1942 MI5 were shown ISOS reports. There had been good reason to conceal them: they indicated that the Abwehr had become suspicious of *Tricycle* because of the poor quality of his otherwise excellent reports. Speculating why the reports were substandard, his Abwehr controllers speculated that *Ivan*, as *Tricycle* was known to them, had become a double agent since arriving in the United States.

This was extremely bad news. It must be remembered to what extent the B1a cases were linked. If *Tricycle* was suspected, so would be his sub-agents *Gelatine* and *Balloon*. Through Plan *Midas*, *Tate* would also have to become a suspect. If this occurred, the Germans would have cause to investigate all the other cases operating out of the United Kingdom.

In view of this potential crisis, Liddell went out to America to meet with the FBI and try to impress upon them the opportunity presented by *Tricycle*. On 4 July Liddell met *Tricycle* and then went to see FBI Assistant Director, Percy E. 'Sam' Foxworth, who was considered 'by far and away the ablest and most intelligent representative of the FBI' by the British. He came away disappointed by the interview.[15]

Unfortunately, there was a fundamentally different view of double agents. Foxworth argued that *Tricycle* had cost the FBI a great deal in terms of money and information passed to the enemy, but they had got little back in return. Liddell explained that they had got a great deal out of the case. *Tricycle* was, he told Foxworth, 'an insurance policy against penetration' by additional German spies. If *Tricycle* was giving the Germans what they wanted, they would not need to send others. In addition, those that might already be operating there would eventually become known to *Tricycle* and thus be revealed to the FBI.

In the end Foxworth wasn't interested. It must be recognized that the pressures that had caused the Twenty Committee to come into being were mostly absent in the United States. America was not in imminent danger of German invasion as Britain had been in 1940 when the importance of stopping the reports of agents was paramount.

Therefore, with the Americans and the British agreeing to disagree, on 3 August *Tricycle* was passed back to British control.[16] Before *Tricycle* could be allowed to return to Europe and face his German employers, he had to come up with a plausible account to explain why his time in the United States had been so unproductive. Quitting his apartment and moving to the Waldorf Astoria, it took some time for *Tricycle* to piece together an account. He was warned that the Germans might go rough on him in Lisbon, or even try to send him to Germany where the Gestapo might interrogate him, but the brazen *Tricycle* was all set for a showdown with his German bosses.

He arrived by plane in Lisbon on 14 October and arranged a meeting with his controller, von Karsthoff. Berlin had warned von Karsthoff that at the first indication the Yugoslav's story did not appear plausible, they were to break off contact with the agent immediately. However, von Karsthoff was somewhat taken aback by *Tricycle*'s aggressive stance. The double agent laid the blame for the mission's failure at the Abwehr's door, claiming they had given him inadequate funds for his mission. Von Karsthoff shot back, insinuating that the agent had spent too much time frolicking with movie stars. Also, apparently, a photograph of *Tricycle* with Simone Simon had appeared in the press. This was hardly the sort of low-key approach secret agents were supposed to maintain. In turn, *Tricycle* pointed out that in the United States Hollywood stars were like royalty, and thus presented a crucial opportunity to break into important society circles.

Tricycle then played his trump card – he threatened to resign. Although von Karsthoff menacingly pointed out that espionage was not the sort of game you could just walk away from without consequence, he did back off a little. Again, the weakness of the Abwehr was that too many people's prestige and income were linked to keeping their agents in the field. The loss of an agent meant the loss of that prestige and income, which might in turn result in a posting somewhere undesirably cold. This is perhaps what had saved *Snow*, *Celery* and *Tate* and what now saved *Tricycle*. Three days after his arrival, the agent was given the all clear from Berlin. On 21 October he returned to Britain to rebuild his case with his slate wiped clean. By then, *Tricycle*'s star had been replaced by another: the greatest double agent of them all – *Garbo*.

7

SPANISH INTRIGUES

IN WHAT WAS STILL A comparatively early stage of development, B1a was hit with another blow that could have effectively spelled the end of the organization before it moved onto the offensive in the war of deception against Nazi Germany.

With the demise of *Snow*, the cases of *Biscuit* and *Charlie* were also lost, as was that of *Celery* not long afterwards. Some attempts had been made to run *Celery* with the view of enticing Georg Sessler to defect, but these had come to nothing and *Celery* passed from the pages of espionage and into the world at large. Of the original 'Welsh' ring the only agent to survive the spring of 1941 was the former policeman, Gwilym Williams, or *GW* as he was codenamed. Fortunately *GW* had branched out away from *Snow* and had begun to build his own independent network of sub-agents. His principal contact was Piernavieja del Pozo, a Spaniard who allowed him to pass bulky documents unsuitable for wireless transmission to the Germans through diplomatic bags from the Spanish embassy in London. Del Pozo had materialized on the scene in September 1940. He came to Britain as a press correspondent for the Spanish Institute of Political Studies and was sponsored by the British Council. Ten days after his arrival in Britain, he had contacted *GW* and gave a prearranged password that the Welshman had agreed with the Abwehr. *Snow* contacted the Abwehr to establish his credentials and was told that del Pozo was bringing him some money. *GW* went off to meet the Spaniard and received £3,500 in cash, along with instructions to provide weekly reports on the Welsh National Party and armament production in Wales. When MI5 took this large sum of money away from *GW* the Welshman was outraged and threatened to resign. It was only after a visit by Marriott that *GW* calmed down and agreed to continue his deception.

Del Pozo was codenamed *Pogo* by the British and put under close observation. It was discovered that he was writing espionage reports in secret ink on the back of articles he wrote for the Spanish press. His telephone calls were tapped and Liddell's diary from October 1940 also revealed that MI5 were contemplating putting microphone bugs in his apartment and were trying to get a Spanish-speaking stooge to move into the same block of flats. The bug plan initially stalled after MI5 failed to get *Pogo* out of the flat by having

Malcolm Frost invite him to lunch with the BBC. The idea was that MI5 technicians would break into the apartment and do the necessary, but on the day in question *Pogo* failed to materialize for lunch with Frost and so the plan was scrapped, although they did manage to set up a telephone tap.

While Liddell was wondering what to do with the Spaniard, he learned *Pogo* had been making enquiries about writing an article on Bomber Command and about accompanying a British crew on a Berlin raid. Liddell's eyes lit up at the idea of this and decided that once *GW* had no further use for him *Pogo* would be allowed to go up in a bomber. If he returned from the raid, and there was a fair chance he wouldn't, *Pogo* would be interned for the rest of the war. To cover his disappearance, it would be put out that several bombers had been lost on the raid, including the one carrying *Pogo*.

Alas, the opportunity to carry out this ruse was snatched from MI5. In December 1940 the Ministry of Information decided they'd had enough of *Pogo*, who had got drunk and told the *Daily Express* he was hoping Germany would win the war. The Ministry made moves to have the Spaniard sent home and there was little MI5 could do to prevent this. They did not intern *Pogo* as this might compromise *GW* at a time when *Snow* was still very active. *Pogo* was thus allowed to return to Spain in February 1941.

Under MI5's prompting, *GW* found a new contact at the Spanish embassy, which allowed him to continue passing the secret documents. *GW* contacted the embassy porter, who suggested that he might like to contact Luis Calvo, a noted Spanish journalist who had been working for Spanish and Argentine newspapers in London since 1932. Calvo had not cropped up on MI5's radar until that point, and they found his involvement surprising. Calvo's flat was bugged and, along with certain obscenities in which he engaged with his Russian mistress, MI5 were able to build up a picture of the journalist's contacts.

In the meantime, in July 1941 a Spaniard named Angel Alcazar de Velasco was admitted into the United Kingdom by the Foreign Office, despite MI5's protests, which were delivered through Lord Swinton. Although he was officially a press attaché, it was believed that Alcazar was a German agent. This was confirmed when Alcazar handed *GW* £50 which *Pogo* had owed him. This established a link between *Pogo* and Alcazar, which was further confirmed when Alcazar paid *GW* an additional £160 for a bogus document showing divisional markings.[1]

On 4 November Guy Liddell had a meeting with Robertson and Dick Brooman-White, head of B1g (Spanish espionage). Brooman-White wanted Calvo arrested, but Robertson disagreed, claiming that this would cause an adverse action against *GW*. With the collapse of *Snow* and the uncertainty over *Tate*, Robertson again described B1a's position as 'slightly dicky' and he did not want anyone to throw a spanner in the works.

The pressure to have Calvo arrested began to mount. On 6 November the subject was raised at a Twenty Committee meeting. Ewen Montagu said that the DNI would be extremely upset with this, because both *GW* and Calvo had been used to transmit false information to the Germans. If Calvo was arrested then it might make the Germans suspicious about the traffic provided by *GW*'s Spanish network. This meeting was attended by Valentine Vivian, who sat in for Felix Cowgill. He told Montagu that everyone present had to accept there was a certain risk in putting information through these channels as agents were notoriously liable to be compromised at any time.

After this meeting Lord Swinton came to see Liddell to discuss the Richter case. Earlier in the summer, pressure had again come from the top to see German spies put on trial and executed. On 15 August Josef Jakobs had been executed by firing squad and the demand for additional victims was growing. Since then Richter had been put on trial in camera and had been sentenced to death.

Liddell had written to Swinton and urged him not to carry this sentence out. He wanted the chairman of the Security Executive to put out a statement to the House of Commons that it was government policy not to comment on the capture and execution of spies and that the House should not assume that just because nothing was being publicized, nothing was happening. Although Swinton saw sense in the arguments, he was afraid that if Richter was granted a reprieve, people would wonder why, and subsequent enquiries might be detrimental to B1a.

At that, Swinton left and Robertson came into Liddell's office. Liddell had a gut feeling that if the Germans read about Richter's trial in the press they might reassess all the traffic coming out of Britain. Richter was closely linked with *Tate*, who was linked to *Tricycle* and *Rainbow*. In turn *Tricycle* was linked with *Balloon* and *Gelatine*. There was also the problem that Richter knew *Tate* was working under government control and had made an appeal based on that information. Faced with the risk of even worse publicity if Richter was allowed to appeal, Liddell and Robertson decided it was probably best for justice to take its course and to allow Richter to face execution. Karel Richter was hanged at Wandsworth Prison on 10 December 1941, at the age of 29.[2]

With the end of Richter, focus now swung back to the Spanish ring. On 5 January 1942 Liddell revealed that two documents planted on Calvo had been discovered by a secret source. The nature of that secret source was deleted in this diary, but was undoubtedly a practice known as *Triplex*.

To digress for a moment, the sanctity of diplomatic bags is accepted as an inviolable courtesy between states. Nonetheless, the British intercepted them and opened them as often as possible. Information derived from this illegal censorship was codenamed *Triplex*. In his memoir *My Silent War*, former MI6 man Kim Philby described the system in detail. The diplomatic bags of neutral states and some of the 'minor' Allies like the Poles, Czechs, Greeks and Yugoslavs, along with the Spanish, Portuguese and the South American states, were considered fair game for interception. The trick was to persuade the carrier of the bag to part with it long enough for it to be opened in secret. During the war, all diplomatic bags were carried by air. If the British wanted to look inside a particular bag, they would engineer a delay in take-off. The courier would arrive at the airport to be told there was likely to be a lengthy delay – for one reason or the other, but usually blamed on the weather or a technical fault. Faced with an infinite wait, the courier could either sit hen-like on the diplomatic bag at the airport, or go to a nearby hotel. If the courier opted for the latter option, a security officer would offer to lock the diplomatic bag up for safe keeping and would even extend the courtesy of allowing the courier to watch it being placed in a secure locker. Philby recorded that a 'surprising number' of couriers fell for this trick, especially when the airport security had fixed them up with a prostitute at the hotel. As soon as the courier was safely out of the way, a team of experts would descend on the baggage, measuring and photographing every knot and seal, before opening the bag, photographing the contents and replacing everything as it had been found. Philby reported that the Russians were exempt from this treatment because they always sent two couriers with the luggage and because the bags were thought to contain bombs. Perhaps suspecting what the British were doing, the Polish chemically treated their seals so that they changed colour when opened and nothing could be done to reverse the effect. Fortunately for the British, when they first fell foul of this trick the bag in question had been entrusted to them for transport without a courier. The Polish were duly notified that bag had unfortunately gone missing in transit![3]

Returning to Calvo, it slowly dawned on the British that Calvo was part of a major Spanish espionage organization controlled by Alcazar, who was feeding information to the Germans, and also the Japanese, who entered the war on the side of the Axis after the attack on Pearl Harbor. The growth of this network was further highlighted by MI6's theft of Alcazar's diary with a list of names and addresses of contacts. Although the diary turned out to be a fraudulent description of Alcazar's activities used to extort money from the Abwehr, it pointed the finger at Calvo and José Brugada, the Spanish press attaché in London.[4]

Liddell believed that an attack on Alcazar's network had to be mounted, and Calvo was the obvious weak link. Unfortunately this put Liddell at odds with B1a, who were using Calvo as a means for *GW* to pass over bulky documents that were unsuitable for radio transmission. Robertson and Masterman argued vociferously against their chief, but in vain.[5]

Calvo had returned to Madrid in January, but was expected to come back after being put in direct contact with two German agents by Alcazar. MI5 learned about this contact through ISOS intercepts and arranged to arrest the Spaniard as he landed at Bristol airport on the evening of 12 February.[6] Before that night was out, Calvo found himself at Camp 020, apparently stripped naked and facing the fury of Tin-Eye Stephens in full flow. At 6.45am Calvo signed his first confession, admitting that he had been an 'unwilling intermediary' in espionage. Within a few days of incarceration Stephens reported that Calvo was 'a broken man'. The Spaniard saw out the rest of the war as the prison librarian.

After the arrest of Calvo, pressure was put on the Spanish embassy to stop using diplomatic bags for espionage purposes. Pressure was also put on Brugada, who was recruited and given the codename *Peppermint*. However, the arrest of Calvo spelled the end of *GW*. Masterman described this loss as a 'disaster'. Firstly they lost an important means of getting documents across the Channel; secondly his elimination put the other agents in jeopardy.[7]

The crisis led Robertson to draw up a memorandum on the possible ramifications of Calvo's arrest.[8] Writing on 26 February, Robertson tried to look at the arrest from the point of view of a German intelligence officer. The Germans knew Calvo was linked to *GW*. The Germans should assume that Calvo would talk, and this would lead to *GW*'s arrest. In a bid to spare his own neck, *GW* would then reveal he was in touch with *Snow* and that he received large sums of money from *Pogo* in September 1940. This information would almost certainly lead to the arrest of *Snow*. If *Snow* was arrested then he could finger *Tate*. In turn, *Tate* could give away an address used by *Rainbow*, 166 Lordship Road. He could also mention that he was given almost £20,000 by a certain Eric Sand in an office in Piccadilly. This lead might take the British to *Tricycle*. If the Yugoslav was picked up then that would blow *Balloon* and *Gelatine*. Calvo's arrest really did threaten to send the whole double cross system tumbling down like a house of cards.

T. A. Robertson, 1945. (Private collection)

The indomitable Colonel Robin 'Tin-Eye' Stephens, commandant of the secret interrogation centre Camp 020 at Latchmere House. (HU66769, IWM)

The first of a remarkable series of photographs: captured spy Karel Richter is led back to his landing ground to recover his parachute and equipment. Dressed in civilian clothes Richter is led to Colonel Stephens (in forage cap, right foreground). (HU66762, Imperial War Museum)

Richter looks for his parachute under a hedge. (HU66763, Imperial War Museum)

While Richter looks away, the parachute and equipment is recovered by the 020 team. (HU66764, Imperial War Museum)

Richter points in the direction he travelled after stashing his equipment. Unfortunately for Richter, his detention raised too many difficulties. He went to the gallows on 10 December 1941 struggling to the last, breaking the leather straps binding his wrists. (HU66766, Imperial War Museum)

Tate posing with his radio set. (National Archives)

Stills from a secret film taken of the rendezvous between Mitinory Yosii and *Tate*. The first two show *Tate* and the Japanese courier waiting for the 16 bus after getting off at the wrong place. The third is where Yosii was followed back to the Japanese embassy. (National Archives)

Norwegian spies John Moe (left) and Tor Glad (right), better known as *Mutt* and *Jeff*. (National Archives)

John Moe (right) receiving radio training in a house in Oslo. Taken by Tor Glad. (National Archives)

Dusko Popov, double agent *Tricycle*. (National Archives)

Johann 'Johnny' Jebsen, Popov's Abwehr recruiter. An
anti-Nazi, Jebsen was recruited by the British and
codenamed *Artist*. His arrest in 1944 almost led to
the collapse of the double cross system.
(National Archives)

Safebreaker, womanizer, adventurer and unlikely
hero, Eddie Chapman aka agent *Zigzag*.
(National Archives)

View of the 'damage' inflicted on de Havilland's Mosquito production plant in Hatfield. This skilful arrangement of wreckage and painted canvas was carried out overnight by members of Colonel John Turner's department. From the air it would appear that Chapman had knocked out the electricity supply to the plant. (National Archives)

Double agent Lily Sergueiev, alias *Treasure*, and her Abwehr controller Major Emile Kliemann. (National Archives)

The dog that nearly ruined D-Day, *Treasure*'s pet dog Frisson. (National Archives)

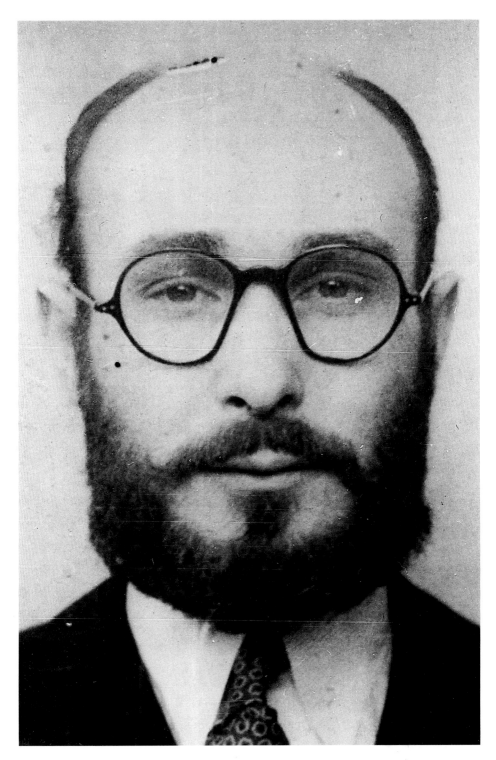

Juan Pujol García alias *Garbo*. He grew this beard after D-Day while pretending to be on the run from the British authorities. *Garbo* included this photograph in a letter to his controllers in Lisbon for approval on 22 February 1945. (National Archives)

There was a silver lining in Robertson's memo, on which all their future hopes were based. He wrote: 'There is, however, a fairly good chance that we may be able to rely on the German psychology to assume that we shall not be able to find *Tate*, and that if *Tate*'s traffic continues roughly on the same level as is the present moment, this factor should help them to reach the conclusion that he remains undetected. It must also be remembered that anyone running an agent will defend that agent against criticism through thick and thin and unless he has definite proof that he has gone bad, will always believe in his integrity. One can only hope for the best.'

What Robertson could not have realized was that all these difficulties were about to be dispelled by the arrival of another agent. This new agent's career would become the crowning glory of the double cross system, making all the teething troubles of the previous year worth the effort.

XX

Back in the dark days of 1940, before Russia and the United States joined the war against Germany, Britain had at least one friend in the world. This ally was not a nation, but a humble Spaniard who saw in Britain the only chance of restoring normality to a world gone mad with extremist ideologies.

During the Spanish Civil War of 1935–38, Juan Pujol García had first sided with the Republican forces against General Franco. However, his loyalty was soured by the Communist firebrands who sought to dominate the Republican movement. He therefore jumped ship and went over to the Falangistas – Franco's supporters, who were ultimately victorious.

Recently married and 28 years old, in 1940 Pujol turned sour on Franco. With the Nazis victorious everywhere, and Mussolini greedily looking to expand Italy, it appeared that Europe was divided into two camps: fascist or communist. To Pujol, and many like him, neither camp appealed. Pujol saw something inherently evil in Nazism with its racist policies and in particular Hitler, whom he branded a 'psychopath'.

Late in 1940, the Spaniard left for Lisbon and toyed with the idea of taking his wife to the United States to start again. But something in Pujol's make-up compelled him not to walk away from this latter-day Dark Age. Although unable to express his feelings clearly, he knew that he had to do something, to make a 'contribution towards the good of humanity' as he later put it.[9] He therefore returned to Madrid and determined to do his bit on behalf of the British cause. In what must have been an unusual domestic discussion, to say the least, Pujol sat his wife down and explained to her that he wished to become a spy for the British. With his Civil War credentials, he reasoned, he should have no trouble in getting posted to Germany or Italy, from where he could make reports.

Mrs Pujol accepted her husband's choice and supported him in it. She went as far as visiting the British consulate in Madrid and told an official that she knew a man who was willing to travel to the heart of the Nazi beast in order to spy for the British. Alas, she was rebuked. The British official had no time for this sort of nonsense and sent her on her way.[10]

Pujol did not become disheartened and the rebuke served only to inspire him further. Unfortunately, even he later admitted that his attempts to work for the British were at best confused. He had no grand scheme, and very little idea of what would make him an acceptable candidate. Thrashing around for ideas, Pujol came up with the idea of infiltrating the German secret service and then going to the British having achieved this.

In February 1941 Pujol telephoned the German embassy, offered his services to the 'New Europe' and asked for an interview. This call led to an interview with a German calling himself Federico in which Pujol offered to go to Lisbon as a spy. On their second meeting Federico told Señor Lopez – to use the alias Pujol gave him – that they were not interested in Lisbon, but if he could work out a way to get to England, they would be all ears.

Pujol accepted the challenge and came up with a scheme that was so labyrinthine in its complexity, so Byzantine in its design, that it could occupy several chapters of a book in itself. In essence, Pujol had to come up with a reasonable excuse to get permission from the Spanish authorities to travel from Madrid to Lisbon, and, once there, convince the Germans he had a plausible means of getting to England.

The first step was relatively easy. Pujol knew Franco's Spain was strapped for cash. The Bank of Spain would literally bend over backwards to get its hands on foreign currency, so, in order to get his visa for Portugal, Pujol pretended that his father had left him shares in Britain, the details of which were in a safety deposit box in a Lisbon bank. Expanding on the currency ruse in more detail, Pujol told the Germans he had earlier made contact with a British subject in Lisbon called Damal and between this character and a member of the Spanish secret police, Pujol told the Germans he had found a way to get to Britain. At this news Federico enlisted Pujol as agent *Arabel* and put him on a crash course of espionage, teaching him to use secret ink and giving him a series of miniaturized questionnaires, along with $3,000 in cash for expenses. His Abwehr contact also told him that if he got into trouble Luis Calvo was working for them in London and that he could arrange to send documents back using diplomatic bags. At this news, Pujol feigned offence. He said he did not want to know anyone's name and he certainly did not want the Germans telling any third party his name either. Pujol would work alone, or not at all.

In July 1941, Pujol left for Portugal, ultimately bound for England, as the Germans believed. Suspecting the Germans would check up on him in Lisbon, on arrival Pujol went straight to the British embassy and applied for a visa, saying he was a journalist. Because he had next to no chance of getting his visa, Pujol upped the ante still further by pretending to the Germans that he had travelled to England and was reporting from there. He achieved this stunning piece of duplicity by enlisting a friend's help. Pujol told Dionicio Fernandez he was having an affair with a woman in Madrid and needed an address where she could send letters to him. Pujol's friend offered his own address. When the friend later moved away from Lisbon, Pujol set up a second cover address, a safety deposit box in a Lisbon bank under the name of Mr Smith Jones – the only two English names he had heard of.

Pujol then wrote to Federico, telling him he had left Lisbon on 12 July and was living in England with a Spaniard. On his way out to England he had become friends with a Catalonian official working for KLM, which flew the Lisbon–London route. For a dollar a throw, this official had agreed to carry Pujol's letters to his wife in his pocket from London to Lisbon where he would post them on to Madrid, thus avoiding British censorship. In order to receive information, the Germans could write to his friend's address in Lisbon and the letters would be handed to the KLM official on his way back to England. Several weeks later, Pujol received a satisfied reply from Madrid commending him for establishing such a successful means of communication.

Armed with this letter, Pujol went to the British embassy in Lisbon again and was eventually granted an interview in which he revealed that he had penetrated the German secret service and was willing to hand over his secret ink and questionnaires, if only someone would take the slightest bit of notice of him. No one did. The British official told Pujol he would meet him with a colleague in a pub that night. They did not turn up.

At last Pujol's frustration began to surface. He visited the embassy again and hearing the official's lame excuses, he walked out in disgust. Pujol started to feel the strain of the lies he had told. There was every chance that the intricate knot of deceit he had tied would either come undone, or tighten yet further to the point of strangling him. There he was pretending to be in England, a country he had never set foot in, with a language he could barely speak a word of, and he was sending the Nazis a pile of nonsense derived from a Baedeker tourist guide, Bradshaw's railway timetable and a map of Great Britain.

At this point most people would have thrown in the towel, but not Pujol. In fact, on 17 August he thickened the stew by telling the Germans he had recruited a sub-agent, a Portuguese named Carvalho. Pujol reasoned that if the Germans accused him of providing false information, he could blame Carvalho and promise not to use that source again. He then 'recruited' a Swiss sub-agent named Gerbers in Bootle, Liverpool and another one, an unnamed Venezuelan based in Glasgow.

Agent *Arabel* developed a mesmerizing, verbose writing style when submitting his reports. Each was filled with personal observations, his thoughts, his belief in German victory and buried somewhere in the prose would be a snippet of information – mostly on fictitious convoys or factories – sparked into creation by something he might have read in a Lisbon library or seen in British newsreels being played at the cinema. Often Pujol would just make up a story – for instance the amphibious tanks he reported seeing on Lake Windermere, where he also reported large army camps and men carrying out landing practices. Another of his classics was derived from his study of his railway timetable. Where he found a busy rail line he decided that the British would probably think it important, so he reported to the Germans that he had seen pillboxes and barbed wire being erected along the track.[11]

However, Pujol's imagination should not have stood up to close scrutiny. The fact it did showed how poorly informed – or lazy – Pujol's German controllers were. Pujol made some tremendous gaffes that anyone with the slightest knowledge of the British Isles should have picked up on. The first was his assumption that dockworkers in Glasgow shared the Spanish custom of drinking wine. He wrote: 'There are men here [in Glasgow] who would do anything for a litre of wine'. Firstly, he would have found few dockworkers piling into the pub after a long shift to quaff wine; and secondly, Britain did not then have the metric system – the British measured their drinks in pints not litres. Then came the British pre-decimal currency. Pujol could not work out the relationship between pounds, shilling and pence. If he had known there were 12 pence to a shilling, and 20 shillings to a pound, he might have been able to add up his rail fare expenditure – but he couldn't. Instead he sent an itemized list without totalling it and informed his controllers that he would submit future expenses in dollars, the currency in which he had been paid.[12]

Towards the end of October 1941, Pujol again visited the British embassy without much luck. This was partly Pujol's fault, because he told the official there that he was using an alias and would not give his real name. The official, a Mr Thompson, refused to believe that the miniaturized questionnaires Pujol offered him were genuine, which was a huge missed opportunity, because the questionnaires clearly showed that the Japanese were fishing for information on British Far East possessions for a coming attack. Pujol was so dispirited he applied to emigrate to Brazil with his wife and son.

In the end, it was Pujol's wife who saved the day. Without speaking to her husband she went to the American embassy in Lisbon and contacted the assistant naval attaché, Rousseau. She told Rousseau she had information about someone engaged in espionage against the United States and would sell the information for $200,000. Having got Rousseau's attention with the high figure, Mrs Pujol produced a letter she had written using her husband's secret ink. Rousseau contacted the British SIS in Lisbon and invited him to meet Mrs Pujol. At the next meeting she brought one of the miniaturized questionnaires, but did not show it to the two officials as the Spanish-speaking Englishman belittled her in her native tongue. The SIS man then added insult to injury by producing 20 escudos and thumping them down on the table to pay her fares.

Fortunately for the British, the American smoothed things over with Mrs Pujol, who then came clean and admitted that it was her husband who was the German spy. On 15 January 1942 Pujol was at last interviewed by Rousseau, who accepted him as genuine. It still took until March for Pujol to be introduced to SIS in Lisbon for an interview.

By this time the case had already come to the attention of MI5 in London, who were then in the middle of the Luis Calvo case. As Pujol's letters were forwarded on from Madrid by the Abwehr they were being picked up and were being read by the British as ISOS decrypts. MI5's B Division were rightly concerned by the reports, as they purported to come from a source in the United Kingdom with several sub-agents. On 22 February Pujol's existence was revealed to MI5 almost accidentally in a conversation between Tommy Robertson and Ralph Jarvis from SIS Lisbon.[13] Comparing notes, Robertson asked Jarvis if any of SIS's agents corresponded with Madrid. In return Jarvis asked Robertson if the address Apartado 1099 in Madrid meant anything. Robertson's ears pricked up at this, as the address was known through another double agent. Jarvis contacted Felix Cowgill to ask permission to tell Robertson about Juan Pujol García. Cowgill agreed and Jarvis explained the Pujol story – how the Spaniard was believed to be in England by the Germans but was in fact still hiding in Lisbon. Suddenly the bizarre messages on ISOS made sense. If they emanated from Pujol, who was not in England, that would explain their wild inaccuracy. This was fortuitous because *Tricycle*'s sub-agent *Balloon* had been asked to confirm some of Pujol's reports by the Germans and MI5 were considering using *Balloon* to discredit the mystery source.[14] If Robertson and Jarvis had not had their little chat, one of the key players in later Allied successes might never have seen the light of day.

That said, the fact Cowgill's Section V had not told the Twenty Committee about this double agent sparked off a major turf war. Liddell wrote to SIS demanding that he be given a full report about Pujol. On 12 March, at the 62nd meeting of the Twenty Committee, the first mention of the Pujol case cropped up, giving him his British codename *Bovril*. In the meeting it was explained that *Bovril* was believed to be Spanish and that his brother had been arrested in Paris and had died in a German concentration camp, hence he 'has a down on the Germans'.[15] What was of most significance to 'Twenty' was that *Bovril* claimed to have two sub-agents and a courier (KLM pilot) working in England.

Two weeks later, Cowgill announced to the Twenty Committee that he wanted to bring *Bovril* to Britain. Much to Liddell's annoyance, Cowgill disclosed that *Bovril* had been known to Section V since the previous December. Cowgill revealed that he had a copy of all *Bovril*'s back traffic and thought that the Spaniard would be very reliable. There was a caveat to bringing him to London. Before Cowgill would accede, he made a condition to Liddell. *Bovril* would only be brought over if B Division agreed to let him return to Lisbon afterwards. This was a difficult one for Liddell. He wanted *Bovril* in Britain working as part of the double cross set up. He told the head of Section V he knew next to nothing about *Bovril* except that he had posed as the chief German spy in the United Kingdom and for that reason alone, it was probably best to keep him in the United Kingdom. However, Cowgill was plainly being obstructive and was guarding his new agent jealously. Liddell gave a non-committal answer. He asked Cowgill to bring *Bovril* over and decide his fate afterwards. Liddell left Cowgill furious at what he perceived as the SIS man's narrow-minded pettiness. In his diary he remarked that the sooner MI5 took over SIS's Section V, the better.

Before this clash, MI5 had been lobbying for control of all counter-espionage. As it stood, MI5 was only responsible for domestic counter-espionage. Anything more than three miles beyond the borders of the British Empire came under the jurisdiction of MI6 Section V. This three-mile limit harked back to the old convention of recognizing territorial waters extending to that limit. What frustrated MI5 was that almost all enemy espionage in the United Kingdom emanated from outside this limit.

To make matters worse, Cowgill's overworked, or rather underfunded and understaffed Section V was so important to B Division's work that MI5 felt obliged to lease a number of officers and secretaries to the SIS in order to help out. On 17 April Sir David Petrie made his move and sent 'C' a memo asking for Section V to be transferred and amalgamated into his B Division. Menzies was having none of it. He claimed that MI5 did not have the necessary local knowledge to run double agents based overseas. And there the bone of contention firmly remained.

In the meantime the decision to bring *Bovril* to England was taken and the Spaniard was smuggled out of Lisbon on 10 April 1942. He went by ship to Gibraltar and then by seaplane to the United Kingdom, arriving in Plymouth on 24 April. He was met by Cyril Mills[16] of B1a, Jock Horsfall, MI5's breakneck-speed driver and Tomás 'Tommy' Harris[17] from B Division's Iberian section (B1g). After a night in Plymouth the four men drove to MI5's safe house in Crespigny Road, now vacated by *Mutt* and *Jeff*, where Pujol's long interrogation began.

With Harris acting as an interpreter, Mills (posing under the name Mr Grey) and Desmond Bristow of Section V in attendance, the interrogation of *Bovril* lasted until 11 May. Copies of his letters to the Germans were examined, as were their replies to him. Before long it was clearly evident that *Bovril* was the source of the mysterious ISOS decrypts. As Masterman later recorded, what was so incredible about Pujol was that he had done the hard part in creating and establishing his own espionage agency; all B1a had to do was operate and develop a system that was already in place and trusted.

A clear example of this trust was demonstrated by a report Pujol sent on 26 March of a 15-ship convoy bound from Liverpool to Malta. The whole convoy was a figment of his imagination, but the Germans believed the report and acted upon it, diverting valuable resources towards intercepting it and giving beleaguered Malta a brief respite from bombing while the German aircraft were searching for the phantom convoy. This was the sort of deception the Twenty Committee had been trying to set up since its inception over a year before.

Although *Bovril* had been promised he could return to Lisbon after one month, he agreed to remain in Britain and work for the XX system, provided his wife and child were brought over to the United Kingdom as soon as possible. *Bovril* was assigned Tommy Harris as his case officer and the two men struck up a fantastic partnership. In view of *Bovril*'s performance to date, it was suggested that the codename *Bovril* should be changed in homage to 'the best actor in the world'. From then on he would be called *Garbo*.

8

'A' FORCE

WHILE THE BATTLE OF BRITAIN had raged and the Abwehr's espionage offensive had floundered, events in the Middle East took on extreme importance. While Masterman was still hinting at the future possibility of large-scale deception operations against the Axis, by the end of 1940 the British in the Middle East were already putting such measures into practice independent of London.

At the start of the war Britain had maintained a significant military presence around the Suez Canal, allowing it an influence in the Middle East that stretched from Egypt across the Sinai peninsula into Palestine and as far afield as Iraq. The region as a whole was vital to the British for two major reasons: firstly, speedy communication with India through the Suez Canal and, secondly, oil. If Egypt was lost and the Canal Zone occupied, the British Empire would in effect be cut in half. Shipping would be forced to make the long voyage round the Cape, lengthening supply lines and making shipping more prone to attack from German U-boats and raiders. Of equal importance, if the oil reserves of the Middle East fell into German hands the result did not bear thinking about.

At the end of the 1930s, the greatest threat to Britain's Middle Eastern possessions was fascist Italy. Having become Prime Minister of Italy in 1922, Benito Mussolini had deluded himself with the idea that Italy's natural playground was the Mediterranean. Like the ancient Roman emperors before him, he, *Il Duce*, decreed that the Italians should have a mighty Mediterranean empire. To this end, during the 1930s Mussolini set up a puppet government in Albania and consolidated Italian control over Libya. His most infamous piece of colonial expansion came with the brutal conquest of Abyssinia (modern Ethiopia) in 1935–36. This conflict led to Italy's falling out with the League of Nations, which in turn forced Mussolini to seek closer ties with that other European pariah state – Nazi Germany.

Mussolini's conquest of Abyssinia left Egypt's King Farouk in a sticky position. Although Britain had granted Egypt independence in 1922 and stated that it accepted Egyptian sovereignty, Farouk could not actually get the British to leave. Now, with Italy's rampant expansionism clear for all to see, Farouk was threatened by another European power. Probably quite wisely,

Farouk opted for the devil he knew. In 1936 Britain and Egypt signed a treaty limiting Britain to 10,000 troops around the Canal Zone, and in which Britain would help to train the Egyptian Army and assist in the defence of the country should there be a war.

This treaty did not go down well among Egyptian nationalists, who wanted full independence for their country. So, when war broke out in 1939, there was a lot of sympathy for the Axis in Egypt among the nationalists and members of the royal court. This sympathy was entertained under the misguided assumption that the enemy of their enemy was their friend. In their eyes, anyone who would help them get rid of the British could not be all that bad. While a full insurrection was still a premature idea, a sizeable Fifth Column was in the making. It is believed even some members of Egypt's first family became involved in espionage for Italy and that wireless transmissions were emanating from several of King Farouk's palaces, which also served as secure meeting places for Axis agents and couriers. Recognizing King Farouk had a weakness for female companionship, the Italians supplied him with a steady stream of belles who of course spied on him and everyone around him.[1]

All this was known to the British Middle East commander-in-chief, Archibald Wavell, but there was not much he could really do about it. Although Britain and Germany had been at war since September 1939, Italy had not yet joined the conflict and London was hopeful that the country might go the way of Franco's Spain and remain neutral. Wavell was therefore told not to do anything to provoke the Italians, and to refrain from any mass round ups of Italian nationals in Egypt, or from putting spies into Italian Libya or Abyssinia. All that could be done in the meantime was to draw up a list of enemy aliens for internment and plan to introduce a censorship organization should war spread to the Middle East.

At the outbreak of the European war, security in the Middle East was the responsibility of the Defence Security Officer (DSO) at Cairo. The DSO was an MI5 officer who acted as a link between the security services in London and the British garrison overseas. In addition to the DSO, MI6 was also very active. Firstly, SIS carried out covert espionage activity against the Egyptian government and institutions. Secondly, MI6 had a prerogative for counter-espionage overseas, which was set as being beyond the three-mile limit of the British Empire. In Egypt there was some conflict of interest between the DSO and SIS's Section V – the department responsible for counter-espionage.

In September 1939 the War Office in London instructed Wavell to set up a central authority to control the existing secret services in that theatre. In June 1939 Wavell had already set up the Middle East Intelligence Centre

(MEIC) in Cairo – a body that coordinated military intelligence from the three armed services: army, navy and air force.[2] Wavell proposed that all matters relating to espionage, censorship, subversion and propaganda should be coordinated by a security section within MEIC. Unfortunately, although the unification of all intelligence agencies and interested parties into one organization might have made sense on paper, the SIS objected to any encroachment on its turf, as did the Foreign Office, which did not want to see censorship and propaganda move from civilian to military control.[3]

It was not until December 1939 that a compromise was reached and a body known as Security Intelligence Middle East (SIME) was formed. This new body was placed on the staff of GHQ Middle East. It was principally responsible for watching and counteracting enemy agents in the Middle East. To prevent a turf war with the established services, an SIS representative was attached to the section to watch out for its interests, while its chief, Raymund Maunsell, was a former DSO from MI5.

XX

Italy declared war on Britain and France on 10 June 1940. Having no scruples about kicking an opponent already on the floor, Mussolini ordered his troops to cross the French Alps and grab what land they could before the French surrendered. In Egypt the Italian declaration of war came as somewhat of a relief to Wavell, who could at last start taking action against the Italians. While a series of hit-and-run raids were launched across the Libyan border to shoot up Italian positions and supply convoys, in Cairo the security services got to work against potential Fifth Column activities.

With a native population largely indifferent to Britain's survival, security was never going to be anything near as tight as MI5 achieved in Britain. Nevertheless, Italian citizens were interned and suspected agents were rounded up off the streets of Cairo and Alexandria. Following these measures, although there were some nefarious individuals still at large, SIME reported no large-scale enemy networks still at work. The only big concern – and this was also true in London – was the firm evidence that the neutral Japanese consulates in Cairo, Alexandria and Port Said were procuring military and shipping intelligence for Rome and Berlin. Until the Japanese declaration of war in December 1941, nothing legitimate could be done about closing down this source of information to the Axis.[4]

Despite initial successes, Wavell was far from in a comfortable position. His opponent, Marshal Rodolfo Graziani, had considerable forces ranged against the British. In Libya there were 250,000 troops, with another 100,000 more in Abyssinia commanded by the Duke of Aosta. Wavell's position was further weakened by the surrender of France on 25 June. With the setting up of the Vichy regime, Graziani no longer had to worry about the French behind him in Algeria. In fact, it was Wavell's turn to worry about his rear, fearing a move against Palestine from Vichy-controlled Syria and Lebanon. The only thing in Wavell's favour was that the Italians were not really up to fighting a war against a modern European force. Even when France had been on the point of collapse, French troops had inflicted a bloody nose on the Italian troops who came over the Alps. Wavell's men were well trained and certainly up for a fight.

Whatever reservations Graziani had, Mussolini was adamant his troops should capture the Suez Canal and on 8 August, amid much thumping of his chest and posturing to Hitler, he ordered an attack. A month later, nothing had happened. Embarrassed by the delay, Mussolini told the reluctant Graziani he would be sacked unless he got his skates on. Thus on 13 September 1940 Graziani began his advance into Egypt with seven Italian and Libyan divisions. They met little resistance from Wavell's forces and steamrollered forward to Sidi Barrani, approximately 60 miles inside the Egyptian border. At this point the Italian advance came to a juddering halt. At Sidi Barrani Graziani adopted a defensive posture in order to consolidate his supply lines, which he feared were already overstretched. His forces dug in and awaited reinforcements and supplies.

Unfortunately for Graziani no reinforcements were forthcoming, as Mussolini had decided to invade Greece and was up to his neck in trouble because the Greeks had decided to fight back. A victim of his own posturing, Mussolini insisted Graziani push on to take Alexandria whatever problems he believed he faced.

The lull in the Italian offensive was enough to hand the initiative back to Wavell, who drew up plans to recapture Sidi Barrani. To balance the odds, Wavell resorted to a series of measures to deceive Graziani about the direction, strength and timing of his main attack. This would be the first proper and large-scale use of deception on the battlefield by the British in World War II, and provided much of the inspiration for what occurred in the rest of the war.

The roots of Wavell's deception ploy can be found in World War I. Wavell had served under General Edmund Allenby during his campaigns in Palestine against Germany's Turkish allies. Specific examples of Allenby's deception ploys at work can be seen in the third battle of Gaza (November 1917) and the battle of Megiddo (September 1918). These examples are worth examining at this point because they form the basis of many of the cover plans behind the largest operations of World War II.

In the first case, although Allenby could not disguise the fact that he was about to launch a major offensive, he hoped at least to disguise the timing and direction of his attack. His first aim was to pin down Turkish reserves in Syria by threatening to invade the north of that country from Cyprus. To make this a credible threat, Allenby went through the motions of a troop build up on the island. There was increased signals traffic, a build up of supplies, food and horses – all things that would occur if the rumours were true.

The main direction of Allenby's attack on land would be towards Beersheba. Again, he could not disguise the build up of troops, but what he wanted the enemy to believe was when the attack at Beersheba was delivered, it was a diversionary ruse. Allenby wanted the Turks to believe Gaza was his true objective and thus to hold back their reserves from Beersheba anticipating this move.

To ensure the Turks took the bait, Allenby's intelligence officer, Major Richard Meinzerhagen, set up what passed into military folklore as the 'haversack ruse'. In one of the most famous deception operations in history, Meinzerhagen dumped an army haversack in a place where it was picked up by Turkish soldiers. It contained a series of false documents outlining a plan to attack Gaza with a two-pronged land and amphibious assault, with a diversionary attack on Beersheba. The documents suggested that the attack would commence in mid-November, when in fact the date of 31 October 1917 had already been decided upon.

To add further credence, a cipher book was placed in the pack, allowing the Turks to read British radio traffic. If the Turks took the bait, they would intercept a lot of frantic messages about finding a missing haversack and perhaps enjoy hearing how Meinzerhagen was in deep trouble for losing it. They would also hear messages making it clear that an attack would not begin until 19 November, as Allenby was in Egypt on leave and was not expected back until 7 November. In addition to bogus signals traffic, false troop movements were designed to throw the German–Turkish High Command off kilter. A week before the battle, hundreds of Egyptian workers were paraded and loaded onto ships by day and quietly disembarked again at night.

It must be said that the enemy High Command was able to see through a number of these ruses. A Turkish reconnaissance force was sent to Cyprus and was able to deduce that the invasion threat was false. They were also able to realize that something was wrong about Allenby's supposed plan to attack Gaza. But enough of the deception worked for the Turks to be taken off balance by the scale of the British attack at Beersheba.

The following year, Allenby was at it again, using deception to assist in his breakthrough at Megiddo in September 1918. This time the British chief wanted to give the impression he was preparing an advance east of the river Jordan.

To confuse enemy agents, Allenby made it look as if he was transferring his headquarters to Jerusalem, by taking over a hotel and installing telephone lines. At the same time, troop billets were marked out and rumours put around the population that there would be a large troop concentration in the area. Troops marched down roads by day and were then secretly bussed back in trucks at night, and local headquarters continued to send out wireless traffic even though their troops had been sent elsewhere. To complete the sham, Allenby threw additional bridges over the river Jordan and went to the extraordinary length of creating 15,000 dummy horses made of canvas. To simulate the dust cloud of the horses going to water, mules were made to drag sledges through the sand.[5]

What was most important about these operations, interesting in their own right as they are, was that Wavell had seen them first hand, had studied them after the war and then had written about them in his history and critique of the Palestine campaign published in 1928. He was convinced enough of their usefulness to revisit them in his campaign against Graziani.

The counter-offensive to recapture Sidi Barrani was codenamed Operation *Compass*. Wavell hatched a cover plan indicating the notional weakening of British forces in Egypt in order to support Greece. To back this up, Wavell began taking measures to suggest the embarkation of a large number of troops from Egyptian ports. This movement was endorsed by simulated radio traffic indicating a general withdrawal from the Western Desert. To reinforce the dummy radio traffic, misleading information was planted on suspected Axis spies in Cairo and the Japanese consulate, which was suspected of working with the Axis intelligence agencies.[6]

Although it is hard to measure the effectiveness of this cover plan on the Italians, it was perhaps no accident that when the British launched their offensive on 9 December, they achieved complete surprise. Wavell drove Graziani back to Libya, taking in the region of 115,000 prisoners as he went.

Following this success, Wavell began to plan the defeat of the Duke of Aosta's forces to the south. He also began devising a cover plan for the operation, which he codenamed *Camilla*. Grasping the importance of deception in military operations, Wavell decided to form a special operations section on his staff that would deal exclusively with implementing deception, both in the physical sense with the fabrication of life-sized models, and also in the realms of intelligence, through the planting of false information on enemy spies and other channels.

To lead this secret section, officially designated as Advanced HQ A Force, on 15 November Wavell sent a telegram to London requesting the presence of Lieutenant Colonel Dudley Clarke. Writing an introduction for Clarke's autobiographical 1948 work *Seven Assignments*, Wavell revealed how he first noticed Clarke's many talents while commanding him in Palestine in 1937–38. He wrote: 'I had on my staff two officers in whom I recognized an original, unorthodox outlook on soldiering; and I pigeon-holed their names if ever I commanded an army in war. One was Orde Wingate, the second was Dudley Clarke.'

At the time Wavell wrote this introduction, his deception operations were still classified information, and as an autobiography the book encompasses the period up to Clarke arriving to assume command of A Force. However, Wavell said of this secret 'eighth' assignment: 'I can only say that I have always believed in doing everything possible in war to mystify and mislead one's opponent, and that I was right in judging that this was work for which Dudley Clarke's originality, ingenuity and somewhat impish sense of humour qualified him admirably.'[7]

Dudley Wrangel Clarke was born in the Transvaal, South Africa, in 1899 just before the outbreak of the Boer War. As an infant he survived the siege of Ladysmith and went on to serve during World War I in the Royal Flying Corps as a pilot. In 1939 the outbreak of war found him working in the War Office. His adventures before joining A Force are detailed in *Seven Assignments*, but perhaps the most of important of these was the creation of the Commandos after the debacle of Dunkirk.

With the loss of Denmark, Norway, Holland, Belgium and France, Britain was left without a toehold anywhere on the Continent from which to strike at the Germans. Reflecting on his knowledge of military history, Clarke dwelt on the example of Boer Commandos during the war in South Africa at the time of his birth. These Commandos had tied up almost a quarter of a million British troops for two years with their hit-and-run tactics. They were not regular soldiers, but hand-picked groups held together by the charismatic leadership of their chiefs and armed with weapons taken from the enemy. Clarke imagined forming similar groups of men in Britain. Instead of mounting raids on horseback, they would come in by sea, picking and choosing the site of their attacks at will. Clarke described the men he was looking for as being a mix of Elizabethan pirate, Chicago gangster and Frontier tribesman.[8] Working on the project with Hollywood actor and former soldier David Niven, Clarke commandeered the United Kingdom's entire stock of 40 Tommy-guns and set up the first Commando raid into France. Unable to resist the lure of action, Clarke went along and ended up the only casualty when a German bullet almost sliced one of his ears off.

After his success with the Commandos, Clarke received his orders to travel to the Middle East, a journey that took him through Lisbon, the Canary Islands and then across Africa. Arriving in Cairo on 18 December, Clarke's activities were shrouded in secrecy. His office was in the Kasr-el-Nil near the Groppis coffee house. At the time of his arrival, the building in question was being used as a brothel, and, anxious not to deprive the ladies of their income, Clarke courteously allowed them to ply their trade upstairs while he set up shop below. His office was in a converted bathroom off the inner courtyard of the building, which was largely hidden from prying eyes.[9]

Among the complement of two officers and ten other ranks, Clarke was ably assisted by Major Vivian Jones, an expert in visual deception techniques. At the head of a team of carpenters and tradesmen, Jones was able to knock up anything from a column of wooden tanks to squadrons of plausible aircraft. The courtyard at A Force HQ quickly came to resemble the back lot of a movie studio, with military 'props' and parts of dummy vehicles stacked in every corner.

Clarke's first mission in the Middle East was to implement Wavell's Plan *Camilla*. At the time the British were reading around 90 per cent of the Italian radio traffic they intercepted.[10] This allowed Wavell and Clarke to gauge what the Italians were most afraid of, and exploit those fears. One of the Italian concerns was an airborne landing behind their lines. At the time the British did not have any airborne troops in the theatre, so Clarke hinted at the arrival of the fictitious 1st SAS Brigade through leaks and bogus signals traffic. He also had Major Jones knock up dummy gliders to fool any enemy airborne reconnaissance.[11]

As for *Camilla*, it was Wavell's intention to strike at the Italians in Eritrea and Abyssinia from the north and south, using bases in the Sudan and Kenya respectively. What Clarke had to do was convince the Italians that Wavell was going to attack from the east by an amphibious assault on Italian-held British Somaliland. Using elaborate dummy radio traffic and by directing diversionary air and naval operations against Somaliland, Clarke was able to keep Italian attentions fixed on their eastern border. Again, the ensuing East African campaign resulted in a major British victory with the surrender of the Duke of Aosta and his forces on 19 May.[12]

XX

In the meantime events had unfolded that would spell disaster for Wavell. Although a great success, Operation *Compass* had taken its toll on Wavell's forces. Much of the armour had broken down and casualties could be ill afforded. Just at the point when it looked as if his forces would drive the Italians out of North Africa, Churchill ordered Wavell to halt the advance into Libya and send troops to support Greece, which had come under German attack. As Wavell relented in Libya, the Germans were able to support their Italian allies with the Afrika Korps under General Erwin Rommel who landed in Tripoli on 12 February. With Wavell trying to juggle his commitments on two fronts, the net result was losses on both by the end of April 1941.

In the confusion of defeat, the opportunities for A Force to mount deception operations became extremely limited. Much of the work carried out by A Force was in league with MI9, the escape and evasion organization, planning escape routes and devices for Allied POWs. One morsel of success came to A Force after the disastrous fall of Crete in May 1941. From the British point of view, the next obvious step for the Germans to make in the Mediterranean theatre was the capture of Cyprus. Although this move did not figure in German planning, the British did not know it, so A Force concocted a series of ruses to deter any would-be attackers. The first scheme was to spread the rumour that there was an outbreak of plague on Cyprus. This idea was vetoed, probably sensibly, and instead A Force fell back on the types of ruse that would have been more in keeping with Allenby's portfolio of tricks.

A Force built up a bogus '7th Division', which was equipped courtesy of Major Jones' engineers, who worked overtime building dummy encampments, vehicles and tanks. In what was by now a well-used routine, fake signals traffic filled the airwaves with all the chatter expected of a relocating division. To put the icing on the cake, A Force in Cairo 'accidentally' mislaid a set of defence plans for Cyprus, which found its way to Rome via the usual suspects, and which was later discovered in captured Italian documents at the end of the desert campaign.

On 21 June Wavell left Egypt for India and was replaced by General Auchinleck. Wavell had not got on with Churchill and the reverses at the hands of Rommel hastened his departure. Throughout the remainder of 1941 Dudley Clarke spent much of his time creating 'channels' through which future deceptions could filter their way through to the Germans.

First up was a trip to what became a major stalking and hunting ground for A Force: Turkey, where the Abwehr had stations in Ankara and Istanbul. Then, when it appeared Turkey might be dragged into the war because of the Nazi advance into the south of the Soviet Union, Clarke went to Lisbon to secure additional channels that could be used in reserve.

As had already been realized in London, perhaps the best channel for deception purposes was the use of double agents. Completely independently of MI5 in London, SIME began to build up a portfolio of double cross cases, of which Dudley Clarke was only too happy to make use. Chief among these masters of espionage was the innocuously named agent *Cheese*. This case became one of the most successful of all the Allied double cross operations in the war. Although the codename initially applied to a single agent, the codename *Cheese* would become the umbrella term for a network of agents used in the Middle East.

The case opened in December 1939 when the Abwehr approached an Italian Jew named Renato Levi and tried to recruit him. Levi had little love for the Nazis. Accordingly, he went to the British consulate in Genoa, told them of the Abwehr's approach and was put in touch with MI6. The British secret service told him he should accept the German offer and keep in touch.[13]

Levi became operational in early 1940 after being sent off to France by the Abwehr. Once inside France he made contact and worked as a double agent for the French Deuxième Bureau.[14] After the fall of France, Levi went to Genoa and joined the Italian Servizio Informazioni Militare (SIM). To ingratiate himself with his new employers, Levi falsely told them he had extensive contacts in Egypt among anti-British elements of the army and also among Italian residents in the country.

In October 1940 the SIM decided to send Levi to Egypt via Turkey with a radio operator and a suitcase full of counterfeit £5 notes. From Turkey the two agents were meant to work their way through Vichy-controlled Syria and Lebanon before finding a discreet method of entry beyond British lines into Palestine. Once there, Levi's radio operator was told to collect a wireless set that would be sent to them in a diplomatic bag through the Hungarian embassy. When they had recruited and built up an extensive espionage network, Levi was then to return to Italy to make his report.

We have already seen a number of well-laid espionage plans fall at the first hurdle and this was no exception. Almost at the beginning of their adventure, Levi and his companion were arrested by the Turks for passing counterfeit banknotes in Istanbul. While incarcerated, Levi was able to contact his friends in MI6 and explain his plight. The British arranged for Levi to be released and he continued on his way to Egypt with their assistance.[15] As for the radio operator, this unforeseen incarceration in a Turkish dungeon put paid to any notions of adventure he once entertained and he wisely went home upon his release.[16]

Finally reaching Cairo in February 1941, Levi reported to MI5's counterpart in the region, SIME, who had already been told about his case by MI6 in London.[17] Levi again explained to his new employers that as a Jew he found the Italian alliance with Hitler incompatible with his conscience. He also revealed that he had spent some time in Australia before the war. If he helped the British he hoped they would allow him to settle there after the war. As for his supposed contacts in Egypt, this was a yarn he had spun for the benefit of the SIM. The contacts he had reported to the Italians were entirely notional, which was excellent news for the British as they did not have to involve anyone with real Axis sympathies in the case.

Once set up in Cairo, Levi, or *Cheese* as he was now codenamed, asked his Italian employers to provide a wireless set and also a list of reliable contacts he might approach in the Egyptian capital. In the meantime, while waiting for these to be provided *Cheese* dedicated himself to the pursuit of women, gaining quite a reputation for his conquests in Cairo's bars and night spots. He is variously described as about 35, intelligent, resourceful and well travelled, although one source reported that he was lazy, carefree and with little concept of the risks involved in the dangerous game he was playing.

After a time blowing his espionage funds on loose women, it became clear that the Italians were not going to provide their agent with a radio set. Rather than allowing the case to run cold, *Cheese*'s case officer and Maunsell's deputy, William Kenyon-Jones, decided that the agent should obtain a radio himself, notionally from his Egyptian contacts, but which would really be provided by the British.

After some cold shouldering from GHQ Signals, Kenyon-Jones was introduced to a Sergeant Ellis from the Royal Corps of Signals who had been an amateur radio ham before the war. In order that *Cheese*'s set would not be identified as one belonging to the British Army, Ellis built it from scratch. Ellis was then assigned as *Cheese*'s radio operator and given the codename *Lambert* by the British. In order to make the deception complete, Ellis' radio-operating alter-ego was given the notional identity of a Syrian national of Russian descent called Paul Nicossof, the name apparently a pun on 'knickers off' or 'nick (steal) it off' (Dudley Clarke called this alter-ego Fornikov). This agent was given the background story of being an anti-Soviet White Russian who saw the Axis as Russia's only hope of salvation from communism.

Towards the end of May, with *Lambert* up and running, *Cheese* was now given a cover story which would allow him to return to Italy as planned. *Cheese* would report that Nicossof had constructed the radio out of parts obtained from his contacts with dissidents in the Egyptian Army, and that he would broadcast his messages in French, that being his strongest language after Russian.

Cheese embarked at Haifa and returned to Italy, where he was greeted with some suspicion. He was actually arrested in November 1941 and imprisoned for alleged black market offences. He was not heard of again for another three years. Fortunately for the British, the Italians' suspicion of *Cheese* appeared to stem from SIM's rivalry with the Abwehr who had originally controlled the agent – or at least had believed they did so.

In July 1941 Kenyon-Jones and Ellis received a signal from an Axis control centre in Bari. The *Cheese* network was operational. This would prove a major coup in the long run, with 432 signals sent before the end of the war.[18]

At first a few small scraps of low-grade intelligence were thrown to the Italians – mere chickenfeed. Gobbling this up, the Italians became more and more inquisitive and their questions became more specific. Facing the same problems encountered by MI5 in London, Kenyon-Jones was forced to go to headquarters and ask their advice on what replies to send. This was extremely well timed, as while Kenyon-Jones and Ellis had been getting their project started up, the new British commander in Egypt, General Auchinleck, was planning a counter-offensive against Rommel, codenamed Operation *Crusader*.

Lambert and the channels opened by Dudley Clarke in Turkey played an important part in making Rommel believe that an attack was imminent through the summer, whereas the British were in no fit state to launch anything until the autumn. Although the attack was not launched until 17 November, *Lambert* set dates in August and September before changing tack and telling the Italians that the offensive had been postponed until after Christmas. *Lambert*'s prime source for this information was reportedly a man named Piet, who was an anti-British South African NCO who worked as a clerk for an unnamed general in GHQ.[19]

The success of the bluff behind *Crusader* convinced the British that the *Cheese* network must have been blown by it and that the Italians and Germans must have realized it was feeding them with false information. The danger now was that if the Italians continued to communicate with them, it might be because they were playing a trick of their own. When *Cheese* was arrested in November 1941 and imprisoned for alleged black market offences, by rights the network should have been consigned to the dustbin. In fact, it was to make a miraculous recovery in 1942.

XX

Dudley Clarke's contribution was deemed so useful that Wavell had sent him to London in September 1941 in order to elicit support for deception. On 2 October he addressed a combined meeting of the JIC and the Joint Planning Staff (JPS) at the War Cabinet Offices.[20] At this meeting Clarke gave an impressive description of A Force's activities and argued that a similar body should be set up in London. This topic was discussed and on 6 October the JPS endorsed Clarke's proposal sanctioning the recruitment of a Controlling Officer of Deception who would coordinate deception operations across the globe, developing the cover plans for operations and using existing services to help implement them, including the Army, the Security Service, the Political Warfare Executive (PWE) and the camouflage and decoy units.

The first incumbent of the post was Colonel Oliver Stanley. A veteran of World War I and holder of the Military Cross, Stanley had entered politics and had served in Chamberlain's government, most recently as Secretary of State for War. He was given the cover title of Head of the Future Operations Planning Sections (the FOPS) and a small staff, the future of which will be discussed in the next chapter.

Clarke's visit also had a big impact on MI5 and the Twenty Committee. Clarke was introduced to Guy Liddell on 29 September as the linkman between Maunsell's SIME and the General Officer Commanding (GOC) Eighth Army. Liddell recorded in his diary that Clarke had 'many double cross schemes' and controlled 'rumours and purveying false information through Maunsell's channels' – i.e. SIME double agents like *Cheese* and *Lambert*. Hearing an account of his work, Liddell was impressed with the deception operations in British Somaliland and Cyprus and noted that Clarke had managed to set up channels for his rumours in Lisbon and Istanbul. What Liddell was most excited about after their meeting was that in the Middle East the operations staff seemed to be the ones going to the local equivalent of the Twenty Committee with plans for them to implement. In Britain it was the Twenty Committee that came up with plans, to which no one appeared to pay much attention. Liddell complained that he had told the Service Directors at the start of the XX project that 'they had a machine but did not make proper use of it'.[21]

Following Clarke's meeting with Liddell, he was invited to attend a meeting of the Twenty Committee at St James's on 2 October 1941. At that time MI5 had little contact with SIME over the running of double agents and even less idea of how A Force was using double agents as a channel for deception. Until then the Twenty Committee's own attempts at deception had not been very successful. In addition to the plans already outlined in previous chapters, there had been a number of, in some cases, slightly madcap experiments to deceive the Germans.

Plan *I* was a scheme for getting the Germans to bomb a dummy ammunition dump in an area of woodland. *Tate* reported the site to the Germans in March 1941, but the Luftwaffe ignored it. One of the more outlandish ideas was the so-called *Blue Boot* Plan. Here the Germans were informed that British troops had been issued with tins of blue paint and would, in the event of an invasion, paint their right boot blue to be able to identify one another. Almost as farcical was Plan *Guy Fawkes*, which was a scheme for *Mutt* and *Jeff* to carry out a sabotage mission that would be reported in the press and therefore establish their credentials in the eyes of the Germans.

In the early hours of 9 November, an incendiary bomb was placed in a food store in Willesden. Although the Ministry of Food and the Commissioner of Police at Scotland Yard were in on the act, one local war reserve policeman unexpectedly turned up at the scene on his bicycle. He saw Christopher Harmer waiting in the getaway car and started asking awkward questions. In the end Harmer had to tell the 'bobby' to refer the matter to the superintendent at Scotland Yard and not mention a word of what he had seen to anyone. Unfortunately he lingered around the site, and when the incendiary bomb went off, the policeman was able to put out the fire before it had even had a chance to destroy the suitcase it was hidden in. A second attempt was then made in a less populated area in the New Forest. To make it look like the work of foreign saboteurs, evidence was left behind on the scene, including *Mutt*'s Norwegian compass. Unfortunately, this time the explosion was so successful it destroyed all the carefully laid evidence and MI5 were forced to send 'investigators' to the scene to 'find' more clues.[22]

Compared to the sort of thing A Force had been getting up to, B1a's attempts were quite feeble, so having a real, successful, practitioner of military deception like Clarke in their midst was considered an excellent opportunity. Masterman welcomed Clarke to the Twenty Committee formally and gave a brief outline of the work that was being done by him in the Middle East. Expanding on his own experiences with using double agents as channels for his deception schemes, Clarke was keen to see if the Twenty Committee could assist him on two very important points.

1. Could the committee arrange to plant a document on the Germans?

2. Could he be given information about what the Germans knew or thought about Middle Eastern matters?

Clarke was informed that there were several channels open to the committee if he wished to plant a document on the Germans, but there was a condition to this. The document had to be available in the United Kingdom and a reasonable story had to be concocted in order to account for its availability to the selected agent. As for the second question, the committee agreed to keep Clarke informed about anything that came up at their end relating to the Middle East.

The day after this meeting, Liddell followed it up with a second meeting with Dudley Clarke to which Tommy Robertson and Gilbert Lennox were invited. Lennox was the representative of MI5 and MI6 on the Inter-Services Security Branch (ISSB), the body responsible for operational security, codenames, cover plans, and so on.

This meeting fleshed out the details of how London and the Middle East were going to communicate on matters relating to XX work and deception planning. It was decided that because Maunsell could not visit London in person, Clarke would act as the go-between. In future Clarke was to let them know everything he was planning and what he expected London to do in return.[23]

With the blessing of MI5 sending him on his way, Dudley Clarke was now confirmed as a very important player in the secret war against the Axis. Inside his head he now carried knowledge of A Force and the existence and functions of the Twenty Committee. It is uncertain to what degree he knew of Bletchley Park, but it is quite possible he had at least some inkling that the British were able to read German radio traffic to some extent. In other words, he was not the sort of man that could risk falling into German hands and should have played it safe on his journey back to the Middle East. Unfortunately he did not, and Clarke seriously blotted his copybook on the way to Cairo, raising a number of eyebrows and causing serious questions about his judgement to be asked in high places, including by the Prime Minister.

Clarke's route back to Cairo was supposed to take him via Lisbon, Gibraltar and Malta, but for some reason he decided to take a short trip to Madrid on the way. In the Spanish capital Clarke was arrested disguised, or rather dressed, in woman's clothing. The Spanish propaganda bureau put out a story that the man arrested in women's clothing was 'Wrangal Craker' and was *The Times*'s correspondent in Madrid. Spanish police photographs show Clarke in a floral patterned dress, with opera gloves, what appears to be a fashionable cloche hat, necklace, high heels, stockings and a clutch bag. He apparently also had female underwear on at the time of his arrest. There is nothing to suggest that the life-long bachelor Clarke was fulfilling a personal need or fetish by acting this way, but in the conservative world of the British establishment in the 1940s this sort of behaviour led to questions being asked of his sanity.

The details of Clarke's release by the Spanish gave more cause for concern. When previously in Lisbon, Clarke had posed as a journalist working for *The Times*. Looking for channels to pass his deception schemes through, Clarke had befriended a fellow he believed to be a Lisbon-based German agent. At the time of Clarke's arrest in Spain, this contact happened to be in Madrid. Believing Clarke to be an important potential agent for the Germans, this unnamed agent supposedly intervened with the Spanish police and got Clarke released. He was enormously lucky not to have been bundled into the back of a car on his release and taken to Germany for further questioning. If that had occurred, and Clarke had broken under interrogation, the Nazis would have scored a significant success and at the very least would have scrapped their entire espionage network in Britain and the Middle East and started again.

Instead, Clarke travelled to Gibraltar and was put on a ship bound for England where he was expected to face stiff questioning about his antics. Guy Liddell remarked in his diary: 'Nobody can understand why it was necessary for him to go to Spain. Before he is allowed to go back to the Middle East he will have to give a satisfactory account of himself. It may be that he is just the type who imagines himself as the super secret service agent.'[24]

On his way back to London, Clarke suffered more misfortune when the ship he was travelling on was torpedoed. Forced back to Gibraltar, Clarke's position appeared further weakened when the subject of his arrest was brought to the attention of Winston Churchill. On 31 October 1941 the Chief of Imperial General Staff, Field Marshal Sir John Dill, informed the Prime Minister that Clarke had been arrested in Madrid dressed as a woman. He advised Churchill that Clarke should be interviewed by Lord Gort, the governor and commander-in-chief of Gibraltar, and 'if he considers his story is reasonable and that he is sound in mind and body, to send him on to the Middle East by the first possible aircraft as he is urgently required there'.[25]

Gort interviewed Clarke and produced a report that was summarized by Sir John Dill for the Prime Minister on 18 November. The language used suggests the extreme seriousness with which the incident was viewed:

The Report clearly shows that Col. Clarke showed no signs of insanity but undertook a foolhardy and misjudged action with a definite purpose, for which he had rehearsed his part beforehand. As a result he gravely risked undoing some of the excellent work already done in the UK and en route there. I feel the following extract from Lord Gort's covering letter paints a true picture:-

'... he seems in all other respects to be mentally stable. I also feel that we can reasonably expect that this escapade and its consequences will have given him a sufficient shock to make him more prudent in the immediate future.'

With Clarke's story deemed 'reasonable' he was allowed to continue on to the Middle East, obviously feeling severely chastised. As a further embarrassment Churchill's personal assistant, Charles Thompson, received copies of the photographs showing Clarke dressed in drag from the naval attaché in Madrid, Alan Hillgarth, who said that Churchill wanted to see them. The letter from Hillgarth is marked with a note saying that the 'PM has seen'.[26] Liddell concluded of the whole messy business: 'It would be much better if these people confined themselves to their proper job.'[27]

There is one last interesting footnote to Clarke's arrest. MI6 officer Kim Philby was head of Section V's Iberian office and a frequent visitor to MI5. He was also a Soviet agent reporting secrets back to his contact in the Soviet embassy almost as fast as he could write them down. Hearing about the Clarke affair he wrote a slightly bemused report to his controllers about Clarke, saying that the case was 'shrouded in the greatest secrecy'. Part of it read:

The above mentioned very important member of AUCHINLECK's staff was arrested in Madrid ten days ago, wearing women's clothes. I do not know his rank or title, but his function is Chief of the 'strategic deception unit' attached to GHQ Cairo. DUDLEY CLARKE has under his command three dummy infantry divisions, 1 dummy tank brigade and several squadrons of dummy aircraft. His position is therefore of great importance from the intelligence viewpoint.[28]

Therein lies one of the great ironies of World War II. Although they may have fooled the Germans, the British intelligence community and its secrets were an open book to the Soviets. Fortunately nothing appears to have found its way to Berlin through this wide open back door. If it had, the course of the war might well have turned out very differently.

9

THE CONTROLLING OFFICER

BEFORE HE GOT HIMSELF ARRESTED in Madrid, Dudley Clarke's visit to London had set in motion the formation of a controlling section for deception. Although caught up in Clarke's enthusiasm for deception, no one in London was quite sure how to make such a section work, least of all the man who was put in charge of it.

Colonel Oliver Stanley was instructed to form a staff of three officers, each representing one of the armed services. To represent the army, the War Office sent Lieutenant Colonel Fritz Lumley, a one-legged veteran of World War I. With the air war and the battle of the Atlantic in full swing, the RAF and Royal Navy were less enthused about losing senior officers. While the navy dragged its feet finding a candidate, the RAF sent a civilian to the post rather than losing a group captain.

The well-known author Dennis Wheatley had served as a gunner on the Western Front during World War I and had been injured in a German gas attack. Invalided from the Army, he took over his father's wine-making business in 1926, but was later forced to sell it during the economic slump of the 1930s. It was then that he turned to writing the occult thrillers for which he was best known. At the beginning of World War II his second wife Joan joined MI5 and, at her suggestion, Wheatley was commissioned to write a number of papers on subjects relating to invasion defences and the conduct of the war.[1] These papers were widely read by members of the Joint Planning Staff (JPS) and the Chiefs of Staff Committee and, in some cases, were even passed to the King.

In November 1941, when looking for a recruit to send to the deception section, the Director of Plans (Air), Group Captain William Dickson, invited Wheatley to lunch and introduced him to Stanley as a possible candidate to represent the Air Force. A formal interview took place shortly afterwards and Wheatley was accepted into the deception planning fraternity.[2]

According to Wheatley's memoir *The Deception Planners*, the first months in the controlling section were frustratingly dull. The department occupied two offices on the third floor of the War Office overlooking St James's Park.

Although the offices were grand in design, the real business of running the war went on in the basement of the building. Secluded in its upper-storey offices, the deception section struggled to be noticed. Oliver Stanley did not help matters. He was so obsessed with secrecy that he appeared unwilling to let anyone know that his department existed. Wheatley very correctly suggested that Stanley ought to hold weekly meetings with all the parties interested in deception, namely ISSB, PWE, MI5, SIS, MEW, the Special Operations Executive (SOE), and so on, but the Controlling Officer declined the idea. By doing so, he condemned the department to a slow and lingering death.

In defence of Stanley, during that dark part of the war things appeared to be going badly on every front. With no offensive operations planned, there was little scope or requirement for cover plans to be developed by his organization. At this early stage there was still some confusion between the new section and the ISSB, the body responsible for operational security. The controlling section's sole success in this period was in the development of Operation *Hardboiled*, a notional assault against Stavanger in Norway. This was the first of many successful attempts to pin down frontline German forces in Norway and it played on a very real concern Hitler had for this northernmost of his conquests. Although *Hardboiled* was never intended to go ahead, the operation was planned as meticulously as if it had been real and actual troops were assigned to it. Although the Germans appeared to take the bait and strengthened their Norwegian garrisons, *Hardboiled* died a death after the troops earmarked for it were transferred to an operation against Madagascar.

This setback caused a loss of impetus and by May 1942 the department had more or less fallen apart. Lumley spent most of his day on *The Times* crossword, dreaming of postings elsewhere. When he eventually secured a posting to SOE in West Africa he was ecstatic. At the time of Lumley's departure, Stanley's wife fell terminally ill and he went on leave to care for her. Increasingly frustrated at his inability to make inroads of any kind, Stanley asked Churchill for permission to be released so that he could re-enter politics.

At this make or break point in the development of organized deception, the creating force behind A Force again played a leading hand. General Wavell arrived in India in July 1941 and by the spring of 1942 was heavily engaged against the Japanese. He decided to set up a deception organization for the Far East on very similar lines to A Force. This organization was initially known by the designation GSI(d), but later came to be better known as D Division.

In the Dudley Clarke role was Lieutenant Colonel Peter Fleming, elder brother of Ian Fleming who then worked for Naval Intelligence and would only later rise to public celebrity for writing the James Bond novels. Before the war Peter Fleming was an acclaimed travel author and had been a special correspondent for *The Times* and the literary editor of *The Spectator*. At the beginning of the war Fleming had been instrumental in setting up the first of the so-called Auxiliary units in Kent during the 1940 invasion scare. The Auxiliaries were a prototype resistance guerrilla force, trained to allow the German Army to roll over their positions and then come out of hiding to attack their supply lines from the rear. According to Wheatley, Fleming taught the men unarmed combat and was well suited to the role, the novelist likening his appearance to that of a jaguar.

At the beginning of 1941 Fleming was asked to go to Egypt by Colonel George Pollock, the head of SOE in Cairo. The plan was for Fleming to make a tour of Italian POW cages and to recruit potential resistance agents from among anti-fascist prisoners. These would then be dropped into Italy by SOE to bring about an uprising in Italy. When this plan failed to develop, Fleming was charged with raising the 'Garibaldi Legion'. This would be a force at least a thousand strong that would accompany the Allies when they landed in Italy. Despite great willingness on Fleming's part, the Garibaldi Legion failed to attract recruits and the plan collapsed. Fleming spent the next few months in Cairo doing very little and growing increasingly frustrated. The time would have been entirely fruitless had he not become acquainted with A Force and Wavell, who had read his travel books and was very taken by him.[3]

When it became clear that the Germans were on the verge of invading Greece, Wavell agreed to let Fleming travel there with a team to organize a post-invasion resistance, much the same as he had done in Kent in 1940. Despite a complete lack of local knowledge and having no one in his party of desperadoes who could speak Greek, Fleming travelled to the Monastir Gap, one of the expected invasion routes. Unfortunately Fleming arrived too late to carry out his mission and instead spent his time blowing bridges and railway locomotives during the retreat, before returning to London.

Despite his lack of success he was not forgotten by Wavell, who requested that he join him in India. Fleming had to wait until February 1942 before he could leave the United Kingdom, travelling from Glasgow to Freetown in Africa on the aircraft carrier *Formidable*. From there he made his way to Cairo and reacquainted himself with A Force, spending time reading through the records of their operations, learning how the art of deception had been successfully employed to date. He arrived at Wavell's HQ in Delhi in March 1942 and took over GSI(d) just at the point when Imperial Japanese forces appeared poised to strike into India.

One evening after dinner Wavell explained to Fleming the principles of the Meinzerhagen haversack ruse used in Allenby's 1917 campaign against the Turks. Taking note of the lesson, towards the end of April Fleming abandoned a car near the advancing Japanese position, in which some documents were deliberately left behind. Among the letters were some false reports indicating that a strong reinforcement of two armies was expected in India and that a secret weapon had been developed for use against the Japanese. There was also a letter to Wavell from his friend Joan Bright in the Cabinet Office in London deliberately filled with all manner of indiscreet tittle-tattle on military matters.[4]

Whether the documents were ever found by the advancing Japanese and if the ruse actually came to anything was never established by its creators, but it did spur Wavell into writing to London on the subject of deception. On 3 May he wrote to Sir Alan Brooke, Chief of the Imperial General Staff (CIGS) describing the ploy and then again, on 21 May, he wrote to Churchill urging him to ensure deception was taken seriously in London.

This intervention was later described by Masterman as the 'real turning point' in the campaign to implement an energetic, globally linked deception plan.[5] To what extent Wavell's letter was provoked by observations made by Fleming on the state of deception in London following Dudley Clarke's mission the previous October is uncertain. However, the timing of Wavell's letter does indicate that Fleming passed on some information about the malaise surrounding Oliver Stanley's small team. In his letter, therefore, Wavell told the Prime Minister that deception in the Far and Middle Eastern theatres would be effective only if it was part of a widespread deception plan worked out in advance by London and Washington together.

The letter was spectacularly well timed because at that moment the British and Americans were making their first plans for offensive action. In a 'knocking heads together' exercise, Churchill circulated Wavell's letter to the Defence Committee of the Cabinet and the Chiefs of Staff, who referred it to the Joint Planning Staff.

The same day the letter was written, Lieutenant Colonel John Henry Bevan was appointed as the successor to Lumley. At the age of 46, Bevan was perhaps best known as a stockbroker and the son of a chairman of the Stock Exchange. A veteran of World War I, Bevan had served as an infantry subaltern on the Western Front where he gained a Military Cross. In 1918 he was given a rare opportunity to make his mark. Summoned to Versailles, he was asked to make an appreciation of the German order of battle, taking into account the German forces freed up by Russia's exit from the war following the Bolshevik revolution of 1917. Given access to secret intelligence and allowed as much clerical assistance as he required, Bevan delivered his appraisal before an assembly of top Allied politicians and 'brass'. Seated before him at his presentation was the Prime Minister Lloyd George, Churchill, Haig, Clemenceau, Foch, Pershing and all the various Allied army commanders. As it turned out, Bevan's predictions were accurate to within three divisions and his forecast for the point of attack was good to within ten miles. Churchill was suitably impressed and summoned Bevan to his quarters at the Paris Ritz to discuss his views in more detail.

With this past link to Churchill and with the coincidental arrival of Wavell's letter on deception, it should come as no surprise that by the time Johnny Bevan arrived at the War Office on 1 June to replace Lumley, he was instead given the top job, Churchill having accepted Stanley's request to go back into politics. Arriving at what became officially known as the London Controlling Section (LCS), Bevan invigorated it. The name of the department was deliberately vague and it was mostly referred to by the initials LCS. Even if someone had worked out what the initials stood for, they would still have little idea what this London section actually controlled. As the new Controlling Officer of Deception Bevan acted as a stimulus to the department, which began to develop very rapidly, moving from secluded isolation to a post of paramount importance in the Allied war effort.

The advancement of the department was built on 'old school tie'-style networking and informal chats with the right people over agreeable dinners. Here Wheatley excelled in promoting the interests of the department. Relatively low in rank, Wheatley would enter a superior officer's office very formally, stand smartly to attention and observe all protocols. Once the officer asked Wheatley to sit down, things would become much less formal. Wheatley was the same age as many senior military figures and a lot of them had read his books. With the ice broken, Wheatley would somewhat impertinently offer to take them out for lunch. If that went well, he would invite them to dinner at his home. Because most officers had sent their wives out of London to escape the bombing, the domestic setting with Wheatley and his wife was all the more attractive to them – and Wheatley was well-known for providing a good table.

By the time of Bevan's arrival, Wheatley's unofficial dining club consisted of top generals, admirals and air commodores. Wheatley naturally introduced Bevan into these circles and the new Controlling Officer made his own invitations for them to dine at his expense. Thus between the two deception officers and their dinner services, they had access to some of the highest authorities in the land.

Bevan was also keen on country pursuits, much more so than Wheatley, and found that Chief of the Imperial General Staff, Sir Alan Brooke, shared his interest in bird watching. This gave Bevan an excuse for lunch with Sir Alan two or three times a month. Through his sister, Bevan was also brother-in-law to General Sir Harold Alexander, who would become Commander-in-Chief of the Middle East and an important player in the war. According to his secretary from February 1944, Lady Jane Pleydell-Bouverie, Bevan became great friends with Churchill's Chief of Staff, General 'Pug' Ismay and 'C', the head of MI6. On a periodic basis Bevan was also sent for by Churchill to discuss deception plans in person, the Prime Minister retaining a strong interest in the subject throughout the war.

This intensive social networking was what made the difference between the Stanley era and the new one under Bevan. Later in 1942 the opportunities to network were greatly increased by the recruitment of Ronald Wingate as Army representative. Ronald Wingate was the son of the noted Sir Reginald 'Wingate of the Sudan' and cousin to Major General Orde Wingate, the legendary Chindit commander in the Far East. Like his predecessor Lumley, Wingate had made his career in India. However, where Lumley had remained a relatively obscure figure, Wingate had risen to some significance, becoming the governor of Baluchistan, a rank equivalent to lieutenant general and entitling him to an escort of lancers. Wingate had also negotiated British protectorates with a number of oil sheikhs in the Persian Gulf.

To compensate for his service overseas in all manner of 'lice-ridden hovels' in the king's service, Wingate took an extended leave every two years.[6] He would return to Europe and motor round the major resorts on the Continent, becoming an expert on hotels and fine dining. With extensive social networks and certain monarchs numbered among his friends, Wingate was naturally in good stead with his new colleagues in deception. His knowledge of politics was unbridled and his negotiating skills and cunning made him perfect for weaving his way through the cluttered halls and offices of the War Office.

The other key members of the team who joined in 1942 were Major Harold Peteval and Commander James Arbuthnott RN. Peteval was also a World War I veteran and had gone on to manage a soap factory. At the start of the war he had enlisted and had been at Dunkirk, where he was known for his calmness under shellfire. Despite this Wheatley remembered Peteval as being shy and extremely reluctant to leave the office to attend conferences. Instead he was studious and, like Bevan, worked extremely long hours, while Wheatley and the others would generally knock off at 6pm.

Arbuthnott was another veteran from the Great War and had since gone on to become a tea planter in Ceylon. Before joining the deception section Arbuthnott spent a year in GHQ Cairo. When in London, he was quizzed about what he knew of Dudley Clarke and A Force from his time in Cairo. Such was the security surrounding Dudley Clarke's outfit that Arbuthnott confessed that although he had heard the organization mentioned he had absolutely no idea what it did.

One of Bevan's first acts was to move the section's offices from the third floor of the War Office to the overcrowded basement where the planning staffs were located. Amid the noise of air conditioning and the glare of electric lights, the basement was like a dungeon. Wheatley tried to brighten the place up by pinning giant maps to the wall and bringing some of his own furniture into the office, including some Persian rugs and a boardroom table complete with a Graeco–Roman-style statuette in the centre. By planting himself in the middle of a rabbit warren of decision-making, Bevan ensured the LCS would not be overlooked or forgotten.

Bevan's next move was to draft a directive for the section, giving it a purpose and a goal. On 21 June the directive was endorsed by the Joint Planning Staff, formally setting out Bevan's mission:[7]

1. Prepare deception plans on a world-wide basis with the object of causing the enemy to waste his military resources.
2. Coordinate deception plans prepared by Commands at home and abroad.
3. Ensure that 'cover' plans prepared by the ISSB fit into the general framework of strategic deception.
4. Watch over the execution by the Service Ministries, Commands and other organizations and departments, of approved deception plans which you have prepared.
5. Control the support of deception schemes originated by Commanders in Chief, by such means as leakage, propaganda.

In addition, the directive confirmed that the LCS was not to limit itself to strategic deception, but to include anything 'calculated to mislead the enemy wherever military advantage may be gained'. This was perhaps an open invitation for Bevan to concern himself with intelligence-led plans rather than just operational ones. To that end, the LCS was to open and maintain links with JIC, PWE, SOE, SIS and other government organizations and departments, one of which, although not mentioned in name, would be the Twenty Committee.

XX

While Bevan was assembling his team, the Twenty Committee was making equally positive steps to ensure the future of the double cross system. In June 1942 the question of access to the decrypts coming out of Bletchley Park was finally resolved. There had been a long-running turf war between Liddell's B Division and Felix Cowgill's Section V over the distribution of what was called Ultra or the 'Most Secret Source' (MSS), with the Security Service very critical of the SIS's apparent mania for withholding information derived from decrypts relating to the double agents, even if it was to the detriment of their cases.

This led to an unreal situation developing over the *Garbo* case.[8] At face value, *Garbo* looked like a fraud. His story was so outlandish, so implausible, that the service representatives on the Twenty Committee would not agree to provide information for the case. It was only when *Garbo*'s story was seen in the light of the ISOS decrypts that it was clear he had been telling the truth and that he was highly prized by the Abwehr. However, with the exception of the Admiralty and the SIS and MI5 representatives, the members of the Twenty Committee were not privy to MSS and therefore the army and air force representatives remained sceptical of *Garbo* to say the least. On 5 June Masterman wrote to 'C' and explained the problem to him. Fortunately the head of the SIS saw sense in the argument and on 11 June agreed that in future, all decrypts relating to the double agent cases would be made available to the Twenty Committee at its weekly meetings.

Buoyed by this concession, Tommy Robertson raised the stakes still further by drafting a memo for consideration by the W Board on Wednesday 15 July. In the memo he claimed that MI5 controlled the only active German espionage networks operating in the United Kingdom, and that it was 'inconceivable' that an unknown major network was functioning. It was a bold statement but there were a number of important clues to support this assertion. Firstly the RSS intercept service had not picked up any illicit radio signals other than those under B1a's control, nor had mail censorship discovered anything indicating contact with known Abwehr cover addresses. There had been no attempts to pay anyone from the £18,000 that *Tate* had pocketed after Plan *Midas*, and most importantly of all, there was nothing indicating unknown spies on ISOS decrypts of the Abwehr's wireless traffic. Taking this into account Robertson concluded that a valuable opportunity existed to begin deceiving the German High Command on a grand scale.

This opportunity would not be realized unless there was a change at the heart of how B1a did business. Since the formation of the committee, agents and their case officers would submit reports to be vetted by the various service representatives on the panel. What Robertson believed should be happening was the reverse: that the service representatives ought to be providing the agents with misleading information to be passed to the Germans. To do this the service representatives should be allowed to work on XX full time, not just the two hours a week then allocated at the time.

Perhaps the most radical of his proposals was that the Twenty Committee ought to be attached to the Operations branch of the services rather than Intelligence. This would allow the Twenty Committee to get its deception schemes into operational planning at the earliest possible stage.

Robertson passed the memo on to Liddell, who met with 'C' and the DMI on Monday 13 July. Liddell explained the nature of the memo and Robertson's call for the service representatives to work full time on deception. The DMI was unhappy with the proposal, fearing the service representatives would find themselves discussing the existence of the Twenty Committee with their colleagues on the operational staff and before long the secret would be out of the bag. Instead the DMI smartly suggested bringing Johnny Bevan onto the W Board and making him fully acquainted with the work of the Twenty Committee, something that had been withheld from Oliver Stanley. The following day, Liddell took Robertson's proposal to the DNI, Director of Air Intelligence and Findlater Stewart. The Directors of Naval and Air Intelligence supported Robertson's proposal and agreed to allow their members to work on deception full time. They confirmed this at the actual W Board meeting on Wednesday 15 July, also endorsing the DMI's suggestion to make Bevan *au fait* with the secrets of the double cross system and Signals Intelligence.

Johnny Bevan quickly became flavour of the month. In addition to being invited to join the Wireless Board, in August the DNI suggested that Bevan might like to take over chairmanship of the Twenty Committee from Masterman and that the whole double cross system ought to be a spin-off from deception. Masterman was against this, although apparently not for any personal motives. On 5 September he wrote to Liddell explaining that the Twenty Committee was not only interested in deception and that only MI5 was in a position to run double cross agents.[9]

On 24 September the W Board met with all members in attendance plus Bevan and Tommy Robertson. It was at this point that Bevan became fully indoctrinated into the double cross secret. 'C' opened proceedings by reading out a note that Liddell suspected had been drafted by Cowgill, designed to inflate the role of MI6 in the enterprise and show that MI5 was not solely responsible for the double agent organization. Liddell explained to Bevan that the present network had begun with the agent *Snow* and developed through the arrival of different parachute agents and other arrivals, along with several agents who were recruited in the United Kingdom. The system had originally been devised for counter-espionage purposes, to capture German spies and, by running them as double agents, to alleviate the need for the Germans to send more to the British Isles. It also had a practical purpose for the intelligence service, both in terms of code-breaking and also in gleaning German intentions from the nature of the questionnaires sent to their agents. Deception had only been envisaged as a subsidiary advantage, but was one that now presented very useful opportunities. In summing up, Liddell cautioned Bevan that the counter-espionage purpose of the system meant that the Director General of MI5 retained the right of veto over any information given to the double agents to pass on that might put the network at risk.[10] As for the DNI's suggestion that Bevan should become chairman of the Twenty Committee, this was quashed. Bevan did not want to burden himself with the day-to-day running of the agents, something that was beyond his remit as Controlling Officer and at which B1a was far more accomplished.[11]

According to Montagu, C also promised to furnish Bevan with the relevant 'Special Material', by which he meant Bletchley decrypts. The initial rewards of this were more of a trickle than a flood and so Montagu very improperly went to his boss the DNI and asked Admiral Godfrey if he might cut a few corners and pass Bevan anything he felt might be useful. This was against MI6's strict orders on the propagation of MSS, but Godfrey very rightly did not believe in allowing red tape to become a hindrance to the fighting of the war. Montagu continued to supply Bevan until the flow from MI6 increased to a more reasonable level.[12]

To preserve secrecy, Bevan divided his department into two parts: Operational and Intelligence. All the secret intelligence/double cross work was undertaken by Harold Peteval in isolation from the others. Peteval attended the weekly meetings of the Twenty Committee on Bevan's behalf and was also privy to the information supplied by Bletchley Park, where his wife worked. An indication of how tight security was surrounding the 'Most Secret Source' was that it was two years before Peteval realized that his wife's work at Bletchley was in any way connected with his own.[13]

XX

At their September meeting with Bevan, the W Board solved an additional problem by agreeing to make an approach to the Americans. General Eisenhower and Admiral Stark were each asked for an officer from their respective services to be appointed to approve information relating to American forces, something on which the German questionnaires were focusing more attention. To this end the Americans set up a body known as Joint Security Control consisting of Major General G. A. Strong of the US Army and Captain George C. Dyer of the US Navy.

Meanwhile, Bevan asked the DMI for an officer who could go to Washington and try to explain the concept of strategic deception to the American Chiefs of Staff and maintain a presence there for liaison with the LCS. The DMI put forward Major Michael Bratby for the post. A relatively young officer by LCS standards, in his early thirties, Bratby did not make a good impression on Bevan or Wheatley. The problem was in his dress, which was sloppy. Bevan was always immaculate and was described by Wheatley as having the best-polished shoes in the British Army. He did not appreciate the idea of being represented in Washington by a scruff. As it turned out, Bratby had worked with the Americans while posted to Iceland and proved to be a great success in Washington. Direct links were also set up with Eisenhower when he arrived in England to take command of Operation *Torch*, the planned Allied landings in French North Africa set for November 1942. The LCS's main contact with his staff was through the British brigadier Eric Mockler-Ferryman. Better known as 'the Moke', he charged former Mid-West railway executive Lieutenant Colonel Goldbranson with keeping in touch and assisting the LCS.

Operation *Torch* was the first real test for Bevan, who was tasked with providing a cover plan for the operation. Since the United States had entered the war against Germany, the British and Americans had been arguing over the merits of how best to prosecute the war in Europe and bring it to as speedy an end as possible. For the Americans there was one clear objective: take Berlin and remove Hitler. Confident that their mighty economic and industrial potential would defeat Germany, the Americans developed a plan for a direct assault across the English Channel into north-west Europe. This they aptly codenamed *Sledgehammer*.

Churchill was opposed to *Sledgehammer* for a number of reasons. It was unclear if the Americans appreciated quite how tough German opposition was going to be. The large-scale Allied raid on Dieppe in August 1942 was an absolute bloodbath and showed in no uncertain terms how strongly the

Germans would resist any such invasion attempt. Churchill believed that *Sledgehammer* would lead to a repeat of the 1914–18 war and the slaughter of the trenches. Churchill favoured using the Mediterranean to attack 'the soft underbelly of the Axis'. He had advocated a similar course in World War I and the resulting Gallipoli campaign was a disaster. Despite this he pressed his argument, knowing that the security of the Mediterranean would reap as much reward politically as it would militarily. Britain's supply route through the Suez Canal with the eastern half of its empire would be secure and a powerful message would be sent out to the Italians that they would be next.

Eager to get American troops into action against Germany before the end of 1942, and thinking that *Sledgehammer* would not be ready before that deadline, Roosevelt went against his advisors and agreed to Churchill's request on 24 July 1942. Three days later Bevan was told to prepare a cover plan for the operation, which would keep as many German troops tied up in north-west Europe for as long as possible and prevent them from being sent to the Mediterranean or to the Russian Front.

On 5 August Bevan submitted a plan for a series of deception operations that would achieve these ends. They included a bogus cross-Channel invasion codenamed *Overthrow*, a threat against Norway codenamed *Solo*, a notional plan to relieve Malta codenamed *Townsman,* and *Kennecott*, a cover plan for the actual destination of the invasion convoys once they were under way.

Operation *Overthrow* was a continuation of the discarded *Sledgehammer* plan. Bevan wanted to encourage the Germans to believe there would be further major cross-Channel attacks in 1942. Landing platforms or 'hards' for invasion craft were built on the Thames and Medway and rumours were put out through the usual channels that the Dieppe raid had been a dress rehearsal for a much larger attack.

In the development of this cover plan it was agreed that a number of double cross agents would be used, including some who were relative newcomers to the B1a stable. With the passing of *GW* after Calvo's arrest, the only one of the early spies still in business was *Rainbow*, who was now working as a pianist in a dance band in Weston-super-Mare. Held on ice for long periods, *Rainbow* eventually developed into an important agent and moved to London in February 1942, where he could get work in a factory. He thus became an important channel for misinformation on industrial and economic topics. Of the other early spies, *Gander*'s career had proved very short lived and *Summer* and *Snow* were locked away for the duration, along with *Jeff* who was notionally posted with the Norwegian forces but whose traffic was in reality now all handled by *Mutt*.

Tate continued to send his colourful messages to Hamburg. He had notionally been posted to work on a farm, travel from which was infrequent and which limited his ability to spy. He reported to the Germans that he had a girlfriend called Mary who worked for the Admiralty and was on loan to the US Naval Mission. She supposedly introduced *Tate* to a number of officers, many of whom would stay at their flat and indiscreetly leave documents out for inspection. *Tate* thus became one of the most important channels for naval deception.

In August 1941 *Tricycle* had been sent by his Abwehr controllers on a mission to set up an espionage network in the United States, and therefore he played no part in the *Torch* planning. However, his two sub-agents *Balloon* and *Gelatine* were still active, the latter reporting on gossip she notionally picked up from her society friends in the services.

Of those agents yet to be introduced, the longest serving was codenamed *Dragonfly*. Born to German parents, Hans George was contacted by the Abwehr as early as April 1940. He reported this contact to the British authorities and in November of the same year, acting on MI5's instructions, accepted the Abwehr's offer during a business visit to Lisbon. He returned to England with a radio set hidden in a gramophone player and instructions to report on the RAF and to send meteorological reports. Working under MI5 control under the codename *Dragonfly*, this new double agent established radio contact with a station in Paris in March 1941. Although his primary importance was in sending meteorological information, he was used by the Germans to help another spy communicate with them.

This spy was the double agent known as *Father*. Arriving from Lisbon in 1941, *Father* was a distinguished Belgian Air Force pilot called Henri Arents. He had returned to Brussels after the fall of France in search of means to travel to England. To that end he offered his services to the Abwehr, offering to travel to England, using the cover of having stolen a German aircraft. Unsurprisingly the Germans did not agree to the loss of an aircraft and instead suggested that Arents travel to America and get work as a test pilot there. Arents travelled to Lisbon in December 1940, where he applied for a travel visa. When it appeared that this would not be forthcoming, Arents suggested he should go to England, steal an RAF plane and fly it back to France. This idea was appealing and Arents was allowed to travel to the United Kingdom to carry out his mission. Unluckily for the Abwehr, Arents had contacted the Belgian government in exile in Lisbon and explained his story. His arrival in the United Kingdom was not therefore unexpected and he was quickly turned to double cross work and codenamed *Father*, writing his first letter to the Germans the day after he arrived in June 1941.

It was a similar story with Agent *Careless*, a Polish airman shot down and wounded in 1939. He managed to escape to France and then Spain in April 1941 where he allowed himself to be recruited by the Abwehr, who knew him by the name Clark Korab. He was sent to Britain with a questionnaire on Air Force matters, in particular the supply of aircraft from the United States. He came to Britain by sea and was denounced by three Polish refugees who had travelled with him. Luckily for *Careless*, he had already revealed his contact with the Abwehr to the ship's captain and after interrogation by MI5 was retained as a double cross agent. Once set up, his prime focus became anti-aircraft defences, although a number of indiscretions on his part saw him locked up in Camp 020.

The star performer was *Garbo*, who reported that he had found himself freelance work with the BBC and the Ministry of Information. These jobs afforded *Garbo* some access to official circles and helped explain how he was able to recruit so many sub-agents. The first of *Garbo*'s notional contacts was officially designated Agent J1 and was known only as the 'Courier'. He was an unsavoury character who worked for an unspecified airline company and used KLM employees to smuggle *Garbo*'s letters to Portugal. The 'Courier' was also said to be involved in smuggling and operated a money-laundering racket for members of the British underworld.

In addition to the 'Courier', *Garbo* had 'recruited' the first three of his imaginary sub-agents while still working in Lisbon. The first recruit was Agent 1, Carvalho, a Portuguese commercial traveller living in Newport from where he was able to report on activities in Devon and Cornwall. He was followed closely by Agent 2, William Gerbers, a Briton of Swiss-German descent. Based in Merseyside, Gerbers was responsible for high-grade naval reports. Agent 3 was 'Pedro', a Venezuelan of private means educated at the University of Glasgow.

Once actually in Britain, *Garbo* increased the size of his organization by recruiting more fantasy figures with the help of his case officer Tommy Harris. Agent 4 was said to be 'Fred', a Gibraltarian waiter. Reporting that his confidence in Fred had been built up over seven months, *Garbo* added him to the payroll in May 1942. Due to the shortage of hotel workers, Fred was highly employable and could work more or less anywhere in the country. *Garbo* asked the Germans where they wanted him to work and from their response the British were able to see what area the Germans were most interested in: in this case the north-east. *Garbo* also reported that Fred had acquired a wireless transmitter on the black market in London. *Garbo* explained that he knew nothing about radios, but if the Germans wanted, he would purchase it. Fred had a friend who was a wireless mechanic employed at the EKCO factory, who could operate the radio on his behalf, believing it was in the cause of Spanish Republicans. This, however, was one piece of bait the Germans did not seize upon straight away, and so *Garbo*'s principal means of communication remained secret letter writing.

Another nameless agent was J2, an RAF officer based at Fighter Command to whom *Garbo* had become close. As notional as his colleagues, this agent allowed the British to pass material from the Air Ministry to the Germans. Next in line came Agent J3, a high-ranking official in the Spanish Department of the Ministry of Information where *Garbo* worked. Although never named as such, Agent J3 was based on the real head of the Spanish section, as the Germans would have realized had they enquired more deeply. Agent J3 had been introduced to *Garbo* by Agent 6, a South African called *Dick* who hated Communists. In return for his services *Garbo* had promised *Dick* a prominent place in the New World Order and was thus assured his constant and unwavering loyalty.

In addition to this complicated web of spies, *Garbo*'s unique style of writing must be emphasized. Where *Tate*'s messages were short to the point of being rude, for every line of useful information given by *Garbo* the poor German decrypting the message would have to wade through ten lines of waffle, of which the following is but a tiny example. In a long letter complaining that he was short of funds he inserted the following:

> All this has worried me a great deal and I want you to know that if it were not for the esteem which I feel personally for you, which I feel you reciprocate, as well as the interest which I have in helping our cause for which I have fought for three years during our war, and continue to fight for, though in a more responsible position in order to terminate this plague of Reds, I must tell you that in all sincerity, and as a friend, that I would have returned to Spain some time ago.[14]

Garbo's letters were littered with such pieces.

For the *Overthrow* operation *Garbo* cautioned the Germans not to be misled by reports that the Allies lacked enough ships to mount an invasion. In fact there was talk, he reported, that the Allies were planning to use all manner of smaller craft in a cross-Channel dash at several points. Taking the bait, the Germans instructed the eccentric Spaniard to learn more. By 5 October even Hitler was convinced something was afoot and began issuing directives to strengthen the Channel coastal defences and that troops stationed along the coast should be put on high alert.[15]

While Hitler suspected the Allies had their sights set on Cherbourg, the German Commander-in-Chief West, von Rundstedt, was concerned that Normandy and the north coast of Brittany might be targeted. In keeping with the rumours coming out of Britain, von Rundstedt believed Dieppe had been no more than a dress rehearsal for bigger things to come and by 12 October was predicting that the attack would come at any time. Also that month rumours began to circulate through Kent that civilians were being evacuated from the coast and that hospital beds were being prepared. In a clear indication that the Germans had no idea what the Allies were planning, towards the end of October *Garbo* was sent an urgent message instructing him to send agents to the south coast, in particular the Isle of Wight and south Wales, to locate troop concentrations and storage areas.[16] It was not until the winter settled in that von Rundstedt finally ruled out an Allied operation against him in 1942.

With forces successfully pinned in France, Bevan was also successful in keeping the Germans busy in Norway. Following the earlier *Hardboiled* plan, the LCS hinted that Trondheim and Narvik were the target of the troops mustering on the Clyde and earmarked for *Torch*. This cover plan was codenamed *Solo I*, an obvious anagram of Oslo, the Norwegian capital. It played upon a long-held German suspicion that the Allies would attempt to wrest Norway back from them. Although the *Mutt* and *Jeff* double act was put on the case, *Garbo* again played the leading role in this ruse. According to Tommy Harris the *Garbo* network reported that Canadian and Scottish troops were training in the vicinity of Ayr and Troon. Their target was said to be a mountainous country and large supplies of anti-freeze, snow chains and skis had been gathered.[17]

Bevan now had to explain the enormous build up of supplies in Gibraltar. The place was packed with men and war materials and it was inconceivable that this build up was not being reported on by Axis agents planted among the large numbers of Spanish who worked there. To explain it, he commissioned Plan *Townsman*, which hinted that the British were going to relieve the beleaguered island of Malta.

Bevan asked the DMI to provide him with a trustworthy officer who could go to Gibraltar and Malta and brief the respective governors on the cover plan about Malta. The officer selected was Major David Strangeways. Unlike the DMI's previous offering, Michael Bratby, Strangeways immediately endeared himself to Bevan and Wheatley by turning up dressed in an absolutely immaculate uniform. Wheatley invited him out to dinner and was equally impressed with his blue undress uniform. Strangeways was a professional officer who liked being in the thick of it. At Dunkirk he had got his men home on an abandoned Thames barge that he sailed back to Dover, before rushing up to London and meeting his wife for dinner at the Savoy that same evening. He was clearly the 'right sort' and would become a major player in due course.

After a few days being briefed by the LCS, Strangeways set off on his mission to brief Lord Gort at Gibraltar and General Mason MacFarlane at Malta. He was also given a number of despatches, which he was to take on to Cairo and give to the new Commander-in-Chief of the Middle East, General Sir Harold Alexander – Bevan's brother-in-law. Strangeways was also given a little deception mission of his own to carry out.

Wheatley was friends with Henry Hopkinson, the foreign advisor to the British Minister of State in Cairo. Giving Strangeways an autographed copy of his latest novel to pass to Hopkinson, Wheatley slipped a letter to his friend inside the book. It was common knowledge that German spies were to be found among the Spanish hotel staff working in Gibraltar. Any British officer spending a night in a Gibraltar hotel was almost certain to have his luggage rifled and any loose documents copied. Wheatley's letter was written on Cabinet Office headed notepaper and contained all manner of indiscreet information about his new job in Planning and speculation on what the build up for stores on Gibraltar was really all about.

Strangeways accomplished his missions in Gibraltar and Malta without a hitch. He travelled on to Cairo with his important despatches, delivered them and was introduced to Dudley Clarke. Returning to the United Kingdom he was quickly raised to the rank of lieutenant colonel and was told that he had been poached by A Force. Rather than the action posting he desired, he was given orders to go to Tehran to head A Force operations with PAIFORCE – the British forces in Persia and Iraq. He was genuinely quite disappointed.

Meanwhile the governor general of Gibraltar, Lieutenant General Mason Macfarlane, was deliberately indiscreet, travelling to Malta and making a show of the arrangements for the island's relief. This still did not explain the growing quantity of landing craft at Gibraltar. These, or so the rumour went, were earmarked for an operation against the port of Dakar in French West Africa.

This part of the deception was codenamed *Solo II*. The actual troops based in Britain earmarked for *Torch* were told their destination was Dakar. During mid-September the troops were told to expect a long sea voyage, were issued with mosquito nets and were vaccinated for tropical diseases. On 18 October, agent *Dragonfly* was asked by his German controllers where he thought the operation was going to occur: on the Atlantic or against Africa. Lending some credence to *Overthrow*, the agent replied that some soldiers expected an attack similar to Dieppe on the north French coast, but on a larger scale. There were no indications of an operation against the Atlantic or Africa on the south coast that he had seen, but *Dragonfly* reported press speculation and rumours about Dakar.

By hinting at Dakar the LCS had made a bit of a rod for its own back. It was important not to put too much credence on an attack against the Vichy French, or their forces would be put on high alert at the time of the landings and no one was sure to what extent the landings would be contested. Vichy France was still extremely upset with the British for sinking its ships at Mers-el-Kebir in 1940 and despite clandestine political overtures, it was expected that the French would resist the landing. To put the Vichy French at ease, the LCS and Dudley Clarke's A Force began hinting that the actual invasion might be against Sicily and Italy. To back up the usual channels, British diplomats began making enquiries about how Italian ex-pats in the Middle East would react to an Allied invasion of Italy. Even the Vatican was consulted about the political situation in Sicily.

At the end of October 1942 the Axis was anticipating an invasion anywhere from Narvik to Dakar. The German appreciation of the situation was interesting. Some speculated that the fleet was destined for Sardinia, Sicily or Malta. If the fleet arrived at Malta, it was then expected to make an assault on Libya to attack the rear of Rommel's forces in North Africa, then engage against the British close to Alexandria. Strangely this eventuality was about the only thing the LCS had not speculated upon, perhaps because they thought the idea was too ambitious.

The two Allied convoys set sail for Africa, the one from Britain sailing 2,760 miles (4,442km) and the one from the United States making a journey of 4,500 miles (7,242km) to reach its target. There was great tension in the map room as hour after hour passed with the members of the LCS waiting for news of an enemy response.[18] It was a miracle that both convoys passed through U-boat-infested waters undetected and were unobserved until they reached the Straits of Gibraltar on 6 November.

On the following day, 7 November, the Axis air forces still did not materialize. Although reserves of bombers had been rushed to Sicily, their commander, Kesselring, held the Luftwaffe back expecting the convoys to pass the narrow straits between Sicily and Tunis as if going on to Malta. Kesselring believed he could smash the Allied convoys with his aircraft as they passed close to his bases. It was a similar story with the U-boats, which were ordered to the eastern Mediterranean to lie in wait. Instead the British convoy turned about and the assault went in at Algiers without a hitch, taking everyone by surprise.

It is difficult to gauge the effect of military deceptions. Masterman sounded a note of caution about any perceived successes over *Torch*. The Twenty Committee chairman believed the Germans were, if anything, guilty of deceiving themselves, erroneously believing the Allies did not have enough shipping to pull off such a large expedition. It was in fact a triumph of security, as the real plans were not deduced. In this case, the value of the control of the double agents was not in sending misinformation, but in not sending real and valuable information.

Perhaps the biggest dividend of the operation, albeit a long-term one, was the strengthening of the *Garbo* case in German eyes. When the convoys were sighted, elaborate plans went into action to protect *Garbo* from any fallout relating to his failure to report the convoys coming from England. On 29 October *Garbo* made a report about the sailing of one of the *Torch* convoys from the Clyde. The letter was sent on to Lisbon with instructions that it was not to be posted to the German safe house until after the Admiralty reported that the enemy had spotted the convoy. A second letter was written on 1 November and posted on the 4th. This letter said that Agent 3 had reported troop transports and warships leaving the Clyde with Mediterranean colours. *Garbo* also reported that he had personally seen a secret Ministry of Information directive about a landing in French North Africa. This letter was not sent by air mail until the day the landings took place.

By holding up the information until it was too late to be of any operational use, *Garbo* convinced his German employers that he had tried to warn them, but had not been able to do so because of his lack of a radio. This embarrassed them because they had not agreed to let *Garbo* buy the transmitter offered to him by 'Fred' the Gibraltarian.

Garbo also reported he had been handicapped by the mysterious silence from his Liverpool-based sub-agent Gerbers (Agent 2) who should have been in a prime position to warn him of ships from the Mersey. After an investigation into the matter, *Garbo* reported that Gerbers had unexpectedly died on 19 November as a result of illness. As proof he forwarded the obituary notice that had appeared in the *Liverpool Daily Post*, planted there by the British secret service. This account was believed and condolences were passed on to Gerbers' widow.

The Spaniard's standing with the Abwehr now rose to a level above and beyond that of all the other agents. His reports were described as 'magnificent', and there was a promise that a radio link would be set up for him as had been previously suggested.

10

EL ALAMEIN

BEFORE THE *TORCH* LANDINGS THE position of the British and Commonwealth forces in North Africa had been precarious to say the least. Through 1941 and the first half of 1942, war in the desert had continued to seesaw between thrust and counter-thrust. When Auchinleck's *Crusader* offensive ran out of steam in early 1942, Rommel counter-attacked. The ensuing battle of Gazala saw the British put into flight on 14 June, with the Eighth Army scrambling back towards Egypt to avoid encirclement and capture, while the previously indomitable garrison of Tobruk surrendered on 21 June. The British and Commonwealth forces continued their headlong retreat until they reached El Alamein, a choke point on the way into Egypt.

Here the coast road and railway passed through a 40-mile (64km) gap bordered by the Mediterranean to the north and the Qattara Depression to the south. This wasteland of salt marshes and soft sands was impenetrable to armoured vehicles and prevented Rommel from making the sort of spectacular, sweeping flanking move that had brought him success at Gazala. Beyond the British line at El Alamein, the desert opened up and the way to Alexandria, Cairo and the Suez Canal was clear. Unfortunately for Rommel, by the time his soldiers began trying to force themselves through El Alamein on 1 July they were absolutely shattered, having endured five weeks of constant advance and battle. Trying to seize back the initiative, Auchinleck took personal command of the Eighth Army and counter-attacked the Afrika Korps. It was to little avail.

For the remainder of July the two exhausted adversaries faced one another until both sides called a halt to their operations. For Auchinleck it was desirable for the stalemate to be as prolonged as possible. New Sherman tanks were on their way from America and reinforcement by the 51st Division was expected shortly. On the flip side, Auchinleck knew that Rommel was also waiting for reserves before recommencing his drive into the Nile Delta. If Rommel's reserves arrived first, the British commander had scant forces available and many of his vehicles were in repair shops. The only thing he had left to hand was deceit.

Auchinleck turned to his Director of Camouflage, Major Geoffrey Barkas, and asked for every dummy gun, truck and tank they could lay their hands on to be placed behind the front line, suggesting to Rommel's scouts and photo-reconnaissance that the troops at El Alamein were only the forward posts of a much stronger army.

By trade Barkas was a film director, producer and writer, having directed the 1928 film *Q-Ships* about a British merchant ship in World War I with hidden armaments used against German U-boats. As was the case with Colonel Turner's decoy organization, professionals from the world of cinema dealt daily in the art of tricking the human eye through a lens and thus proved extremely adept at military deception.

In addition to cinema, the art of camouflage had long been the preserve of artists. Most attribute the modern concept of camouflage to the American artist Abbott H. Thayer, who made a study of defensive coloration in the animal kingdom in 1896.[1] During World War I Picasso's geometric Cubist style influenced French *camoufleurs*, and it was the British painter Norman Wilkinson who devised the concept of 'dazzle ships' in April 1917. Pointing out that there was no way of hiding a large ship on the horizon through a German periscope, Wilkinson demonstrated it was possible, by painting ships in Cubist-like angled blocks of greys and blues, to distort the view of the ship through the periscope and thus confuse or 'dazzle' the aimer about its direction and speed. Before long, thousands of vessels were painted in the striking manner conceptualized by the artist.

In 1940 the War Office established the Camouflage Development and Training Centre at Farnham Castle in Surrey. It was the preserve of a mixed bag of individuals including Hugh Cott, a distinguished Cambridge zoologist who applied the coloration found on animal skins to guns and tanks. From the art world there was the Surrealist artist and friend of Picasso, Roland Penrose, who wrote the *Home Guard Manual of Camouflage*. Penrose's party trick was successfully to hide his lover, the acclaimed American model, photographer and war correspondent Lee Miller, in a garden, naked, camouflaged from prying eyes with body paint and netting. He reasoned that if he could hide a naked woman in a garden full of people, anything could be hidden.

Perhaps the most famous of the British *camoufleurs* was the popular stage magician Jasper Maskelyne. Following the publication of his memoirs in 1949, Maskelyne has long been seen as the leading light in the deception world. However, the truth about the 'war magician' appears somewhat less fantastic under scrutiny. Maskelyne arrived in Cairo on 10 March 1941 as part of a detachment of 12 camouflage officers sent to work with Barkas. He spent much of his time performing magic shows for entertainment purposes and later went on to work for the escape and evasion department MI9, where he helped in devising concealed escape devices for POWs.

Maskelyne's actual involvement in military deception appears to have been a bit of a sham. Curiously enough, people appeared much more confident with the dummy vehicles when they were told they had been devised by a well-known illusionist. It also appears that Dudley Clarke encouraged Maskelyne's boasting to some extent, because it diverted attention away from A Force and himself. Somewhat ironically, then, Maskelyne's main contribution to deception may have been to provide a cloak behind which others could work in secret.[2]

Maskelyne's more limited role is also suggested by the artist Julian Trevelyan, a fellow graduate from Farnham. An interesting character in his own right, Trevelyan was a member of the British Surrealist movement and before the war had experimented with injections of hallucinogenic synthetic Mescalin crystals, an experience which led him to exclaim: 'I have been given the key of the universe.' His feet firmly back on the ground, Trevelyan was sent from the United Kingdom on a fact-finding mission to the Middle East to witness the deceptions being carried out there by Barkas's department.

In March 1942 Trevelyan visited Tobruk and then went to Barkas's Camouflage Training and Development Centre at Helwan near Cairo. He was generally impressed with what he saw, except perhaps with a dummy railhead complete with dummy rolling stock and station, which he claimed that the Germans complimented by dropping a wooden bomb on. Having witnessed the hand of Barkas at work, the artist remarked: 'It is thanks to Barkas, principally, that the formidable technique of deception has been elaborated. You cannot hide anything in the desert; all you can do is to disguise it as something else. Thus tanks become trucks overnight, and of course trucks become tanks, and the enemy is left guessing at our real strength and intentions.'[3]

Returning to the situation at El Alamein, Barkas followed Auchinleck's orders to congregate his dummies behind the main lines and was overjoyed that he, for the first time, received the magic words 'operational priority' to assist him.[4] Operation *Sentinel* saw the land between El Alamein and Cairo become dotted with camps, complete with smoke rising from cookhouses and incinerators. Canteens were set up with dummy vehicles parked outside while their imaginary drivers were inside enjoying an equally notional 'brew'. To thicken the defensive positions, the craftsmen at Barkas's school at Helwan developed a wide range of decoys, including batteries of field guns that could be stowed inside a single truck. Within three weeks of starting the build up Barkas was simulating enough activity to indicate the presence of two fresh motorized divisions in close reserve to the main line.

XX

A Force also played a part in Operation *Sentinel*. With Dudley Clarke on numerous and prolonged absences during 1941, A Force had been the victim of some detrimental organizational changes. In July of that year Wavell formed a new body designated GSI(d), as mentioned earlier. Under the command of Major Wintle, Royal Dragoons, GSI(d) was made responsible for spreading 'alarm and despondency' among the enemy with deception and tricks. Wintle was an interesting character. Before arriving in the Middle East, he had been the subject of a scandal after threatening to shoot the Director of Air Intelligence. Wintle had been asked to rejoin his regiment, but instead wanted to be seconded to the French Army. Having been an instructor in France, Wintle believed he could instill some fighting spirit in the French if he was allowed to go out there. The Director of Air Intelligence made a quip Wintle interpreted as an insinuation of cowardice, at which point he drew his pistol. Wintle was put under arrest and faced a court martial. When challenged that he had pulled a gun and said words to the effect that certain ministers and Air Force officers ought to be shot, Wintle admitted it. He then produced a list of ministers he believed ought to be shot for the way they were running the war. Reaching the seventh name on his list, Wintle was stopped and the proceedings were brought to a speedy conclusion.

Perhaps the best known of GSI(d)'s ruses was the manufacturing of defective German ammunition. Instead of propellant, inside the cartridge case Wintle's men would write defeatist messages, allegedly penned by German factory workers. The organization also pioneered the use of sonic deception at Halfaya on 24 December 1941.[5] This technique saw an Egyptian film company record the sound of tanks moving through the desert – the recordings of which were played back through amplifiers mounted on trucks.

With the initiative very much in German hands and with the British in retreat, much of GSI(d) and A Force's time was spent with the escape and evasion organization, MI9. It was through this association that the magician Maskelyne had his name linked with Clarke's secret organization; it also saw Wintle arrested in Marseilles while unwisely trying to set up an escape network from France.

Clarke's return from Gibraltar after the Madrid affair was a godsend to A Force. While absent, much of A Force's control over tactical deception had been taken away. Clarke lobbied General Auchinleck to restore A Force's control over all tactical and strategic deception, arguing that the two were inexorably linked and required a single chief coordinating them. In March

OPERATION *BERTRAM* – THE COVER PLAN FOR EL ALAMEIN

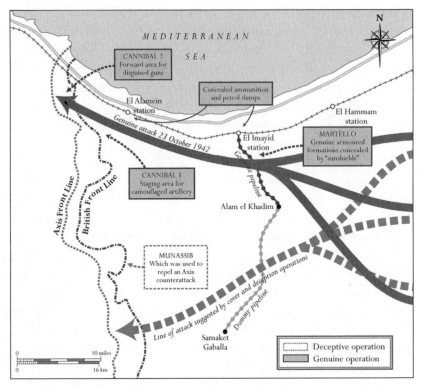

1942 Clarke began an operation that was to prove the cornerstone of later successes. Operation *Cascade* was the build up of a fake order of battle making the British appear much stronger than was the case. A Force had already built up a number of notional units, including several SAS brigades, the 10th Armoured Division in the Western Desert and the 7th Division in Cyprus. *Cascade* aimed to add three armoured and 11 infantry divisions to the Allied order of battle.

Achieving this was not simply a case of adding a few more formations to a list; it involved real administration. Divisions would need to be assembled, transported to Egypt and quartered, and all this would take mountains of paperwork. The divisions would need a physical imprint – camps, staging and training areas, real insignia, real radio traffic and so on. All this was provided and a phantom army began to grow. What was so fabulous about *Cascade* is that when the Germans learned of a new formation and entered it on their appreciation of the British order of battle, that unit would remain in existence, in many cases until the end of the war.

One of the best channels for *Cascade* and other deceptions was the double-agent network *Cheese*. After misleading the Italians over *Crusader*, by all the rules the *Cheese* link should have been discredited beyond further use. Sure enough, the Italians at SIM were suspicious and allowed the channel to stagnate. However, a new SIME case officer, the novelist Captain John Simpson, persisted in sending the Italians messages from *Cheese's* fictional White Russian sub-agent *Lambert*.

As the Twenty Committee had found in London, the best way of establishing an agent's standing was to have them demand money from their controllers. The fact that none was forthcoming in this case did not bode well. Unfortunately for *Lambert*, Rommel had other means of getting information out of Cairo and *Lambert's* services were simply not in demand. The prime source of information for Axis forces was in fact the US embassy in Cairo. American military attaché Colonel Frank Bonner Fellers was charged by Washington with providing reports on the actions and plans of the British in the Middle East. To that end Fellers was a frequent visitor to British GHQ and to frontline units. Fellers' reports were transmitted in the so-called 'Black Code' used by American missions abroad. Unknown to the Americans, this code had been fatally compromised by the Italian SIM. Before America's entry to the war, a SIM agent had picked the lock on the safe in the office of the US military attaché in Rome. The agent photographed the 'Black Code' and put everything back in order without anyone noticing. The Italians then passed the code on to the Abwehr. From that point on, most of what Fellers told Washington ended up on Rommel's desk.[6]

Another important source of information for Rommel was his wireless intelligence service commanded by Captain Alfred Seebohm of the 621st Signals Battalion. In the broad expanse of desert warfare, radio communications were the only practical way for a modern army to communicate. Unfortunately for the British Eighth Army and the Desert Air Force, in the chaos of the fighting with Rommel, their radio security had become somewhat lax. Unknown to the average Tommies, as they chattered away to their command posts and colleagues, Seebohm was listening in, and the German had an uncanny knack of deducing British intentions from the origin and intensity of the chatter he intercepted.

These secret sources had given Rommel the edge in the desert battles and played no small part in his success. Unfortunately for the German field marshal, this success was not to last. Acting on Bletchley Park's Ultra intercepts, on 10 July the British launched a surprise attack on two Italian infantry divisions at Tel-el-Eisa. Caught up in the attack was part of the 621st

Signals Battalion including Seebohm. Rather than flee, Seebohm set up a defensive perimeter around his vehicles and prepared to fight it out. In the ensuing combat about one hundred members of the 621st were captured, along with a large cache of important documents. Seebohm was mortally wounded in the attack and later died in a hospital in Alexandria.

The loss of Seebohm was a catastrophe for Rommel, who was furious to learn he had been so near the front line.[7] Not only had he lost the officer, but the captured papers would reveal the extent to which Seebohm had been aware of British call signs, map reference codes and radio codes. It also confirmed suspicions about the 'Black Code' having been broken. The British informed Fellers of the breach, but asked the American to keep using the code as a channel for deception traffic.

Thus, at the time Rommel was on the verge of breaking through the last British defences at El Alamein, his most important secret sources dried up. Coupled with the collapse of these sources, the British were able to demonstrate mastery of the skies over Egypt, making German aerial reconnaissance dangerous and sporadic. With the lights switched out, and desperate for news of British intentions, the Germans had no choice but to rely on their agents on the ground.

Unfortunately for Rommel these agents were a mixed bag of no-hopers and unfortunates. The key agent network in Cairo was known as the *Kondor* mission. All sorts of legends have grown up about *Kondor*, but the truth is that as a source of intelligence the mission was a disaster. *Kondor* consisted of two German spies smuggled into Egypt by the Hungarian adventurer, Count Laszlo Almasy. Famous as a pioneer of desert travel, Almasy was recruited by Major Nikolaus Ritter (alias Dr Rantzau) for his knowledge of the Middle East to help infiltrate spies into Egypt. As with almost everything else Ritter was involved in, the result was a dismal failure.

The first mission was to pluck the Egyptian chief of staff, General Aziz Ali Masri Pasha, from behind British lines and take him to a conference in Berlin to discuss an anti-British uprising. Ritter provided Almasy with two Heinkel He111s and a crew, but the link up never materialized and Ritter had his arm broken in a plane crash and went back to Europe. Masri fared no better. When he tried to flee, the RAF forced his plane to land at Almaza airport and he was taken into custody. This attempted flight was reported in the *New York Times*, which correctly speculated that Masri was trying to cross over to the Germans in Libya to offer them his expertise in desert warfare.[8]

Almasy's next mission fared little better. Operating under the codename *Salam* (a part anagram of his surname), Almasy recruited a spy ring in Paris known as the *Pyramid* Organization. The network comprised of two men, Mohsen Fadl, the head of the Egyptian tourist office in Paris, and Elie Haggar, a student in the French capital and the son of the head of the Egyptian Police Force. Both were infiltrated into Egypt via Istanbul in October 1941 and told to report on political matters. Unfortunately neither was provided with any means of communicating with the outside world and both were eventually caught in 1943 after very little gain.

With no news from the *Pyramid* Organization, Almasy came up with the *Kondor* scheme. This time the explorer would drive two German agents from Tripoli through the southern desert into Egypt. Despite much celebrity, the mission was another in a long line of German secret service disasters.

The *Kondor* agents were *Max*, 29-year-old Heinrich Sandstede, an English-speaking former employee of the Texas Oil Company, and the lead agent, *Moritz*, 28-year-old Johannes Eppler, who also went by the name Hussein Gaafar. Eppler had been born to German parents, but was raised in Cairo by his stepfather, an Egyptian judge. As such he was credited with enough local knowledge to make the mission a success. Instead it was doomed to failure from the start because as early as December 1941 Bletchley Park began picking up signals relating to it. The British code-breakers listened in as the team was assembled, as it received six Ford V8 lorries, and as it set out from Jalu Oasis 250 miles (402 km) south of Benghazi on 12 May. *Moritz* and *Max* were dropped off seven miles (11km) from Asyut and then made their way to Cairo by train. Arriving in the Egyptian capital, the two agents painted the town red with £3,600 of forged British banknotes they had been given to buy information. The pair never got their radio set working and, despite many claims that the two agents were Rommel's top spies in Egypt, no messages were sent. After several attempts to set up their operations in brothels, the pair were put up in a houseboat on the Nile by the famous Egyptian belly dancer Hekmet Fahmey. The star of the Kit Kat Club at Cairo's Continental hotel, Fahmey had links to the nationalists Gamal Abdul Nasser and Anwar el-Sadat, both future presidents of Egypt and then members of the anti-British Free Officers' Movement. In a bid to procure more funds and establish contact with Rommel's HQ, Fahmey introduced the pair to Sadat. Their presence in Cairo was also advertised to Victor Hauer, an Austrian employed by the Swedish embassy to look after the concerns of interned Germans. Hauer was told to look after the German agents, but instead he was taken into custody on 21 July and spilled the beans to his interrogators. Eppler and Sandstede were arrested along with Fahmey and some of the Egyptian officers – Sadat included. The failure of *Kondor* left the Germans with just one last source: *Lambert*.

Lambert's script writer, Captain Robertson, had given the notional agent an address in the Rue Galal in Cairo. From there he sent a stream of news about the fictional order of battle build up that A Force was creating in Operation *Cascade*. *Lambert* was also used in trying to divert Axis resources away from Malta, which was then in a state of blockade, and to deter reserves being sent to Rommel. From a fictional sub-agent, *Lambert* began sending reports that the British were planning an attack from Cyprus against the Greek islands. As the script unfolded, this notional attack became focused against Crete. To support *Lambert*'s messages, dummy landing craft were constructed in Cyprus and dummy gliders were built in Egypt to hint at airborne support for this bogus operation.

When *Lambert* reported that the invasion force might have already left Cyprus, a detachment of the Italian Navy blockading Malta was sent to intercept it. While the Italian ships were away a British convoy managed to reach Malta with much-needed supplies. Although his warnings had not materialized, this was enough to build *Lambert* up in the eyes of his controllers.

The fictional White Russian was handed over by the Italian SIM to the German Abwehr. Whatever suspicions the Italians had harboured did not seem to be shared by his new German bosses, whose opinions of *Lambert* were being read by Bletchley Park. On 4 July ISOS decrypts revealed that *Lambert* was thought of as a credible source by the Abwehr and by 12 July Bletchley Park could report that *Lambert* was considered 'trustworthy'. After the failure of the *Kondor* mission to report in and the loss of Seebohm, the Abwehr instructed *Lambert* to step up his transmissions from twice a week to daily. His eagerly awaited reports were then sent by the Abwehr direct to Panzer Army HQ where they were dissected by Rommel's staff. This was an incredible success for the British.[9]

With *Lambert*'s new lease of life confirmed, SIME decided to add another fictional character to the *Cheese* network by giving *Lambert* a notional girlfriend, a Greek girl they codenamed *Misanthrope*. This fictional woman was portrayed as young, brave and intelligent with a hatred of the British. She showed no scruples in befriending officers for the purpose of extracting secrets from them. *Lambert* revealed to his eager Abwehr controllers that he was teaching the girl to use his radio set in case he fell ill. Again the British showed a deep understanding of the cunning necessary in secret service work. Every radio operator sounds different over the air when typing out Morse code. To ensure *Misanthrope* was distinguishable from *Lambert*, the British recruited an ATS officer (Auxiliary Territorial Service, the British Army's female support service) as a substitute radio operator.

Suddenly the Germans were keen to send money to *Lambert* and worryingly they asked him to have a face-to-face meeting with one of their agents in order to be paid. *Lambert* replied that this was impossible, but he would send his girlfriend instead. To this end SIME recruited and schooled a Greek girl to play the role of *Misanthrope*. The girl was known as the *BGM* (Blond Gun Moll) as it was rumoured she had shot someone in the past, and it was SIME's knowledge of this act that allowed them to blackmail her into complying with their requirements. In fact the 'gun' part of her nickname was inaccurate, as she had actually pushed the poor fellow off a building rather than shot him.[10]

Despite her schooling and background the *BGM* was reluctant actually to meet with an Abwehr agent face-to-face, so a system was worked out whereby the Axis courier would leave the money inside some milk bottles in a cupboard outside the house in the Rue Galal. They remained empty as a succession of couriers failed to materialize. This should not be read as a lack of interest in *Lambert*; on the contrary, the bogus Russian remained, along with *Garbo*, one of Germany's most trusted spies until the end of the war.

XX

Having ordered his deceivers to commence work at the beginning of July, Auchinleck did not remain long enough in theatre to witness their eventual success. While en route to Moscow on 5 August 1942, Churchill visited Auchinleck at his desert HQ. Churchill was unhappy that 'the Auk' had taken direct control of the Eighth Army and believed that should have been left to a subordinate while he concentrated on commanding the whole theatre. The British Prime Minister wanted a new commander for the Eighth Army and, against the advice of Auchinleck and General Sir Alan Brooke, the Chief of the Imperial General Staff, he appointed Lieutenant General William 'Strafer' Gott.

An aggressive desert veteran popular with his troops, Gott never took up this post, as the unarmed transport aircraft he was travelling in was shot down on 7 August. Although the aircraft crash-landed and the pilot escaped, Gott did not escape the wreck. Somewhat ironically considering Gott's nickname, after a forced landing the transport was strafed on the ground by the German fighter and caught fire. The following day the Eighth Army command was offered to Lieutenant General Bernard Montgomery (Monty), the preferred choice of Brooke, but then still a relative unknown to many. On 8 August Churchill also replaced General Auchinleck as Commander-in-Chief Middle East with

General Harold Alexander. Churchill was pained to replace Auchinleck and told Alexander that sacking his predecessor was 'like killing a magnificent stag'.[11] However, with the succession of reverses and Rommel's growing reputation as an unbeatable military wizard, such a cull was necessary.

Alexander's first appreciation of the military situation in the Western Desert was precise. If the Alamein position was lost, then the whole Nile Delta was indefensible. A German advance beyond that point would precipitate a huge withdrawal. This view was shared by Montgomery, who pinned his colours to the defence of El Alamein. This would be his Thermopylae and the word 'withdraw' was henceforth expunged from Eighth Army vocabulary.

Greatly assisted by Bletchley Park's decrypts of Rommel's situation, Montgomery was able to resist the final Axis attempt to break through the Alamein line and drive into the Delta. The battle opened on the night of 30 August with a determined German effort to hook round the British from the south and to occupy the ridge of Alam el Halfa, which gave the battle its name. Warned by Bletchley Park, the Desert Air Force was able to hit Rommel's tank and vehicle concentrations as they were bunched up passing through the dense British minefields. This same air force also bombed and strafed Rommel's supply lines to the point where, on 4 September, he had to give up his advance.

General Alexander put part of the success at Alam el Halfa down to a ruse, which in essence was a variation of Meinzerhagen's haversack ploy described in Chapter 8. It concerned the planting of a bogus 'going' map in a damaged armoured car that was left behind to be captured by the Germans. A 'going' map was a specially coloured map produced by the Survey Branch showing what parts of the desert were possible for vehicles and which areas were impassable. The map was specially drawn up to show that a wide flanking move around the Alam el Halfa position would be hard 'going', while an advance against the south of the position would be relatively easy 'going'.

The map was 'aged' with folds, creases, tea and oil stains and given to an 11th Hussar armoured car reconnaissance. The patrol drove within sight of the Germans and attracted some fire, at which point the crew of the armoured car faked a breakdown. The crew bailed out, ran away to the safety of another vehicle in the patrol and sped off, leaving the map and several other documents behind.[12]

According to Alexander, the Germans found the map and altered their plans from making an outflanking manoeuvre to a direct assault on the ridge, which was repelled. Although many believe the Germans did not make the flanking move because of a lack of fuel, Alexander claimed that confirmation of the role of the map was given by General von Thoma, who was subsequently captured by the Allies.[13] It has been pointed out that von Thoma was not in the theatre at the time of Alam el Halfa and only arrived later. Although it is not beyond the realms of belief that the captive general learned of the German planning after his arrival, his absence during the battle has left the door open for sceptics.[14]

XX

After his failure to break through the Alamein line Rommel was forced onto the defensive. With an impatient Prime Minister anxiously watching proceedings, the British made their preparations for a counter-attack scheduled for 23 October. To cover this attack, two cover plans were developed, Operations *Treatment* and *Bertram*.

Shortly after Montgomery took command of the Eighth Army on 13 August he held his first meeting with Colonel Dudley Clarke and was given an appraisal of his command's activities, which centred on maintaining a notional threat against Crete. Montgomery did not disapprove of Dudley Clarke's tactics; in fact he endorsed them. When planning the counter-offensive, in addition to the notional threat against Crete, Montgomery wanted A Force to use its intelligence channels to make the Germans believe the start date, or D-Day, for the forthcoming Allied desert counter-offensive would be 6 November, two weeks later than actually planned. This A Force ruse was codenamed *Treatment*.

At the time, Dudley Clarke was heavily involved with the planning for Operation *Torch*. In October he was called to attend a meeting with the London Controlling Section, which was set up to ensure Anglo-American cooperation in deception once the US forces began operating in North Africa. As he would be away from Egypt at the crucial time, Clarke handed over management of *Treatment* to his deputy, Lieutenant Colonel Noël Wild.

Having been acquainted with him for some time before the war, in April 1942 Clarke had poached Wild from his job as a staff officer at GHQ Cairo. The circumstances of his recruitment were somewhat irregular. One evening Major Wild went to a Cairo hotel to cash a cheque and was ambushed by the A Force chief, who bought him drinks to celebrate Wild's promotion to lieutenant colonel as Clarke's deputy. When Wild enquired what the promotion entailed, and what exactly Clarke did, he was met with evasive replies. The only certainty was that Clarke wanted someone he knew and trusted in the post.[15]

After a night's sleep Wild accepted the position and was indoctrinated into the weird and wonderful world of A Force. By the time of *Treatment*, Wild was well enough versed in its techniques to use the A Force channels to hint that there were no plans to commit to a major offensive against Rommel. As long as German forces continued to advance into the Caucasus through the Soviet Union, the British were said to be apprehensive about their rear. Instead, Montgomery's sole purpose was to use the lull in the fighting to train and test his troops for future operations. According to information sent out by the *Cheese* network, if there was going to be any major British attack it would be against Crete. This information was taken so seriously that Hitler ordered the island's garrison to be strengthened on 23 September. He reiterated this order on 21 October, just two days before the British offensive was due to open.

To divert attention away from the last week of October, a conference was scheduled in Tehran. In attendance would be the British Commanders-in-Chief Middle East, PAIFORCE (Persia and Iraq) and India. This conference was scheduled for 26 October, three days after D-Day. In Egypt the last week of October was left open for officers to take leave and many had hotel rooms booked in their names.[16]

The tactical counterpart to *Treatment* was codenamed *Bertram* and was given to Lieutenant Colonel Charles Richardson to devise and implement.[17] An engineer by training, Richardson had only recently joined the planning staff of Eighth Army HQ after having spent a year with SOE in Cairo. Privately he was dismissive of the dummy tanks Auchinleck had used in *Sentinel* as a 'pathetic last resort'. Richardson was sceptical about the chances of fooling the Germans, in particular the Luftwaffe and its photo-reconnaissance interpreters.

Richardson was summoned by Montgomery's chief of staff, Freddie de Guingand, and received the outline of the British plan, which was a direct assault along the coastal road, on the right of the British position. He was then told to go away and come up with a suitable cover plan that would conceal the intention of the offensive for as long as possible, and when that was no longer possible, to mislead the enemy over the date and sector in which the attack was to be made.

For this purpose Montgomery wanted a plan that advertised false moves in the south, while concealing his real moves in the north of the sector. Pondering the situation from Rommel's point of view, Richardson thought that the German field marshal might 'buy' the suggestion of a British attack from the south, as it was the sort of tactic he might resort to himself.

The other thing Richardson had to consider was how to persuade Rommel the attack was not going to be delivered on 23 October, as was the case. The preparations for the battle were so vast that Richardson supposed they could only stall the enemy's thinking by about ten days. The way he proposed to do this was ingenious. His idea was to construct a dummy pipeline bringing water to the southern flank. German reconnaissance would no doubt spot this pipeline and, by gauging the speed with which it was being constructed, they would be able to project the date on which the British would be ready to begin their operations. This date would be set at ten days after D-Day. Richardson took the plans to de Guingand, who approved them, and passed them on to Monty for his final endorsement.

With official approval granted, Richardson needed someone actually to implement the plans. Richardson was aware of A Force's existence, probably through de Guingand, who had until recently been the Director of Military Intelligence in GHQ Cairo. However, Richardson was reluctant to use A Force because he believed Clarke's work was so 'stratospheric and secret' it was best to keep well out of it.[18] Instead Richardson used GHQ's Camouflage Department under Barkas.

On 17 September Barkas and his deputy, Major Tony Ayrton, were invited to de Guingand's caravan and warned that what they were about to hear was top secret. The Chief Engineer of the Eighth Army was about to make a number of bulldozed tracks running from an assembly area codenamed *Martello* towards the front line, running parallel with the coast road and railway. Shortly afterwards large concentrations of vehicles and tanks would begin concentrating at *Martello* along with vast quantities of stores and munitions. Beyond *Martello*, but about five miles behind the front line, a great number of field guns would be marshalled at an area codenamed *Cannibal 1*. These would then be moved closer to the front line to deliver an opening barrage from positions directly behind the front line codenamed *Cannibal 2*. De Guingand wanted to know if the Camouflage Department was able to assist with the following objectives:[19]

1. To conceal the preparations in the north.
2. To suggest that an attack was to be mounted in the south.
3. When the preparations in the north could not be concealed, to minimize their scale.
4. To make the rate of build up appear slower than it actually was, so that the enemy would believe there were still two or three days before the attack commenced.

Although sobered when told he had about a month to achieve all this, Barkas was inwardly jubilant that at last Camouflage was about to make a 'campaign swaying' contribution.[20]

Barkas and Ayrton left the caravan to formulate their plan and took a stroll along the beach where their voices were drowned out from prying ears by the waves breaking on the shore. Two hours later, having typed up an appreciation and report on the subject, they went back to de Guingand, offering to suggest that two armoured brigade groups were concentrating to the south. When Montgomery's reply was delivered a few days later, Barkas was told to make provision for an entire phantom armoured corps in the south.

This entailed making 400 dummy Grant tanks and at least 1,750 transport vehicles and guns. Barkas was given ample resources, including three complete pioneer companies, a transport company and a POW unit. While he masterminded production of the material and devices, Barkas charged Ayrton and his colleague, the former *Punch* illustrator Brian Robb, with the actual deception work on the battlefield.

The deception scheme was composed of a number of separate plans, their component parts coming together to form a veritable symphony of deceit. The first problem was the approach tracks that were bulldozed from *Martello* to the front line. Although there was absolutely no hope of hiding their existence from the Luftwaffe, their purpose could be concealed. Ayrton went up in an aircraft to enact the role of a German reconnaissance pilot taking photographs. Ayrton's solution to the problem of the tracks was ingenious. He called in at the Chief Engineer's with annotated aerial photographs and suggested that rather than starting at *Martello* and driving directly to the front, the bulldozers should complete only patches of the track and join them together only much closer to D-Day.

More solutions were found to disguise the stores. Over 3,000 tons of stores had to be hidden at El Alamein train station, about five miles behind the front line. This included 600 tons of supplies, 2,000 tons of petrol, oil and lubricants and 420 tons of engineer stores.[21] A similar amount required concealment at a second station about 15 miles to the east. In the forward area the most pressing problem was finding suitable storage for the cans of petrol. Ayrton and Robb found that there were about a hundred sections of slit-trenches in the area, all of which were lined with masonry. Supposing that these trenches were already well known to Germans from reconnaissance photographs, it was decided to line the trenches with a single course of petrol cans on each side. This slight reduction in the width of the trenches did not appear to change the shadows cast by the trenches, so 2,000 tons of fuel was successfully stored overnight. Confirmation of their success came when British air observers were sent out to locate the new fuel dumps and failed.

The food supplies arrived at the dumping ground in trucks by night. The trucks were met by guides and led to pre-arranged unloading sites in the open, featureless piece of terrain. As they were unloaded, the stores were stacked in such a way that they resembled three-ton trucks covered by camouflage netting. Further stores were stacked under the apron of the net, with the remaining boxes stacked and hidden under soldiers' tents. To complete the illusion of a park of thin-skinned vehicles, a small unit of soldiers was moved into the area to animate it and real trucks were diverted to drive through it to create tracks and demonstrate the sort of activities associated with a vehicle park. Similar arrangements were made for the concealment of ammunition and other military stores close to the rail stations at El Alamein and also further back.

The British offensive was to be opened by an enormous barrage of around 400 25-pounder field guns. These guns had to be hidden at their assembly point and then again at their barrage positions. It was not simply a case of hiding the guns, but also their limbers and the distinctively shaped quad tractors used to transport them. It was found that by backing the limber up to the gun and rigging a canvas dummy vehicle over the top with the limber and gun's wheels protruding, the effect was to produce a convincing three-ton truck. In turn the quads had a rectangular tent put over the back of them to make them also appear as trucks. Each gun crew was then trained in making the transformation from assembly area (*Cannibal 1*) to the barrage point (*Cannibal 2*) – the codename *Cannibal* deriving from the way the dummy 'swallowed' the thing it was protecting. When the time came to move the guns into position, the transition occurred at night and the gun crews had their tents and covers in place before the sun came up.

As for the *Martello* staging area, the problem was collecting hundreds of armoured vehicles in an area just 12 x 8 miles (19 x 13km). Since there was no way of hiding such an assembly, it was decided to fill up the *Martello* area with as many thin-skinned vehicles and dummies as quickly as possible. The Germans would no doubt notice this concentration area, but because nothing appeared to be happening there, they would come to ignore it.

Meanwhile, each tank that was destined to arrive at *Martello* was assigned a special point where it would be concealed. Each tank was provided with a 'sunshield', an invention that Barkas attributed to Wavell, who had earlier shown him a sketch of a tank with a canopy over it. The idea was that each tank would have a quickly detachable cover to make it look like a truck. In all,

772 'sunshields' were issued before El Alamein. The tank crews were trained how to use them and then taken up to *Martello* and shown their hiding place in advance. On the night of 20–21 October Xth Armoured Corps began moving from its staging area to *Martello*. On arrival the crews had their 'sunshields' rigged before first light. Back at the staging area, the track marks were obliterated, the empty fuel cans were collected and a dummy tank was erected where the real tank had previously stood. From the point of view of German photo-reconnaissance, nothing had changed since the previous day, except the arrival of more trucks in an already busy assembly area behind the British lines.

The main focus of the build up in the south, where Montgomery wanted Rommel to think the attack was coming from, began on 26 September with the start of the dummy water pipeline codenamed *Diamond*. A five-mile-long section of trench was dug and a 'pipeline' laid parallel to it. The actual 'pipeline' was constructed from crushed, empty petrol cans laid along the ground in a line. Overnight the trench would be filled in and the 'pipeline' gathered up to be reused in the next section of trench. Dummy pump houses were built at three points along the line, complete with overhead tanks and can filling stations. To add further credence to the illusion, these areas were populated by dummy vehicles and mannequins of soldiers.

To the east of *Diamond*, an area codenamed *Brian* (after Brian Robb) was set aside for the build up of dummy stores. Despite a sandstorm and the unexpected arrival of a horde of British tanks on field manoeuvres, two days before D-Day Barkas's men had created what appeared to be a huge stockpile of stores.

With the real artillery hidden to the north dummy batteries were set up at the eastern end of what was codenamed the Munassib Depression. This area was chosen for the site of a series of dummy gun batteries, which were set up on 15 October. They were camouflaged exactly the same way a genuine battery would be hidden, but after a few days the camouflage was allowed to lapse so that the Germans would realize the guns were dummies. Shortly after D-Day, the dummy field guns in Munassib were replaced with the genuine items, much to the surprise of a column of German armour which decided to probe against what it thought was a harmless decoy position.

Last, but by no means least, at the opening of the battle a non-existent amphibious landing was staged behind German lines between El Daba and Sidi Abd el Rahman. This operation saw the use of sonic deception – where battle sounds were played over loudspeakers mounted on fast motor torpedo boats operating just off shore. This technique was still in its early stages, but had been pioneered by GSI(d) almost a year earlier. Barkas was not overly impressed with sonic deception, complaining that the recordings of gunfire sounded like dustbins being struck. However, better amplification was being developed by movie companies in the United States and so the ruse would be used again later in the war.

XX

The night of 23 October was clear and brightly illuminated by a full moon. At 9.40pm, the calm was ruptured by the detonation of hundreds of British field guns. For 15 minutes, just short of a thousand British guns pounded the German batteries in front of them. There was a five-minute pause before the barrage recommenced at 10pm, this time targeting German forward positions. Behind the barrage Allied infantry began advancing through the Axis minefields.

At the opening of the battle Rommel was not in Egypt. He had been in poor health since August and had returned to Germany in September on leave. On 3 October he was presented with his field marshal's baton in Berlin and declared that he was at the gateway to Egypt and had no intention of being flung back.

His understudy was General Georg Stumme. On the night of 23 October Stumme and his chief signals officer went forward on a reconnaissance towards the British lines. It was an ill-chosen adventure moments before the opening of the British attack. In the opening barrage the signals officer was killed by machine-gun fire and Stumme suffered a heart attack. He was unused to the climate in North Africa and had been overworking: the shock of the barrage and the close proximity of the signals officer's death finished him off. It was some time before he was missed and the body recovered. Meanwhile in Berlin it was a full 24 hours before the seriousness of the situation was realized and Hitler ordered Rommel to return and resume command.

With the charismatic field marshal missing for the first 48 hours of the battle and overwhelming Allied superiority, the end result of El Alamein was never really in doubt. The Axis troops fought hard but were gradually worn down in a battle of attrition. When a renewed offensive began on 2 November Rommel realized the game was up. Despite being told to stand and fight by Hitler, by 4 November the Afrika Korps began to retreat to the west. Four days later the *Torch* landings began.

The victory at El Alamein is often described as the turning point of the war against the Nazis, or, as Churchill put it, 'the end of the beginning'. Along with the surrender of the German Sixth Army at Stalingrad on 31 January 1943, El Alamein marked a point in the war when the balance swayed in favour of the Allies, and one on which all future successes were built.

Although one might speculate that the German defeat was down to a lack of air superiority, a lack of operational intelligence, the inferiority of their numbers and the disruption of their supplies, the success of *Treatment* and *Bertram* cannot be overlooked. Barkas modestly and rightly noted that none of his colleagues was 'so foolish' as to think that El Alamein had been won 'by conjuring tricks, with stick, string and canvas' and attributed the success to the bravery of the fighting men. However, in a speech in the House of Commons on 11 November Churchill acknowledged the importance of 'surprise and strategy' in the battle:

> By a marvellous system of camouflage, complete tactical surprise was achieved in the desert. The enemy suspected – indeed, knew – that an attack was impending, but when and where and how it was coming was hidden from him. The Xth Corps, which he had seen from the air exercising fifty miles in the rear, moved silently away in the night, but leaving an exact simulacrum of its tanks where it had been, and proceeded to its points of attack. The enemy suspected that the attack was impending, but did not know how, when or where, and above all he had no idea of the scale upon which he was to be assaulted.

For the first time on a large scale, the planning of a cover for an operation involving camouflage, decoys, bogus signals traffic and double agents, had been successfully achieved. With varying degrees of success, this same recipe would now be applied to every major Allied operation in the build up to the Normandy invasion in 1944.

THE DEVELOPMENT
OF AGENT CASES

AFTER THE SUCCESSES OF El Alamein and *Torch*, in December 1942 Colonel Bevan travelled to the United States to make arrangements for the long-term cooperation between the Allies in deception planning. As a result of this visit it was agreed that the LCS would control deception in Europe, North Africa, the Middle East and India, while the American Joint Security Control would be responsible for the Western Hemisphere including Canada, the Pacific, Australia, New Zealand and China.

Although the Middle East and North Africa remained the sole preserve of A Force, organizational changes were required to keep up with developments in the war. With the entry of America and the arrival of General Eisenhower in North Africa, the weight of command had shifted from Cairo to Algiers. This posed A Force some trouble as its spidery links were mostly based on channels built up with contacts in the Egyptian capital.

To protect these channels and maintain a credible threat against the eastern Mediterranean, A Force left its main HQ in Cairo. In Algiers A Force set up an 'Advanced HQ' working directly for Eisenhower. It was put under the dual command of Colonel Goldbranson of the United States Army and Lieutenant Colonel Michael Crichton. Already known to Dudley Clarke before the war, Crichton had been recruited into A Force from a staff position with the 7th Armoured Division. There was good news for Lieutenant Colonel David Strangeways when he was rescued from his earlier posting to PAIFORCE in order to run A Force's new 'Tactical HQ', which was posted with General Alexander. Finally a 'Rear HQ' was set up in Nairobi for maintaining A Force's channels in East and South Africa.

A Force's deceptive web now extended from Cairo to representatives in Algeria, in Nairobi and Kilindini in Kenya, in Cape Town, in Khartoum, with the Eighth and Ninth Army HQs, and with XXV Corps HQ in Cyprus. There were also five 'special correspondents' stationed variously in Turkey (at Ankara and Istanbul), in Portuguese East Africa (Lourenço Marques), in Asmara in Eritrea and on Malta.

In December 1942 Dudley Clarke received authorization to set up a series of regional double cross committees in Cairo, Beirut and other places. Known as 'Thirty' Committees, each had three members: a representative of A Force who took the chair, an MI6 officer acting as secretary, and a member of SIME. Policy was set by A Force, who supplied the text of the messages to be relayed by the various agents. SIME provided the case officers and MI6 provided the ciphers, funding and controlled agents outside areas of Allied control. By the end of the war there were 21 of these committees (numbered 30, 31, 32 etc) at work in various parts of the world, running agents who were perhaps even more exotic than their counterparts controlled by the Twenty Committee in London.

The prime double agent source in Cairo was known as *Cheese* after the founding member who arrived in 1941. Since *Cheese*'s return to Italy the case had passed to his sub-agent, the notional White Russian Paul Nicossof, codenamed *Lambert*. Subordinate to *Lambert* were a number of equally notional informants, including his fiery girlfriend *Misanthrope* and the Afrikaner Piet.

In the Levant, there were a number of star players who assisted with the ongoing false order of battle build up codenamed *Cascade*. Strategically poised near to the Aegean Sea, these agents also played the important role of pinning down German troops in Greece and the Balkans by suggesting a long-term threat of invasion through the region and a link up with Soviet forces through the Balkans. Controlled by the Thirty-One Committee in Beirut, the two most important double agent networks were assigned the codenames *Quicksilver* and the *Pessimists*.

Quicksilver was a Greek Air Force flight lieutenant wireless operator who accepted an offer to spy for the Abwehr as a chance to go over to the British. He was given two assistants. The first was *Rio*, a brutal thug hired by the Gestapo as 'local muscle' and then sacked for his overzealous interrogation techniques. With a knife in the ribs waiting for him if he ever walked the streets of Athens again, *Rio* volunteered to join *Quicksilver*'s espionage mission. The second recruit was codenamed *Gala*, politely described as a 'secretary' but in fact the former mistress of an Italian intelligence officer who wanted to offload her somewhere distant and preferably dangerous. It was thought that *Gala* would find no end of work in the Middle East and would be able to fund the expedition from her immoral earnings.

The British security services were forewarned by ISOS that three agents had set out from Greece bound for Syria and the party was duly picked up in a small boat off Latakia. While *Quicksilver* was whisked away for double cross work, the two stooges were locked up and allowed only a notional existence in the world beyond their prison bars. Thus the thuggish *Rio* ostensibly joined the Hellenic Navy and served on board a destroyer, while *Gala* set herself up as a high-class prostitute in Beirut, mixing with British officers and showing additional favour to those who provided her with information.[1]

Quicksilver, or 'George' as he was informally known by his controllers, was set up in a house in Beirut guarded by a company of East Africans whom Mure described as speaking 'no known language'. For company the Greek officer shared the house with the other great Levantine performer, one of the previously mentioned *Pessimists*.

The origin of this second Beirut star can be traced to the summer of 1942 just after *Lambert* sparked off the bogus Crete invasion scare. Three Greeks were intercepted in northern Syria, having landed by boat. The captives became known in British intelligence circles as the *Pessimists*. It is believed that the chief, codenamed *Pessimist C*, was bringing money to *Lambert* when he was captured. *Pessimist C* had previously been in contact with MI6 in Athens and there is a theory that he did a deal and agreed to work for SIME in exchange for a large percentage of the cash he had been carrying. His two companions, Costa and Basile (*Pessimists B* and *Z* respectively), were deemed undesirable and were thrown in jail – although, as in the *Quicksilver* case, they were notionally left at large in order to supply their chief with information to send back to Sofia by wireless. *Pessimist C* was known to the Germans as *Mimi* (short for Demetrios) and by the British as 'Jack', as in the phrase 'I'm all right, Jack.'[2] Mure described him as a fat, oily slob, while his A Force case officer described him as 'a greedy devious shit and a stirrer'. Notionally stationed in Damascus, but in reality lodged in respectable comfort with *Quicksilver* in Beirut, 'Jack' was nevertheless a brilliant double cross agent, albeit one who strained the nerves of those in his direct vicinity.

The Thirty-One Committee (Beirut) also ran several purely notional agents who were the brainchild of MI6 officer Michael Ionides, whom Mure believed was the same man who facilitated *Cheese*'s passage from Istanbul to Cairo in 1941. The first of these agents was *Humble* – a notional source of information that was passed to the Axis through a Turkish customs official known as *Smooth*. This official had got himself into debt and was bailed out by MI6 in return for a favour. As far as *Smooth* or anyone else knew, all he had to do was deliver the occasional letter to an Abwehr contact, and ask no questions. The background story for *Humble* was that he ran a grocery in Aleppo and was contracted to provide fruit and vegetables to British Army camps. Ostensibly perched at the entrance to his shop smoking a hookah, *Humble* became an excellent channel to promote A Force lies.

Ionides' other fictional masterpiece was *Alert*. Supposedly employed as a civilian orderly in an Army HQ in northern Syria, *Alert* was said to be the bastard son of an Australian sergeant-major who had raped his mother in World War I. Unsurprisingly *Alert* was anti-British and sent his letters to the Germans via *Crude*, a British double agent who was supposedly an Abwehr informant working as a janitor in the British consulate in Istanbul.[3]

Switching between the control of Thirty-One and the Thirty-Three Committee in Cyprus, two other groups of agents are worthy of note. The *Savages* were an Abwehr team of three intercepted on their arrival in Cyprus in July. While his companions were thrown into prison, *Savage I* reported to his German controllers that he had moved to Cairo with his wireless transmitter set and had obtained employment in the Allied Liaison Branch of GHQ.[4] More worthy still were the *Lemons*. A Greek sailor, *Little Lemon* was named thus for his visual resemblance to that fruit. His hair was white and his skin complexion was a pale yellow. *Little Lemon* was accompanied by his companion *Big Lemon*, who was a Greek Cypriot and part of Enosis, the movement wishing to bring about the union of Greece and Cyprus. Their original destination had been Syria, but they were captured by the British when the skipper of their boat lost his nerve and took them to Cyprus instead. Operating out of Nicosia, *Little Lemon*'s early messages were filled with his fear that he had contracted syphilis. *Little Lemon* had in fact contracted VD almost as soon as he arrived and was experiencing considerable discomfort. His principal informants were a string of girls from Axis countries who had been interned by the British. These had been released from detention to work as cabaret dancers for the enjoyment of Allied officers based in Nicosia. The girls were real enough, but each was given a notional alter-ego: the Austrians *Helga* and *Trudi*, *Gabbi* the Hungarian, *Marki* the Bulgarian and two Romanians, *Maria* and the aptly named *Swing-Tit*. While the real dancing girls performed their routines, their notional counterparts fed *Little Lemon* tasty morsels of information picked up and overheard from the Allied officers in the club.

Moving further afield, it was important that wherever the Germans had a listening post, there would be some organization in place to deceive it. At the beginning of the war the Abwehr maintained a station in Kabul from where it could monitor British and Soviet activities in the region. In 1943 an excellent channel was opened up to feed this station with deceptive material by the recruitment of a Hindu codenamed *Silver*. Guy Liddell described *Silver* as the 'only valuable double cross case' in the region.[5]

Bhagat Ram Talwar was a communist activist and had helped the anti-British politician Subhas Chandra Bose escape from Delhi to Berlin in 1941. After the German invasion of Russia, Talwar was found in Kabul. Now that Britain and Russia were allies, his services were offered to Peter Fleming's

GSI(d) Division in India. Codenamed *Silver*, he returned to Kabul in January 1943 posing as the head of a notional body called the All India Revolutionary Committee. *Silver* claimed that this organization had branches all across the sub-continent, providing him an excellent network of informers and spies. In fact all the information was provided by Fleming's organization in the hope that the Germans would pass it on to Berlin and that it would be relayed to Tokyo.

Silver was one of the more colourful spies at work during World War II. At one point he was seen in Delhi in the company of British officers by an Afghan who knew him in Kabul. The British feared *Silver* would be blown and advised him not to travel back to Afghanistan. *Silver* disagreed and went back. He found the man who could identify him and arranged to have dinner with him. Before the meal, *Silver* laced the Afghan's curry with a deadly dose of poisonous chopped tiger whiskers.[6]

XX

The opportunities for double cross work were extended further by the collapse of the Vichy regime in North Africa following *Torch*. In early 1943 the resources and skills of the French Deuxième Bureau in North Africa were placed at Eisenhower's disposal. In order to cooperate to the maximum, the Forty Committee was formed in Algeria consisting of representatives from A Force, MI6, MI5 and the Deuxième Bureau. Again there were the usual misfits expected in double cross work, not to mention the occasional rough, but very valuable, diamond.

Throughout the Nazi occupation of France, the Deuxième Bureau was credited as a hotbed of organized resistance and even as the curtains fell on the Third Republic in 1940, the Deuxième Bureau committed itself to continuing anti-German counter-espionage. The French counter-espionage organization was disguised as the Travaux Ruraux (Rural Works) or TR programme. The purpose of TR was to continue counter-espionage against the Germans and record acts of collaboration and treachery by Frenchmen who would be called to account for their crimes after liberation.

In terms of counter-intelligence used for deception purposes, the key man in the French organization was Major Paul Paillole. A professional soldier, in 1938 Paillole became chief of the Deuxième Bureau's counter-espionage German Section. He thus became a key, albeit unwitting, player in the eventual development of the Twenty Committee. Before the war Paillole met Sir Stewart Menzies and had an excellent working relationship with his counterpart in MI6, Felix Cowgill. As noted previously, Masterman credited the Deuxième Bureau with influencing MI6 on the possibility of running double agents for deception purposes. This appears to be borne out by Paillole's memoirs.[7] The secret service chief reveals how in 1939 Cowgill was so impressed with his insight into what the French called the 'intoxication' of the enemy intelligence service with disinformation that he twice invited the Deuxième Bureau officer to come to London to brief his officers on technical information relating to double cross work.

Continuing to play his role after the fall of France in 1940, Paillole left France in December 1942, crossing over the Pyrenees after learning he was being investigated by the Gestapo. He made his way to Gibraltar and came to London to renew his acquaintance with Menzies, who explained what had been going on in terms of deception. Paillole then travelled to Algiers, arriving on 3 January 1943. He was joined there on 8 January by Felix Cowgill of Section V. Knowing Paillole's background in deception, Cowgill very wisely set up a meeting between the Frenchman and Dudley Clarke on 10 January. This gave Paillole a clear indication of the deception policy, which he could complement with the Deuxième Bureau's own network of agents who had penetrated the German secret service.

At a further meeting with A Force on 7 April 1943, the Deuxième Bureau was given the new Allied disinformation directives.[8] The first priority was to break the dogged resistance of the tenacious Afrika Korps in Tunisia under General von Armin, who had replaced Rommel to help the latter save face in the event of the Korps' defeat. As an immediate measure, the French put three double cross agents at A Force's disposal. The first was based in Le Kef and worked as a war correspondent for the newspaper *L'Echo d'Alger*, while another well-placed agent worked for air traffic control at Maison-Blanche airport. The third agent was the pick of them all, Chouali ben Larbi. A sergeant in the Algerian Tirailleurs, Chouali had been taken prisoner by the Germans in November 1942.[9] During his interrogation the Germans offered him the chance to spy for them. Chouali's nonchalant reply was: 'Why not? We'll see what happens.' He was then transferred to an espionage training camp in southern Tunisia where an Abwehr agent came to meet him. After mastering the basics, he received additional training in Naples before going to Germany for code and radio training. While in Germany Chouali's controller dubbed him *Chinois* (the Chinaman) because of his oriental physiognomy.

On the night of 14–15 February 1943, Chouali dropped from the sky by parachute near to Medea. He buried his wireless set and then went to the local gendarmerie, taking some gold coins as proof of his mission. When they eventually deigned to listen to his story, the gendarmes were less than impressed; but, eventually, at his insistence, they accompanied him to where the radio set was buried. Thus began his career in double cross.

After some teething troubles, he finally established contact with Germany. Spending his nights encoding messages to his controllers, Chouali maintained his cover by day working as a gardener or barber. The Abwehr wanted to know the names of all the boats in the port of Algiers and he duly obliged, providing the names of vessels the Allies wished the Germans to know about. His reports were deemed accurate and increased his standing to the point where he could be used for a decisive stroke.

On the night of 3 May 1943, as the battle for Tunisia drew to its climax, *Chinois* transmitted a message to the Germans that 'a British division was going to move towards the south to force a passage through the German frontline'. A similar story was transmitted by the other double cross agents and A Force staged the movement of a division of British troops from the centre to the south. The trucks were empty, but when the German reconnaissance aircraft took off at dawn to confirm the movement, they were not to know that. General von Armin responded, rapidly moving one of two panzer divisions holding the centre of the Axis line and directing it to the south. The Allies attacked the weakened centre and two days later entered the port of Bizerte. Von Armin surrendered on 12 May, along with a quarter of a million men. Despite this success, Chouali was posted as a deserter by the French, and it was only with some difficulty that he was later acquitted of this crime.

XX

Towards the end of 1942 a new German agent was parachuted into Britain. He was a British citizen recruited by the Abwehr and charged with blowing up the de Havilland works in Hatfield where the Mosquito light bomber was produced. Feted as one of the most colourful characters of the war, the story of Edward Arnold Chapman catches the imagination like few others.

Chapman had been discharged from the Coldstream Guards in 1933 for desertion. He quickly descended into a life of crime and stormy affairs with women often on the fringes of society. Soon after his dishonourable discharge he was arrested and convicted of theft and obtaining money by false pretences. Shortly after his release he was again in trouble, this time for having behaved 'in a manner likely to offend the virtuous public' – or in other words, found *in flagrante delicto* in the middle of London's otherwise respectable Hyde Park.

His pursuit of women became somewhat of an obsession. When later interrogated by the British authorities, Chapman boasted about his conquests and his unchivalrous treatment of the fairer sex. He admitted having had a friend take illicit photographs of him with female acquaintances and then blackmailing them with the pictures. He also admitted without any remorse to having infected an 18-year-old girl with VD, and then having blackmailed her by saying he was going to tell her father she had passed it on to him. More arrests followed, and in 1938 he was wanted on a safe-breaking charge in Edinburgh. Arrested again, he jumped bail and fled to the island of Jersey, where he was arrested on charges of burglary and house-breaking. This time the one-man crime wave was put to an end, and he received two years' hard labour the day after war broke out in 1939.

It was in solitary confinement that the Germans found him after they occupied the island in July 1940. Chapman was moved to a prison in France where he manufactured a skeleton key allowing him to make night-time visits to the women's block. Unsatisfied with his role of unofficial prison gigolo, Chapman made an approach to the Germans, offering to work for them as a spy. Chapman told them he could be trusted and was unlikely to betray them as he was a wanted criminal on the British mainland and could expect harsh treatment if he ever contacted the authorities there. This appealed to Teutonic logic, and his new employers arranged for him to be sent to a spy school in Nantes to be trained in espionage, sabotage and radio transmitting.

His principal mentors became Hauptmann von Groening and Hauptmann Praetorius, the Abwehr talent scout also behind the recruitment of *Summer* and *Tate*. The two took Chapman under their wing and named him *Fritzchen* (Little Fritz). They pandered to his ego by giving him a German uniform and admitting him to the officers' mess, where he picked up some of the language and became somewhat of a celebrity. In return he became an able student in the dark arts of the spy school.

Meanwhile, on the other side of the Channel mentions of *Fritzchen* began appearing on ISOS decrypts. From April to December 1942 there were 160 messages relating to Chapman, his training and his missions, all of which became known to MI5. By December 1942 MI5 knew he would shortly be coming over and so Operation *Nightcap* was put in place to receive him once he parachuted in. An MI5 representative was sent to Fighter Command to identify the likely aircraft on radar so it would not be shot down. Secret instructions were sent to all the RSLOs and police forces around the country; at the same time a team of bloodhounds was prepared to hunt him down.

In the event, bloodhounds were not necessary. Chapman made landfall in the early hours of 16 December near Littleport in the Isle of Ely in

Cambridgeshire. After gathering his parachute and stacking his equipment, he went to the nearest house, and, posing as a crashed British airman, telephoned the police. He was taken into custody, disarmed and strip-searched. With something like a 14-year stretch waiting for him at the hands of the British penal system, Chapman was understandably uncomfortable in the presence of the police. He asked them to put him in touch with the secret service instead, and before long Operation *Nightcap* was in full swing. He was collected and rushed to Camp 020 in a Black Maria.

Having been subjected to the preliminary medical examination, mugshot and prison uniform, Chapman was taken before the camp's formidable commandant for interrogation. One of the curious things about the Chapman case is the way in which Tin-Eye Stephens quickly developed something close to admiration for him. Given Chapman's less than salubrious past, such feelings may appear somewhat surprising, but Tin-Eye had detected in Chapman a genuine, albeit inexplicable, deep-rooted vein of patriotism and, as Tin-Eye put it, 'a streak of hatred for the Hun'.

Without much introduction, Chapman told his interrogator everything he could remember about the Abwehr, its techniques, the officers he had met, and the nature of his mission. Everything matched or complemented what MI5 had learned about the man from ISOS. Indeed, their knowledge of Chapman was so great that they were able to identify him as *Fritzchen* from intercepted dental reports after an accident in parachute training. By 2.30pm on 17 December, Tin-Eye had recommended Chapman for XX work.

The key to Chapman's becoming a successful double agent was to get him on the air as soon as possible. Too long a delay and his controllers might begin to suspect that their resourceful spy had been intercepted. He was set up with his wireless transmitter in a riding club not far from 020 and sent out his call sign. This message was greeted with toasts of champagne back in France. When the Germans replied to his message, there was equal excitement in the British camp. On 22 December, Chapman was handed over to B1a to begin active service under the codename *Zigzag*.

For the Germans to believe *Zigzag* was credible, he would have to complete his sabotage mission at de Havilland's factory at Hatfield. Of course, there was no question of *Zigzag* actually causing any real damage to such a vital plant – the damage would have to be faked. Case officer Ronnie Reed and *Zigzag* visited the factory and identified an electricity plant as the best target to put out of action. On the night of 29 January 1943, camouflage experts from Colonel Turner's department transformed the plant using painted canvas sheets, papier-mâché models and carefully placed rubble to made it look as if it had been destroyed. To complete the illusion a detonation rang out in the night air, marking the culmination of *Zigzag*'s successful mission.

Next morning Robertson and Colonel Turner came to inspect the damage and were suitably impressed. From a distance one of the factory workers had been convinced the factory had taken a direct hit. On 1 February news of the 'attack' was printed in the 5am edition of the *Daily Express*, which talked about a factory explosion, reporting that 'investigations are being made into the cause of an explosion at a factory on the outskirts of London. It is understood that the damage was slight and there was no loss of life.' This edition was the one that was sent to Lisbon by air every day, so without doubt, when *Zigzag* radioed the successful completion of his mission, his report would be complemented by the newspaper account.[10]

According to his orders, *Zigzag* was now meant to return to occupied Europe to take up his mission to the United States. At first he was told that a submarine would come and pick him up, but then he was instructed to make his own way home. To accomplish this he was enrolled as an assistant steward on a ship bound for Lisbon, and shown how messages to him would be hidden among the classified ads in *The Times*.

Before leaving *Zigzag* revealed that he had been working on a plan. It was incredible even by his standards. He had convinced his Abwehr boss von Groening that he really was a fanatical Nazi. If his mission in Britain was successful, von Groening had promised to take him to a Nazi rally and to get him a prime seat close to the front where he would be able to see Hitler clearly at the podium. If he got close enough, *Zigzag* offered to assassinate the German leader with a bomb. Reed was understandably taken aback by the suggestion and told the agent it would be a suicide mission. This only seemed to make the mission more appealing to *Zigzag*, who remarked laconically: 'Ah, but what a way out.' His celebrity would be guaranteed forever.[11]

In the end MI5 baulked at the idea. Perhaps they thought that assassinating foreign heads of state was beyond their remit, or perhaps they thought the reprisals would be too terrible. Certainly later in the war SOE's Operation *Foxley* was not given the go-ahead, partly from a fear of reprisals, but partly also because Hitler's erratic leadership was becoming something of an asset to the Allies. But one wonders how the outcome of the war would have changed with Hitler dead almost two years earlier. At the end of the war, Masterman admitted that perhaps they had missed a chance with Chapman; if anyone could have pulled the stunt off it would have been him.

Zigzag boarded the *City of Lancaster* and arrived in Lisbon on 13 March. He had a little surprise planned as a parting gift. Making contact with the

Germans, he procured two bombs hidden inside lumps of coal. He told the Germans that he was going to put them on the ship so they would be scooped up into the boilers. This would be enough to damage the ship, if not sink it altogether. *Zigzag*'s plan became known to B1a through Bletchley Park. Believing that *Zigzag* had betrayed them, Ronnie Reed was sent on the next flight to Lisbon to bring *Zigzag* back, in irons if necessary.

Reed arrived in Lisbon and contacted the captain of the *Lancaster*. *Zigzag* had indeed brought the explosives on board, but had immediately entrusted them to the captain with instructions to hand them over to MI5 for analysis on his return to Britain. When the captain had locked the bombs in his safe, the double agent vanished back ashore and had not been seen since. Reed radioed his relief to London: *Zigzag* had not gone bad after all.[12]

XX

The star player of the XX organization was certainly *Garbo*. Since his warning of the *Torch* landings, his stock ran very high with the Abwehr. In order that his messages need never be delayed again, his German controllers gifted him with what Guy Liddell described as 'perhaps the highest grade cypher ever used by the Abwehr'. On 11 June 1943 he was so impressed by the report on *Garbo* made by GC&CS that he concluded: 'If B1a have done nothing else for the last three years they would certainly have justified their existence with this case.' However, while B1a was giving itself a much-merited pat on the back, *Garbo*'s wife threw a spanner in the works with an almighty tantrum.

Garbo's wife had played an important part in his decision to become a spy and in aiding his recruitment. However, when brought to Britain with their two children, she quickly became homesick. She had never travelled outside the Iberian peninsula and was less than impressed by the austerity of wartime Britain. Coupled to the dismal climate and bland, rationed food, Mrs *Garbo* did not speak a word of English. Her husband was completely absorbed by his work and was neglecting her. At the same time she was not allowed any contact with Spanish people living in Britain, lest her husband's duplicity became known in Madrid. For these reasons, in a violent row on 21 June 1943, she told *Garbo* that she wanted to go home to her mother back in Spain.

Garbo tried to play the whole incident down, actually calling MI5 from a pay booth in the street and apologizing in advance if his 'excited' wife telephoned and verbally abused any of them. However, when she called her husband's case officer, Tommy Harris, and said she was going to the Spanish embassy to reveal all, the alarm was sounded at MI5 HQ in St James's.

Pondering what to do, Guy Liddell's first thought was that she should be locked up and kept incommunicado. He dismissed this as impossible given the law of the country. He then thought about sending the Spanish embassy a description of her, with the message that she was planning to assassinate the Spanish ambassador and that they should under no circumstances let her in. Tommy Robertson thought he should go down and visit 'Mrs G' and 'read her the Riot Act', threatening her with detention.[13] Instead *Garbo* came in and gave an account of what was going on. He did not believe his wife would actually do anything to blow his cover, but agreed to a little charade to calm her down.

Next evening, Chief Inspector Burt arrived at *Garbo*'s residence and informed Mrs *Garbo* that her husband had been arrested. He passed her a note from him in which he asked for his toothbrush and pyjamas. She refused to hand anything over and instead got on the telephone to Harris.

This was exactly what MI5 had hoped for. Harris explained, falsely, that his boss had agreed to let Mrs *Garbo* go back to Spain. The only condition to this was that *Garbo* give up his work against the Germans and accompany her and her children back to Madrid. At this suggestion, Harris said, *Garbo* had flown into a rage and had to be arrested on disciplinary grounds.

Hearing this, Mrs *Garbo* put down the telephone. Her next call was to *Garbo*'s radio operator, Charles Haines, who was called to the house. When he turned up, the gas taps had been left open and Mrs *Garbo* was in an incoherent state. Although he believed she was playacting, he was genuinely worried she might have an accident. Tommy Harris's wife, Hilda, was asked to spend the night with her and ensure nothing happened.

On the morning of 23 June, Tommy Robertson interviewed *Garbo*'s wife and obtained a statement from her saying that on no account would she behave badly in future. To impress upon her the gravity of the matter, Tin-Eye Stephens agreed to put on a little show for her benefit. She was taken to Kew Bridge by MI5 and then met by a Black Maria. She was blindfolded and taken to Camp 020, where she was told how lucky she was to have avoided arrest. She was told that if there was any repeat of the incident she and her husband would be detained for the duration of the war. Her husband was then brought from his cell, bearded and in prison clothing. This had the desired effect. He told his wife he was due to face a tribunal in the morning and asked her to tell him truly if she had been to the embassy. She swore she had not and promised she would not go there.

The following morning *Garbo* was released and reunited with his wife. Although the prison set up had been his own idea, he was somewhat shaken by the whole experience. Still, in riding out this domestic crisis, *Garbo* again demonstrated how far he would go to serve the Allied cause against the Nazis.

12

MINCEMEAT

W ITH NORTH AFRICA CLEARED OF Axis opposition, the Allies planned their next step. At the Casablanca Conference in January 1943 the Allies had agreed that Sicily would be the next target and since then plans for Operation *Husky* had been underway. At the same time *Barclay* – a cover plan for *Husky* – was plotted by A Force within a framework set by the LCS and approved by Eisenhower on 10 April 1943.

On first glance, formulating an effective cover plan was no easy task. From the Allied point of view, Sicily was an obvious target. Convoys passing to the eastern Mediterranean and the Suez Canal came under constant air attack from Axis bases on the island. If they ignored Sicily and attacked elsewhere, for instance Sardinia or the south of France, the presence of Sicily would be like a dagger held to their back. This very same thinking led the German and Italians to come to the same conclusion. As Churchill is alleged to have said: 'Everyone but a bloody fool would *know* that it's Sicily.'[1]

The Allies knew they had little chance of surprising the Axis as they had done with *Torch*. The plan called for a combined force of 160,000 American, British and Commonwealth troops to be landed by a fleet of 3,200 ships. With such large numbers involved it was unlikely enemy air reconnaissance would miss the convoy once it put to sea. Their only chance therefore would be to try to indicate an objective other than Sicily, or to indicate that more than one operation would be mounted. Such then were the objectives of Plan *Barclay*, the cover story for *Husky*.[2]

The existing A Force channels would indicate that the main thrust of Allied operations would come through the eastern end of the Mediterranean, through Greece and into the Balkans. A Force had long been feeding information about Crete. To keep German attention focused there, from January 1943 A Force began feeding its agents with Plan *Withstand*, a notional move against Turkey. The story was that the Allies were so concerned the Germans were preparing to invade Turkey they were contemplating a pre-emptive strike against the Dodecanese via Crete. To support this rumour, British armoured units were moved to Syria, their ranks swelled by the provision of dummy vehicles.

The outline of the plan was as follows: the notional British Twelfth Army in Egypt was planning to invade the Balkans through Greece. Hopefully

Turkey would join the war with the Allies and together they would push up through Bulgaria and link up with Soviet forces advancing into southern Russia. The attack on Greece would be preceded by a diversionary attack on western Crete. Moreover, to prevent the Germans from moving reinforcements from western Europe, diversionary assaults would be launched against the south coast of France by General Alexander and a French army gathering in North Africa. At the same time as these assaults, General Patton would attack Corsica and Sardinia with US forces. From these islands the Allies could come down on Sicily from the northern side, or attack Rome, or take a short cut into northern Italy and up into the underbelly of the Reich. In any case, Axis positions in Sicily and Italy would be subjected to heavy air bombardment. The Allies – or so the cover plan said – did not want to get bogged down in a long and arduous slog up the mountainous Italian peninsula in face of a hostile reception by the locals.

Lending credence to these ruses, beach raids were mounted around the Mediterranean and amphibious training was carried out by Greek troops in Egypt and French troops in Algeria. There were appeals for Greek interpreters and French fisherman who knew the south coast of France well. As the operation approached, all leave was cancelled and then suddenly allowed again. Conferences called for senior commanders were put off and then put on again, all to keep the Germans guessing about when the invasion was scheduled. To conceal the date of D-Day for *Husky*, which was 10 July, local port workers were given a completion date for work two weeks after D-Day, and Tobruk was filled with dummy landing craft.

For the Sicily cover plan the Deuxième Bureau utilized a new 'intoxication' agent: *Gilbert* – a man who would become the cream of French double cross operations. According to Paillole, *Gilbert* was, from the German point of view, the head of the Abwehr's best ever agent network in North Africa. The day after the liberation of Tunis, *Gilbert* unexpectedly presented himself to the French authorities and offered his agent network to the Deuxième Bureau for double cross purposes. Although Paillole was not normally well disposed to 'walk in' agents, in *Gilbert*'s case he made an exception. Paillole had actually met *Gilbert* in France towards the end of 1941 and was quite sure of his loyalty.

Gilbert was described in his case file as 'athletic, middle-aged with greying hair and a military moustache'. He was a bachelor from a good family and had been a career soldier. A graduate of the Saint-Cyr academy, he had fought in both World Wars and had been decorated with the Légion d'Honneur. When Paillole first met *Gilbert* the former soldier was working as the apprentice police commissioner in Lyons. He was forced to resign from this post in 1942 because of 'ideological differences' with his superiors. *Gilbert* was a rabid anti-communist, so much so that he joined the LVF (Légion des Volontaires Français), a French volunteer regiment in the German Army recruited to fight against the Soviet Union. He quickly fell into intelligence work through the French fascist Parti Populaire Français (PPF) and set up a front business cover in Paris for sending PPF members to carry out sabotage, propaganda and secret intelligence missions in North Africa. Receiving financial backing for his activities from the Abwehr, *Gilbert* volunteered to lead a secret 'stay behind' mission into Algeria codenamed *Atlas*. The idea was that *Gilbert* and four sub-agents would allow the Allied advance to roll over them after which they would spring up and begin transmitting. Accordingly he reached Tunis with four men on 25 April. He was given a cover story to show he had in fact been living an an address in Tunis since the previous December and that he was a refugee escaping from the Germans after they occupied Vichy France in 1942 to protect the southern coast. After arriving *Gilbert* quickly established contact with local Muslim officials and PPF sympathizers, all of whom would provide him and his team with intelligence once the Allies took control.

When *Gilbert* gave himself up, he explained how he had planned the whole mission deliberately to deceive the Germans. He knew the Axis was finished and he saw this mission as a chance to wipe the slate clean with the Free French. Of his four companions, *Gilbert* could vouch for only one of them: *Le Duc*, his second in command, whom he had personally recruited. *Le Duc* was the *nom de guerre* of Duthey Harispe, an apparently idle man in love with gambling and horseracing. Accepting *Gilbert*'s decision to work for the Allies, *Le Duc* was given a posting in French Headquarters.

The *Atlas* team's radio operator *Albert* was an altogether different story. Known by the name Blondeau, *Albert* had been recruited by the PPF and was assigned by them to *Atlas*. The Abwehr had made a recording of his Morse style and so it was going to be difficult to mimic him. It was decided that *Albert* never needed to know that *Gilbert* had gone over to the Allies; as far as he was concerned his mission was to tap out the messages *Gilbert* provided. For that reason, *Albert* was left in a state of ignorant bliss, happily serving the new world order. He found a job working as an electrician for a man in Tunis, never realizing that his employer was a Deuxième Bureau informant who had offered him the job in order to keep tabs on him. The third member of the team, *Falcon* the radio mechanic, was also left in the dark and found an innocuous job at a repair depot.

The fourth member of the team was a problem. Hired as the team's expert in sabotage, *Duteil* was incorruptible from the Allied point of view. The alias of Joseph Delpierre, a 26-year-old former Parisian pimp, *Duteil* was a fully fledged member of the PPF and had been sent along to keep an eye on *Gilbert*, with orders to liquidate him if he betrayed the mission. As he was surplus to *Gilbert*'s requirements in terms of using the radio transmitter, it was decided that a very speedy end should be arranged for him.[3] *Gilbert* introduced *Duteil* to an officer friend of his who had a deep Gallic dislike of his Anglo-Saxon counterparts. As *Gilbert* suspected, the two got on like a house on fire. One night after dinner *Duteil* visited his new friend's office at the local divisional HQ. While the pair were rifling through a stack of papers they were discovered by some unusually alert sentries, who roughly dragged them, kicking and screaming, off to the cells.

Isolated from his companion, *Duteil* was confronted with a list of his crimes. The depth of knowledge of his interrogators must have frightened the wits out of him. In the face of such omnipotence, there was no use trying to deny anything so *Duteil* blabbed ... and blabbed some more. As a direct result of his confession, about a hundred Vichyist collaborators and sympathizers were rounded up along with a number of Abwehr and SIM informants, a police superintendent included. *Duteil* betrayed *Gilbert* and the rest of the team, never thinking for a moment that it was his chief who had betrayed him. He also revealed the whereabouts of a frighteningly large stash of sabotage equipment that he had buried without *Gilbert*'s knowledge. Clearly *Duteil* was too hot a potato to be allowed to stay in the region. If he escaped it would bring an end to *Gilbert* and throw suspicion on many other double cross cases that the Deuxième Bureau were running. The last Paillole heard about *Duteil* was that he had been sent to England. According to Ronald Wingate he was executed. As far as the PPF ever knew, he had fled North Africa trying to find a route home through Spain.[4]

On the same day that *Duteil* was arrested, 10 June 1943, *Albert* established radio contact with the Abwehr. *Gilbert* claimed to have reacquainted himself with several old colleagues who were now high up in Tunis and were proving excellent sources of information. *Gilbert* explained that the Allies were collecting a large quantity of invasion barges at the port of Bizerte. A Force backed this up with the usual show of dummies and the Germans obliged them by sending photo-reconnaissance aircraft overhead. With only token flak sent up to prevent the Nazi airplanes accomplishing their mission, it was not long before Bizerte was visited by a large force of bombers. The dummy invasion fleet took a hammering while the real preparations continued at Sousse 90 miles (150km) to the south east.

XX

The most celebrated ruse linked to *Husky* came not from the LCS or A Force, but from the Twenty Committee. Generally speaking the Twenty Committee kept out of the Mediterranean war and focused on maintaining a threat against northern France and Norway (see Chapter 14). However, the members of the Twenty Committee were men of great imagination and it was one of their number who came up with the idea behind Operation *Mincemeat*.

The inspiration for *Mincemeat* came from Twenty Committee's secretary, Flight Lieutenant Cholmondeley, who proposed the idea. Cholmondeley had earlier come up with the idea of dropping a dead body on a parachute into occupied France. The body would be supplied with a radio transmitter and a full set of codes. The idea was to see how the Germans would run a double cross operation themselves. The idea was immediately shot down in flames because the Germans would quickly establish that the man was already dead before hitting the ground. Undeterred, Cholmondeley suggested a modified version of the plan on 4 February 1943. He said:

> Why shouldn't we get a body, disguise it as a staff officer, and give him really high-level papers which will show clearly that we are going to attack somewhere else. We won't have to drop him on land, as the aircraft might have come down in the sea on the way round the Med. He would float ashore with the papers either in France or in Spain; it won't matter which. Probably Spain would be best, as the Germans wouldn't have as much chance to examine the body there as if they got it into their own hands, while it's certain that they will get the documents, or at least copies.[5]

The idea was not as far-fetched as it might appear. In September 1942 an aircraft had come down near Spain and documents found on a recovered corpse were forwarded to the Abwehr by the Spanish authorities. The committee therefore thought it was an excellent idea, but could see many difficulties convincing the authorities to authorize it. Nevertheless, Cholmondeley and Montagu were told to make all the necessary arrangements first, and when the plan was ready to go, then it would be submitted.

Developing the idea, Cholmondeley suggested buying a corpse from a hospital and having its lungs filled with water as if the person had drowned. Finding a suitable body presented the first stumbling block for the operation. True enough, in wartime London there was no end of corpses to choose from (the going rate was £10 per corpse), but they had very specific requests. The corpse had to be of a man of military age, and he had to have died of a cause not out of keeping with someone killed after ditching an aircraft at sea. This limited their choices considerably. Even if a body was found, there was then the problem of the next of kin. How many families would freely give up the mortal remains of their loved one to a shadowy organization who refused to tell them what they were going to do with it?

At the point where they were seriously considering doing 'a Burke and Hare' (two famous 19th-century bodysnatchers), Montagu was contacted by Bentley Purchase, a well-known coroner. He had come across the corpse of a man who had died of pneumonia but could be mistaken for someone who had drowned. The identity of the corpse was never revealed by Montagu, except that he was a ne'er-do-well. It was not until 1996 that the identity of the so-called 'man who never was' was disclosed, and he was named as Glyndwr Michael. About as far removed from the role of war hero as could be imagined, he was an unemployed Welsh down-and-out, living rough on the streets of London. On 26 January 1943, Michael broke into a warehouse and helped himself to a large portion of phosphorous rat poison. He was admitted to hospital but died two days later aged 34.

In order to check if the corpse would be convincing, Montagu went to the pathologist Sir Bernard Spilsbury. Over a glass of sherry at the Junior Carlton, Sir Bernard was told only that a body in a Mae West lifejacket was to be floated onto a foreign coast as if it had come from a ditched aircraft. Spilsbury asked what country this would be and was told Spain. His reply to this was somewhat immodest: 'Oh that's all right. Although such a man would almost certainly die of exposure rather than drowning, he would swallow a good deal of water. There will be pleural fluid in the lungs of your body and to detect that it wasn't sea water would take as good and careful a pathologist as I am and they haven't got one in Spain.' He advised Montagu to keep the body in a mortuary until needed and then to pack it in an airtight container filled with dry ice. This was not to keep the body frozen, but to exclude air from the container as air would speed up the decomposition process.[6]

As for the corpse's notional identity, Montagu and Cholmondeley went into great detail to construct a background for him. This man would have to be provided with a name and a rank, with family, friends, colleagues, a girlfriend or wife, all of whom would miss him dearly once news of his death was announced. For security reasons Montagu initially wanted the man to be a naval officer, but there was a practical consideration here. Naval officers wore tailored uniforms and Montagu could not simply take the body to be fitted out. To alleviate this problem, the corpse would be dressed as an officer from the Royal Marines, in standard-issue battledress. He was given a name: Major William Martin. This was not a name plucked at random. All naval officers had their names recorded on a published list. If Montagu came up with something outlandish, it should not be very difficult for an Axis agent, perhaps a member of one of the neutral delegations, to obtain this list and check Martin's name. The name was selected because there were a number of W. Martins on the list, all of whom were about the right age and rank to be confused with the fictional character.

With a name chosen, great pains were taken to make Major Martin as real as possible. Firstly he was given a love interest. A female clerk in MI5 took on the role of 'Pam', Major Martin's fiancée, and wrote two love letters to him. In the meantime, the more attractive girls in the office were asked to pose as 'Pam' for snapshots and one of the pictures was placed in Martin's wallet. The scenario Montagu developed was that Martin had only met Pam in April and had proposed to her almost immediately – nothing unusual in wartime. He had a bill for the engagement ring, this time unpaid, and a stern letter from his father disapproving of wartime weddings.

THE COVER PLANS FOR OPERATION *HUSKY*

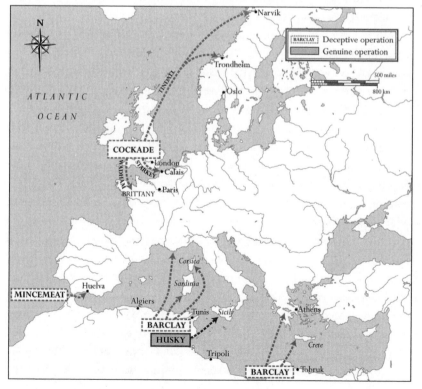

In addition to the letter from his father, there was a warning letter from his bank manager about his overdraft, a bill for a shirt, two theatre ticket stubs for 22 April indicating he could not have left England before 23 April, a letter from his solicitors confirming that they had drawn up his will, a bill for lodgings at the Navy and Military Club where he was made a temporary member, some keys and a packet of cigarettes. Montagu used his own fingerprints on the documents, so that there would be a matching set on each one. He reasoned that Major Martin would be buried before anyone thought of checking fingerprints. He also opened and creased the personal letters, carrying them around in his pockets to give the impression that Major Martin had read them several times.

The only real difficulty they found in creating the identity was in taking a photograph of 'Martin' for his identity papers. Montagu mused that although it is often the case that living people can look like corpses in photographs, it is impossible to make a corpse look like a living person – in particular when the corpse has been held in deep freeze for a period of time. A substitute was required and so Montagu took a photograph of someone in Naval Intelligence. He then spotted an absolute 'dead ringer' across the table at a meeting and retook the photograph. Thus *Zigzag*'s case officer and MI5 radio expert Ronnie Reed became the face of Major Martin.

With the body and identity taken care of, a letter was written by General Sir Archibald Nye, the Vice Chief of the Imperial General Staff, to General Alexander in North Africa. The letter was deliberately informal in style, as if Nye was setting out his thoughts to Alexander off the record. In it he said that there were reports 'the Bosche' had been strengthening their hand in Greece and Crete and that the Chief of the Imperial General Staff felt that the forces earmarked for the assault there were insufficient. Reinforcements were therefore going to be sent to the groups assaulting the beach south of Cape Araxos and the one going to Kalamata. The letter continued that Sicily had been requested as the cover for this operation, which was codenamed *Husky*, but this target was already being used as the cover for Operation *Brimstone*. Instead, the cover for *Husky* should be the Dodecanese. Clearly, then, if the Germans had heard anything about *Husky* they were to infer it related to operations in the eastern Mediterranean.

As for *Brimstone*, the Axis were to interpret this as an assault somewhere in the western Mediterranean other than Sicily. Major Martin was given a second letter, this time written by Lord Louis Mountbatten, Chief of Combined Operations, to Admiral Sir Andrew Cunningham, Commander in Chief of the Mediterranean. Mountbatten instructed Cunningham to make sure the personal letter Martin was carrying reached General Alexander safely. Fleshing out Martin's role in all this, Mountbatten explained to Cunningham that the major was an expert in tank landing craft and had been sent to North Africa to sort out several problems. Mountbatten wrote in glowing terms that Major Martin was absolutely indispensable to him and that he had been proved correct over the Dieppe raid. Martin had been right in his appraisal of that mission and the rest of Combined Ops had been terribly wrong. Finally – most importantly – Mountbatten asked that Martin be sent back to him as soon as the assault was over. He then made a joke that when Martin came back to London he should bring him a tin of sardines as they were rationed in Britain.

The two most crucial elements in Mountbatten's letter were as follows Firstly the joke about sardines clearly linked the forthcoming assault with the island of Sardinia. The second important part of the letter was the mention of how Martin had been right about Dieppe. This was inserted as bait, so that the Germans would gloatingly send this piece of news to Berlin showing that the British had made a mistake in their planning and were inept.

Once the letters were ready and the planning was completed, the Twenty Committee passed the plan over to Major Wingate of the LCS and asked him to show it to Colonel Bevan in order to get higher approval.[7] Bevan took the plan to the Chiefs of Staff who, to use Montagu's expression, 'passed the buck' to the Prime Minister's office. Fortunately Churchill loved this sort of thing and gave the plan his backing. The letter from Nye to Alexander was officially approved by the Chiefs of Staff on 13 April and the green light given.

Soon after, Montagu prepared Major Martin for war. He was taken out of storage and dressed. This proved problematic as the feet had to be thawed by an electric heater before the shoes could be made to fit. The body was then placed in an airtight canister specially designed by Cholmondeley, which was then filled with the dry ice advised by Spilsbury.[8]

Montagu and Cholmondeley were met by driver Jock Horsfall, who had procured a truck for the mission. With Major Martin safely stowed in the back, the three set out for the Clyde, via Cholmondeley's flat where they stopped for dinner. On the way to the flat they passed a queue outside a cinema where people were waiting to watch a spy movie. The three men were reduced to hysterics at the thought of showing the cinema-goers what they were carrying in the back of the truck and telling them about the real secret service caper they had planned.

Arriving in Scotland, Montagu had procured the services of the submarine *Seraph*, commanded by Lieutenant Commander Jewell. This submarine was destined for a number of secret service operations and its departure from the Clyde was delayed in order to take part in *Mincemeat*. The crew were told that the canister contained a secret weather-reporting buoy, although from the size and weight of it, many joked that it contained 'John Brown's body' and dubbed their new shipmate 'Charlie'.

Seraph set out at 6pm on 19 April and, in the early hours of 30 April arrived off the coast of Spain. Montagu had selected a point off Huelva, as it was known there was a German agent working there and a south-westerly wind would help Major Martin's body drift ashore. The British submarine surfaced and Lieutenant Commander Jewell scanned the horizon from *Seraph*'s conning tower. It was an overcast morning and there were a number of fishing boats active in the bay about a mile away from the submarine. The canister was brought up on deck at 4.15am and then all the ratings were told to go back below. Only when the deck was cleared did Jewell tell the other officers what the mysterious canister contained and something about the nature of Major Martin's mission to deceive the enemy. One of them is said to have remarked, 'Isn't it pretty unlucky carrying dead bodies around?' Ignoring this quip Jewell opened the canister and unwrapped the body from a blanket. He checked that the briefcase was still secured to Major Martin's belt by a security chain and that his fingers were clutching the bag. He then inflated the Mae West lifejacket and prepared to send the major on his way.

In an unscripted move, Jewell offered a prayer for the body. As the four young officers removed their caps Jewell murmured words from Psalm 39, traditionally used for burials at sea. This was Jewell's first sea burial and the words of the psalm must have struck him as extremely apt for such a top secret occasion:

> I said, I will take heed to my ways: that I offend not in my tongue.
> I will keep my mouth as it were with a bridle: while the ungodly is in my sight.
> I held my tongue, and spake nothing: I kept silence, yea, even from good words; but it was pain and grief to me.

With that, Jewell gave the body a gentle push and within moments 'Major Martin' was drifting in the direction of the Spanish shore.

In addition to the prevailing wind, the body was given a push in the right direction by the wash of the screws as the submarine began to pull away. After they had gone another half a mile, an overturned rubber dinghy was dropped into the water with a single paddle. The canister that had contained Major Martin was also tossed overboard but would only sink after it was riddled with bullets from a Vickers gun and pistol fire from close range. At 7.15am Jewell signalled that the operation was complete.

Several hours later, at around 9.30am, a Spanish fisherman retrieved the body from the sea just off shore. The body was handed over to an infantry detachment exercising in the area and was then passed to a naval judicial officer who took charge of the documents and personal effects. The corpse was then taken to the mortuary at Huelva and examined by a doctor, who certified that the man had fallen into the sea and that death had come by asphyxiation through immersion in the sea for five to eight days.

Nothing more was heard about Major Martin in London until 3 May, when a signal from the naval attaché in Madrid revealed that his body had been picked up by the Spanish authorities. The naval attaché was then instructed to go to Huelva and told that a wreath from 'Pam' should be placed on the grave and a tombstone erected as soon as possible. The naval attaché was then instructed to take photographs of it to send to Martin's parents and fiancée.

With no mention of any papers being discovered, the Admiralty informed the naval attaché that Martin had been carrying vital documents and that these should be retrieved at all costs. After frantic enquiries these were returned via the Spanish Chief of Naval Staff on 13 May. When the letters arrived back in London from Spain they were sent for scientific analysis and this left little doubt that the letters had been opened by the Spanish.

Sure enough, the letters had been opened, photographed and sent on to Berlin. The first German appraisal was that the letters appeared genuine. It was reported that Major Martin had been in the water for five to eight days and had died from swallowing seawater. German planners already believed that the British were planning a limited operation in Crete, the Dodecanese or southern Greece and the Major Martin documents appeared to confirm this. Between 9 and 12 May, during which further supporting evidence for the document was found, the Germans became more convinced of its genuine nature. On 12 May they acted, making the defence of Sardinia and the Peloponnese the priority over everything else.[9] On 14 May Bletchley Park intercepted a signal reporting 'absolutely reliable' information that Allied landings would be mounted in the eastern and western Mediterranean, with the landings in the east in the Peloponnese codenamed *Husky*.[10] As an indication of how far the *Mincemeat* letters were discussed, on 25 May 1943 Information Minister Joseph Goebbels recorded a discussion about them in his diary:

> I had a long discussion with Admiral Canaris about the data available for forecasting English intentions. Canaris has gained possession of a letter written by the English general staff to General Alexander. This letter is extremely

informative and reveals English plans almost to the dotting of an 'i'. I don't know whether the letter is merely camouflage – Canaris denies this energetically – or whether it actually corresponds to the facts. In any case the general outline of English plans for this summer revealed here seems on the whole to tally. According to it, the English and Americans are planning several sham attacks during the coming months – one in the west, one on Sicily, and one on the Dodecanese islands. These attacks are to immobilize our troops stationed there, thus enabling English forces to undertake other and more serious operations. These operations are to involve Sardinia and the Peloponnese. On the whole this line of reasoning seems to be right. Hence, if the letter to General Alexander is the real thing, we shall have to prepare to repel a number of attacks which are partly serious and partly sham.[11]

Although such inclusions indicate that Cholmondeley's plan succeeded in getting the letters delivered to the German High Command, there has been a lot of speculation about how far *Mincemeat* succeeded in deceiving the Germans. True enough, because of *Cascade* the Germans believed there were 40 divisions capable of participating in the offensive (almost double the real figure) and that the Allies were capable of mounting two attacks, as the Major Martin letters described. It has also been shown that 1st Panzer Division was moved from France to Greece and that it arrived a fortnight late due to attacks on the transport network by the Greek Resistance, which had been called out by the Allies as if in preparation for an assault.

However, one should introduce a note of caution. Whatever Berlin may have initially believed about Allied intentions in the western Mediterranean it soon became clear that Sicily was the most likely target. On 11 June the Allies captured the island of Pantellaria just 62 miles (100km) off the south-west tip of Sicily. From that point on, German communications intercepted by Bletchley Park pointed strongly towards a landing in Sicily, despite agent *Gilbert* telling his controllers not to be alarmed as the attack on Pantellaria was a feint. The fact that Hitler did not reinforce the two depleted German divisions on the island was more because the Germans feared that a general Italian collapse would leave their troops there vulnerable and cut off than because they did not suspect an invasion.

Whatever the reality, the real achievement of *Mincemeat* was the way it kept the Germans focused on Greece even after *Husky* went ahead. When the Allies began making plans to invade Italy, German interceptions showed that Greece was more likely to be a target than the Italian peninsula. In that sense A Force and the Twenty Committee had scored a resounding success.

13

LONDON CALLING

S OMEWHAT SURPRISINGLY THE WESTERN ALLIES had no set plan of action to follow the invasion of Sicily. At a meeting in Washington during May 1943, Churchill urged the Americans to agree to an attack on Italy. Having been pressganged into *Torch* and *Husky* the US Chiefs of Staff were less than enthused about the prospect of more operations in the Mediterranean. However, with the sudden collapse of Italian forces after *Husky* and the fall of Mussolini on 24 July, Eisenhower began planning a dash into southern Italy. It was hoped this would knock Italy out of the war altogether.

A two-pronged attack was planned. In Operation *Baytown* the British would cross the Straits of Messina on 3 September and pin down Axis troops in Calabria. Six days later, Operation *Avalanche* would see US troops land at Salerno with the objective of capturing the port of Naples. To cover these operations A Force developed Plan *Boardman*. This aimed at weakening German forces in the south and centre of the Italian peninsula while pinning down Axis reserves in the Balkans and mainland Greece.

Essentially this was an extension of the objective set out by *Barclay*. The British were said to be planning to take Sardinia while a Franco-American force was heading for Corsica. From these locations the Allies would be in a position to strike against either the south of France or the north-west Italian coastline between Genoa and Livorno. At the same time the British Twelfth Army in Egypt was to be portrayed as preparing for an operation against the Peloponnese. The only real additions to earlier deceptions included an attack on Apulia on the heel of Italy by the British III Corps. Codenamed *Boothby*, this operation also included feints against Gofore on the south Italian peninsula using the full range of signals and sonic deception, plants, decoy bombing and naval activity.

Plan *Boardman* also saw the arrival of another double agent channel in the Mediterranean. Based in Tangiers for a number of years, James Ponsonby was an English commercial attaché and member of SOE. He had a bad reputation and most believed he was a hopeless, washed-up, miserly drunk whose finances were in a precarious state. Despite, or rather because of this reputation, in July 1943 A Force recruited Ponsonby as a channel for passing deception, codenaming him *Guinea* after the British coin.

Tangiers was one of those exotic neutral backyards stalked by secret services of all nations. It was assumed that the Germans already knew *Guinea* had money problems; all A Force had to do was provide him with a plausible source of military information. Over the coming weeks *Guinea* became friendly with the British military attaché. The two men started going out together and drinking immoderately. In fact both men could hold their drink quite well, and so they play-acted as a pair of drunks. After a suitable interval *Guinea* approached a member of the German consulate in Tangiers named Goeritz. Pleading poverty, *Guinea* told the German that he was willing to betray his country in order to pay off his debts. Goeritz told the Englishman that he would pay hard cash for military secrets. Thus another channel for deception was born.

Their first meeting was in the hinterland of Tangiers. *Guinea* drove his motor car in one direction, Goeritz the other. When the two cars met, the windows were wound down and documents passed from *Guinea* to the German, who then sped off. The arrangement remained the same for future exchanges, of which there were many. Later on, Goeritz admitted to *Guinea* that on their first rendezvous there was a German armed guard hiding in the luggage compartment of his car. *Guinea* did not reveal that he had taken a similar precaution at the meeting. As he drove to the rendezvous he had an armed guard hiding in the back of his car too.[1]

At the beginning of September A Force gave *Guinea* a set of false invasion plans. These revealed that the Allies had abandoned the idea of attacking Greece for the time being and that the invasion of Italy would begin on 12 September with landings in the Pisa–Livorno area. These landings would be preceded by landings in other parts of the country, which were designed to draw German forces from the true objectives. Goeritz was impressed and paid *Guinea* 2.5 million francs for his services before sending the message high priority to Berlin. There is an interesting sequel to this episode. ISOS proved that *Guinea* had succeeded and it is recorded that he was awarded the MBE in recognition. However, after his work covering Salerno he was sent to Lisbon on a mission for SOE, where he went off the rails. When told to return to London, he had a breakdown, threatened to kill himself and claimed he would be shot on his return. He demanded £110,000 in compensation, otherwise he would make certain 'disclosures' to the Germans. Eventually he agreed to go back, whereupon Johnny Bevan informed Guy Liddell there might be a case for locking him up. Liddell was more cautious and pointed out that if he was locked up, he would have to be released again at the end of the war. After meeting *Guinea*, Liddell concluded he was 'quite mad'.[2]

Another key performer in the deception plan was the French Forty Committee agent *Gilbert*. With the Allied invasion of Italy under way *Gilbert* reported to the Abwehr that there was an opportunity to get his sub-agent *Le Duc* posted to Sicily as part of the commission for repatriating Italians. The way the system now worked was that A Force fed material to *Le Duc* on Sicily and he copied the information in secret ink and posted it back to *Gilbert*. The Frenchman then dutifully encoded the material and passed it to his distrusted radio operator, who was still unaware of the part *Gilbert* played for the Allies.[3]

On 15 August *Le Duc* reported information he had picked up from members of Montgomery's staff. Apparently the British were looking to land at Crotone on the south-west corner of the Gulf of Taranto. He repeated this warning on 20 August, adding that the troops earmarked for the operation were assembling near Siracusa. The idea was to draw two German divisions away from the Straits of Messina and north out of Calabria. When Montgomery landed in Calabria on 3 September, A Force used its channels to indicate this was only a feint and the real attack would be made against the Gulf of Taranto. The idea of this was to draw German divisions south away from Naples and Salerno before the American *Avalanche* landings, which were scheduled for 9 September.

The net result of the deception plans was not what had been intended. A Force found it increasingly difficult to concentrate German minds on their deception targets. There were so many uncontrolled leaks and rumours doing the rounds in North Africa and the neutral countries that A Force messages were lost in the noise. From the German point of view everywhere appeared threatened at once, so their policy became one of holding back mobile reserves and waiting to see what the Allies actually did before committing to action. When Montgomery landed, the German commander in Italy, Field Marshal Kesselring, was not taken in by the ruse. Rather than move south to contest the landings, Kesselring ordered his troops in Calabria to fall back in front of Montgomery's advance. Therefore, when *Avalanche* began, Kesselring counter-attacked on 12 September and very nearly succeeded in driving the Allies back into the sea.

One of the key Allied objectives during the invasion of Italy was to prevent the Germans from seizing the Italian fleet. There is some evidence that a curious deception ruse was used to ensure that this did not take place. On 10 September 1943 an announcement was broadcast that the Italian fleet should sail to Malta where it would be 'liberated' from the Germans. Under no circumstances, the announcer said, should patriotic Italians allow their ships to fall into German hands, and any order to scuttle their ships was to be ignored as having come directly from Hitler. By all accounts, the Italian ships were said to have obliged, sailed out of Livorno and surrendered to Admiral Cunningham and General Eisenhower at the appointed rendezvous point.

The mysterious broadcasts came from a station calling itself Radio Livorno. On the air since 27 July 1943, it appeared as if the station was being run by members of a secret patriotic association within the Italian Navy opposed to Mussolini and Hitler. The mastermind of the operation was said to be an officer who passed messages to a loyal NCO who then broadcast them from a radio room in one of the Italian warships in the port of Livorno. Actually, Radio Livorno was a put-up job. It was the brainchild of British Naval Intelligence's Admiral Godfrey.[4] The scripts were passed to a top-secret propaganda organization and read by a Maltese officer named Randolph Imozzi. To what extent the Italian Navy suspected Radio Livorno was a front for the Allied leadership is unclear; in any case they were won over by it and denied Germany its ships.

Radio Livorno was one of a number of radio stations the Allies used for communicating with Axis servicemen and civilians. Unlike the obvious foreign service broadcasts of the BBC, these services actually pretended they were German stations emanating from within the Reich itself. Whereas the BBC took a humanist approach, appealing to the sense of reason of those sympathetic to or ruled by the Axis, the 'Black' stations appealed to baser human virtues: self-interest, vice and good entertainment.

Although the main aim of psychological warfare was to lessen the morale of the enemy and to promote anti-Nazi resistance, Black propaganda became a very useful channel for deception purposes, in particular as a channel for putting over rumours, or 'sibs' as they were known, from the Latin *sibilare* 'to whisper'. The British organization primarily responsible for this was the Political Warfare Executive (PWE) and the leading exponent of counterfeit radio broadcasts was Denis Sefton Delmer, the journalist and broadcaster who had defied Hitler's so-called 'last peace offer' to Britain in 1940.

When last mentioned, Delmer was working for the BBC German service, giving German soldiers English lessons as part of the 'burning sea' rumour campaign. Since then he had been recruited by PWE and given free rein to sow discontent among German listeners without scruple or regard to the moral constraints that had handcuffed him while working for the BBC.

Delmer therefore invented the first of what would become a number of bogus radio stations, all of which would gain a cult following among their

Axis audience.[5] This first radio station was GS1, or Gustav Siegfried Eins, to give it its full title. The initials 'GS1' were entirely meaningless, except that German listeners might read something into them. In German 'GS1' could stand for General Staff One (Generalstab Eins) or Secret Transmitter One (Geheimsender Eins). Although the broadcasts could be heard by German civilians, they did not address them directly. Delmer's idea was that people would tune in to eavesdrop on what sounded like the transmission of a clandestine military organization with cells across occupied Europe. Furthermore, the station would be staunchly patriotic and not critical of Hitler. It would instead target local party officials who controlled Germany in Hitler's name and who were becoming increasingly corrupt as the war went on. By adopting this approach, Delmer hoped to hint at a split between the upper echelons of the Army and the Nazi party organs, including the Gestapo. The Army, the broadcasts would demonstrate, was convinced that while it was out fighting the war, party villains were ruining the country behind its back. This had been the Army's excuse in 1918 – that it had lost the war because it had been stabbed in the back by those at home. In that sense it played on some very real fears.

The front man for GS1 was a character Delmer called 'Der Chef' – the chief. From his pre-war days in Berlin, Delmer remembered how Hitler's lackeys had referred to him in this way and so this was a private joke in homage to that memory. The 'Der Chef' character was played by a Berliner called Peter Seckelmann. A writer of detective stories before the war, Seckelmann had come to Britain in 1938 because of the Nazis' treatment of the Jews. He enlisted in the Auxiliary Pioneer Corps under the name Paul Sanders and spent the early war years defusing German bombs with time fuses. As if bomb disposal was not hazardous enough, Seckelmann applied to join the SOE and volunteered to be parachuted behind German lines as a secret agent. Instead, he was introduced to Sefton Delmer and recruited as the voice of GS1.

Seckelmann had a noticeable Berlin drawl to his accent, making him perfect in Delmer's mind for impersonating the type of German officer found in the old guard regiments in the German capital. The scripts provided for Seckelmann were littered with salty expletives and, to begin with at least, descriptions of acts that bordered on the pornographic. David Garnett's official history of PWE explains the reason for this approach: 'The method of imparting news items designed for this purpose was to be that of such newspapers as the *Daily Mirror*, which, by denouncing vice, secure a large circulation among those who wish to read about it.'[6]

Der Chef's first broadcast took place on the evening of 23 May 1941. Delmer and Seckelmann drove to a secret recording studio in a house in the village of Aspley Guise in Bedfordshire. The broadcast began with the repetitive announcement in German of the station's call sign. 'Here is Gustav Siegfried Eins ... here is Gustav Siegfried Eins ...' After 45 seconds, Seckelmann announced that he had a message for 'Gustav Siegfried 18'. The message was in an easily breakable code announcing that someone named Willy should meet Jochen in the Union theatre. Delmer hoped that this message would be intercepted by the Nazi Security Service (Reichssicherheitshauptamt or RHSA, Main Security Office of the Reich) and would lead to chaos as Gestapo agents were despatched to every one of Germany's many Union theatres looking for the two men.

With the preliminaries dispensed with, *Der Chef* began his broadcast in earnest. Twelve days before, Hitler's deputy, Rudolf Hess, had landed in Scotland. *Der Chef* was not pleased by this and launched a tirade against Hess and the other weak-kneed 'parlour Bolsheviks' posing as the Nazi leadership. In a line that was specifically designed to convince German listeners that the broadcast was not a piece of British propaganda, *Der Chef* described the British leader as 'that flat-footed bastard of a drunken old Jew, Churchill'. He then predicted that Hess would be bled dry of information by the British, that Hitler had nothing to do with the Deputy Fuhrer's decision to fly to Scotland and arrests of other traitors would no doubt follow soon. He ended the transmission with a promise that the broadcast would be repeated on the same wavelength hourly at seven minutes to the hour.

After recording the piece, one of the recording engineers asked Delmer if GS1 should have a signature tune played before the transmission. Delmer agreed and chose a suitable piece of pomp from the same German folk song used on the Nazi's own Deutschlandsender radio station.

As Seckelmann grew in confidence and became more practised in the projection of his voice through a microphone, he took on more of the script-writing himself, introducing colloquial Berlin phrases to give the broadcasts more authenticity. One thing that worried Delmer about the broadcast was the lack of an aide-de-camp to *Der Chef*. A man of *Der Chef*'s standing ought to be announced before speaking: such a formality would never have been overlooked by a real German officer. In later broadcasts this sidekick role was played by Johannes Reinholz, a German journalist who had fled Berlin with his Jewish wife on the eve of war in 1939. At the beginning of every broadcast Reinholz's clipped, metallic baritone voice would make all the official announcements before announcing Seckelmann's character with the catchphrase '*Es spricht der Chef*' – 'The Chief speaks'.

To keep the feel of the broadcasts as contemporary as possible, Delmer used a wide range of news and intelligence sources on daily life in the Reich. Scripts were based on interviews and reports from refugees, German newspapers and magazines, censorship intercepts, captured mail, and letters and diaries found discarded on the bodies of dead German soldiers or taken from the wounded. Delmer was also provided information from the highly top-secret Combined Services Detailed Interrogation Centre (CSDIC) reports on recently captured prisoners of war. This information was often obtained clandestinely by secret microphones concealed in the POW cages and even hidden in the gardens where the POWs would walk to talk in privacy. All these reports allowed *Der Chef* to talk about real people and real situations occurring behind enemy lines and to make use of the most up-to-date German service jargon and slang.

This accuracy convinced many of *Der Chef*'s growing German audience that he was broadcasting from inside the Reich, moving from hideout to hideout to avoid capture by the Gestapo. One theory even placed *Der Chef*'s transmitter in a barge on the River Spree. Before the United States entered the war, the staff in the US embassy in Berlin were avid listeners to the show, believing that it indicated the existence of an opposition group within the heart of the Nazi empire. In a secret report to Washington on 8 September 1941, the Americans noted that the radio station had a large German audience and that the information given was in such detail that if false, it would be easily discredited. The station operated daily on the 31.5 metre band and took to the air seven minutes before the hour. The German authorities had tried to interfere with the signal, but during air raids (when German broadcasts went off air so that they could not be used by Allied bomber crews as beacons) GS1 would come across very clearly.

The embassy staff speculated that the station was worked automatically with records, and that when a transmitter was found, another was set up elsewhere to replace it. As for the content of the broadcasts, the report said:

> Using violent and unbelievably obscene language, this station criticized the actions of the Party and certain party-favoured officers, especially the SS. Superficially it is violently patriotic and is supposed by many German officers to be supported by the German Wehrmacht in secret.[7]

Despite the fact that GS1's lewd, guttural approach was judged highly entertaining by its German listeners, others were less impressed. Although the transmissions were intended for a German audience, some locals living close to the transmission sites occasionally picked up GS1 on their wireless sets. About a year after GS1 had been broadcasting, *Der Chef* was brought to the attention of the politician Sir Stafford Cripps, a popular 'silver spoon' Marxist whom Churchill found useful in negotiating with Stalin. A devout Christian, Cripps described PWE as 'that beastly pornographic organization' and complained this style of broadcasting would only appeal to the 'thug section of the Nazi party' and that, in his opinion, PWE should instead concentrate on broadcasts that gave hope and appealed to 'good Germans'.[8] After hearing about a particularly lewd GS1 script involving a German admiral, his mistress, five drunken German sailors and a lump of butter, Cripps complained to the Foreign Secretary, Anthony Eden: 'If this is the sort of thing that is needed to win the war, why, I'd rather lose it.'[9]

Fortunately, common sense prevailed over Cripps' prudishness and Delmer was allowed to carry on broadcasting. As *Der Chef* became better known, Delmer was able to drop some of the worst outrages in his scripts, but Seckelmann contained to use the coarse and abusive language that had become *Der Chef*'s trademark.

Some of the more juicy 'sibs' put over by *Der Chef* included one about Nazi blood transfusion units collecting blood from Polish and Russian POWs without giving the donors a Wassermann test for syphilis. As a result of this a number of German soldiers had contracted the disease, not to mention being 'contaminated' by Slav blood. Another 'sib' came after PWE learned that the Italian envoy to Berlin, Dino Alfieri, would soon be recalled to Rome to consult with Mussolini. Before this news was common knowledge in Germany, *Der Chef* broadcast that a German officer had come home from the front and found the Italian in bed with his wife. The German officer pulled his revolver to shoot Alfieri, at which the Italian went down on his knees and begged diplomatic immunity. Instead of shooting the 'spineless creature', the officer instead beat him black and blue until he was unable to stand and sent him back to the Italian embassy in a car. When it was later revealed on German radio that the Italian had returned to Rome, *Der Chef*'s account appeared to have been true. Even Mussolini heard about the story, and thought it was hilarious.

Der Chef's final broadcast on Gustav Siegfried Eins came on 18 November 1943. Delmer decided that his anti-hero would serve a better purpose as a martyr to the anti-Nazi cause. Delmer scripted a show in which the Gestapo burst into the studio mid-broadcast and machine-gunned down *Der Chef* live on the radio. Sure enough, in the middle of a broadcast, with special effects provided by a Tommy gun, *Der Chef* was heard to be killed. Unfortunately, this ending was the only botched job of what had been a successful and long-running hoax. The recording was broadcast as planned, but then the engineer, not speaking German and not realizing what had occurred on the show, re-broadcast the recording an hour later. *Der Chef* was thus machine-gunned down a second time that day! Delmer quickly realized what had occurred and prevented the mistake from recurring. To his knowledge, nobody else noticed.

<h2 style="text-align:center">XX</h2>

By the end of GS1 Delmer's interests had broadened to another counterfeit radio station: Deutscher Kurzwellensender Atlantik (German Shortwave Radio Atlantic) – or Atlantiksender for short. Just before Christmas 1942 Naval Intelligence asked Delmer to complement GS1 with a 'Black' radio broadcast aimed at breaking the morale of German U-boat crews. Although the BBC already had special programmes for the German Army, Navy and Air Force, Admiral Godfrey wanted a 'Black propaganda' campaign targeting U-boat crew morale. Delmer's broadcasts were to portray service on a U-boat like being in a coffin.

Atlantiksender began broadcasting on 22 March 1943 (although Delmer says 5 February 1943) and was on the air live every night from 6pm until 8am the following day. Where GS1 had relied on the foul language and outrageous antics of *Der Chef*, Atlantiksender attracted its audience by playing the very best and latest dance music interspersed with the occasional newsflash or bulletin focusing on tabloid-style human interest stories and music. The U-boat crews would listen in, not because of the news bulletins, but because the music was better than anything else on the air.

Enormous efforts went into providing the right sort of music. The latest German hit records were specially flown over from Stockholm to Delmer. Songs were specially recorded by German-speaking artists in the United States, including Marlene Dietrich, who had no idea she was recording songs for a purported Nazi radio station, and was pelted with tomatoes in Germany because of this after the war. More hits from America were supplied by the American sabotage and subversion organization, the Office of Strategic Services (OSS) and recordings were made by Henry Zeisel and his band after they were captured by the Eighth Army on a tour of Axis troops in North Africa. The band of the Royal Marines was booked for a secret recording session in the Albert Hall where it performed German songs. Through POWs Delmer had learned the Berlin song '*Es war in Schoneberg im Monat Mai*' was popular with U-boat crews, who had come up with their own lyrics for the piece. The first line of the version recorded for Delmer therefore opened: '*Ich war in Saint-Nazaire in einem Puff*' (I was in a brothel in Saint Nazaire).

As with GS1, Atlantiksender's bulletins and reporting style were greatly assisted by information provided – wittingly or not – by captured German servicemen. A number of prisoners turned out to be highly anti-Nazi and offered their services to the Allies. Among these was Eddy Mander, a disgruntled U-boat radio operator from Hamburg well versed in the 'below decks' slang used by German submariners. To give the impression that the radio station really was a forces' radio show, Atlantiksender employed its very own 'forces sweetheart'. The part of *Vicky* was played by Agnes Bernelle, the daughter of the German playwright and theatre-owner Rudolf Bernauer. Although Bernelle was to lose half her family in Auschwitz, as *Vicky* she would send out loving individual birthday greetings to surprised German crewmen. Acting on tip-offs from Naval Intelligence about which U-boats would most likely have gone out to sea, Delmer would have Atlantiksender play 'special request' music for the crew, which must have unnerved them no end. In addition to music, Atlantiksender was well known for its sports reporting. NID provided the results of football matches between German crews stationed in France including the names of the scorers, all of which increased the audience base of the show.

One of the crowning glories of Delmer's engineers was the way they could patch into genuine German broadcasts. If a live speech by Hitler was on the air, the engineers would pick it up on the German station and relay it through Atlantiksender. The announcer would say that they were interrupting the service to broadcast, along with all the other radio stations in the Reich, an important speech. This made Atlantiksender appear to be under Nazi control.

The subversive element of Atlantiksender was the way in which it reported air raid damage to German cities. After British bombers returned from an air raid, an intelligence officer would contact Delmer and let him know which city had been hit and what ordnance had been used – i.e. high explosives or incendiaries. This would allow Delmer to put out immediate newsflashes over Atlantiksender saying that such-and-such a place was in flames and so on. The next morning the RAF would send over Mosquito fighter-bombers to judge the damage of the previous night's raid. Copies of the photos would be raced by motorcycle to Delmer's team who would pore over the pictures and German city maps, working out which streets had been hit and to what extent. The evening after the raid they would broadcast to the German servicemen in France, giving the addresses of the homes that had been hit and then reminding them that if their home had been bombed they were entitled to take compassionate leave. The accuracy of these reports was very impressive and must have caused enormous anguish to those on the front line. With the ensuing requests for leave, it also left the bases in danger of becoming undermanned.

Atlantiksender was also used for deception purposes by NID. The merits of newly introduced secret German inventions such as automatic homing torpedoes would be discussed on Atlantiksender. Obviously the German High Command knew Atlantiksender was under enemy control and so monitored these technical bulletins to see what the Allies were saying about the weapons. Knowing this would be the case, Admiral Godfrey came up with the following ruse: the Germans had introduced an anti-sonar device known as Aphrodite. In reality the device was practically useless, and Godfrey asked Delmer to run a campaign denouncing it as such. When the Germans realized the British were trying to discredit the device, they deduced this must be because it was working well and the British were afraid of it. Therefore, despite tangible evidence that Aphrodite did not work, the Germans retained it in service.

On 24 October 1943 at 5.57pm a new service was launched: Soldatensender Calais. Using the same wavelength as Radio Deutschland and broadcasting in the evening when Deutschland was off air during the air raids, Soldiers' Radio Calais became an even bigger hit than Atlantiksender. It was aimed at German soldiers in the western command area (i.e. France) and Norway and broadcasted a similar diet of news and dance music to Atlantiksender; even Goebbels would tune in with grudging admiration.

The strength of the broadcast was possible because of the most powerful radio transmitter in Europe: a 600-kilowatt medium-wave monster named Aspidistra after the popular song 'The Biggest Aspidistra in the World' by Gracie Fields. Soldatensender Calais was also broadcast from a small transmitter placed on the British coastline opposite Calais to confuse Germans trying to get a direction fix on the signal's origin. From POWs it seemed that the German public accepted that the radio station was a genuine forces' radio station and that the news reports were genuine. When the Germans tried to jam the signal, the German public believed the jamming came from the English who were trying to block what they thought was a German station.

In addition to music and coverage of air raid damage, Soldatensender Calais began softening up the German garrison of France for the forthcoming invasion. According to Soldatensender, France was regarded as an operational backwater for inferior quality troops and weapons. The real war was on the Russian Front and even in the event of an Allied invasion, no reinforcements would be sent to France. The units there had already been effectively written off. At the same time, Soldatensender Calais would warn its military listeners that units showing themselves in any way efficient or individuals gaining promotion would be whisked off to the Russian Front with immediate effect.

XX

Moving away from the world of propaganda, the Aspidistra transmitter was also used in the air war against Germany. The Assistant Director of Intelligence (Science), Professor R. V. Jones, recalled how Aspidistra was used to confound German airmen. Initially the British started making recordings of German air controllers speaking to German pilots. These messages were recorded onto gramophone records and then played back on German channels on different days to confuse fighter pilots. During an air raid on Ludwigshafen, the British succeeded in counterfeiting the German air controller's voice by using Aspidistra to warn all German night fighters to land because of the danger of fog. When the Germans found out what had happened, they substituted women for men to broadcast the commentary, but the British had already thought of that and had German-speaking WAAFs standing by. The Germans then had a man repeat any order the WAAF gave so the pilots would know it was false. All the British had to do was have every order the German woman gave repeated by a man. In the end the Germans were forced to abandon verbal communication and use elaborate musical codes. Pilots hearing a waltz would know the Allied bombers were heading for Munich, while jazz meant Berlin was thought to be the target.[10]

In another ruse of the air war, Professor Jones recalled how his first assistant, Harold Blyth, was sent to work on intelligence matters with Kim Philby at MI6 (V). Blyth told Jones he would like him to meet one of the officers involved with security. Jones called this man 'George' in his memoirs, but it was almost certainly XX member Charles Cholmondeley.[11] In any case Jones was given the use of the double cross spies in order to deceive the Germans over a new direction-finding device the RAF were trialling. This new system was known as *Gee* and had been shown greatly to improve bombing accuracy.

Bombers had previously been guided to their targets by converging radio beams. The bomber would follow a beam until it crossed a second beam. This indicated the bomber was over the target area and should drop its load of bombs. The downside to such systems was that the beams could be detected by the enemy and the likely target guessed in time to divert night fighters. With the *Gee* system, there was no fixed beam, only a series of pulses, which did not give the target area away.

Unfortunately an aircraft had been lost somewhere over Hanover on 13 August 1941. Jones was told that although a self-destruct device had been put in place, there was a chance the Germans might find some of the system intact or that captured crewmen might talk. If the Germans were alerted to *Gee*'s unique characteristic, a counter-measure might be developed before the system was properly introduced. With nothing else in the pipeline to replace it, Jones was asked to come up with a way of throwing the Germans off the scent over the *Gee* system.

The war scientist believed the only way to protect *Gee* was to suggest to the Germans that they were planning to use beam systems in the future. He had some navigational beams used for directing targeting on Brest moved to the east coast of England. These he called *Jay*, hoping the German pronunciation would confuse the codenames *Gee* and *Jay* enough for them to believe they were one and the same thing. 'George' then offered Jones the double cross agents as a channel for planting the *Jay* information on the Germans.

Jones suggested that one of the agents could overhear a conversation at the Savoy on the evening of New Year's Day between two RAF officers about the introduction of the *Jay* beam against German targets, its trials having worked so well over Brest. The agent would then describe how the two officers demonstrated the use of *Jay* moving salt and pepper pots over the table. Another agent was asked to report that a 'Professor Ekkerly' had been giving instruction lectures to RAF personnel about a navigational system called Jerry. Jones hoped that the Germans would think either that Jerry stood for *Jay*, or that Jerry would be taken in the sense of its slang meaning, i.e. that it was going to be used against Germans.

Jones noted that the agents were thanked for their information and that no questions about the *Gee* system were asked. When the new system came into service on 8 March 1942, the Germans had no contingencies in place to stop it and took five months to successfully jam the signal.[12]

14

THE *FORTITUDE* PLAN

AT THE CASABLANCA CONFERENCE OF January 1943, Churchill and Roosevelt committed themselves to mounting a cross-Channel invasion of France in the spring of 1944. While the main effort in 1943 was concentrated on the Mediterranean theatre, British Major General Sir Frederick Morgan was appointed on 12 April 1943 as Chief of Staff to the Supreme Allied Commander (COSSAC). At the head of an Anglo-American team, Morgan was responsible for drawing up plans for a full-scale invasion in the spring of 1944, codenamed *Overlord*. In addition to planning *Overlord*, COSSAC was ordered to draw up a series of deceptive plans that would keep alive the possibility of a cross-Channel attack during the summer of 1943.

Previously, in the build up to *Torch* in 1942, the fledgling London Controlling Section had sought to keep German forces from being redeployed from north and western Europe to the Mediterranean by indicating operations against France (Operation *Overthrow*) and Norway (Operation *Solo I*). These threats were maintained and adapted to fulfil Morgan's objectives, and became known under the umbrella name Plan *Cockade*. This was a series of schemes to deter the Germans from detaching troops either to the Mediterranean or to the Russian Front, by threats to northern France and Norway. Expanding on what had already been attempted, *Cockade* was supposed to culminate in an ambitious mock invasion of the Pas de Calais, the narrowest crossing point from England to France. In addition to tying down German troops, it was hoped this feint would draw the Luftwaffe out of its bases and into a pitched battle over the English Channel.

With the assistance of the LCS, these cover plans were drawn up by Colonel John Jervis-Read, who had been put in charge of a section under COSSAC called Ops.B. Unfortunately Jervis-Read was given nothing like the access, priority or resources available to Dudley Clarke's A Force, the body which Ops.B was theoretically meant to emulate. It appears that Morgan viewed A Force with some suspicion as a 'private army' and had no intention of allowing anything similar to develop in his own neck of the woods. Jervis-Read was more or less a one-man show, forced to beg what help he could from other service departments. It was not an arrangement with which Colonel Bevan was satisfied.[1]

The most important element of *Cockade* was Plan *Starkey*, an Anglo-Canadian attack on the port of Boulogne scheduled for between 8 and 14 September 1943. According to the deception plan, after the bridgehead was established by *Starkey*, a second attack would follow, codenamed *Wadham*. This time an American force would attack the port of Brest in Brittany, supported by the arrival of troops sailing directly from the United States. In the grand deception plan, the Allies would cancel *Starkey* and *Wadham* at the last minute and instead put all their resources into an invasion of Norway by five divisions, codenamed *Tindall*.

In the original version of *Starkey*, the infantry contingent was to be complemented by a strong naval force that included two older battleships, over 90 other naval vessels, whatever merchant ships could be found, and a large fleet of landing craft. When this shopping list was presented to the First Lord of the Admiralty Admiral, Sir Dudley Pound, he refused to allow his battleships to join in. The French coast along the Pas de Calais was bristling with heavy-calibre German coastal batteries. It was very unlikely the battleships would be able to knock any of them out, but they would almost certainly take fire and sustain damage themselves. No matter how much the Navy approved of deception, losing two battleships for no reward would be a hard thing to explain to the British public. There was also a problem with the number of landing craft available. With an urgent need for landing craft in the Mediterranean, only 360 could be mustered on the south coast. To these were added 100 dummy assault landing craft, called 'Wetbobs', and 75 dummy tank landing craft, known as 'Bigbobs'. The name 'Wetbob' came from Eton College and signified someone in one of the water sports teams, as opposed to those in land-based sports teams, who were called 'Drybobs'. 'Bigbobs' were so called because they were bigger. According to Sir Freddy Morgan, the prototypes of these decoys were first constructed on the London Metropolitan Water Board reservoir near Shepperton.[2] These dummy craft were very convincing, even from close range, and were embellished with small details like smoke coming from non-existent engines and laundry hung on washing lines by their equally bogus crews. Even if there were not enough landing craft to suggest a full-scale invasion, when the decoys were mixed in with the real thing, the undertaking appeared larger than the Dieppe raid.

With the prospect of delivering the Luftwaffe a bloody nose, Fighter Command appeared very enthusiastic about the mission. Between the British and American commands, 60 fighter squadrons were earmarked for the planned battle with the Luftwaffe. Unfortunately, without the battleships acting as a lure, Fighter Command did not believe the mission had much chance of success. Further scorn came from Air Chief Marshal Sir Arthur 'Bomber' Harris. When asked for several thousand heavy bomber sorties in support of *Starkey*, he protested very strongly and in the end permitted only inexperienced crews and medium bombers not capable of hitting targets in Germany to take part. Harris did not like anyone interfering with his master plan for bringing about a German surrender through area bombing, especially when Fighter Command appeared to stand most chance of gaining credit from the mission.

There was also the problem of the French Resistance. It would be catastrophic if the Resistance believed that the invasion attempt was genuine and came out en masse, only to be left in the lurch. So, while on the one hand the Allies promoted the idea of an invasion, they were very careful to tell the Resistance not to come out unless they received the official green light from London. It was a similar story for the British press. Reporters would no doubt get wind that something big was being planned, and it would be terrible for public morale if *Starkey* was reported as a real invasion attempt that had failed. Everything about the operation was a tightrope act performed in a blustery gale of inter-service politics.

Despite the disappointments and internal politics, *Starkey* pushed on. To complement the preparations, Colonel Turner's department was called in to provide camouflage and decoys for the mission. Lighting was used to simulate traffic and divert bombs away from the major Channel ports, including Southampton, Portsmouth, Newhaven and Dover. At the same time military camps were simulated with lighting effects and dummy installations. The airfields were also packed with somewhere in the region of 400 dummy gliders and large numbers of decoy Spitfires and Hurricanes. Radio deception was also used to simulate the chatter of the formations earmarked for *Starkey*, many of which were entirely fictional additions to the order of battle.

Although German reconnaissance flights did spot some of the preparations, the best way of drawing the Germans' attention to *Starkey* was again through special means, in particular the Twenty Committee's double agents. Of those most involved, *Tricycle* is already well enough known. Having re-established his credentials after the fiasco of his mission to America, in July 1943 he again returned to Lisbon and took a mass of information on the supposed Allied plans, all of which increased his standing with the Germans. His reports were augmented by those of *Gelatine*, his sub-agent who reported on invasion gossip picked up at society gatherings.

These reports were echoed by those of another socialite codenamed *Bronx*. The daughter of the Peruvian chargé d'affaire in Vichy France, Elvira

Chaudoir had lived in England since the beginning of the war. She lived life on the wild side, attending weekend parties where she rubbed shoulders with members of the government and aristocracy. *Bronx* kept a flat in Mayfair, ran up considerable gambling debts and fully explored her voracious sexual appetites with men and women alike. Recruited by Claude Dansey, the deputy head of MI6, *Bronx* was sent to visit her parents in Vichy France, where she allowed herself to be recruited by a German agent who offered her £100 a month to supply economic and political intelligence. This payment was disguised as an alimony payment from the husband she was divorcing. When she returned to the United Kingdom she revealed her recruitment by and love affair with the German agent. After some deliberation, she was enrolled as a double agent.

Other new faces in the XX set up included a trio of businessmen: *Hamlet*, *Mullet* and *Puppet*. The instigator of this network was *Hamlet*, a half-Jewish Austrian who had property in Germany until it was confiscated in 1936. After a brief period of imprisonment, *Hamlet* went to Italy and sent his children to a school in England. He then moved to Belgium where he had a business. It was in Belgium that he agreed to work for the Abwehr, albeit under pain of being handed over to the Gestapo. He was sent to Lisbon and became friends there with an Englishman who had formerly worked in Belgium for an insurance firm. *Hamlet* asked this new friend, whom the British codenamed *Mullet*, to take some valuables to England on his behalf, and to act as his business representative there. He also asked him if he could identify anyone who might be sympathetic to an approach by Germans in the event of the Nazis losing power, presumably after a coup.

Pointing out his Jewish heritage, *Mullet* questioned *Hamlet* about why he was working for the Germans. *Hamlet* had quite a plausible excuse, claiming to be building up an intelligence network that would show German generals that they had lost the war and should ask for peace. He claimed that he had direct access to Canaris and that through a friend he could contact General von Falkenhausen, the military governor of Belgium. The case now came to the attention of the British secret service and when *Mullet* went back to Lisbon in December 1942 he took an SIS officer with him. *Hamlet* was interviewed and it soon became apparent that most of his claims were false. However, the link to von Falkenhausen turned out to be genuine and this go-between received the codename *Puppet*. With *Hamlet*'s children a guarantor of his loyalty, the Twenty Committee decided to risk taking on the network and added them to the stable. With *Mullet* acting as the contact man in Britain, *Hamlet* was able to report on matters relating to the City and government throughout 1943.

The surest means of reporting was still *Garbo*. With order restored to his case following his wife's depression, *Garbo* soon became bombarded with questions about Allied intentions in north-west Europe. After reporting that troop concentrations and exercises were being carried out in Wales, *Garbo* supposedly travelled to Scotland in August in order to investigate rumours about an attack on Norway. While apparently in Scotland, *Garbo*'s notional sub-agents began reporting large troop build ups around Southampton and that assault craft were being collected in the Channel ports. Believing this significant, *Garbo* raced south and reported that he had personally discovered seven divisions in the Brighton area. Hedging his bets, *Garbo* cautioned that this build up might be nothing more than a dummy run for a future operation. On the other hand he would not put the idea to bed completely, as the unexpectedly swift collapse of the Italians in Sicily might have led to a last-minute change in Allied planning. On 5 September *Garbo* received information from his agents that troops were concentrating for an assault three days later.

To back up *Garbo*'s messages, troops were moved to the south coast along with Colonel Turner's dummy fighters and gliders. There was also a number of Commando raids, which were supposed to capture prisoners in the landing areas. Of the 14 raids planned, only eight actually took place and all of them were unsuccessful. In fact, the only captive brought back across the Channel was a sample of barbed wire that one of the teams had come across.

In the two weeks up to 8 September the Allied air forces began stepping up attacks on Calais. Unfortunately bad weather intervened and many of the missions were cancelled. The weather continued to play a part and, when 8 September came, the feint was postponed for 24 hours. On 8 September *Garbo* reported that the troops were being confined to barracks and were being issued four-day ration packs, indicating that the assault was imminent. Next day the troops were marched along the hards to their landing craft. Once there, they turned about, and with disappointed looks on their faces, trudged back to camp, with the exception of the anti-aircraft gunners, who remained to protect the boats from the expected droves of German aircraft. A force of around 30 ships then assembled off Dungeness and headed towards France preceded by a screen of mine-sweepers. Overhead a force of 72 fighters flew over the convoy, accompanying medium bombers, which attacked the German coastal batteries, without much success.

When the force was just ten miles outside Boulogne the ships stopped and waited for the German response. Nothing happened. The coastal artillery did not open up and the Luftwaffe stayed on the ground. According to Morgan's account of the day, the only response obtained was a slightly confused German subaltern who was overheard radioing his commander asking what all the fuss in the Channel was about.[3]

Any notions of a great aerial battle came to nothing. At 9am the convoy made smoke and turned for home. Later that day *Garbo* reported that the operation had been suspended and the troops were returning to barracks. Without the aerial battle the Allies were left in a sticky situation. Something had to be told to the press before the Germans came out and said they had 'scared off' a British invasion attempt. In the end the press were told that a full-scale rehearsal had taken place and valuable lessons had been learned for future operations.

The main remaining hope of deceiving von Rundstedt in France was Plan *Wadham*, the attack on Brittany set for 22 September. Unfortunately this was another flop. The Germans showed absolutely no sign of taking the bait and Morgan asked for it to be cancelled.

With *Starkey* and *Wadham* cancelled, all efforts were put into implementing Plan *Tindall*. When the attacks on northern France failed to materialize, the excuse given by the double agents was that resources for it had been diverted to invade northern Norway and to capture the airfield at Stavanger. Four divisions were to go in by sea, while an airborne division was earmarked for the attack. Detailed plans were drawn up, all of which were dutifully leaked by the double agents, who suggested a landing would take place between 6 and 12 September. This time the Germans did take some of the bait, and no troops were removed from Norway to reinforce the Mediterranean. In that sense, four training divisions in Scotland successfully held down three times their number of trained German troops.

On balance, it took great optimism not to be disheartened by the implementation of *Cockade*. The deceptions against France had clearly failed. The Nazi High Command had made up its mind that the Allied attacks in 1943 would be confined to the Mediterranean theatre. As a mark of how little attention was paid to *Starkey*, von Rundstedt was stripped of ten divisions to stabilize the situation in Italy. There was, however, a small plus to this exercise. Although the German High Command was unimpressed with the British plans, the preparations being carried out in Britain filled von Rundstedt with a sense of foreboding. He concluded that the whole operation had been a 'large-scale preliminary rehearsal for a genuine attack against our west coast'.[4] The embarkation practice and the real deployment of mine-sweepers and aircraft could only be a portent of something much larger to come. True enough, General Morgan went away happy that his troops had practised for an embarkation and that they had appeared quite up for a scrap.

The planning of *Wadham* had proved similarly useful. Only a few Americans involved with the planning knew that this attack with five divisions was a bluff. As the troops began to muster in south-west England, there was chaos as planners were faced with very real logistical problems and struggled to make their final preparations for an assault they believed was going ahead. The lessons learned by US planners during this operation became invaluable when it came to organizing the real show the following summer.

Perhaps at best, like many deception operations carried out by the Allies, it could be said that *Cockade* had done no harm. There had been the usual grumblings from service chiefs over the use of resources for 'pointless' operations, but at least no double agents had been blown and the Germans appeared to accept the inflated Allied order of battle. In that sense it proved a useful learning experience for the following year.

XX

While *Cockade* spluttered along, planning for *Overlord* continued. By the middle of July 1943 an outline had been written with Normandy selected as the target area. It was felt that, of all the options, Normandy offered the Allies the greatest hope of success. The shape of the coast north of Caen was such that the beaches were sheltered from prevailing winds, plus there were numerous exits allowing troops to penetrate inland quickly. It was also considered that it would be easier to gain the deep water ports of north-western France, such as Cherbourg, Brest, Lorient and Saint Nazaire, than it would be to take Antwerp after a landing around Calais. Once these north-western ports were in Allied hands, it would be easier to bring supplies directly from the United States without having to land them first in Britain.[5]

With Normandy selected, COSSAC was instructed to come up with a suitable cover plan for *Overlord*. This was no easy matter. The cover plans for *Torch* and *Cockade* had both indicated that a cross-Channel invasion was imminent. The Allies now wished to convince the Germans this was not the case and that the invasion of France was not scheduled for 1944.

The prevailing mood in COSSAC was that the deception could not be made to work. Morgan was extremely sceptical that anything more than limited tactical surprise could be achieved and told LCS officer Ronald Wingate he did not believe a cover plan for *Neptune* (the cross-Channel attack phase of *Overlord*) would succeed. Wingate was acquainted with Morgan from long before the war, having known him in Baluchistan. This familiarity allowed Wingate to argue the point with some force, urging

Morgan, 'You must let your staff try.'[6] In the event, because of the limited resources then available to COSSAC Ops.B, most of the planning was carried out by the LCS. In August Bevan's section presented their first draft for approval. Plan *Jael* claimed that the Allies had given up on the idea of making a cross-Channel attack and would continue to concentrate on the Mediterranean theatre through the course of 1944, attempting to open a new front in the Balkans. Meanwhile priority would be given to the air bombardment of Germany (codenamed *Pointblank*), which would hopefully bring the Nazis to their knees.

On paper it was a neat idea, playing on the various deceptions already suggesting an attack in the eastern Mediterranean, and the air war was in full swing with round-the-clock bombing of Germany. However, there was one insurmountable weakness in the plan and this meant it failed to get serious backing. Plan *Jael* would not explain the enormous build up of troops in Britain, which the Germans were sure to detect and which, by early spring 1944, would indicate that the Allies were planning an invasion of France between Cherbourg and Dunkirk. For that reason *Jael* was scrapped and Bevan went back to the drawing board.

It was replaced on 16 September 1943 by a plan initially known as *Torrent* but then more simply as 'Appendix Y' of the *Overlord* plan.[7] This assumed the Germans would know an invasion was going to occur in 1944, and that they would be able to predict many of the details of *Overlord* in advance. They knew for example that for the invasion to succeed the landing site would need to be within fighter range of UK bases. Knowing the limits of fighter range, they could make a reasonable estimate of which beaches were most suitable for landings. From a study of the tides and phases of the moon, the Germans would also have a fair idea when it was likely to take place.

The Germans would also know that the Allies needed to capture a deep water port fairly quickly to ensure their bridgehead was sufficiently supplied and reinforced. Therefore they had stationed strong garrisons at Cherbourg and the ports in Brittany, while putting their main strength at the Pas de Calais, the shortest Channel crossing, and the point in France closest for a drive into Germany. The weakest defences in Hitler's Atlantic Wall were along the Normandy coast near Caen because no deep water port existed there. What the Germans had not foreseen, and what became a key element in developing the deception plan, was that the Allies planned to prefabricate port facilities in Britain and float them across the Channel. Known by the codename *Mulberry*, these artificial harbours were perfectly suited to the Normandy beaches where the assault was actually aimed.

With these factors in mind, Appendix Y introduced three key themes that would form the backbone of all subsequent deception plans for *Overlord*. The first was to make the German High Command believe that the Pas de Calais was the target rather than Normandy. Secondly, the Germans were to be left doubting the actual date of the assault, with all available channels indicating that D-Day would be later than was the case. Lastly, and perhaps most importantly, once the assault went in, the deception planners were to try to pin down as many land and air forces as possible to the east of the Pas de Calais for at least a fortnight, by indicating the Normandy landings were a diversionary feint.

Appendix Y remained in draft form until the final details for *Overlord* were agreed at the Eureka Conference held from 28 November to 1 December in Tehran. At this conference Churchill and Roosevelt undertook to open a second front in Europe by launching a cross-Channel invasion of France in May 1944, with a simultaneous landing taking place in the south of France. In order that the Germans would not be able to reinforce France, the Russians pledged to match this commitment with an offensive of their own, also scheduled for May. Given the full details of the invasion, the LCS was asked to prepare a final draft of the cover plan. This was completed and submitted to the Chiefs of Staff, who approved it on Christmas Day 1943.

At Tehran, Churchill had told Stalin: 'In wartime, truth is so precious that she should always be attended by a bodyguard of lies'. With this in mind, the overall deception policy for the war against Germany in 1944 was codenamed *Bodyguard*. It encompassed every theatre of the war, and provided a framework in which a number of subsidiary plans could be developed by the relevant theatre commanders. *Bodyguard* offered a set of general themes and scenarios that would persuade the Germans to distribute their forces in a manner to cause the least interference with *Neptune*. In addition, *Bodyguard* also had to take into account the landing in the south of France, codenamed *Anvil*, and the Russian offensive. *Bodyguard* therefore formed the basis of leaks, double agent reports and physical deception policy, all of which were carefully designed to keep the Germans away from France and the Russian Front, making them focus instead on Italy, southern Germany, the Balkans, Greece and Scandinavia.

XX

The first scenario given by *Bodyguard* harked back to Plan *Jael*. It said that Britain and America were convinced that the war could be won by *Pointblank* alone. As sign of how serious they were about this, they were putting full logistical support behind the transportation of personnel and equipment from the United States to Britain, to the detriment of the build up of ground forces. In the meantime, while the Western Allies built up their strength in Britain, a plan known as *Rankin* was drawn up to exploit any weakening of German forces or withdrawal from any part of occupied Europe.

Continuing on from operations *Tindall* and *Solo*, *Bodyguard* also played on German fears about Norway. This time the threat would include a Russian attack on northern Norway in May 1944 with the objective of securing the northern supply route between the Allies. After the invasion of Norway, the Allies would put political pressure on Sweden to provide airfields for Allied bombers. They would then pressurize the Swedes into allowing them to station fighters in the south of the country, in order to support an invasion of Denmark later in the summer of 1944.

To pin down German troops in the Mediterranean, *Bodyguard* set out the following guidelines. Britain and America intended to launch an amphibious assault against the Dalmatian coast, supported by a British attack against Greece. A third assault would be made by the Russians against the coast of Bulgaria. To outflank the Germans in Italy, more amphibious landings would be made in the north of the Italian peninsula on the Adriatic and Mediterranean coasts. While this was being enacted, overtures would be made to bring Turkey into the war on the side of the Allies in order to gain airfields for the proposed operations. Olive branches would also be offered to German satellite states in order to entice them away from supporting the Nazis. Given these commitments, no cross-Channel invasion could be attempted before mid-July 1944, when the Allies would have assembled at least 50 divisions and have enough shipping available to land 12 divisions in France simultaneously. Given the strength of German coastal positions around Calais, this force was considered the minimum required for *Neptune* to succeed.

With these guidelines set, all the various theatre commanders were called upon to develop subordinate deception plans locally. By far the most important of these was codenamed *Fortitude*, which was the tactical cover plan for the Normandy landings. To understand this plan and its development up to and beyond D-Day it is first necessary to set out the various organizations that had a stake in its design and implementation.

With America the main contributor to *Overlord* in terms of men and material, General Eisenhower was selected as Supreme Commander in December 1943. Planning for the invasion now passed from COSSAC to Eisenhower's staff, Supreme Headquarters Allied Expeditionary Force, or

SHAEF. With prompting by Bevan when this change occurred, Ops.B was expanded and a new broom was brought in from A Force to take control of the section. The post was initially offered to Dudley Clarke, who turned it down and suggested instead his deputy. Noël Wild therefore arrived in England from Cairo on 24 December, having been misled into believing he was about to go on a long-awaited period of home leave. Needless to say he had a bit of a shock when he was lumbered with Ops.B, so much so that at the end of the war Bevan wrote to Wild and apologized for having landed him the job.[8]

Finding little in place to work with, Wild organized his section after the A Force model with two branches: Operations and Intelligence. The former head of Ops.B, Jervis-Read, was retained and became Wild's deputy as well as being put in charge of the Operations branch, covering the physical aspects of deception, including decoys and false radio transmissions. Meanwhile, the Intelligence, or 'Special Means', sub-section was given to the intelligence officer, Lieutenant Colonel Roger Fleetwood-Hesketh, another former student of J. C. Masterman.

With the expansion of Ops.B the LCS began to take a back seat in the development of the strategic cover plan for *Neptune*. Having provided the framework for deception in 1944, the LCS reverted to its role as a coordinating body between Noël Wild, Dudley Clarke and Peter Fleming in the Far East.[9] In fact, for much of the early part of 1944 Bevan was in the Soviet Union trying to enlist Stalin's approval for *Bodyguard* and was in no real position to take a hands-on role in the planning at all.

Noël Wild began working on the *Neptune* cover plan, *Fortitude*. His goal was to deceive the Germans over the 'strength, objective and timing' of the operation once it became obvious that a landing was going to be attempted in 1944. *Fortitude* was itself split into two various scenarios termed 'South' and 'North'. The key to the plan was the southern part. *Fortitude South* suggested an invasion date forty-five days later than was actually the case (D+45) and gave the location as the Pas de Calais. According to the plan, the assault would be carried out by 50 divisions, with enough craft available for shipping 12 divisions simultaneously. The plan was that two divisions would land east of Cap Gris Nez and four to the south of that point, and that these would be reinforced by a further six divisions immediately. Their build up would continue with three divisions a day until all 50 were across. The first phase of the operation would be to secure a bridgehead and to capture the Belgium port of Antwerp. The Allies would then thrust towards the Ruhr, deep into the industrial heartland of Germany.

To keep as many German forces as possible in Scandinavia at the time of *Neptune*, and to reinforce the D+45 timing of *Fortitude South*, Ops.B drew up *Fortitude North*. This plan to liberate Norway relied on a complicated timetable, all of which should have spelled out to an astute German intelligence officer that *Neptune* was scheduled for mid-July. The plan supposed that the liberation of Norway would take at least three months. Given that the climate in Norway prevented an invasion before April in the south and May in the north, if the Allies were intending to finish the conquest of Norway before *Neptune* was launched, then D-Day could not occur until some time in July at the very earliest.

This date was further reinforced by the timing of the Russian summer offensive. The Western Allies let it be known that they would not launch *Neptune* until six weeks after the Russians attacked and drew off German reserves to the east. Again the climate put certain restrictions on operations: the Soviets could not attack in the south until the beginning of May, and the fighting would not develop in the northern sector until the end

OPERATION *BODYGUARD* – THE COVER PLANS FOR NORMANDY

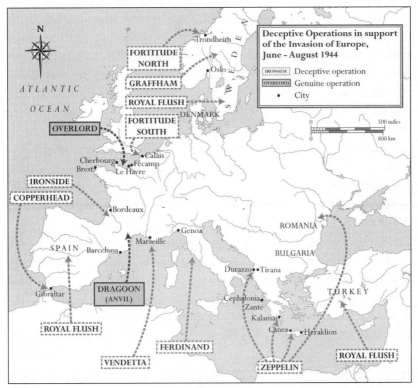

of that month. Again, an astute German might have calculated that *Neptune* was being scheduled for mid-July.

These calculations formed the core of *Fortitude North*. According to the Allied timetable, the invasion of Norway would be launched at *Neptune* D–30 (30 days before D-Day) with an operation against Stavanger. At D–17 a second operation would be launched in the north of Norway in conjunction with Russian forces, with the aim of opening communication with Sweden.

Responsibility for implementing *Fortitude North* was given by SHAEF to Commander-in-Chief Scottish Command, General Sir Andrew Thorne. A former military attaché in Berlin, Thorne was known to the Germans as an experienced general who might be expected to receive an important command. In charge of a partly notional British Fourth Army, Thorne in turn appointed Colonel Rory MacLeod to implement the deception plan. Due to the distance between Norway and Scotland and the lack of German reconnaissance, it was not felt necessary to carry out a major visual deception plan, but instead to rely on bogus signals traffic to suggest the presence of the British Fourth Army. This army was to be portrayed as being in training for an amphibious assault. In reality it was largely fictional and in great part a product of the forces depicted during the *Tindall* operation in 1943. With its headquarters based at Edinburgh, the Fourth Army had elements across Scotland and far away as Northern Ireland and Iceland. To simulate this, a radio deception plan codenamed *Skye* was drawn up. On 22 March Fourth Army HQ went live, followed by the rest of the army two days later.

The messages simulated training programmes, troop movements, the requesting of supplies and equipment, in fact all the noise associated with a busy army preparing for combat. At its peak Fourth Army consisted of only several hundred men, frantically driving round different parts of Scotland with their signals equipment. The men were told that they were engaged in vital deception work and that a single slip might spell disaster. To explain their erratic movements to a suspicious public, they were ambiguously designated No. 12 Reserve Unit. MacLeod complained that at most they had enough to simulate a single corps, but with typical ingenuity manpower problems were solved. One of the means used was to record the signals produced by a real corps on manoeuvres in the south. These signals were then broadcast by being played back on gramophone players.

To complement *Fortitude North* the LCS devised Plan *Graffham*. This was a series of diplomatic deceptions designed to fulfil the part of *Bodyguard* by suggesting that the Allies were trying to bring Sweden into the war. The British minister in Stockholm, Sir Victor Mallet, was briefed about *Graffham* on a trip to London in March. When he returned to Sweden he began trying to get concessions for the use of Swedish airfields for Allied reconnaissance aircraft. He also requested that the Swedish Army should be in a position to seize the Norwegian port of Trondheim if the Allies attacked. According to Dennis Wheatley, Mallet arranged a meeting between the former British air attaché to Sweden, Wing Commander Thornton, and Lieutenant General Bengt Nordenskiöld from the pro-Allied Swedish Air Force.[10] Using the utmost secrecy to make the mission seem important, Thornton explained that if the Allies invaded Norway there would be reprisals on the civilian population. The Allies could not hope to occupy the whole of Norway before the dissidents were murdered, and therefore wondered if the Swedes would enter the country in a peacekeeping role. As Thornton and Nordenskiöld discussed the idea, their conversation was being secretly recorded by the pro-German chief of police. He forwarded a transcript of the conversation to Berlin, where Hitler went into a rage and ordered more troops to Norway.

A measure of the success of *Fortitude North* and *Graffham* is that before they began there were 17 divisions in Scandinavia. These forces were put on full alert at the beginning of May and reinforced by another combat division. In all something like a quarter of a million men were of no use to the Germans at a critical moment of the war.[11]

XX

While *Fortitude North* was being implemented, the southern part of *Fortitude* was also delivered. General Montgomery had been placed in command of the land forces committed to *Neptune* and was therefore responsible for implementing *Fortitude South*.[12] Remembering the success he had enjoyed at El Alamein, Montgomery chose to bring another A Force veteran over from the Mediterranean to run his deception section, which became known as G(D). Colonel David Strangeways had been in Italy since Salerno performing tactical deceptions for General Alexander with Tactical HQ A Force. With direct access to Montgomery and his Chief of Staff General de Guingand, Strangeways developed a reputation for ruffling feathers. Although a relative latecomer to the D-Day deception plan, more than any other person, Strangeways was the real brain behind the cover plan as it was implemented.

Considering Wild's *Fortitude* plan to be in many ways defective, on 25 January 1944 Strangeways began interfering with the planning at an official level. De Guingand wrote a letter to SHAEF with an important amendment to the plan being discussed. Although many, including Dudley

Clarke, believed it was pointless making contingencies for deception after *Neptune*, G(D) disagreed. For them the key was to slow down the arrival of enemy reinforcements to the bridgehead after the invasion took place, in particular the German Fifteenth Army, stationed north of the Seine guarding the Pas de Calais. Wingate emphasized this point, writing in his memoirs: 'At all costs, therefore, the German Fifteenth Army must be kept to the Pas de Calais.'

To achieve this, de Guingand proposed that the Pas de Calais should be represented as the real target after the landings had begun in Normandy. This was a subtle shift in policy, but it was hoped German troops could be pinned down north of the Seine if they believed another attack was coming after Normandy. This amendment was accepted and the plan for *Fortitude* was finally agreed on 23 February 1944.

In this plan *Fortitude South* was presented in two phases. Story A was for the pre-assault phase. This played directly into what the Germans believed might happen. A directive issued by Hitler on 3 November 1943 predicted a cross-Channel assault at the latest by the spring of 1944. Although diversionary attacks were expected, including a large-scale attack against Denmark, Hitler maintained that the main assault would come against the Pas de Calais. This reasoning was based partly on the fact that this would be the shortest crossing point and would allow the best fighter cover, but also on the knowledge that Germany was preparing to bombard Britain with secret V-weapons, the launch sites of which were located at the nearest point to London – in the Pas de Calais. Once the V-weapon attacks began the Allies' first objective would be to overrun the launch sites. Knowing this, *Fortitude* said that an assault would be carried out on the Pas de Calais with 50 divisions at *Neptune* D+45, as discussed earlier.

In the post-assault phase, Story B would follow de Guingand's amendment. The Germans would be told that the Normandy invasion was only a feint designed to draw German reserves away from the Pas de Calais where the main attack was still aimed. When the Germans committed their reserves to Normandy, the main Allied attack would fall somewhere between Ostend and the Somme.

Quite how this deception would actually be pulled off was quite another thing. In much the same way that *Bodyguard* was an overall strategic plan, the *Fortitude* plan of 23 February was only an outline to guide the theatre commander's deception staff. Three days after it was agreed, SHAEF issued what became known as 'the *Fortitude* Directive', which called on the Joint Commanders to implement the deception plan.

The infamous Madrid police photographs of Lieutenant Colonel (later Brigadier) Dudley Clarke, head of A Force. Clarke was arrested in female attire trying to set up a deception channel to the Germans. He was then allowed to change after being photographed. These are the actual pictures sent to Churchill by the British naval attaché in Madrid. (Churchill Archives)

Fitting 'Sunshield' decoy device to disguise M3 US tank as a truck. The 'Sunshield' principle is attributed to General Archibald Wavell. (MH20767, Imperial War Museum)

Fabrication of decoy Crusader tank, showing (1) spray-painting tracks with stencil; (2) painting the turret; (3) the production line; (4) the finished article. (MH20752, 20754, 20755, 20739, Imperial War Museum)

'Trackmaker' device for simulating tank tracks in the desert. (MH20772, Imperial War Museum)

From the A Force war diary: dummy Mosquito light bombers at El Adem in Libya, 1945. (National Archives)

An assembly of dummy landing craft. These decoys were used to disguise real embarkation points and to confuse the Axis over Allied intentions. (National Archives)

'Wetbobs' and a larger 'Bigbob' – dummy landing craft for infantry and tanks respectively. From A Force war diary. (National Archives)

Dummy ships used in *Fortitude* – the deception plan for the Normandy landings. (H42527, Imperial War Museum)

A series of decoys prepared for D-Day. Large parks of these vehicles were used to suggest that the Allies' main force was actually in the south east of England, poised to strike against the Pas de Calais. (H42529, 42530, 42531, Imperial War Museum)

Operation *Mincemeat*: the canister containing 'Major Martin' was airtight and filled with dry ice to preserve the body. The crew of the *Seraph* were told it contained top-secret weather instruments. (National Archives)

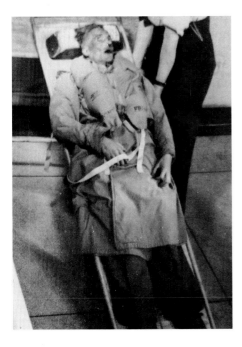

Martin's notional fiancée 'Pam'. This photograph was carried by Martin and was returned by the Spanish authorities. The real identity of this person is unknown except that she was one of the prettier girls working in the office with the planners of this ruse. (National Archives)

'Major Martin' is dressed for action at the morgue. (National Archives)

Surname MARTIN

Other Names WILLIAM

Rank (at time of issue) CAPTAIN, R.M.
(ACTING MAJOR)

Ship (at time of issue) H Q
COMBINED OPERATIONS

Place of Birth
CARDIFF

Year of Birth 1907

Issued by *C.C. Congreve*

At

Date 2nd February 1943.

**NAVAL
IDENTITY CARD No. 148228**

Signature of Bearer

W. Martin

Visible distinguishing marks

NIL.

Major Martin's ID card. The photograph actually shows *Zigzag*'s case officer Ronnie Reed, who Ewen Montagu believed bore a close resemblance to Martin. (National Archives)

Operation *Copperhead*: 'Monty's Double', actor M. E. Clifton James, then a serving lieutenant in the Royal Pay Corps, was found to bear a striking resemblance to Field Marshal Montgomery (opposite). (Getty)

Field Marshall Bernard Montgomery. (TopFoto, 2005)

When Strangeways got his hands on *Fortitude South* he made a number of amendments to how Ops.B envisaged the plan unfolding. His biggest concern was the suggestion that there were 50 divisions in the south-east of England ready to land at the Pas de Calais. These troops simply did not exist, and although some work had been done towards building up a phantom army as A Force had done in the Middle East, for Strangeways there was nothing to suggest it was convincing enough to fool the Germans.

Without the time to build up an elaborate false order of battle, his solution was ingeniously simple. SHAEF would now comprise two separate and distinct armies. The first of these was Montgomery's Twenty-First Army Group. A second army was to be formed around the bones of the First United States Army Group (FUSAG), created in London in October 1943, and given the Pas de Calais assault. Already based in the south-east, the First Canadian Army was notionally taken away from Twenty-First Army Group and assigned to FUSAG. It was joined by the Third United States Army, which was then stationed in Cheshire, but was supposedly sent to East Anglia. This move was simulated by having the real formation maintain strict radio silence, while its transmissions were replicated in East Anglia.

Under Strangeways' management, all plans relating to the Pas de Calais came under the codename *Quicksilver*. In total there were six parts to Strangeways' plan, which were titled *Quicksilver I – Quicksilver VI*. In summary these plans were:

Quicksilver I: Before D-Day it would be said that the Supreme Commander had two army groups at his disposal, Twenty-First Army Group and FUSAG, which comprised of First Canadian Army and Third United States Army. Then, after D-Day, FUSAG was to be described as ready to strike the Pas de Calais once Twenty-First Army Group had drawn German reserves across the Seine towards Normandy.

Quicksilver II: This wireless deception plan was the key ingredient of the deception. After becoming active on 24 April there were 22 decoy units simulating FUSAG's radio traffic in East Anglia and the south east.

Quicksilver III: Dummy landing craft would be erected in case German aerial reconnaissance was sent to substantiate FUSAG forces as reported by special means and by simulated wireless traffic. As a precaution against enemy spies not under MI5's control and neutral foreign observers, road signs would be put in place indicating the various embarkation points.

Quicksilver IV: This was the air plan for *Fortitude*, which called for the air forces to compensate for missions against the *Neptune* area with a similar number of attacks in the decoy area; in fact a ratio of 2:1 in favour of Pas de Calais was achieved, since the various air commands were happy to play their part as it continued to fulfil their strategic objectives of disrupting the rail networks and bridges across the Seine. Training flights were to be undertaken over the Pas de Calais to simulate familiarization flying. Air-sea rescue was to be practised, as was the large-scale movement of aircraft to Kent on D–3. Lastly the airfields in Kent were to be made to appear unready, indicating that the invasion was still some time off. After *Neptune*, air attacks on the Pas de Calais should intensify between D-Day and D+14.

Quicksilver V: An increase of activity at Dover was called for and work was to be carried out to suggest tunnelling and the erection of wireless stations.

Quicksilver VI: Colonel Turner's department was asked to install decoy night lighting from mid-May onwards to simulate decoy hards and to protect the real invasion ports. In all 65 sites were set up and a strict 'lights-out' policy enforced in the real camps.

To implement this plan Strangeways initiated R Force, a UK version of A Force. He chose the letter 'R' so that if anyone was really interested, they might deduce it stood for Reconnaissance. It consisted of three light scout car companies and their support company. Their vehicles were equipped with sonic deception devices by which they could simulate the movement of tanks and sounds of battle though huge speakers. Strangeways also took control of the various Royal Engineer Camouflage Special Field Companies still being trained at the camp at Farnham that had turned out such men as Barkas and others of North African fame. The *camoufleurs* were supplemented by Colonel Turner's department, still in the business of making decoys as it had been since the start of the war. Perhaps the most important servicemen in R Force were the radio operators. To implement *Quicksilver II*, the War Office formed 5 Wireless Group in January 1944. Equipped with recording devices, this group could simulate the radio traffic of an entire corps. Strangeways would provide officers who would write scripts for the normal day-to-day business associated with military formations and these would be recorded. The radio men would then drive about the Kent countryside transmitting the recordings for the Germans' benefit.

Not everything went to plan, however. There was terrible trouble with the dummy landing craft. If the wind became gusty, even the 160ft Bigbobs would break their mooring lines and go flying through the air. If the Germans had happened to notice this, it could have blown the whole operation. Colonel Turner's men also experienced difficulties clambering around the coastal regions, where they had to contend with landmines and inquisitive cows barging the equipment around and chewing on it.

There was also the issue of putting someone in command of FUSAG. The first choice was General Omar Bradley, but he was earmarked to take part in D-Day. As soon as his presence in Normandy was reported, the game would be up. The second choice for this appointment actually became one of the most convincing aspects of *Quicksilver*. It was leaked that General Patton was in command of FUSAG. Patton was the commander of Third Army, which made up part of FUSAG, and this formation was not scheduled to cross into Normandy until at least a month after D-Day.

At the time Patton was in a state of semi-disgrace after an incident in Sicily where he had slapped two soldiers in hospital and called them cowards, and also for the so-called Knutsford incident, where some off-the-record remarks involving Russia were reported by the press. From the German point of view, Patton was the Allies' best commander and certainly the one most likely to be chosen to lead an assault into Germany. They viewed the slapping incident with suspicion and believed it was all a hoax to cover up an important assignment, all of which reinforced *Fortitude South*. In some respects, it made perfect sense to have the more cautious Montgomery lead the Normandy assault and then adopt a defensive posture, drawing the German reserves towards him, with the flamboyant Patton poised like a coiled spring at the narrowest crossing point and on the shortest road into the heart of Germany.

Although these measures did flesh out the bones of FUSAG, the real key to its success was in security. In April a ten-mile exclusion zone was set up along the coast. Travel was permitted only for certain compassionate reasons, and then only by train. On 17 April security was further tightened by the unprecedented step of imposing censorship on foreign diplomats in London. These measures were distinctly un-British and were called into question by everyone, Churchill included. What could not be explained at the time was the need to protect the secret of *Fortitude*. The decoys, camouflage and faked radio transmissions would hopefully take care of the Luftwaffe and Y Service. But what if an observer got to the south coast? They would quickly realize that the real weight of preparations was in the

15

BY SPECIAL MEANS

SINCE THEIR FIRST MEETING IN January 1941, it had been the ambition of the Twenty Committee to use the double agents of B1a in a major deception against the Germans. Now, with Allied aerial supremacy limiting German reconnaissance flights over Britain, the most important and successful means of delivering *Fortitude* directly to German High Command was through the agents under Twenty's control. This was exactly the sort of show that had been envisaged by Masterman in early 1941, for which the double agents had been built up and made to appear plausible to their German employers. The committee was quite prepared to blow all its agents on one big show and *Overlord* fitted the bill perfectly.

The first inkling that the spies would be used in the invasion deception came in the late summer of 1943. At a meeting of the Twenty Committee's parent body – the W Board – in September 1943, Johnny Bevan was co-opted as a member. Still at the planning stages of the invasion cover plan, Bevan asked MI5 and SIS representatives if all the German agents operating in the United Kingdom were under their control. Given that no other networks had been picked up by the RSS through postal censorship or from discussions intercepted by ISOS, they concluded there was still no evidence of any other clandestine German activities.

After this meeting, towards the end of 1943, there followed a review of all the double cross cases, after which the W Board cherry-picked those it believed could be used to support *Bodyguard*. From the continual daily monitoring of ISOS intercepts, B1a were able to report that, in German eyes, the three strongest cases were *Tricycle*, *Garbo* and a relative newcomer to XX work called *Brutus*, who will be fully introduced later. In the second line were *Tate*, *Mullet*, *Mutt* and *Jeff*, and three female agents: *Gelatine*, *Bronx*, and a recent addition to the team codenamed *Treasure*. Taking that as their running order, at the W Board meeting on 21 January 1944 the members authorized the Twenty Committee to go all out on the deception plan for *Overlord*, even if it meant sacrificing all the agents.

Having made this decision, the Twenty Committee took more of a back seat in the invasion deception. It was decided that SHAEF Ops.B would be the approving authority for deception material and that a representative from that body should sit on the Twenty Committee. Since his secondment to Ops.B in April 1943 from Army Intelligence, Lieutenant Colonel Roger Fleetwood-Hesketh, working under Jervis-Read, had become the linkman between COSSAC and 'Special Means'. Through the auspices of the LCS, Hesketh had been made aware of the existence and availability of B1a's double agents. Under COSSAC, approval for 'special means' traffic had been given by a weekly sub-committee known as Twist. Chaired by Bevan, these meetings were used to allocate leakages and other 'special means' information to the best channel for it to reach the enemy. Anticipating the increased workload prior to D-Day, Bevan decided it was best to cut out the middle-man and shut down Twist in favour of direct meetings between Ops.B and B1a. To achieve this, an MI5 officer from B1a, Major Christopher Harmer, was posted to Ops.B to act as a liaison between the two organizations.

From that point on the coordination of the double agents used for D-Day happened extremely informally, with the majority of decisions made after direct conversation between Hesketh and the case officers.[1] Hesketh was based in Eisenhower's headquarters at Norfolk House, 31 St James's Square, just a short walk along King Street to MI5's headquarters at 58 St James's Street. Case officers like Tommy Harris (for *Garbo*) and Hugh Astor (for *Brutus*) would go over to Hesketh at Norfolk House and thrash out the details of messages to be sent by their particular agent. In turn, Hesketh would often visit the London Controlling Section's offices at Storey's Gate on the other side of St James's Park. There he would explain developments to Harold Peteval, who dealt with 'special means' traffic on behalf of Johnny Bevan. As the *Fortitude South* plan developed, Hesketh also had to consult with the deception officer, Colonel Strangeways, before approving anything relating to Twenty-First Army Group. Hesketh therefore had his brother Cuthbert seconded to Ops.B and used him more or less daily as a despatch rider between Norfolk House and Montgomery's Twenty-First Army Group HQ at Southwick Park near Southampton.

<h2 style="text-align:center">XX</h2>

Just as it was on the verge of making its greatest contribution to the war, there were private fears that the whole double cross system might collapse at any point. Having kept the system alive through all the scares from its inception to the spring of 1944 was a great achievement in itself.[2] Partly through the judgement of the case officers, of Masterman, Tommy Robertson, Guy Liddell, and in no small part down to German inefficiency and sheer luck, they had weathered many storms. The stakes were enormously high – perhaps too high for the system to continue. Even at this late hour, if the Germans suspected one of their agents was blown, they could have read the deception messages in reverse and deduced the Allies' real intentions. This eventuality was perceived to be so serious MI5 did consider shutting down all the agent cases except *Garbo*; and even then he too was in grave danger of being shut down by his case officer over fears about the traffic being read the wrong way.

Another problem was that the double cross system was becoming too well known. From a closed circle of acquaintances it now included operators in Canada, Iceland, Ireland, Ceylon and the Middle East. Also, because the Allies expected to find 'stay behind' agents as they advanced into Europe, it had become necessary to indoctrinate a number of front line security officers in how to handle captured agents and play them back. In preparation for the invasion, B1a had been asked to provide training for officers and set up a 'school' for XX work. Sooner or later it was feared someone would let the cat out of the bag, or, after the invasion, would be captured and interrogated.

By 1944 there were also a number of competitors to B1a's spies vying for the attention of the German intelligence service. Although the British controlled all the agents operating in the United Kingdom, several freelance operators working outside Britain were fraudulently selling secrets to the Germans on the back of having informants in Britain. In Lisbon the most successful of these bogus operators was Czech businessman called Paul Fidrmuc, codenamed *Ostro*. By the autumn of 1943 the Abwehr in Lisbon was reporting that *Ostro* had up to five sub-agents in Britain and regarded him as one of their best sources of information. He was highly paid and his messages were sent straight to Berlin for action. When *Ostro*'s reports were transmitted to the German capital they were intercepted by the British Y Service and sent to Bletchley Park for decoding. From the content of the messages the British realized that *Ostro* was not in the United Kingdom, and was making it up. However, he was inventive, and thus a threat. There was always the chance he would get lucky and guess Normandy was the Allied target.

The Security Service was at a loss as to what to do, as *Ostro* was not on its turf. Johnny Bevan suggested having *Ostro* eliminated, while Tommy Robertson was backed by the Twenty Committee when he called for him to be discredited and blown. The only other option was to gamble and try to bring *Ostro* under British control. In the event, 'C' blocked every attempt to do anything against *Ostro* in order to protect the source of their information on him. Although MI6's reluctance to endanger Bletchley Park was understandable, the Twenty

Committee's worst fears were realized on the eve of the invasion. Guy Liddell's diary for 5 June 1944 recorded that *Ostro* did indeed 'hit the target area'. Citing an officer on Montgomery's staff as the source, *Ostro* forecast that the Allies' main assault would be against the Cherbourg peninsula.[3]

The second troublesome operator was a certain Dr Krämer, an Abwehr officer posing as a German press attaché in Stockholm. Karl Heinz Krämer had been an assistant to Nikolaus Ritter in Hamburg during the days of the invasion spy offensive. He had then been sent to Sweden to report on air intelligence and appeared to be quite successful. Setting up a network of contacts in the Finnish, Hungarian and Japanese secret services, Krämer made contacts with the French military attaché's office, a well-placed Swedish businessman and an airline employee who brought information in from Britain, Lisbon and the United States. When reporting back to Berlin, Krämer codenamed all his air-related intelligence *Hektor*, while naval matters were codenamed *Josephine*.

When these two codenames began appearing on ISOS, both MI5 and MI6 feared there were two uncontrolled agents operating in the United Kingdom. *Josephine* in particular proved a worthy adversary and the Security Service was somewhat dismayed to read Krämer's prediction that the invasion would come in June. He also reported some material that obviously related to *Fortitude*, and this, coupled with a number of mistakes in his reporting, allowed MI5 to conclude that his agents were notional. In addition to his normal sources of information, it is believed that Krämer was shown German daily intelligence summaries, which made mention of *Fortitude* material being reported by B1a's agents in the United Kingdom. Krämer embellished these reports with other information picked up in Sweden and regurgitated it back to Berlin. In that sense, unlike *Ostro*, the *Josephine* and *Hektor* reports did at least have their foundation in the Allies' deception plan.[4]

The biggest fear was that something unforeseen would blow the cases before they could make the finish line. More than any other, this fear was realized and a number of the most important cases literally collapsed a matter of days before the invasion began. Experience with agents such as *Snow* and *Summer* proved that the agents could be erratic and suddenly go off track. However, few could have foreseen the major crisis sparked by the most improbable circumstance imaginable: the death of an agent's pet dog in quarantine.

Nathalie 'Lily' Sergueiev was born in Petrograd in 1912, but raised in Paris after her parents emigrated when the Bolsheviks came to power in 1917. Working as a journalist for a German newspaper, she eventually allowed herself to be recruited by the Abwehr in late 1940. Coming under the control of Major Emile Kliemann, Lily volunteered for a mission in Britain on the back of having relatives in the Bristol area. She received extensive training and in June 1943 was sent to Spain from where she sought passage to Britain. Unfortunately for the Abwehr, Lily was unable to get permission to pass through Portugal because of her Russian background. The Portuguese were apparently very wary of communist infiltration and so they denied her access to Lisbon from where she could have flown to Britain.

While in Madrid, Lily made an approach to the SIS representative at the British embassy. She explained her mission, the fact she could not get to Portugal and asked for help, in return for which she would come under Allied control. The British gave her access to Gibraltar and from there things appeared to go more smoothly. Before leaving Spain, Lily Sergueiev made one demand of the British. She knew about the strict quarantine laws for animals entering the country, but she wanted to take her pet terrier Frisson with her. This clause became a major obstacle in the smooth running of the case.

While the British officials insisted the dog would have to undergo six months' quarantine in Gibraltar, Lily fell in love with a USAAF lieutenant, Kenneth Larson. He promised to smuggle the dog to Britain for her. Reassured by Larson, Sergueiev continued with her mission and was given the codename *Treasure* by MI5. She agreed to go to Britain on the strength of Larson's promise and became enormously upset when the dog did not materialize a few weeks later. In December *Treasure* told her case officer, Mary Sherer, that because the British had broken their promise to her she felt able to do the same and would no longer work for them. When Sherer implied that *Treasure* could be forced to work for the British, the spy only dug her heels in more. Sherer explained the dog situation to Tommy Robertson, advising him that *Treasure*'s American boyfriend had let her down; she asked Robertson if they could get the Navy involved to bring the dog over quietly and avoid quarantine.

Robertson's patience must have been worn very thin by such a seemingly unimportant matter as Frisson the dog. Elsewhere that month Robertson had just learned that the cases of *Jeff* and *Summer* might have been compromised. The problem concerned suspected Abwehr officer Erich Karl, who had been taken captive but was then repatriated. Karl had been held with other Nazi German internees at Camp L on the Isle of Man. This camp was dangerously close to Camp WX which held former Camp 020 inmates. Once the two camps became aware of one another's existence, the two sets of inmates began clandestine communications by means as simple as messages tied to bricks thrown between the camps.

Learning about this breach of security, in December 1943 MI5 carried out an investigation that established that Camp WX inmates had probably explained their plight to the inmates of Camp L and that Karl might well have been one of those made privy to the secret messages. If the fate of *Jeff* and *Summer* was known, this would immediately compromise *Mutt* and *Tate*. Because of Plan *Midas*, suspicion of *Tate* would also put suspicion on *Tricycle* and his network. Faced with this dilemma, it was decided simply to ignore the problem. There was no concrete proof that Karl knew anything, and so Robertson's report on the subject to the W Board on 21 January concluded that they had probably got away with it again.[5]

With this as a background, the fate of *Treasure*'s dog might not have been B1a's first priority. However, shortly after the bust up with Mary Sherer, *Treasure* was admitted into hospital. In fairness, the agent's erratic behaviour may have been in part down to a serious kidney illness she was suffering. Soon after her outburst at Sherer, *Treasure* consented to see a doctor. Over Christmas 1943 she was told she had just six months to live unless she agreed to an operation. She refused. Robertson took time out to visit *Treasure* in hospital and tried to convince her to have the operation, which she again refused, claiming that she would not want to die on an operating table in England and be buried in damp British soil. When she broached the subject of bringing Frisson to Britain with Robertson, he simply replied: 'I'm afraid it's not possible.'[6]

Treasure recovered her strength and agreed to go to Lisbon in February to collect a radio. Posing as an employee of the Ministry of Information making propaganda films for the soon-to-be liberated territories, *Treasure* met with case officer Kliemann and received a radio disguised in a gramophone player. She returned to the United Kingdom with instructions to report on the weather and on whether troops were being assembled in the area between Bristol and Salisbury Plain. If the Allies assembled their troops in this area it would indicate they were planning to invade at Normandy. If the troops were on the Channel coast, it would indicate the Pas de Calais.

When *Treasure* returned to the United Kingdom at the end of March, she learned that her pet dog had died in quarantine. She held MI5 squarely to blame for the death of her dog and planned to get revenge. A week after beginning transmissions, on 17 May *Treasure* informed her case officer that she had been given a security code to insert in her messages if she was working under British control. She would establish contact with the Germans and then blow her case at a vital time. Robertson interrogated *Treasure* about this and concluded that she was lying and that no such code existed. However, by now his confidence in the case was at rock bottom. From that point on she ceased to have any involvement in the case and her signals were sent by a substitute.

The panic over *Treasure* came just after the collapse of one of the longest-running and most successful agent cases of the war. Throughout 1943 *Tricycle* had been making frequent visits to Lisbon where he was able to pass information relating to *Cockade* and to expand his network beyond *Balloon* and *Gelatine*. In league with his friend in the Abwehr, Johnny Jebsen, *Tricycle* came up with a ploy to recruit genuinely pro-Allied colleagues in Yugoslavia by having them recruited by Jebsen as German agents.

It was an elaborate game of double, and sometimes triple, bluff, with potential recruits very unsure of what they were getting into, and whose best interests they were actually serving. The way the system worked was this: *Tricycle*'s brother Ivo Popov (codenamed *Dreadnought* by the British) would select potential candidates in Yugoslavia who would travel to England where, he declared, *Tricycle* would take care of them. Once *Dreadnought* had gained their confidence, he would pass them on to Jebsen, who would take them to Berlin for spy training. On graduating from spy school, they would make their way through Spain and Portugal, before continuing on to Britain where they would begin their careers as German agents, albeit under MI5's control.

The first spy out was a Croat officer codenamed *Meteor*. He arrived in April 1943 and began communicating with the Germans through secret letter writing. The next to arrive was the *Worm*, who came in September after causing a security scare as he passed through Europe. The *Worm* had been seen numerous times going into the Abwehr's Paris headquarters at the Hotel Lutetia. Hearing the news, Tommy Robertson thought the *Worm* had turned and warned *Tricycle* there was a good chance his own case had been 'burned'. In typical fashion, *Tricycle* neglected Robertson's offer for him to retire from the field. In fact the *Worm* turned out not to have betrayed the network at all. The simple explanation was that the *Worm* was an irrepressible party animal who had been taking advantage of the Abwehr by running up a large expense account in their name. His frequent visits to the Hotel Lutetia were simply to have them settle his bills.

Taking the escape route idea a step further, *Tricycle* saw a way of satisfactorily explaining his frequent trips to Lisbon. Airline seats between Portugal and Britain were at a premium, so *Tricycle* needed a good excuse for his continued 'business trips'. He told the Abwehr that the British were organizing an escape route for a number of Yugoslav officers who were in Switzerland. As a Yugoslav, the British had offered *Tricycle* the chance to help out and had guaranteed him permission to travel to Lisbon as often as he pleased in order to facilitate this escape route. The Abwehr were sold on the idea because it secured *Tricycle*'s services and presented an opportunity to slip a few spies into those passing through. The first of these agents was Count Nicholas Ruda, who became the subject of mirth after becoming infested with crab lice in a Madrid brothel. Arriving in Britain in December 1943, Count Ruda was unkindly codenamed *Freak* and became the radio operator for *Tricycle*'s network.

The most interesting component of the whole *Tricycle* operation remained Jebsen, whom the British codenamed *Artist*. After *Tricycle*'s visits to Lisbon in the summer and autumn of 1943, he reported that he was certain *Artist* knew he was working for the British. By September *Artist* agreed formally to work for the British and came under SIS control when he was in Lisbon. In November 1943 *Tricycle* returned to Lisbon and stayed until January. During that stay, British representatives had a long discussion with *Artist* and concluded that he was genuinely anti-Nazi and could be trusted.

Through *Artist* the British obtained first-class information on the Abwehr. More importantly in terms of the deception plans, *Artist* was able to act as a weather vane on how *Tricycle*'s traffic was being viewed in Berlin. He confirmed that the Germans believed *Tricycle* had been under Allied control at some point. However, the material he was now delivering was considered so detailed and of such a classified nature that it was unthinkable the British were planting it on him.

Unfortunately, the *Artist* case became very troublesome for B1a. *Artist* gave the British enough information for them to have arrested *Garbo* if he was not already under their control. The fact that *Garbo*'s traffic continued after *Artist* passed this advice meant that it probably became obvious to *Artist* that *Garbo* worked for the British. This was intensely troubling, and in February 1944, case officer Tommy Harris actually recommended that *Garbo* no longer be used for deception work. If *Artist* had a sudden pang of guilt or patriotism, he could blow B1a's two most successful operators out of the water.

As D-Day approached, the vultures began circling *Artist*. As an organization the Abwehr had long been stalked by the Nazi Party's own intelligence service, the RHSA. A branch of the SS, the RHSA was probably justified in claiming the Abwehr was defeatist and incompetent. The RHSA was investigating claims that Abwehr chief Canaris had spent large sums of money getting seven Jewish families to Switzerland. It noted that the Head of Section I, Colonel Hans

Piekenbrock, had resigned in 1943 and volunteered for an active command on the Russian Front because he did not want the Nazis to win the war. His replacement Georg Hansen found the department in such a mess that the obvious conclusion was that Piekenbrock had deliberately encouraged inefficiency in his subordinates. The final straw came in February 1944 with the defection of Abwehr officer Erich Vermerhen and his wife to the British in Turkey. Hitler responded by sacking Canaris and putting the organization under the control of Himmler's SS.

Against this backdrop, *Artist* feared that he was under investigation by the Gestapo and had been tipped off never to return to Berlin. True enough, *Artist* had been carrying out some illegal currency deals on behalf of various Nazi officials in Switzerland. He had also been upsetting some of his colleagues in Lisbon by investigating *Ostro*. As the net drew in, from MI5's point of view *Artist* was now endangering the whole show. The most obvious solution was to get *Artist* out of Lisbon into protective custody. However, this was quickly ruled out. If *Artist* deserted, the Germans would expect him to reveal everything he knew about the German spies in Britain. Therefore bringing *Artist* out would certainly torpedo *Tricycle* and his sub-agents, if not *Garbo* et al.

In the end events overtook them. On 17 April *Artist* was ordered to Biarritz in France to meet with the financial administrator of the Abwehr's foreign stations. When he didn't go, he was kidnapped in his Lisbon home on 29 April. *Artist* was taken to the French resort and then on to Berlin where he was questioned. Although never completely explained, ISOS evidence suggested that the most likely cause for his abduction was the currency scams in which *Artist* had become involved. However, *Artist* was a friend of Vermerhen and the Germans must have feared that *Artist* may have been planning to follow his lead and defect. If he did defect it would blow the Yugoslav ring, which was then considered an excellent source of information at a critical time, just before the invasion. Ironically, *Artist*'s demise was probably a German move to protect *Tricycle*. Johnny Jebsen was never heard from again. It is believed that he was murdered in Oranienburg concentration camp. Importantly, there is no evidence that he betrayed his friend *Tricycle*.

However, in those crucial days of 1944 the British were not to know that *Artist* would be brave enough to hold out under interrogation. Although *Tricycle* protested that his friend would never betray him, the Twenty Committee also saw fit to take precautionary measures. Until such time as *Artist* returned, or his fate was revealed, as a precaution the *Freak* transmitter was shut down along with all *Tricycle*'s other direct sub-agents, who were found various excuses not to be able to carry on reporting.

More drastically, the British feared that *Artist* might wreck the whole deception plan. *Artist* knew that *Tricycle* and *Garbo* were under Allied control. Even if *Artist* had been arrested for a relatively minor offence, under Gestapo interrogation he might blurt out the truth and cause all the agents in the United Kingdom to come under suspicion. The Germans would then realize the Twenty Committee's worst fears by reading the deception messages backwards.

Already the Twenty Committee had started to implement Plan *Premium*, an attempt to draw German attention toward the Pas de Calais. This utilized the *Mullet*, *Puppet*, *Hamlet* set up. Before the war *Mullet*'s insurance company did a lot of business in Belgium and northern France and he was therefore privy to sensitive information on industry sites in the area. *Mullet* told *Hamlet* that his company had been asked to furnish details of these sites on behalf of the government for 'unspecified use', the inference being that it was to gain intelligence prior to the invasion.[7] As a precaution against the Germans reading messages in reverse, this plan was stopped. All mention of an attack on the Pas de Calais by 'special means' was ceased. From then on the threat to Calais would only be implied indirectly, by building up the FUSAG order of battle.

XX

The loss of *Tricycle* was offset to some degree by the growing importance of a Polish double agent called *Brutus*. His real name was Roman Czerniawski, a Polish air officer who had headed a resistance network in France before being betrayed and captured. Curiously, *Brutus* was not maltreated in prison and he allowed himself to be recruited by the Germans to come to Britain to stir up discontent among the large Free Polish contingent there. *Brutus* was allowed to escape and make his way to England in October 1942, where he gave himself up to the authorities and gave them his cover story.

Initially *Brutus* told his interrogators that he had escaped from prison unaided. He later changed this story and explained he was a German agent. In his initial interrogation *Brutus* had been questioned by members of the Free Polish Intelligence Service. Fearing this organization might have been penetrated by German spies, *Brutus* stuck to his cover story. However, once with the British, he produced a document called *The Great Game* in which he outlined how he proposed to double cross the Germans. All this appeared quite plausible. *Brutus* came across as a prima donna, but appeared to be sincere. For that reason, on 20 December he was allowed to begin radio communications with the Germans.

However, there was still a doubt about to what extent *Brutus* should be used for deception purposes. His case was discussed by the Twenty Committee on 31 December 1942, and then by the W Board on 13 January 1943. The main suspicion was *Brutus* might have been an unwitting plant by the Germans to watch how the British would play back a double agent. Throughout 1942 there had been a pervading fear that if one major double cross case was blown the Germans would re-examine all the other cases and conclude that they too were controlled. The Twenty Committee had carefully built up its network with a view to pulling off a major coup at the eventual invasion of France. As each passing month brought the promise of that goal tantalizingly closer they did not want to fall at the final fence. With these considerations in mind, *Brutus* was not considered for deception work immediately. He was given a post with Polish Intelligence and limited to reporting on the Polish armed forces in the United Kingdom. As for his primary mission, the formation of a pro-German faction among Polish soldiers, *Brutus* reported that this was extremely unlikely given the German treatment of occupied Poland.

While visiting Scotland, *Brutus* was notionally arrested by the Polish on a disciplinary charge. Before his arrest he announced to the Germans that he was going off the air and hiding his radio set. In late August he resurfaced and radioed that he was awaiting sentencing and could not be sure when he would open communications. The game continued until ISOS revealed that the Germans considered *Brutus* a reliable source of information. This admission changed MI5's perception of the Pole and it was decided to put him back on the air as quickly as possible. His trial was carried out in December 1943 and *Brutus* received a two-month sentence, which took into account the time he had already spent incarcerated. Given his liberty, *Brutus* swiftly went on to the air and announced that he had recruited a radio operator in the guise of a recently retired Polish Air Force officer who held a grudge against Russia, where most of his family had died. The radio operator was codenamed *Chopin* by the British. The Germans approved of this recruit and rewarded *Brutus* with the announcement that they were planning to send him more money and a new radio set.

In April 1944 *Brutus* announced he had been seconded to a group of Polish troops in Scotland. This posting allowed him to become one of the principal channels for *Fortitude North*. On 12 April *Brutus* reported that he had identified Fourth Army HQ at Edinburgh. Four days later he revealed that an attack on Norway was expected in May. Adding further colour to the build up, he announced the arrival of a Russian liaison team in Edinburgh, all of which fitted in with the general pattern suggested in the Ops.B plan.[8]

In addition to *Brutus*, *Mutt* and, by proxy, *Jeff* also contributed to *Fortitude North* by reporting on troop movements in Scotland. In turn these reports were bolstered by a team of double agents working in Iceland, under the unattractive codenames *Cobweb* and *Beetle*.

The *Artist* crisis meant that B1a's agents required redistributing to implement *Fortitude South*. *Tricycle* had been successful in taking a large number of documents relating to the FUSAG order of battle, but with the collapse of his network the hole needed to be filled. The next spy in line reporting on FUSAG had been *Tate*, but by 1944 B1a had very little idea if the Germans considered the Dane blown or not. The basic problem with *Tate* was that his traffic had been transferred from Paris to Hamburg. Unlike the other double agents whose controllers were based in Lisbon, Madrid, Paris and so on, *Tate*'s controllers were able to communicate directly with Berlin through landlines without the need for wireless transmissions. The absence of radio traffic meant that there was no opportunity for Bletchley Park to obtain intercepts to provide ISOS reports. The verifiable means of monitoring *Tate* was if information he imparted worked its way into the daily intelligence summaries. Although the same handicap was true for *Brutus* and *Treasure*, from the evidence on offer, *Tate* did not appear to be having any effect, even though he was to send his thousandth message by the end of May.

Tate had been portrayed as working for a farmer in Hertfordshire. So that he could report on FUSAG, *Tate* reported being transferred to a farm at Wye near Ashford. The farmer there was a friend of the farmer *Tate* worked for, but he was also an officer in the Home Guard and his military duties were taking up all his time. *Tate*'s employer loaned *Tate* to help out and the spy reported moving into the area on 1 June.[9] Once in position – albeit notionally – *Tate* reported making friends with a railway clerk from Ashford. From this man, *Tate* managed to get his hands on the rail timetable for moving FUSAG from its concentration areas to the embarkation ports. Unfortunately, although *Tate* was feeding all the right pieces of information, the Germans did not seem to be taking the bait. Whether this was because *Tate* was not trusted, or because the Germans had not the wit to draw the conclusions the Twenty Committee expected them to, was uncertain.

Somewhat unexpectedly for the Twenty Committee, it appeared that *Brutus* was, above all others after *Garbo*, the agent most trusted by the Germans. Therefore on 18 May, *Brutus* announced that he was being posted to FUSAG on the 27th of the month. His excuse was that he had been appointed to a small section of Polish officers who would form recruitment parties for Polish workers in German-occupied territories liberated by the Allies. As part of his mission, *Brutus* claimed he had to travel round all the various units about to go into Europe and explain what to do with liberated Poles. From the German point of view, the only downside to the posting was that *Brutus* would be based at Staines, away from the main FUSAG HQ and also away from *Chopin,* who had set up their transmitter in Richmond. This meant that although *Brutus* was on the staff of FUSAG he could not be expected to be privy to everything going on in headquarters.

By the end of May *Brutus* was able to deliver *Fortitude* to the Germans on a plate. Where *Tate* had spelled out the plan with hints and small observations, *Brutus* set his intelligence out in plain terms. On 31 May *Brutus* reported Patton had taken command of FUSAG, not Bradley, as had been first supposed. He also set out the order of battle for FUSAG as he had found it in his travels through Kent and East Anglia. It showed that Patton's HQ was in Wentworth and that, like Montgomery, he was in command of two armies. These were the First Canadian Army, with four infantry and one armoured division, and the Third United States Army, with three armoured divisions and another corps in the process of being formed at Chelmsford.

Brutus finished sending his order of battle report on 4 June and was immediately asked to find out the composition of Montgomery's Twenty-First Army Group. Of course, *Brutus* could only report that he knew very little and was not in a position to find out much. It was a similar story with almost all the double agents. The Germans were desperate to know what was going on in the south west of England, but frustratingly enough, all they ever heard about was the build ups in Kent, East Anglia and Scotland.[10]

XX

The real star of D-Day from the point of view of 'special means' was without doubt the *Garbo* network. By the beginning of 1944 the *Garbo* fictional network had grown in number and complexity, making it the top espionage ring the Germans had.

To recapitulate, *Garbo* had recruited a series of personal contacts, which he classified with the codenames J1–J5. These included J1, the Courier, whom the Germans called Smith but *Garbo* never actually named. An employee of BOAC or KLM, in addition to acting as *Garbo's* courier, Smith had a few other profitable scams on the side. At one point *Garbo* complained that the Courier had guessed he was a spy and was trying to blackmail him. Curiously, the Germans instructed *Garbo* to pay Smith what he wanted, as from the point when he accepted *Garbo*'s money, he would be in the agent's power for evermore. Agent J2 was a talkative RAF officer working for Fighter Command prone to giving away secrets; J3 was *Garbo*'s boss at the Ministry of Information; J4 was a left-wing fanatic working for Censorship; and J5 was a slightly misguided secretary at the War Office who had fallen in love with *Garbo*.

In addition to the early recruits *Garbo* was now served by the fictional *Dagobert* network. This centred on *Stanley*, a rampant Welsh Nationalist who belonged to the improbably titled group 'Brothers in the Aryan World Order'. When *Garbo* first told the Germans he had made contact with an important Welsh Nationalist, they urged him to take extreme caution. They actually believed that *Garbo* had stumbled upon *Snow*'s colleague *GW*. Before agreeing to the new recruit they asked *Garbo* for a physical description of the man, his occupation and his first name. If the man had been *GW* the Germans would have expected the description of a tall, powerfully built ex-policeman with the unusual forename of Gwilym. Instead they were told that *Stanley* was the complete opposite and was a former merchant seaman.

The initial reason for recruiting *Stanley* was that he offered *Garbo* the chance to smuggle letters to the Continent if the radio operator was lost, or if the air link to Lisbon broke down. The secondary consideration was equally important. *Stanley* had seven colleagues in the Aryan group, all of whom could be used as informants and spies. The Germans agreed and codenamed the group *Dagobert*. In addition to a mixed bag of Welsh Nationalists, the *Dagobert* group contained an Indian poet known as *Rags* and his lover, Theresa Jardine, the group's secretary and a serving Wren (member of the Women's Royal Naval Service).

Other than the *Dagobert* agents, *Garbo* was still well served by Agent 1, Carvalho the Portuguese commercial traveller, who was based in south Wales. When Agent 2 (Gerbers) had died, his widow had stayed in touch with *Garbo* and he had taken her under his wing, using her as a housekeeper. She later helped with enciphering messages and as a 'cut out' between some of the agents. Agent 3, Pedro the Venezuelan in Glasgow, had come to be seen as his deputy. Pedro ran the *Benedict* network, an odd group comprising of an RAF NCO (Agent 3(1)), a lieutenant in the 49th Infantry Division (Agent 3(2)) and a Greek communist (Agent 3(3)) who believed that *Garbo* was working for the Russians. Working for Fred the Gibraltarian was another group of sub-agents, including Agent 4(1), the network's radio operator. Fred also recruited a guard at a military depot hidden in the Chislehurst Caves (Agent 4(2)), along with Agent 4(3), the son of a senior American officer on Eisenhower's staff working in the US supply service. Agent 5 was the brother of Pedro, and had relocated to Canada where he picked up an American sub-agent codenamed *Moonbeam*. Agent 6 was *Dick*, a British-hating South African employed at the War Office, but who was tragically killed in an air crash in North Africa in July 1943. By any standard, *Garbo*'s network was impressive, reaching right round the country and taking in a number of important civil and military organizations (see Appendix B).

Alas for the Germans, it was all false. None of the above persons ever existed, except J3, the unnamed senior official in the Spanish section of the Ministry of Information who gave *Garbo* part-time work. J3 was actually based on W. B. McCann, the real head of the Spanish section. McCann was informed about his alter ego and had some idea of the *Garbo* case, but the rest was a hoax. Nor were there secret depots in the Chislehurst Caves. Even the 49th Division was completely fictitious.

In addition to the size of the network, it is also important to emphasize how personally involved *Garbo* was in the creation of material passed over to the Germans. In other cases the agents had little choice in what was being said, but *Garbo* was different. The precautions of the early days had fallen by the wayside. The MI5 officers who dealt with him no longer used aliases as they had done in the early days, and *Garbo* went by the name Juan García, using his mother's surname. The Spaniard was a frequent visitor to Tommy Harris's home and was well acquainted with his wife, Hilda. As their workload increased before D-Day, *Garbo* was given an office in Jermyn Street, just round the corner from MI5's home in St James's Street. There he had a secure telephone link to MI5 and SHAEF headquarters at Norfolk House and would spend the day writing cover letters that would then have messages written between the lines in secret ink. Although *Garbo* never visited MI5's offices and was never told about the existence of B1a or the Twenty Committee, he had a fairly good idea of how his messages were vetted by the service departments concerned. Quite often Harris would telephone Hesketh for last-minute corrections to messages with *Garbo* present. *Garbo* was given an accurate description of the cover plan for D-Day and was aware which military formations were real and which were bogus. He was also told the intended date of the landing several weeks in advance.

Between January and D-Day, over 500 wireless messages were sent by the network, at a rate of four per day. When they were received, Madrid would immediately forward them to Berlin where they would be distributed to the relevant intelligence section. Although no one in London knew it at the time, a high proportion of the messages was then sent to von Rundstedt, who would also see them repeated as part of the daily intelligence summary reports and the fortnightly intelligence bulletins on Allied intentions.

On 5 January 1944, the Germans asked *Garbo* to discover the dates of any attacks being planned on northern France, the French Atlantic coast, the Mediterranean or in the Adriatic. They also instructed him to make studies of all the various embarkation points in Britain and to count the number of landing craft, along with the number of warships available to protect operations. More questions followed, and on 14 January the Germans revealed their hand when they asked *Garbo* to explore the south west of England and southern coast between Weymouth and Southampton. If the Allied invasion was to come at Normandy, the Germans knew these would be the areas used for concentrating and embarking the Allied forces. If, however, this area appeared clear and the troops were gathering in the south east and east, then it would be the Pas de Calais.

Herein lay the foundation of the double cross system's success and all its worth. If the Germans had possessed genuine spies in the United Kingdom, it is unlikely that they would have missed the vast build up of men and material in the areas now called into scrutiny. Equally, if all the German spies had simply been captured and shot previously, because the Allied air supremacy was so strong the Germans would have been forced to infiltrate new spies into the British Isles to find out what was going on. However, because the Germans believed they had a well-established and trustworthy espionage network in the United Kingdom, they did not feel it necessary to go to the time and trouble of recruiting and training a new set of agents. So when *Garbo* received this request he simply moved his imaginary pawns around to suit German requirements.

Of course, he had no intention of revealing the truth. In the same way that Gerbers had been sacrificed to protect *Torch*, Agent 1 had to be got rid of before D-Day. Based in Newport, south Wales, Carvalho spent much of his time in the south west, which was too close to the genuine build up area for Twenty-First Army Group. The excuse given for his departure was that a letter was intercepted by censorship during Plan *Starkey* and a number of arrests had followed. Although Carvalho had remained free, his nerves began to fail him and he offered his resignation. Investigation of the south and west was therefore entrusted to two members of the *Dagobert* network, agents 7(5) and 7(6).

Unfortunately for the Germans Agent 7(5) turned out to be a big let down. He was an unenthusiastic spy and nervous at the best of times. On 17 May he reported that he was at Exeter, inside the prohibited zone along the coast.

Although he had so far wangled his way round the security checks, he informed his chief that he saw no possibility in remaining there for very long without discovery. Sure enough, on 2 June Agent 7(5) was apparently arrested for being in Exeter without the correct documentation. He was sentenced to a month in jail – a month that conveniently left *Garbo*'s network blind in a crucial reporting area. He had even less success with the next nearest placed, Agent 7(6). In April *Garbo* told the Germans that the reports from 7(6) were 'stupid' and concluded he could not be trusted on military matters.

16

VINDICATION

WITH D-DAY APPROACHING, TENSION in the Allied camp grew, as the operational planners wondered if tactical surprise would be achieved, and if the assault troops would be able to secure a foothold. By the end of May there were worrying reports that the Germans were looking more and more at Normandy as the site of the coming invasion. Through 'Most Secret Source' British Intelligence intercepted the details of a conversation between Hitler and the Japanese ambassador to Berlin. In it the latter reported to his superiors in Tokyo that Hitler believed there would be a succession of diversionary operations against Norway, Denmark, France's southern Atlantic and Mediterranean coastlines. The Allies would also seek to establish a bridgehead in Normandy and Brittany before commencing the main attack across the Straits of Dover against the nearest part of the French coast.

This appreciation was both good and bad news for the deception planners. On the one hand it showed that Hitler had swallowed much of the *Bodyguard* plan and accepted that the Allies had enough troops in England to mount several large operations. On the downside was his belief that the launching of the main invasion against the Pas de Calais would depend on the success of the Normandy landings. This suggested that the Germans would go all out to defeat the first landing with a view to deterring the second.

This view was supported by the news that several German divisions were being transferred south of the Seine, where they would be able quickly to strike at the Allied beachhead. The most worrying of these movements involved 21st Panzer Division, which was confirmed as being at Caen on 21 May. At the same time there was news of considerable reinforcements being moved into the Cotentin peninsula to protect Cherbourg.[1]

These deployments were a grave cause of concern to Montgomery's staff and a suggestion was made by Twenty-First Army Group to implement some 'hot deception' to move the Germans away from Normandy. This suggestion was rejected by Tommy Robertson, who explained to his superior, Guy Liddell, that changing course at such a late stage would be counter-productive. In order to bring about the movement of German troops it would mean having the spies tell such an enormous falsehood that it would blow them for good. Although Twenty-First Army Group's request was understandable, Robertson believed that *Garbo* should be preserved for after the invasion. It was clear that Hitler believed there were still enough Allied reserves to launch a second operation. He would, therefore, be obliged to hold back considerable reserves north of the Seine, and it would be *Garbo's* job to keep them there.[2]

From the point of view of deception, everything in those last few days had to be done to maintain the credibility of *Garbo*. As the date of the invasion crept closer, *Garbo* insisted that one of his agents should give advance warning of the invasion, even if, as had been the case with *Torch*, the warning arrived too late to be of operational use to the Germans. This advance warning would reinforce the Germans' trust in him and put him in a good position to put over the FUSAG deception. The matter was put before Eisenhower, who agreed, saying that the message could be sent 3½ hours before H-Hour, which was set for 6.30am.

This put *Garbo* and Harris in a quandary. Their contact in Madrid shut down at 11.30pm each night and did not come back on the air until 7am the following day. A way needed to be found to keep the Germans on the air without causing any suspicion. The agreed scenario was an important development in the *Fortitude North* saga. As D-Day approached, *Garbo* reported that Agent 3(3) was due to arrive from Glasgow with important news about the build up of troops on the Clyde. When the agent arrived there was no real news, only that the agent believed that something was about to happen. A furious *Garbo* gave the agent a dressing-down and sent him back to Glasgow to watch the ships. If the troops there began embarking, 3(3) was to telephone *Garbo* with a prearranged codeword. On the evening of 5 June, *Garbo* reported to Madrid that he was anticipating a call from Glasgow some time during the night and therefore asked Madrid to be listening at the agreed emergency time of 3am.

In the early evening of 5 June, all over England soldiers, sailors and airmen were sitting anxiously waiting for the battle to begin. Likewise, in London a small gathering collected for dinner at Tommy Harris's house before setting off to do battle in a very different way. After the meal and a bottle of good wine, Harris, *Garbo*, Robertson and Hesketh were driven up to Hendon to the old safe house at 35 Crespigny Road. Waiting for them there was the wireless transmitter set and Sergeant Charles Haines, who posed as *Garbo's* radio operator. According to the Hesketh report, the 'Special Means officer' from SHAEF was also there.[3] One can only speculate, but as Robertson drove up to witness the event, there may well have been a moment of reflection back to early 1941 when Masterman had presented his memo on the double cross system, outlining the plan to build a credible network of double agents who would all be willingly blown to pull off some great deception at a critical time.

At 3am on 6 June, already several hours after Allied parachutists had begun landing in Normandy, but still well before the German coastal troops had glimpsed their first sight of the vast invasion armada heading towards them, Haines tapped out the message in Morse.

Typically of *Garbo*, he did not state outright that the invasion had begun. The gist of the story went something like this: while waiting for news from Agent 3(3), *Garbo* had been contacted by Agent 4, Fred the Gibraltarian waiter. Fred worked at one of the armed forces' NAAFI clubs. In April he had been posted to Hiltingbury camp in Hampshire. This was one of the troop concentration areas for the troops earmarked for *Neptune*, and Fred had watched with interest as cold rations and vomit bags had been issued to the 3rd Canadian Division three days before. He then learned that this division had embarked and he joined two American deserters who were running away from the embarkation points, broke camp and made his way to London clandestinely. From this message it was hoped the Germans would understand the inference of what 'the 3rd Canadian Division has embarked' meant.

Haines tapped out the message and waited for the response from Madrid. Everyone sat around expectantly, but nothing happened. Fifteen minutes later Haines typed out the message again; and again, and again. To everyone's disappointment Madrid did not come on the air until 8am. It had turned out to be an awful anticlimax.

XX

While the *Garbo* team were still preparing to contact Madrid, shortly after midnight on 6 June Allied paratroopers went into action in Normandy. Among the thousands of parachutes that opened and fell to earth that night were 450 inflatable dummies. Operation *Titanic* was developed by the SAS as a deception plan to cover the airborne landings. Large numbers of dummy parachutists would be dropped to spread confusion and alarm among the German defenders. The parachutists were nothing more than an inflatable cloth bag that gave the silhouette of a real parachutist. When the dummies hit the ground they activated fireworks, simulating anything from rifle or machine-gun fire to exploding grenades.

Alongside the dummies were eight SAS troops principally armed, improbable as it might seem, with battery-powered gramophone players and flare-firing Very pistols. Their mission was to attract the attention of German soldiers by playing recordings of soldiers' voices and small-arms fire. Then, once they had attracted attention, they were told to head for the safety of the Allied beachheads, causing as much chaos as possible on the way.

Four *Titanic* missions had been planned for D-Day. The first simulated the landing of an airborne division north of the Seine, 30 miles from Dieppe. The second mission was intended for the east of Caen, but was cancelled because the skies were too congested. *Titanic III* and *IV* were successful and landings were simulated south west of Caen and towards St Lo respectively, to cover the real airborne landings nearby.

Given the confusion of night, it is difficult to assess the success of *Titanic*. It is reasonably sure that the commandant of Le Havre was spooked by the mission and at 3am sent a message to Berlin that he had been cut off from Rouen and did not know what to do. The SAS team belonging to *Titanic IV* landed to the south of the Cherbourg peninsula, near to Marigny. By chance the local commander had just finished an anti-parachutist exercise and was switched on to the threat of parachute landings. Hearing the commotion caused by the SAS troops, the German officer ordered a brigade into the local woods to flush the paratroopers out before they had time to organize. Thus another German unit was absent from the beaches on D-Day.[4]

More confusion came from broadcasts made on the Allied-controlled German service radio stations. The first news that many people in occupied Europe heard of the invasion came from the Soldatensender Calais radio station. Sefton Delmer and company had prepared for an all-out assault on the German defenders in France. During the early morning broadcast on 6 June the regular beat of dance music was interrupted with news that the invasion had begun. Fifteen minutes later a more detailed report followed partly using intercepted transmissions from Goebbels' DNB (Deutsche Nachrichtenburo) news agency. Soldatensender and its sister station Atlantiksender had been issued themes to put across to support the D-Day operation. The most important of these were that coastal divisions would be deliberately sacrificed and that there were no more reserves for the West.[5]

These themes were expanded by PWE's newspaper for German soldiers, *Nachrichten für Die Truppe*. Something like 800,000 copies of this newspaper were printed every morning and dropped from American planes on German positions at night. Like the Soldatensender, the editorial of *Nachrichten für Die Truppe* was not overtly pro-Allied and much of the information in it was straight down the middle in tone and content. As with all deceptions, this was necessary to build confidence and to allow the occasional falsehood to be slipped in and believed by its audience. A few hours after the invasion began, the newspaper's headline proclaimed that in addition to combat with Allied parachutists and commandos, the Atlantic Wall had been breached in several places and Allied armour had penetrated deep into the interior of France. It reinforced the concept that there were no reserves on the way and troops were dying in vain.

XX

Brutus's immediate response to D-Day was to register his surprise. None of the troops in FUSAG had taken part in it, which was interesting because he believed FUSAG was ready for an attack, but thought it would be independent of Montgomery's operation. Through *Fortitude* the German response had been programmed to believe that there might be several Allied attacks before the main event took place. On the evening of 6 June German Military Intelligence in the West concurred with this view, reasoning that FUSAG had not been employed in the attack, and that there were more troops in Scotland yet to be committed to the action.

Garbo's first action on D-Day was to complain that Madrid had not been on the air as requested. On the following morning he continued his complaint with a strong message of protest:

> I am very disappointed as, in this struggle for life and death, I cannot accept excuses or negligence. I cannot masticate the idea of endangering the service without any benefit. Were it not for my ideals I would abandon the work as having proved myself a failure. I write these messages to send this very night though my tiredness and exhaustion due to excessive work which has completely broken me ...'[6]

Naturally enough, the Germans tried to soothe and placate *Garbo* by telling him that his work in the weeks leading up to the invasion had meant they were not taken by surprise, which of course was a pack of nonsense. Surprise had been achieved, although this was more due to the bad weather than to any deception.

The tiff put to one side, the Spaniard reported going back to work at the Ministry of Information and finding the place in a state of excited chaos. There was much interest in how news of the invasion was commented on by the Allied leadership. Of most interest to *Garbo* was a secret PWE guideline about reporting on the invasion. It declared that the Normandy operation was part of an ongoing attack on 'Fortress Europe' and that the press should avoid all speculation on future operations, the inference being that future attacks were planned.

Although they accepted the warnings meant that more attacks were to come, the Germans were surprisingly quick in releasing their armoured reserves to Normandy. On 3 June SHAEF had made a projection of the German response to *Neptune* and how fast they could expect reserve formations to arrive. It forecast that between D+1 and D+7 the German Fifteenth Army would detach three Panzer divisions from north of the Seine. These would be the 1st SS Panzer, 2nd Panzer, and 116th Panzer. In addition Fifteenth Army might detach three infantry divisions, the 84th, 85th and 331st, all of which were expected to arrive in Normandy by the end of the first week with somewhere in the region of 30,000 men. To the south and west of France it was predicted that 2nd SS Panzer and 11th Panzer Division would also be sent to Normandy within seven days.[7]

Once the invasion took place von Rundstedt requested the immediate release of all available armoured reserves. The 1st SS Panzer Corps, comprising 12th SS Panzer, 17th SS Panzer Grenadier Division and the Panzer Lehr Division, was released, as were two Panzer divisions under Field Marshal Rommel's direct control: 2nd Panzer and 21st Panzer. On 8 June, when it was clear how strong the Allied bridgehead was becoming, the remainder of the armoured reserve was released at 10.30pm. This included the entire 1st SS Panzer Division and one regiment of the refitting 116th Panzer Division. In addition to this release, von Rundstedt was allowed to select two infantry divisions from Fifteeenth Army to redeploy in Normandy.

Now came the major test for which the double agents had been built up. With almost all the available German armoured divisions in northern France heading for Normandy, could any of them be stopped their word alone?

Approaching D-Day, the feeling of the Twenty Committee was that if even a single German division could be held up for 48 hours then all the effort they put in would be worth it.[8] Eisenhower was more blunt in his expectations. After Noël Wild took over Ops.B Eisenhower told him: 'Just keep Fifteenth Army out of my hair for two days. That's all I ask. That will give us time to establish ourselves firmly in the bridgehead.'[9]

Before D-Day, Eisenhower had been consulted about when the message should be sent confirming that Normandy was only a feint for the Pas de Calais. Eager to have all the assistance he could as close to D-Day as possible, the Allied Supreme Commander authorized them to send this message as soon after *Neptune* as they saw fit. However, Tommy Harris argued that they should wait two days before sending the message. The reason for this was that if the Germans could be tricked into recalling troops they had already ordered to Normandy, they would be unlikely to change their minds again. This supposition proved entirely correct.

On the evening of 8 June *Garbo* signalled Madrid with important news. He confirmed that the British 3rd Infantry Division was already in Normandy and that the British Guards Armoured Division was also about to come over the following day. This message was designed to increase *Garbo*'s standing and confirm him as an excellent source in preparation for the main punch. The infantry division was easily verifiable by Army Intelligence units at the front, and the Guards Division was considered something of an elite unit by the Germans. Actually, the Guards were not due over for another week. The message originated as a piece of deception from Montgomery's HQ and was designed to make the Germans put more weight against the British sector and lighten the burden on the Americans who had come ashore at Omaha Beach. Nevertheless, news that the Guards were on their way to Normandy was considered very important by von Rundstedt, who demanded more intelligence of the same.[10]

At the end of the message *Garbo* requested that Madrid listen in again later that evening. Shortly after midnight, Sergeant Haines began sending a message that took over two hours to transmit. The length of this message should have aroused suspicion in itself. How on earth a real secret agent could stay on the air transmitting for so long in wartime conditions was unbelievable. British SOE agents operating in Europe were told to keep transmissions to less than five minutes in order not to be detected. However, this was not questioned.

Until this time it had been a matter of policy not to spell out hard and fast forecasts to the Germans. The British deceivers wanted to present the Germans with a series of facts that would allow them to make their own deductions. It is debatable if this was the right approach, as rivals *Ostro* and *Josephine* took the direct method and were considered excellent sources. For this long message, *Garbo* changed tack and gave his opinion on the invasion to the Germans. He explained that after D-Day he had summoned his agents for a secret crisis meeting. From their information he could now confirm the following facts. He listed all the military formations still in Sussex, Kent and East Anglia, as well as mentioning the landing craft on the Suffolk coast for the first time. He agreed that the landing in Normandy was a major operation, but considering the heavy aerial bombardment of the Pas de Calais, and the fact that 50 Allied divisions had not been committed to Normandy, not to mention the strategic advantages of a landing on what would be the shortest road to Berlin with the best air cover, *Garbo* concluded that Normandy was a feint intended to draw German reserves away from the main thrust. This intelligence was clearly of the highest importance. It was exactly what Hitler had been telling his generals would occur, and therefore could not be doubted.

Before being sent on to High Command, *Garbo*'s message was summarized by Madrid in the following manner:

> After personal consultation on 8th June in London with my agents [D]onny, Dick and Dorick, whose reports were sent today, I am of the opinion, in view of the strong troop concentrations in S.E. and E. England which are not taking part in the present operations, that these operations are a diversionary manoeuvre designed to draw off enemy reserves in order then to make a decisive attack in another place. In view of the continued air attacks on the concentration mentioned, which is a strategically favourable position for this, it may probably take place in the Pas de Calais area, particularly since in such an attack the proximity of the air bases will facilitate the operation by providing continued strong air support.

At 10.20pm the message reached Colonel Friedrich Krummacher, the intelligence officer who provided the link between the German Intelligence Service and High Command. Somewhat fortuitously, before *Garbo*'s message arrived Krummacher had received two other important messages that day. The first had arrived in the early afternoon and claimed that a secret activation code had been broadcast to the Resistance in Brussels signifying the imminence of an Allied landing. At the time Krummacher was not entirely convinced by this message and did not consider it worth passing up the chain to Jodl. However, later on, at 6.10pm, a second message arrived from the uncontrolled agent *Josephine* in Stockholm. This report said that it was highly likely that 'a second main attack across the Channel directed against the Pas de Calais is to be expected'.[11]

With this in mind, when *Garbo*'s message arrived, it appeared to be a confirmation of the previous two messages. Krummacher underlined the part of the message suggesting a 'diversionary manoeuvre' and added his own thoughts to the end of the message: 'confirms the view already held by us that a further attack is to be expected in another place (Belgium?)'[12] He then sent the message to Jodl, who, in the early hours of 10 June, underlined the words 'in S. E. and E. England' and took it in to show to Hitler.

Although no record survives, the Führer's interpretation of the messages cannot be called into doubt. The head of OKW, Field Marshal Wilhelm Keitel, personally telephoned von Rundstedt, who responded by issuing an alert for Belgium and northern France at 7.30am on 10 June. Most crucially, 1st SS Panzer Division was ordered to halt and was redirected from its lodgements north-east of Bruges to reinforce Fifteenth Army at the Pas de Calais. It was held there and did not move again until 17 June, by which time the Allies had established their bridgehead and any chance of German tanks driving the invasion back into the sea had passed.

It is also worth remembering that the Allied planners expected Fifteenth Army to detach three infantry divisions to Normandy in the first week. The decision to put Pas de Calais on the alert saw the cancellation of the orders for the 85th Infantry Division and the 16th Luftwaffe Regiment, which had been ordered from the Fifteenth Army to Normandy. It also affected the march of the Grossdeutschland Regiment from the 116th Panzer Division, which had earlier been ordered to Normandy. The fact that all these troops were held back to defend the Pas de Calais from a phantom invasion force is further vindication of the work carried out by the Twenty Committee and the deception planners.

Many commentators with first-hand knowledge of the battle for Normandy agree that the retention of Fifteenth Army in the Pas de Calais was a key factor in the Allied success. Eisenhower's intelligence chief, Major General Sir Kenneth Strong, wrote that the Germans' obsession with Calais was an 'unparalleled blunder ... Had they moved their divisions from the Pas de Calais to Normandy in the early days when bad weather hampered the build up and the air support, the Allied invasion would have been in great jeopardy.'[13] Referring obliquely to the *Fortitude/Quicksilver* plans, Eisenhower also commented on the late arrival of elements of Fifteenth Army across the Seine to join the battle. In his book *Crusade in Europe* the Allied Supreme Commander wrote: 'They were too late. Every additional soldier who then came into the Normandy area was merely caught up in the catastrophe of defeat, without exercising any particular influence upon the battle.'[14]

Buoyed by this success, it now became a matter of interest to see how long *Fortitude* could be kept afloat.

XX

Although early results showed the deceptions were having a tangible effect on the German response to the invasion, there was little time for self-congratulation for B1a. On 13 June two officers of the Joint Planning Staff were taking the short walk from Storey's Gate for lunch at one of the service clubs in Pall Mall. Just as they reached Waterloo Steps they heard the strange sound of a motor in the sky. The noise suddenly cut out and the two officers threw themselves face down on the ground. They had guessed that this might be one of Hitler's secret weapons, a rocket that Allied scientists believed might be capable of carrying a devastatingly large 20-ton warhead. As the two officers lay prone, two civilians passed them by nonchalantly. An instant later there was an explosion in the distance and one of the civilians said to the other: 'I suppose that's this new secret weapon we've heard so much about.'[15]

As this anecdote suggests, the Allies had been expecting this new threat since the spring of 1943, when intelligence sources informed them about a secret weapon programme at the German research base at Peenemünde. There had also been warnings that something was up through information passed through the double agents. In September 1943 *Tricycle* had been warned against living in London, after which *Garbo* began making enquiries about rumours he had heard about a new secret weapon. At first his controllers told him not to be concerned, but towards the end of the year their tone changed. In a message of 16 December they warned *Garbo* he should be prepared to leave London and stay in touch with the Ministry of Information when London was evacuated, as well as to obtain a second transmitter and an additional radio operator. Despite constant probing by his case officer, nothing more was established until May 1944 when *Garbo* was informed, indirectly, that he would be called upon to report on the fall of the weapons.

After the elation of D-Day, the sudden advent of German secret weapons raining down on the British capital had the potential to be disastrous for civilian morale. For the first time in five long years, the British public had been given something in the Normandy invasion that was near to home and tangible. Now, ten days after D-Day, on the night of 15–16 June, the strange and new V1 offensive really began in earnest. That night 217 V1 rockets were fired at Britain, with 45 hitting central London.

On 16 June *Garbo* received messages from his controllers asking for information on the location of the crash sites and exact times of impacts with similar requests made to *Brutus* and *Tate*. *Garbo* was instructed to use the Pharus map of London and to inform them of the squares in which the bombs landed and the times. The messages were to be kept as short as possible and prefixed '*Stichling*' (stickleback) so Madrid would know to forward the information directly to Arras, where the rocket command was established.

If given this information, the Germans would be able to adjust their aim and correct any shortfall. The only trouble was that there was no plausible reason why the double agents could not report this information with a high degree of accuracy. The bomb impacts would quickly become common knowledge among Londoners and most likely reported in the press, which the Germans had access to through neutral capitals. As Masterman pointed out, if St Paul's Cathedral was hit, 'it would be useless and harmful to report that the bombs had descended upon a cinema in Islington'.[16]

Garbo began his counter-offensive to the rocket threat by complaining at not being pre-warned about the attack, which had put him and his network at risk. Madrid had to explain they had not been informed about the attack either, as Berlin had decided to keep it a secret from everyone. For the next few weeks, while the British were trying to figure how to play the rocket threat, *Garbo*'s main tactic was to play for time. The first official line to reporting V1 hits was agreed on 18 June, when it was decided to adopt the same approach as during the Blitz, with the double agents not trying to influence what targets the Germans went for. Instead they would report the damage reasonably accurately and minimize the effect they were having on civilian morale. This had been all well and good in 1941, but now the Germans expected exact reports from their well-established agents. Already *Garbo*, *Brutus* and *Tate* were being pushed for specifics. Simply reporting that the rockets were having no effect and everyone in London was walking round with smiles on their face was not going to be adequate.

On 22 June *Garbo* reported several well-publicized incidents, including the terrible hit on the Guards Chapel in which 121 had been killed at prayer on Sunday 18 June. In terms of other reporting, it had been decided that *Garbo* should not give the times of the explosions and should report mostly on those rockets that fell in the north west of London, giving the impression the Germans were overshooting the target area. Also on 22 June *Garbo* wrote one of his heartfelt, long, rambling letters to his controller in Madrid, Karl Kuhlenthal. The letter was marked 'personal' and was intended as a heart-to-heart between two comrades, long into the war, used to suffering the privations and perils of the secret conflict. It was not intended for Berlin, *Garbo* wrote in his introduction, but if Kuhlenthal believed it was worth showing to the higher command, then all the better.

To précis the letter, *Garbo* concluded that the new secret weapons were a complete waste of time. Their military effect was 'nil', *Garbo* complained, and they also failed as a propaganda weapon. For the first three or four days they had an impact on the morale of the British public, but when they saw that the damage caused by the weapons was comparatively small compared to the great Blitz, they had more or less dismissed the wonder weapons and all the accompanying propaganda. *Garbo* told his controller that the Germans could broadcast about London being reduced to a smouldering ruin, but for the average Londoner this was obviously false. Now, rather than being terrorized into fleeing their capital, they even ignored the air raid sirens. *Garbo* wondered if the resources used for the development and research of such a weapon would have been better spent on conventional weapons that could have made a difference and led to victory in the field.

Until the end of the month, *Garbo* maintained his stalling tactics by pointing out that the Pharus map of London used by the Germans had been out of print in England since 1908. The only copy of this out-of-date map that he could find was in the British Library. He instructed the Germans that he was using the Stanford map, but as this did not have coordinates printed on to it, he was going back to the British Library to copy the Pharus coordinates on to the newer one. This caused no end of confusion and wasted another week. In the end the Germans asked *Garbo* to get hold of a copy of the Baedeker London map.[17]

While *Garbo* played for time the British were hard at work assessing the new threat. It was guessed that the Germans had set their target area in the heart of London, at Charing Cross station near Trafalgar Square. By studying the fall of the V1s, the British worked out that the majority of German rockets were falling two or three miles short of this and landing to the south and east of that target, with the 'mean point of impact' (MPI) given as the area around North Dulwich station. Facing up to the fact that the bombs had to land somewhere, it was suggested to try and foreshorten the Germans' aim still further, so that the flying bombs landed in less densely populated areas outside the city centre. With this in mind, a team was put together comprising of Dr R. V. Jones of Air Intelligence, along with the Twenty Committee members Charles Cholmondeley and the Home Defence Executive representative, John Drew. Their conclusion was to allow the double agents to give the correct impact coordinates for rockets that had overshot the target area and landed in north west London, but to assign them the times of impact from those rockets falling short of the MPI. By doing this the Germans would hopefully correct their aim and cause the MPI to move further south and east of the centre, where the bombs would be less disruptive to the running of the war. A meeting of the Twenty Committee on 29 June heard this proposal and agreed to back it. The proposal was then submitted to the Chiefs of Staff by W Board member Sir Findlater Stewart on 7 July. Despite 2,415 flying bombs being fired at

London in the course of June, and with no end to the bombardment in sight, the Chiefs of Staff were not sure what to do with the idea, and, frustratingly, asked Stewart to go away and come back with a more detailed plan.[18]

XX

In addition to combating the V1 menace, through the remainder of June *Garbo* and *Brutus* maintained a steady flow of information on FUSAG and American reserves arriving in Britain. FUSAG, or Army Group Patton, as the Germans called it, maintained its poise ready to strike them as soon as Fifteenth Army was weakened in favour of Normandy. From the German point of view, now the V1 offensive had begun, overrunning the rocket sites in the Pas de Calais must have been high on the Allied priorities. Although *Garbo* had been playing down the damage caused by the V1s, the uncontrolled Lisbon agent *Ostro* had been telling a different story. He told the Germans that London was a wasteland and had been largely evacuated in the face of enormous casualties.[19] Unable to make aerial reconnaissance, the Germans had preferred *Ostro*'s version of events to *Garbo*'s and thus believed the Allies would pull out all the stops to overrun the launch sites.

Moving into July *Fortitude* faced its first big hurdle. The Third United States and the First Canadian armies were about to fulfil their intended role and be shipped to Normandy as reserves. With their connections, both *Garbo* and *Brutus* should have been able to report this move and pre-warn the Germans before front line intelligence units noticed their arrival in the field. Excuses therefore had to be made for both agents to be absent at the crucial time. With *Brutus*, it was fairly easy to send him off to Scotland for a week on an assignment, but with *Garbo* it was more complicated. Not only did Ops.B want him to miss the transfer of the two armies to Normandy, the Twenty Committee wanted him to avoid answering questions on the V1 until Sir Findlater Stewart could get approval for the MPI deception.

The answer to the problem turned out to relatively simple: *Garbo* was arrested. On 30 June *Garbo* was instructed that his primary concern was troop movements and that reporting on V-weapons was only to be considered a secondary mission. Unfortunately for the Germans, since expressing his misgivings about the V-weapons, *Garbo* had now taken it upon himself to turn them into a success. He informed Madrid that the success of the bombardment required him to undertake the investigation of the bomb sites personally, as the reports of his sub-agents had been lacking in zeal.

On 4 July there was an ominous silence from the *Garbo* network's radio transmitter. The following evening Agent 3 appeared on the air and explained that *Garbo* had been missing since the previous day. He feared that *Garbo* might have been the victim of a flying bomb and reported that Gerbers's widow had been sent to *Garbo*'s wife to find out if there was any news. On 6 July Agent 3 reported that *Garbo* was still missing and even his wife was unsure of his whereabouts. On the 7th, the news that everyone feared the most was confirmed. *Garbo* was being held by the police. Madrid ordered Agent 3 to take over the network. In the short term he was told to cease transmission, get out of London and try to preserve anything of the network he could. By ordering the transmitter to shut down, the Germans were now robbed of any news on the redeployment of the FUSAG troops to Normandy.

On 12 July Gerbers's widow reported that *Garbo* had been released from detention, but was still unable to throw any light on what had occurred. Agent 3 was instructed by *Garbo* to take a ten-day holiday and to inform Madrid that he would be in contact with them by post with an explanation of what had occurred. The wily Spaniard explained that he had been picked up at a bomb site in Bethnal Green by an alert plain clothes policeman. Even though *Garbo* had been seen swallowing a piece of paper with incriminating notes, he would not admit to any wrong doing and solicited the help of his friend Agent J(3) at the Ministry of Information to vouch for him. On his release, *Garbo* reported that he had been sent several letters by the Home Secretary apologizing for the confusion and his arrest. Writing all this down on 14 July, *Garbo* enclosed these official documents with his letters to the Germans. They had been forged by MI5.

On 29 July the Germans replied. Not only was *Garbo*'s story believed, they informed him that in view of his bravery Hitler had awarded him the Iron Cross. The Germans also told *Garbo* to keep away from the V1 bombardment and to concentrate all his energies on troop movements and military intelligence, or in other words, propagating *Fortitude South*. This was exactly what the British had been hoping to hear. As an additional boon to the exercise, *Brutus* was told to drop investigating the V1s and concentrate on developments with Patton's FUSAG. In future, reports on the flying bombs would be made by *Tate* and the recently returned agent *Zigzag*.

The indomitable Eddie Chapman had more or less disappeared from view since jumping ship in Lisbon two years before. However, in the early hours of 28 June Agent *Zigzag* parachuted back into Britain with a long list of questions to which the Germans required answers. On landing Chapman came down hard on a road and was knocked out. He groggily took himself to the nearest police station where, after some difficulty, he managed to contact MI5. *Zigzag* was quickly whisked off to Camp 020, where he delighted Commandant Tin-Eye with fantastic tales of hard drinking and deceit. The Germans had feted him as a hero, awarded him the Iron Cross, paid him a fortune and sent him to Norway where they gave him a yacht and asked him to work as a consultant sabotage expert for trainee spies. Colonel Stephens applauded *Zigzag* as a patriot and recommended that he be pardoned for all his crimes. The Security Service let it be known that *Zigzag* was to be treated as a returning friend and not made to feel under scrutiny or suspicion.

His debriefing was therefore held next morning over a large breakfast at the In & Out Club on Piccadilly. His hosts were Tommy Robertson and Ronnie Reed, Chapman's previous case officer. While they ate, Chapman poured out a wealth of detail on his time behind enemy lines. He said that Berlin resembled Pompeii and that Goebbels was vainly trying to convince the German people that the same was true of London. He had collected a lot of information on German forces in Norway, radio codewords and numerous potential bombing targets. He also revealed that he had brought back an undeveloped film containing the portraits of numerous Abwehr officers.

As the debriefing process continued, without prompting *Zigzag* proved his loyalty by giving the names of two Icelandic spies he had trained, and who, unknown to him, had already been picked up by the British. Perhaps the most interesting piece of information was that he had a Leica camera and £1,000 sterling for another spy working in Britain. From what *Zigzag* had been told, this spy was one of the most valuable agents the Germans had working in Britain. Known to Chapman as Hubert, the mystery spy was actually *Brutus*, the Polish officer reporting on FUSAG. This raised a problem. If Chapman was allowed to fulfil his mission it would mean linking the *Zigzag* and *Brutus* cases. Although an agreeable character, Chapman was not in the same league as *Brutus* in terms of the deception campaign. *Zigzag* was still very much a wild card and despite Colonel Stephens' plaudits, he could only be trusted so far.

Zigzag revealed he had been having a steady relationship with a Norwegian woman called Dagmar Lahlum. He explained that Dagmar had connections with a resistance network in Norway and he had told her the truth about his mission lest she was denounced as a collaborator by the Resistance for being with a German officer. Before leaving for England *Zigzag* had asked his German case officer, von Groening, to make sure Dagmar was well looked after in his absence. From B1a's point of view, this left Chapman vulnerable to blackmail. Nevertheless, on 30 June *Zigzag* went on the air and made radio contact with his employers. One of his first concerns was reporting on V1 sites.

As previously mentioned, the Twenty Committee had been trying to get approval for the rocket deception campaign. Having been rebuffed by the Chiefs of Staff on 7 July, Sir Findlater Stewart revisited his proposal and submitted it in more detail on 18 July. In the new version he reiterated the need to shift the target area away from critical government areas and out to the suburbs. He also pointed out that the double agents working on *Fortitude* were being asked to supply information on the V1s, so that if they failed on that front, it might harm the wider deception campaign. The Chiefs of Staff nodded in approval, but then decided that the matter was so serious that it had to be passed to the Prime Minister's office for approval. The deception plan was thus thrown into the murky world of politics, where it remained until the end of the month.

At a meeting to discuss the V1 deception plan on 28 July, the Home Secretary and Minister for Security, Herbert Morrison, stood in for Churchill. Morrison was a native of south London and had a constituency in Hackney, in the East End of London. If the aim of the V1s was reduced, his constituency would be one of those to suffer most, so naturally he was completely against it. Although the flying bombs would not hit central London, they would still land in built-up areas and would cause significant damage to life and property. Morrison argued that central London was more used to bombing than the proposed area and better prepared to withstand it. Moreover, he felt that the whole thing smacked of people playing God with other people's lives. He ruled that the Twenty Committee's proposal would be 'an interference with providence' if the Germans were supplied information that led to people being killed who would otherwise have survived.[20] Although unspoken, there was also the political consideration of how such a decision would be viewed if the policy was revealed at a future date. It would take a very brave politician openly to endorse a policy that saw the targeting of poorer areas to protect the seat of government.

Stewart was therefore forced to the inevitable compromise. Morrison agreed that in essence nothing would change and as much confusing information would be sent over to the Germans as possible to prevent the MPI from being moved north. R. V. Jones was aghast when Charles Cholmondeley reported this decision. From the scientist's point of view the bombs had to land somewhere and, however unpalatable such decisions might be, he believed the deception would be worth it. He was fully alive to the dangers of redirecting the bombs, as his own parents still lived in south London near to the MPI. From his point of view there was a way forward. Taking inspiration from Horatio Nelson, with whom he shared the same birthday, Jones decided to turn a blind eye to the politicians, ignore them and continue the deception anyway.

This proved a brave and fortuitous decision. Unknown to the British, a small percentage of the flying bombs were fitted with a radio-transmitting device. These transmissions clearly indicated that the V1s had a tendency to fall short. When Oberst Wachtel, the commander of the Flak-Regiment 155(W) responsible for launching the flying bombs, compared the agents' reports with the radio device readings, the conclusion he came to was that there must be a fault with the device fitted to the bombs. Wachtel was told that the agents were particularly reliable and ought to be trusted. If Wachtel had relied on the devices alone and not been led astray by the double agents, there is every reason to suppose that he would have made the necessary adjustments. In this case, it was later calculated that deaths and injuries would have increased by at least 50 per cent. From R. V. Jones's perspective, his 'Nelson moment' may have helped to save over 10,000 people from death or serious injury.[21]

17

MEDITERRANEAN SWANSONG

HAVING BUILT UP HIS ORGANIZATION for more than three years, it was inconceivable that Dudley Clarke would allow A Force to miss out on the biggest show of them all. As conceived in the *Bodyguard* plan, deceptions in the Middle East, Mediterranean, Adriatic and Italy would play a key role in supporting the *Neptune* landings by deterring the Germans from moving reserves to Normandy. They also had an important part in paving the way for the *Anvil* landings in the south of France scheduled for mid-August.

The part of *Bodyguard* covering the eastern Mediterranean was codenamed *Zeppelin*. It was drawn up by Dudley Clarke and authorized in February 1944. The operation was, Clarke ordered, to be A Force's swansong. With every mission A Force had thus far attempted, there had always been a note of caution to preserve the organization for a future date and therefore not to do anything that would seriously compromise its special means agents. With *Zeppelin*, every stop was to be pulled out to keep the deception rolling for as long as possible, no matter what the cost in terms of agents blown and so on. This was the big one they had been waiting for and, as the self-styled guru on deception, Clarke did not want to disappoint.

Zeppelin's aim was to retain as many German troops in the Balkans and Greece before *Neptune* as possible, and for as long as possible afterwards. The first stage was set for 23 March 1944, when the British would attack Crete and western Greece or the Dalmatian coast. It would be supported by a Russian attack on 21 April somewhere in the Black Sea.

The British attack would be carried out by the Twelfth Army, which was in large part notional, the fruit of the long-running *Cascade* deception. This army consisted of only five real divisions, but was swollen by three factual brigades posing as full divisions, and four entirely notional divisions that existed only in terms of the double agent reports, collections of dummy vehicles, camps and the requisite amount of radio chatter provided by small teams of specialist radio operators driving round the theatre in trucks.[1]

Tobruk became the base from which a notional attack on Crete was planned. The harbours in Cyrenaica were filled with dummy landing craft, the airfields were packed with decoy aircraft and radio transmitters worked overtime, simulating a hive of military endeavour. An appeal went out for local guides and maps of the target area were churned out by printers known for their lax security and anti-British sympathies. In terms of providing 'special means', the star performers in *Zeppelin* were the A Force agents *Lambert* (still operating the *Cheese* transmitter), the *Lemons*, *Pessimist C* and, in particular, the Greek double agent, *Quicksilver*.

Greek troops were given extensive assault training and their zeal to liberate the homeland was freely reported in the local press. Bombing missions were carried out in the Balkans and beach reconnaissance patrols were sent to spy out potential landing grounds in Crete. Meanwhile the British sabotage organization, SOE, and its American counterpart, the OSS, contacted local resistance groups and tried, with occasional success, to arm them in preparation for the Allied attack, although unfortunately this led to a state of virtual civil war between various resistance groups in Greece. To lend credence to the idea that the attack would be coordinated with a Russian assault in the Black Sea, exchange visits were noisily arranged between British and Soviet officers. As the target dates for *Zeppelin* approached, the double agents suddenly reported a delay, which they put down to the stalling of the Allied advance in Italy. A new target date was set for the British attack of 14 April, with the Russian assault postponed to 21 May. However, due to Russian insistence that the attacks ought to be synchronized, the British attack was again postponed in April and set back to 21 May. This change of strategy was blamed on the mutiny of Greek troops in early April. Apparently Greek politicians had been arguing about the exact nature of government and whether or not there should be a plebiscite to determine the return of the exiled King George II. This had unsettled the troops and when they learned that the invasion had been postponed tensions spilled over, forcing the British to surround the Greeks with tanks. The insubordination was so bad that some of the Greek units, it was said, had had to be disbanded completely.

On 8 April *Quicksilver* reported 'great trouble', saying that the army and part of the navy had mutinied and the Provost Marshal had been shot dead in Cairo. On 16 April he speculated that the British were so upset with the Greeks that they were considering offering the Turks a free hand in north-eastern Greece if they joined the Allied cause. *Quicksilver* was particularly worried by this development because his family lived in Thrace, the area most threatened by a Turkish invasion. Time and time again, *Quicksilver* implored his German case officer to make sure his family were evacuated in the event of an invasion. All of this, of course, was a figment of Dudley

Clarke's imagination. To support *Quicksilver* he had *Pessimist C* report that the British were sending tanks and guns to Turkey.[2]

As the 21 May deadline approached, a new plan was fed to the double agents. Following the nonsense with the Greeks, it was said that the original plans were cancelled and that the Americans and British now planned to land in Istria on 19 June. On the same day, the Russians would assault Varna on the Black Sea and the Seventh United States Army would attack the Gulf of Lyons. This took the deception past the crucial *Overlord* D-Day and successfully helped pin German forces in south-eastern Europe as planned.

Zeppelin can be considered a genuine success, and probably the high point of everything A Force had worked towards. At the end of the mission Dudley Clarke could report that no German divisions had been sent north before *Neptune* and that those sent afterwards arrived too late to be of decisive help.

The reason it was successful can be explained by real German fears for the Balkans and Greece. The Germans feared that their supporters in south-east Europe might defect at the sight of the first Allied tank, and one of the outcomes of *Zeppelin* was the German occupation of their supposed ally, Hungary, on 19 March 1944. It was also clear that the Germans had taken in the long-running order of battle deception, which had proved the keystone for all A Force's successes. In February 1944 Operation *Cascade* had been replaced by Plan *Wantage*, an even more obvious hoax calling for 26 bogus divisions in the run-up to *Neptune*.[3] Of these 21 were found in German reports as genuine. In fact, across the whole Mediterranean theatre, the Germans had been led to overestimate Allied strength by something like a quarter of a million men.

XX

In the western Mediterranean, the cover plan had somewhat different problems. On the one hand the planners had to tie down German troops ahead of *Overlord*, but at the same time they had to make sure there were not too many in the south of France to oppose the *Anvil* landing scheduled for August. Eisenhower's replacement in supreme command of the Mediterranean, General Sir Henry Maitland Wilson, therefore commissioned three cover plans: an attack on the Bay of Biscay codenamed *Ironside*, and two false operations in the Mediterranean codenamed *Vendetta* and *Ferdinand*.

In addition to the Fifteenth Army, the Germans held considerable reserves south of Normandy around Toulouse in the form of 2nd SS Panzer Division Das Reich. To keep these troops from being sent north, Operation *Ironside* maintained that Allied troops sailing directly from the United States were going to invade France from the Bay of Biscay and land in the vicinity of Bordeaux.

This plan almost immediately started coming apart at the seams. Bordeaux was well out of the range of Allied fighter cover and lacked plausibility as a landing site from that respect. Unlike the other plans being developed as part of *Bodyguard*, the Navy and Air Force could not spare any resources to provide either the shipping or the preliminary air bombardment that would have been required for such an expedition. Without a tangible, physical deception the Twenty Committee and A Force were both hesitant to lend much credence to the plan in terms of special means traffic. It was felt that if any of the front-rank agents staked their reputations on the plan, they would be lost to the detriment of better-supported operations.

However, not wishing to leave the plan dead in the water, the Twenty Committee authorized one of its second-string agents to be used. The main protagonist in the plan therefore became *Bronx*, the Peruvian socialite with family ties to Vichy France. When recruited, *Bronx* had refused to take a radio set to Britain, claiming it was too hazardous. Instead she communicated with the Germans by letter. She was highly trusted and had sent more than 60 letters to a cover address in Lisbon by April 1944.

As D-Day approached the Germans realized that if *Bronx* picked up news of the invasion from her social contacts, the letters would arrive too late to be of any use. They therefore devised a code based on an innocuous telegram to be sent to Antonio de Almeida, the General Manager of the Bank of Espírito Santo in Madrid, a bank with strong links to the Deutsche Bank. The code assigned various sections of the French coast to monetary values. If a request for money was made for the dentist, this would indicate that the information was certain; if it was for her doctor, it indicated the information was almost certain. If *Bronx* then requested the money be sent 'straight away', it meant the invasion was due in less than a week; 'urgent' meant within a fortnight; 'quickly' stood for in a month, while 'if possible' meant the exact date was vague.

On 29 May *Bronx* cabled the bank manager with the message: 'send £50 quickly. I have need of a dentist.' From this request for the quick despatch of £50 sterling, the Germans were to interpret the message as being that the invasion of the Bay of Biscay was certain in one month.[4] As an insurance policy the telegram was then backed up by a letter dated 7 June, which the Germans probably did not receive for three weeks. In the letter *Bronx* explained that she had got talking with an intoxicated captain at a cocktail party at the Four Hundred Club. He told *Bronx* there would be interesting news in the morning, as there was going to be an airborne assault against

Bordeaux that night in preparation for the invasion. Next morning the captain had contacted *Bronx* and confided in her that the attack had been put back a month and she was not to mention it to anyone. Writing the day after D-Day, *Bronx* explained that there must have been a change in the Allies' plans, or that the airborne attack on Bordeaux was still to occur.[5]

To reinforce *Bronx*'s telegram, *Tate* also sent a message, this time based on intelligence received from his notional girlfriend, Mary, who had just returned from Washington. Lastly, on 5 June, the eve of D-Day, *Garbo* sent a somewhat sceptical message in which he reported news of an American division assault-loaded at Liverpool, which was to be joined by a large army sailing directly from the United States.

Oddly enough, this is one deception where the Allies appear to have missed the boat. The most successful deceptions were those that played most directly into Hitler's thinking; hence the deceptions against the Pas de Calais, Norway and the Balkans were taken seriously. Hitler also believed there was a credible threat to the Bay of Biscay and might have taken the bait if more energy had been expended on *Ironside*. Instead, the mission of delaying the Das Reich regiment's march to Normandy fell principally on SOE and the resistance networks. This task was performed admirably, but with awful consequences for the French civilian population, notably at Oradour-sur-Glane, where the entire population of a town was executed in reprisal for partisan action. In the face of constant harassment and sabotage, Das Reich famously took two weeks to arrive in Normandy, a transfer that should have taken three days.

It also appears that the 15 May message did little harm to *Bronx*'s reputation. Almost a year later, in March 1945, the Germans gave *Bronx* an almost identical code, asking her to report on the possibility of Allied landings in Norway, Denmark or north-west Germany, or an airborne drop west of Berlin. Masterman concluded that if the Germans had not been satisfied with *Bronx*'s performance in May 1944, it is unlikely they would have asked her to repeat it.[6]

One less well-known ruse relating to *Ironside* was hatched by 'C', the head of MI6. The British Secret Intelligence Service had been monitoring an agent's radio set known to have been captured by the Germans and played back to the British. As D-Day approached, the German impostor operating the set asked where would be the best place for escapers and evaders to head. MI6 replied that all such resisters should head towards Bordeaux by 15 June, where they would have a good chance of being picked up. Hearing about this ruse in June, Guy Liddell noted that the deception might have worked as there had been a large concentration of German U-boats sent into the Bay of Biscay to protect the approaches to Bordeaux. These 30 submarines were therefore unavailable in the Channel on D-Day.[7]

XX

Supplementing *Ironside* in its support role for *Neptune* was Plan *Vendetta*. Initially, the Allies had planned to invade the south of France at the same time as Normandy. However, due to logistical problems, in March 1944 the Combined Chiefs of Staff decided that the invasion of southern France, Operation *Anvil*, would not take place until after the Normandy beachhead was firmly established. In lieu of this, they ordered Wilson to mount a threat to the area in order to deter German troops from being redeployed to Normandy.

Wilson passed this task to A Force, which developed *Vendetta*, a simulated assault on the coast of southern France scheduled for 11 June. To lend credence to this threat, A Force decided that some real troops should be earmarked for assault training. It must be remembered that security in the Mediterranean theatre was nothing like as tight as in Britain. Whereas the homeland was an island with a mostly sympathetic indigenous population, the shores of North Africa were very different. In addition to undetected spies in the local population, there was the ever-present problem of gossip. The Free French were considered amazingly lax in this regard, so much so that de Gaulle was kept in the dark by the Allies about the date of *Overlord* right up until the last possible minute. Therefore Clarke was right. To simulate a threat, real troops would have to be observed.

The fall guys were the 91st United States Infantry Division. Actually bound for Italy, the 91st was told it was going to France, along with the 65th Puerto Rican Infantry Regiment. They would be joined in this endeavour, they were told, by the Seventh United States Army, which at that time was comprised of nothing more than administrative personnel and a number of genuine French colonial divisions.

Blissfully unaware of the reality, this division began practising amphibious training near Oran. Aerial photographs and maps of the French coast were issued to it, and French lessons were given to the troops. Unlike *Ironside*, this time bombing missions were carried out, as disruption to the road and rail network from the Midi to the north of France was seen as directly benefiting *Neptune*. To heighten the tension and indicate that something was about to happen, the border between French and Spanish Morocco was closed. As the target date approached, the assault date was put back by eight days to 19 June.

The bait was taken and the Germans maintained 11 divisions in the south of France, none of which were withdrawn until D+24. Even by D+52 there were still nine divisions in the south, although two of them had been sent there from Normandy to rest and regroup. However, by the end of June, once the 91st was in action in Italy, *Vendetta* was wound down. Only then was it explained to the soldiers of the 91st why they had been trained for France but instead sent to Italy. It may have been a relief that it was not, as they probably suspected, due to the incompetence of their leaders.

Mention should also be made of a plan to support *Vendetta* codenamed Operation *Copperhead*, a ruse perhaps better known as 'Monty's Double'. It was another brainchild of Dudley Clarke, who had noticed how German agents in Algeciras equipped with telescopes could observe all the comings and goings at the Gibraltar airfield. Taking this a step further, Clarke wondered what would happen if, through the reports of these agents, the Germans believed that Montgomery was in the Mediterranean at the time of D-Day and not in Britain at the head of his army. Surely the Germans would not expect an attack to develop with the British commander absent from his troops.

Of course, borrowing the real Montgomery would be out of the question, so the search was on for a substitute. Back in London the LCS went to an acting agency in Wardour Street and went through several volumes of photographs showing the actors on their books. One actor was found to have a resemblance to Montgomery, a certain M. E. Clifton James, a serving lieutenant in the Royal Pay Corps. James was duly telephoned by the actor David Niven and asked to come to London for an interview at the War Office about a special part they had lined up for him.

The likeness was truly uncanny. Without quite knowing what he was getting into, James signed up and was posted with the real Montgomery to study his mannerisms and mimic his speech. A typical thespian, James was wracked with self-doubt and stage fright, no doubt made worse by having to refrain from smoking and drinking, both habits Montgomery shunned. However, he was coaxed through his role, with various members of the deception staff directing him as if Hollywood professionals.

Every detail was considered. When they learned that James had never flown before, Johnny Bevan told Wheatley to take him up in an aircraft to find out if he was prone to airsickness.[8] He was issued with a complete outfit and Montgomery insisted that while James was imitating him, he should draw the same pay as a general, which was a considerable improvement on his lieutenant's wage.

Amid much pomp, on 28 May 'Monty' arrived in Gibraltar accompanied by Noël Wild. He was met by a car sent by the governor, General Mason McFarlane, and taken to his residence. A Spanish spy called Molina happened to be visiting the governor general at the time. He was kept in a room where he could clearly see 'Monty' through a window in deep discussion with the governor. This matter was quickly reported to Berlin.[9]

After Gibraltar 'Monty' arrived in Algiers, where he was received by the Mediterranean Supreme Commander and given a parade to inspect. He also met Dudley Clarke, who forwarded him on to Cairo for a week's leave. James was met in Cairo by Michael Crichton who provided him with a bottle of whisky. Crichton left James with the bottle and later returned to find the actor snoring contently with an empty bottle by his side. He had probably earned a drink for his endeavours.[10]

The success of the ruse is somewhat harder to judge. Informed about the mission, Guy Liddell was worried that the hoax had been played too early, considering that it should have happened nearer to D-Day.[11] Certainly none of the B1a agents played along with the gag, although some of the A Force agents did. It seems that *Copperhead* caused quite a stir at the lower levels of the German intelligence service, but did not carry so much weight at the top. In fact it appears that *Copperhead* was torpedoed by *Josephine* reports from Sweden. On 19 May this source falsely reported that talks had taken place in Gibraltar on 14–15 May between the various commanders in the Mediterranean theatre. From the German point of view, if Montgomery had wanted to meet with Maitland Wilson he would have done so while he was at Gibraltar and not waited ten more days and incurred the necessity of having to go to North Africa. When captured after the war, the German report on *Copperhead* was marked with the query 'Deception?' Colonel Krummacher, the liaison officer between the Abwehr and the German High Command, actually pencilled his reply in English: 'Who knows?'[12]

XX

Diplomacy played an important part in implementing *Bodyguard*, real or otherwise. The threat of Russian cooperation was key to several plans so it was felt that the Soviets should be told what was going on. With careful lobbying the Chiefs of Staff felt that there was always the chance that they might even help out. Bevan had serious misgivings about telling the Soviets about Allied deception methods lest they became known to the Germans, but he was overruled.[13]

On 30 January Bevan took off to sell *Bodyguard* to the Russians. The mission started badly. Travelling in an unpressurized Liberator bomber, Bevan passed out from lack of oxygen during the flight and had to be resuscitated by his American colleague Colonel William Baumer of the US Joint Security Control.[14] Bevan hit a stumbling block when negotiating with General Kuznetsov of the Soviet General Staff. He wanted the Russians to mount a threat against Bulgaria to support *Zeppelin*. The only trouble was that although Bulgaria was at war with Britain and America it was not actually at war with Russia. The Soviets offered Romania as an alternative, but Bevan knew that this would not suit Dudley Clarke. For A Force, the beauty of selecting Bulgaria was that the Russians would be able to make a surprise landing unopposed, because no state of war existed. In the case of Romania, defences were already prepared and for the Russian threat to be taken seriously, the Soviets would have to demonstrate that they had enough assault craft for the job. Such equipment was entirely lacking, therefore it was unlikely the Axis would take the bait.

Complex negotiations between Bevan, Baumer and their Soviet hosts, the Foreign Office and so on, continued slowly, with haphazard interpretations between the English- and Russian-speaking parties. The Soviets argued every point, and then suddenly on 6 March decided to agree to the whole of *Bodyguard* without change. Quite what prompted this change of heart has never properly been understood. Unfortunately by then time was running out. Rather than helping with *Zeppelin*, the Russians' main contribution was to *Fortitude North* and *Graffham* by putting pressure on Norway and Sweden.[15]

In terms of deceptive diplomacy, Ronald Wingate was the author of an interesting plan he codenamed *Royal Flush*. The plan supposed that certain neutral countries might provide the Allies with facilities after an invasion. The countries considered to be worth approaching were Spain, Sweden and Turkey. In Sweden's case, *Royal Flush* was more or less a continuation of *Graffham*. Likewise, the pressure put on Turkey to join the war on the side of the Allies had been a long-running theme.

The really interesting case with *Royal Flush* was Spain. There had been a number of ideas about dragging Spain into the war, either by invading it, or by goading the Germans into occupying the country. There had even been talk of mounting a royalist coup to get rid of Franco. In all these cases the plans had been quashed. Anyone with an inkling of knowledge of military history knew that Spain had never taken kindly to invaders. As Napoleon had found out, resistance to an invader would be intense. Anyway, even if the Allies could become established there, the Germans had a natural line of defence in the Pyrenees, stopping the Allies from moving into France.

However, *Royal Flush* called for something entirely different. On 3 June the US ambassador approached the Spanish government and asked if they would allow the evacuation of wounded personnel and the supply of food through Spain if the Allies invaded the south of France. In terms of practicality the idea was a non-starter, but it was hoped someone in Spanish government circles would hear about it and tell the Germans. They would conclude that an invasion of the south coast was imminent and refrain from sending their troops there north to Normandy.

To reinforce the deception, on 5 June the British ambassador repeated the approach. As the negotiations continued, the Spanish actually agreed in principle to provide humanitarian assistance, but would only formally do so once the invasion in the south had taken place. This charade was maintained with the Spanish well into July, when the Allies thanked the Spanish for their trouble, but explained that Normandy had been so successful that the invasion of the south had been cancelled. By turning down the Spanish offer, the diplomats provided cover for the real *Anvil* landing, scheduled for mid-August.

XX

Having drawn German attention to the south coast of France with *Vendetta* and *Royal Flush*, the Allies now had to backtrack and divert German attention elsewhere before their invasion on 15 August took place. A Force developed a cover plan called *Ferdinand*. It was quite simple and said that all the preparations were for a direct assault on Genoa to outflank the Germans' position on the so-called Gothic Line in Italy.

Perhaps the most vital double agent for *Ferdinand* was the Frenchman *Gilbert*. Since the Salerno landings, *Gilbert* had been very busy trying to maintain his cover. Late in November 1943 an Abwehr agent named Caron was parachuted in near Tunis. Exhausted by his journey, he quickly located *Gilbert* and was given a bed in a safe house. *Gilbert* had met Caron before, knew he was an out-and-out collaborator and guessed that he had been sent to check up on him and *Le Duc*. While Caron caught up on his sleep, *Gilbert* rifled his clothes and discovered a code hidden behind a seam, which he duly copied and replaced.

When Caron awoke, he told *Gilbert* he had come to take control of encoding all the messages broadcast by the team's radio operator. Forewarned of Caron's coming, the Deuxième Bureau had had the foresight to remove *Albert*, the group's Vichy radio operator, who still had no idea of

Gilbert's duplicity. It was found that the hapless *Albert* was eligible for the draft and he was quickly despatched to far-flung French West Africa for his basic training.

The scene was now set to deceive Caron. Messages would continue to arrive from A Force, via the hands of *Le Duc*, and be passed to *Gilbert* for encryption. This was now supervised by Caron, who was as clueless to the origin of the intelligence as *Albert* had been. Perhaps a more astute man would have realized that *Gilbert* was double crossing his masters, but Caron spent all his time in high-class brothels and what little cross-examination he carried out on *Gilbert* and his *Atlas* team was quickly conducted between orgies of the most extreme kind.[16]

As the fighting in Italy continued, *Gilbert*'s main task was in promoting A Force's deception plan for Anzio, codenamed *Chettyford*. This plan indicated that a pincer move was about to be mounted by the Seventh United States Army under Patton against Pisa on the west coast and Rimini on the east coast, with the objective of containing German reserves to the north of the country. When it came to providing cover for *Anvil* a similar tactic was used. From June 1944 *Gilbert* began sending messages about an Allied attack in the Bay of Genoa and a push for the Brunner Pass and Austria. The Germans were no doubt eager to learn more and, so as not to jeopardize the Frenchman's reporting, informed him that the Luftwaffe were henceforth prohibited from bombing Tunis and Bizerte.

The Germans also decided to send *Gilbert* some help in the guise of three agents who took off from Athens on 27 July 1944. *Gilbert* had been asked to provide a welcoming committee for these agents. He heard the drone of the aircraft engines, ignited the beacons and spent half the night waiting in vain. He returned back to his hideout and from there began sending an aggrieved message to Paris, complaining about the incompetence of the pilots. As he finished transmitting there was a knock at the door and in walked one of the three missing spies.

The man called himself *Le Moco* and claimed that he had parachuted in miles off course from the drop zone. On landing he had twisted his ankle and hurt his ribs. *Gilbert* listened wide-eyed as *Le Moco* explained how an Italian lorry driver had seen him land and had come to his rescue. *Le Moco* explained that he gave the Italian a bit of a pep talk about his fascist duties and was rewarded with a lift into town. *Gilbert* asked the spy if he knew where the Italian lived. Unluckily for the said lorry driver, *Le Moco* confirmed that he knew this and told *Gilbert* where. Before long the charitable Italian found himself arrested and sent to spend the rest of the war in solitary confinement in a prison somewhere in southern Tunisia, with no idea of the spider's web he had just blundered into.

Gilbert then asked what had happened to the two other spies. *Le Moco* told him that they had bailed out some miles south east of Tunis with their radio sets. They were under orders that if caught they were to agree to transmit under Allied control by inserting the letters QBU into their messages. Sure enough, the two spies were picked up after both of them presented themselves with their luggage and radio sets to the first police station they encountered. The prospect of running two double agents whom the Germans knew were under Allied control was an intriguing opportunity for the Deuxième Bureau, but with such little time until *Anvil*, it was felt that nothing could be done to get a triple cross operation properly established.

Le Moco could be used, however, and he was somewhat relieved when *Gilbert* explained he was actually working for the Allies. Until that point *Le Moco*'s entire ambition had been to avoid getting shot and to go back to his family in one piece. On the other hand he was only too pleased to work against his former employers.

After recovering his equipment and codes, an opportunity presented itself for *Gilbert* to get rid of Caron permanently. *Le Moco* had brought a radio set and instructions from Paris for Caron to go to Algiers and report from there. Caron bade farewell to the brothel and took a flight to Algiers where he was promptly, and seemingly randomly, searched and the wireless transmitter set discovered. With Caron under arrest, the Deuxième Bureau asked MI5 if they would lock him up in England at Camp 020, but Liddell was not enthused by the prospect. The French complained that if they kept him they would have to present a legal case, and that would blow *Gilbert*.[17] As remembered by Ronald Wingate, the eventual solution to the problem was quite simple: a few weeks later Caron found himself in a ditch facing a firing squad.

Meanwhile *Gilbert* continued to implement *Ferdinand*. With *Le Moco* firmly on board, and *Le Duc* reporting that he formed part of the force bound for the coming operation, the German intelligence services were led up the garden path yet again.

At the beginning of August, A Force had the codename of *Anvil* changed to *Dragoon*, as it was believed that the Germans knew what *Anvil* signified.[18] All the reports suggested that a large invasion force was coming up from North Africa and southern Italy, bound for Genoa. On the night of 13–14 August the armada assembled off Corsica and then made all speed towards the Italian port. However, three miles from the port, the invasion force made a sharp turn and presented itself at sunrise off the French coast.

18

THE FINAL DECEITS

WITH THEIR CHIEF BACK IN OPERATION following his arrest, *Garbo*'s agents began explaining away the changes to FUSAG since they had last been on the air. The formations leaving for Normandy were being replaced by the arrival of the Fourteenth United States Army in Liverpool. This new formation was earmarked for FUSAG along with the British Fourth Army, which had been used in *Fortitude North*, but had now been notionally redeployed to the south. With the exception of a few units in the latter formation, both these armies were largely imaginary. To bolster the volume of radio chatter and give more credence to the threat posed by FUSAG, the very real Ninth United States Army was temporarily added to the order of battle while it waited to be deployed in Normandy.

More complex still, Patton assumed command of the Third United States Army now that it was in Normandy. This made Patton a subordinate of General Bradley, and certainly inferior to Montgomery. Quite how Patton was supposed to go from Army Group commander to subordinate general required some explaining to the Germans, but again, *Garbo* was up to the task. On 20 July he explained that Eisenhower had begun siphoning off troops from FUSAG to reinforce Montgomery, because the going in Normandy was slower than predicted. This had made Patton furious and he had exploded, making an angry outburst aimed at the Supreme Commander. Having supported Patton through his previous indiscretions this time Eisenhower demoted him on the spot. Once tempers cooled, Patton was offered a subordinate command and given the opportunity to restore his tarnished reputation. To back up *Garbo*, the circumstances of Patton's apparent demotion were also reported by the letter-writing socialite spies, *Gelatine* and *Bronx*.[1]

To maintain a credible threat, Patton would have to be replaced by an equally senior US general. The choice candidate was Lieutenant General McNair, then Commander-in-Chief of Land Forces USA. He was ordered to Europe to assume an important command in the field and given FUSAG. Unfortunately, before anything could be made of McNair's appointment, tragedy struck. Soon after he arrived in Britain, McNair asked if he might visit Normandy and see how the troops were performing in action. On 24 July, while visiting troops near the front line, McNair was caught up in an air raid. The USAAF had been called in to soften up a German defensive line but they accidentally bombed their own troops instead. McNair received a direct hit and was killed instantly.

Undeterred, the deceivers turned McNair's demise to their profit. Before news of the accident was made public, *Brutus* leaked the whole McNair story to the Germans. He explained that McNair had gone over to France to have a closer look at German defensive techniques in preparation for FUSAG's attack across the Channel. When the news of McNair's death was eventually made public, it confirmed exactly what *Brutus* had already said.

To continue the deception, an equally senior figure had to be found to replace McNair. Such a person was found in General John DeWitt, Director of the Army and Navy Joint Staff College in Washington. On 9 August news of DeWitt's appointment was mentioned in an intercepted German report. The appointment was seen by the Germans as vindication of the importance of FUSAG, which they now believed to consist of 'thirty-two large formations'.[2] Actually, by then von Rundstedt had already realized that the Allies would be content with their gains in Normandy and would probably not require any further large-scale landings. On 27 July the German High Command had at last authorized the Fifteenth Army to release two infantry divisions for Normandy. Two more followed on 31 July and 1 August respectively. By then it was far too late for them to stem the tide.

Fortitude now moved into a new stage. No one had seriously believed that the hoax would last as long as it had thus far, and it was even more unbelievable that none of the double agents had yet been blown. All the indications were that although FUSAG was now unlikely to be used against the Pas de Calais, the Germans still considered it an important threat. When the Ninth United States Army crossed over to invest the port of Brest, the composition of FUSAG was changed. *Garbo* reported that it now consisted of the British Fourth Army and the First Allied Airborne Army. Both armies were fictitious, but were portrayed as being made ready rapidly to exploit any sudden German withdrawals, or to make a combined operations assault somewhere along Europe's North Sea coast.

This was to prove the last important coup delivered by *Garbo*. The killer blow came from a Spanish associate of the Abwehr named Roberto Buenaga. Seeking a cash reward, Buenaga contacted the British SIS and told them he knew the name of the top German radio agent in England. This put the British in a pickle. They were certain the name would be *Garbo*, but they had to be sure and so asked Buenaga to name him. It was *Garbo*.

If *Garbo* was not arrested, Buenaga would suspect the truth about *Garbo's* allegiances. On the other hand, if *Garbo* was arrested it would spell the end of the whole network. Although there were some calling for the double cross system to be wound down after the success of *Overlord*, others like Masterman were not so sure, and thought the system ought to be kept running for as long as the Germans appeared to believe in it. The agreed solution was for *Garbo* to be tipped off and for him to go into hiding. This would allow the network to maintain contact under the leadership of Agent 3(1) Pedro, whose identity was unknown to the Germans and could not be checked because he did not exist.

On 12 September *Garbo* explained that 'the Courier' had warned him that an individual named Buenaga had betrayed him to the British SIS. *Garbo* instructed the Germans to suspend all correspondence and money transfers and informed them that he was going to take refuge in a safe house in south Wales with Agent 4, who was on the run after going AWOL the night before D-Day. From there, *Garbo* would do his best to watch over the organization while his wife would tell the British he had fled back to Spain. At first the Germans were slightly puzzled as to why a British SIS officer would have told the crooked courier about Buenaga in the first place, but they failed to push the enquiry very far. Thus *Garbo's* war came to an effective end.

There was one last hurrah still in the bag for FUSAG. Picking up where *Garbo* had left off, *Brutus* was still in place to deliver. On 10 September Montgomery had set out his plan to use paratroopers to seize a crossing over the Rhine at Arnhem and cut off the retreating German Fifteenth Army. That same day *Brutus* followed up *Garbo's* report on the First Allied Airborne Army, revealing that it consisted of four airborne divisions. In his estimation these, along with the British Fourth Army, were being prepared for what seemed to be an attack against the north-west German coast. Somewhat cryptically he mentioned that a second force was also being prepared for action, but he could not find out where and had little detail on the subject. This second force was in fact the real airborne troops being prepared for Montgomery's Operation *Market Garden*, the plan to seize a bridge over the Rhine at Arnhem.

In essence it was a re-run of the Pas de Calais story. It was hoped that once the real airborne landing took place in Holland, the Germans would remain cautious of committing their reserves lest the Allies pounce with FUSAG in their rear. From the point of view of the deception planners, the plan was a success in the sense that the Germans took notice of it and were alive to the possibility of a second attack. Unfortunately, from the point of view of the average soldier parachuted into Holland the mission was a total disaster. Faulty British intelligence underestimated German strength in the Arnhem area, so although tactical surprise was achieved, the battle for Arnhem was lost with heavy casualties sustained. In that sense, the German Fifteenth Army gained some small measure of revenge for having sat on its hands through the battle for France.

It also proved the last time *Brutus* could be safely used. As France was liberated, many of his former colleagues and enemies in the Resistance started to come out of the shadows. It was surely only a question of time before he was denounced as a German stooge or otherwise investigated. After the Arnhem deception his case was allowed to peter out. There was, however, almost a reprieve for the case at the end of the year. At the end of 1944 Noël Wild asked for one of the double agents to pull off a deception to counter the German Ardennes offensive. This deception plan was going to be so drastic the agent's cover would quickly be blown. *Brutus* therefore appeared to be the perfect choice. In the end, he was not required and his last message was sent on 2 January 1945. He was awarded the OBE by the British for his secret service.

Garbo also received an award around this time. On 21 December 1944, the day before Noël Wild asked for an agent to sacrifice on his deception plan, *Garbo* was awarded the MBE. It was presented by the Director General of MI5 in the presence of Tommy Harris, Robertson, John Marriott, Masterman and others.[3] The party then went off to enjoy lunch at the Savoy, during which *Garbo* made a heartfelt acceptance speech in English. He had come a long way since his early ridiculous messages about Glaswegian dockers drinking wine. He truly was one of the most remarkable characters of the war.

XX

In terms of deception in the field, as the war in Europe entered its last phase opportunities for implementing grand schemes grew increasingly sparse. With German resources already stretched to the limit and with the net closing in, there were fewer opportunities for the British-based B1a agents to try and influence the course of the war. What deception could be practised was mostly of a physical nature rather than intelligence-driven.

To some extent this problem had already been anticipated before *Overlord*. Through signals interception the Allies knew that the Germans were planning to leave stay-behind agents all over the occupied territories to spring up behind the lines. With the fast-moving situation, it would be unwieldy to attempt to try to run these agents from Britain, so MI5 helped with the formation and training of Special Counter-Intelligence Units (SCIUs), which were posted with the British Twenty-First Army and the American Twelfth Army Groups to capture and play back enemy agents.

The British SCIUs were run by Ops.B, while the American equivalent in 12th Army Group was run by a shadowy outfit known as X-2. This was the counter-espionage branch of the OSS, which was in essence a cross between Britain's SIS and the SOE sabotage organization. It had been formed in June 1943 after the British had lobbied the Americans to form a central agency to deal with counter-intelligence matters. Until then such a service had been split between the FBI and various service intelligence staffs, none of which appeared willing or able to take a lead in the matter. The British actually lobbied for the FBI to take the lead and to place Assistant Director 'Sam' Foxworth in the lead role, but Hoover resisted. He did not want Foxworth as a rival and so vetoed the idea, thus paving the way for OSS to own the project.

OSS X-2 was based in London, but did not share the headquarters of its parent body in Grosvenor Street. Instead it was housed in the same Ryder Street building as MI6's Section V. To begin with, X-2 was almost entirely reliant on the British secret service for everything. Although there had long been a turf war between Section V and MI5, this did not apply to X-2. Its officers were allowed unfettered access to Ultra and access to the index card system that was the cornerstone of the British intelligence service. This card system contained information on everything and everyone that had come to the attention of the secret service. It showed who could be trusted, who could be approached and where potential threats might exist, or enemy agents lurk. Without this huge resource the Americans would have been effectively blind.

As part of the build up to *Overlord*, in early 1944 MI5 opened its doors to X-2. Officers were assigned desks at the B1a office and were given open access to the case histories of the double agents and the traffic being passed by them. The X-2 officers were taught all the techniques of double cross and about their rivals in the German intelligence services. They were shown the interrogation methods used by the Germans, often from people who had been through the experience, and also shown the British style of interrogation practised at Camp 020.

One of the most important features of X-2 work was providing the training for the SCIUs that would accompany American armies in the field. Through Ultra and other intelligence, the SCIUs were provided with information on the German intelligence services and police, and known and suspected stay-behind agents, collaborators and potential allies among the local population. The information was so detailed it included maps pinpointing the last known locations of all known German agents and espionage centres, and a wish list of items and people the intelligence services wanted seized. This ranged from German intelligence officers down to seemingly mundane but vitally important items like German telephone directories.

When the Allies began liberating France, they were often aware of the location of enemy agents. If the opportunity allowed, these agents would be quickly sent to England for interrogation at Camp 020, and, if believed fit for purpose, sent back to Europe to be run as double agents. Although the primary purpose of this was for counter-intelligence, in other words, using spies to capture spies, there was always the possibility of double cross opportunities arising.

This possibility eventually led to the various SCIUs (American and British, naval and air force) forming the 212 Committee in August 1944. Based on the Twenty Committee, 212 allowed the SCIUs to coordinate their activities and pool data. For deception policy, and as an approving authority for material to be transmitted by the captured spies, 212 relied on Ops.B at SHAEF. In practice, though, the Allied advance after the breakout from Normandy was so rapid that it proved difficult to implement deception plans on the scale of *Fortitude*. By the middle of September SHAEF decided that the 212 Committee would only be used for counter-intelligence purposes, not deception. Double cross work therefore remained the preserve of the established agents in Britain.

XX

On 8 September the first V2 rocket landed on British soil. Unlike the V1, which could be shot down in the air, the V2 was more or less immune from air defences of the day. When launched, the rocket would hurtle up into the air and then, on the edges of space, flip over and begin its descent. It would plummet down on its target faster than the speed of sound, delivering a payload of 2150lb of high explosive. It was only after impact that survivors would hear the sound of something like an express train hurtling towards them as the V2's sonic boom caught up.

In terms of potential for harm, the V2 was clearly a bigger threat than the V1. Initial estimates speculated that the V2s might kill as many as

100,000 people a month, and steps had therefore been taken to evacuate London and the seat of government if necessary. Confidentially Guy Liddell told Tommy Robertson that there was a secret plan to threaten Hitler with atomic retaliation if the V2 was deployed as a weapon.[4] In fact, the V2 proved somewhat less of a problem than feared. Although they were deadly to those in the vicinity of their blast, compared to the number of bombs being dropped on German cities, the amount of explosive carried by the V2s was modest. In addition, the suddenness with which the weapon struck was perhaps less psychologically troubling than the sound of the V1 'Doodlebugs' spluttering by and then suddenly cutting out as they fell to earth.

Initially the V2s were fired from extreme range and mostly fell in East Anglia. However, by the end of October, the launch sites had been moved closer to the front line and began to find their range, landing on London. Unable to carry out air reconnaissance of the damage, the Germans again relied on their agents to provide information that would allow them to correct their aim. This reopened the whole debate about what information to provide the Germans, and if the agents' reports should be used to divert the rockets from striking central London. On 9 November the Twenty Committee wondered if they should not implement a deception similar to the one proposed for the V1. This meant locking horns with the politicians again, and officially the request was turned down. Official policy was that the agents should send only the bare essential information to maintain their cases, and nothing more.

It was odd, then, that the fall of the bombs began to creep eastward. Again the Twenty Committee decided (or was secretly authorized) to implement the deception in the face of official disapproval. Montagu admitted that the Twenty Committee's mandate on the V2 deception was phrased very vaguely 'for political reasons'.[5] It was decided that the agents should mix the location of incidents where the rockets landed in central London with the time of those falling 5 to 8 miles short.

Of the agents available to implement this deception, *Zigzag* might have been the obvious choice, but he had unfortunately had to be sacked in November. When *Zigzag*'s case officer Ronnie Reed was transferred as a liaison officer in France he was replaced by Michael Ryde, a former RSLO for the Reading area. Ryde and *Zigzag* took an instant, mutual dislike to one another and Ryde almost at once began trying to have the case shut down so he could be rid of his charge.

Despite the best efforts of Masterman and Robertson to iron out some of *Zigzag*'s excesses, it was only a question of time before Ryde got his way. The first problem was the revelation that *Zigzag* had told his girlfriend Dagmar the truth about working for the British; then there was his continued attachment to von Groening, his German case officer. The planned meeting to provide *Brutus* with money and a camera had then collapsed because *Brutus*'s German case officer would not cooperate, declaring *Zigzag* unreliable. The final nail in the coffin came when Chapman began drifting back into criminal circles. Ryde believed that the spy had told his underworld drinking companions the truth of his existence and the source of his money. If this was the case, Robertson had no choice but to agree to cut him loose: *Zigzag* was just too unpredictable. He was asked to sign the Official Secrets Act and was threatened with retaliation if he ever told anyone about his secret service. Of course, true to form he started touting his story to publishers and journalists almost straight away!

Of course, *Zigzag* had never been a key player in B1a's stable of deception agents. His departure was more than compensated for by the arrival of a new double cross agent codenamed *Rover*. This was a young Polish sailor and one-time professional boxer who had been captured by the Nazis and subjected to forced labour in Hamburg. As a way out of this unpleasant occupation, he joined the German secret service and agreed to go to Britain as a spy. He was well trained in Morse and instructed in how to build his own wireless transmitter set once he arrived. *Rover* reached Gibraltar via Spain and came clean to the authorities. They sent him on to England, where he arrived in May 1944 and was put to work as a double cross agent.

Unfortunately the Germans did not return his calls and so *Rover* was handed over to the Polish Navy. Almost as soon as his services had been dispensed with, the Germans began trying to call him. Rather than bring *Rover* back and have to explain everything to the Poles, B1a decided to use a substitute. The Germans did not notice the change and from 9 October the British secret service had yet another means with which to bamboozle their opponents.

Before returning to the V2 deception, a disaster befell the man imitating *Rover*. He fell ill, was packed off to hospital and promptly died. By this time the V2 offensive was in full swing and *Rover* was considered the best source on the subject after *Tate*. A second substitute was found, who tried to imitate the style of the previous substitute. The match was not perfect, but an excuse was developed to cover this. *Rover* reported that he had been off the air because he had been in hospital. He claimed to have been hit by a lorry during the black out and had sustained damaged ribs and a broken shoulder, which made tapping out Morse messages difficult. It appears this incapacity was accepted as a valid reason for the subtle change in Morse style and the *Rover* channel was allowed to continue.

The main trusted source on V2s was *Tate*. Before D-Day B1a had been unsure how favourably *Tate* was viewed by the Germans. There had been so many near misses with the potential to blow the case that B1a wondered if the Germans believed he had been blown, or was simply out of favour. However, once the invasion took place, *Tate*'s importance was confirmed when his German case officer told him that his messages were so important they might 'even decide the outcome of the war'.[6]

At a Twenty Committee meeting on 18 January, Masterman pointed out that the Germans appeared to paying an awful lot of attention to the reports of *Tate* and *Rover* regarding V2 hits. At the next meeting, a week later, Masterman pointed out that the V2 MPI was shifting and this was probably down to the two agents deceiving the Germans. A few weeks later, Masterman believed that from 20 January to 17 February the MPI had moved eastward by two miles a week and had ended up outside the boundary of London altogether.[7] Strangely, none of *Tate*'s V2 reports have survived in British files, and none were thought to have survived on the German side. However, what did become certain at the end of the war was that the Germans plotted the majority of their hits fairly centrally in the middle of the capital. In fact the majority of the hits were east of the River Lea, and north of the River Thames in the districts of East and West Ham, Leyton, Barking and Ilford. Again by the actions of the agents, Londoners were spared another probable 11,000 killed or maimed – unofficially or not.[8]

XX

Perhaps more important than his work with the V2s, *Tate*'s biggest contribution to deception was the last successful project of the Twenty Committee.

The steady flow of ships bringing supplies from Britain and America into mainland Europe proved an irresistible target for German U-boats. Even with the Allies knocking on the borders of Germany, the outcome of the war was still not guaranteed, as the German Ardennes offensive in December proved. If German U-boat attacks continued and the flow of supply ships and troop transporters was disrupted, the Allied advance might be forced to halt. Escort vessels were overstretched with the increase in shipping since June 1944 and the Germans had introduced technical innovations to their submarines. Previously, German submarines had been forced to surface to take on fresh air and recharge their batteries. Vulnerable to detection and attack from the surface, the Germans designed a device called a *schnorkel*, which allowed the submarine to perform these maintenance actions while still submerged. This allowed U-boat crews to sit in busy Allied shipping lanes, submerged and undetected, waiting to pounce.

British Naval Intelligence was extremely puzzled as to how the Germans managed safely to navigate through the treacherous shallows around the south west of the British Isles. Without surfacing they were unable to follow the standard practice of determining a fix on their position from the stars, or by tuning in to land-based radio transmitters. Head of the Admiralty's U-boat Tracking Room, Captain Rodger Winn, believed that the Germans were using depth sounders to pilot their way along a certain part of the seabed south of the Irish coast. Close to the Fastnet Rock, the contours of the sea floor were so unique that it was relatively easy for German captains to follow and gave them an accurate fix of their position prior to entering the Irish Sea.

The obvious answer would have been to sow this part of the ocean floor with mines. Unfortunately for Winn, the only available mine-laying ships were too busy in the Channel protecting the supply route to Normandy. Previously dismissive of deception, Winn swallowed his pride and asked Ewen Montagu if he could find a way to stop the Germans from getting their positional fixes. The obvious choice of double agent for Montagu was *Tate*. The Dane had already been set up with a notional girlfriend, Mary, seconded to the American Naval HQ in London's Grosvenor Square. Still flush with cash from Plan *Midas*, *Tate* was able to purchase hard-to-come-by booze on the black market and held parties for Mary's colleagues.

After one of these imaginary parties, *Tate* explained how one naval officer had had one too many drinks at the flat. The officer served on board HMS *Plover*, a mine-layer. He indiscreetly boasted that the Allies were going to bag themselves a lot of U-boats from a new minefield they had just laid. The officer was not specific about where this new minefield was, describing it as being 'south of Ireland in a place where they go to fix their position when they're snorting [the British term for a U-boat using a *schnorkel*]'. It was hoped this off-hand description would be all too obvious to German Naval Intelligence.[9]

As with so much else, the British were able to gauge the success of this deception through Bletchley Park. On 1 January 1945 the Germans ordered all their U-boats to steer clear of the area. Several other messages were intercepted to the same effect, but it was unclear if the Germans believed there was a minefield, or were merely remarking that this was a possibility.

At this point Lady Luck played her hand. A German U-boat crew was washed up on the southern Irish coast, having scuttled its sub after striking a deep sea mine. Although the U-boat had obviously not hit *Tate*'s imaginary minefield, the point at which it was scuttled was in the right area to suggest that this might be the case. Naval Intelligence was quite sure that the U-boat crew had not made a distress signal or sent word of their plight, so it was decided that *Tate* would use the incident to reinforce his earlier deception. He made contact with his controller, and in one of his blistering communiqués claimed he felt like giving up spying. The British naval officer had recently stayed at the flat after a night out celebrating sinking a U-boat in the new minefield. *Tate* asked his controllers what was the point in him taking risks to gather and send intelligence if he was going to be ignored.

This had the desired effect. On 13 March Bletchley Park deciphered a message confirming *Tate*'s minefield. All U-boats were ordered to avoid an area some 3,600 square miles wide, or, if they found themselves there, to proceed at a depth of less than ten fathoms if they blundered into it. Thus a safe route for Allied shipping was opened, and the German crews were pushed out into deeper waters that were genuinely mined. *Tate* was confirmed as a loyal German spy, remaining in contact with his controllers until 2 May 1945, the same day German forces in Berlin surrendered to the Russians.

EPILOGUE

WITH THE WAR IN EUROPE at an end, on 10 May the W Board met. Masterman attended and gave an account of the Twenty Committee's activities since the beginning of 1944. Since *Overlord*, Masterman explained, the Twenty Committee had naturally begun to wind down its work. There were now only five active double agents: *Tate*, *Bronx*, *Rover*, *Gelatine* and *Garbo*, who was notionally in hiding, but still in contact with Madrid. Of these cases the only one who might prove genuinely useful in the post-war world was *Garbo*. It was intended that *Garbo* should go off to Madrid and make contact with his former employers to monitor the new German secret service when it was formed. Although Masterman said that B1a should maintain its links with the various service departments to act as approving bodies for double cross material, he reported that the actual Twenty Committee had served its purpose and should be dissolved. Thus the Twenty Committee ceased to be. The final, 226th, meeting was held later that day.

One by one the members around the table expressed their appreciation for the work of the secret committee. The Director of Military Intelligence said that as chairman of the W Board, he would write to MI5 and the SIS to express the board's thanks. Guy Liddell graciously returned the compliment and thanked the Directors of Intelligence for the wireless deception campaigns that gave credence to *Garbo*'s phantom army. The last word went to Johnny Bevan.

The Controlling Officer of Deception had already made known his feelings on the usefulness of the double agents. On 25 October he had written to the Director General of MI5 and applauded the work of his organization as 'outstanding'. He added, 'I believe it will be found that the German High Command was, largely through the medium of B1a channels, induced to make faulty dispositions, in particular during the vital post-*Overlord* D-Day period.'[1] Since then more information had come to light. A German map dated 15 May 1944 had been found showing the German appreciation of the armies in Great Britain. Even a cursory glance showed that the Germans had completely accepted the double agents' fake order of battle. Further proof came from the interrogation of POW German Intelligence officers. They had firmly believed there was a concentration of troops in south-east England poised to strike across the Channel at the Pas de Calais. As final proof, a cache of daily intelligence summaries had been discovered. A study of the documents showed that *Garbo*'s reports had been one of the primary sources of information used to compile them.

As all the agents were shut down and arrangements made for their ongoing security, B1a had one final act: to secure *Garbo* for future use. The last message from Madrid to *Garbo* had been sent on 8 May 1945. It spelled out the end for Germany, but also gave *Garbo* a cover address in Madrid where he could make contact. First *Garbo* had to get back to Spain, and this was complicated. *Garbo*'s arrival in England had not exactly been legal, the Spaniard having been secretly smuggled out of Lisbon to Gibraltar without the requisite paperwork being completed. Therefore, to deter suspicion about his long stay in Britain, a way had to be found to get a new passport which did not have a British stamp on it.

Tommy Harris came up with the solution. *Garbo* would go to America posing as an art student. From there he would travel to Latin America, lose his passport and apply for a new one from the local Spanish embassy. Harris was well connected in the art world, so he was able to obtain letters from the Courtauld Institute indicating *Garbo* was making a study of the influence of Spanish art in the Americas. Harris also arranged for *Garbo* to receive a series of lectures in the subject by art historian and secret Soviet spy, Anthony Blunt. *Garbo* was then accompanied to America by Tommy Harris. While there, he met FBI Chief Hoover before applying for various visas in Latin American countries. He was given permission to go to Cuba, from where he travelled on to Venezuela. It was here that he obtained a resident's permit, which allowed him to apply for a new Spanish passport and visa. He travelled back across the Atlantic and arrived in Spain on 9 August 1945. After landing in Barcelona he set off on his final mission for Britain.

Garbo located his old case officer, Kuhlenthal, and renewed his offer to work for Germany should the secret service be restored. During their reunion Kuhlenthal gave no indication that he was suspicious of *Garbo*. He only expressed regret that he had been unable to secure the Iron Cross award for *Garbo*. Due to his Spanish nationality, there had been various bureaucratic difficulties. Hitler had apparently agreed to let *Garbo* have the award, but the end of the war came before the necessary paperwork could be completed.

Their reunion ended after three hours. Kuhlenthal asked *Garbo* what he planned to do next and hinted that he himself might need some help getting out of Spain and going into hiding. *Garbo* said he would probably go to Portugal and then head for South America. Knowing the difficulty of crossing into Portugal, the German quizzed him about how he would get across the border. *Garbo*'s response was fittingly cryptic. He simply replied: 'Clandestinely'.[2]

APPENDICES

APPENDIX A – THE MASTERMAN MEMO

SECRET

MEMORANDUM ON THE 'DOUBLE AGENT' SYSTEM

A fairly extensive 'double agent' system has been built up by M.I.5. and M.I.6., but there is considerable difficulty in keeping it in existence, mainly because the Service Departments (for obvious reasons) are chary of releasing sufficient information to the enemy for him to retain confidence in the agents. We submit, however, that it is possible to secure that the losses involved in releasing information are outweighed by the gains accruing from the successful working of the system.

ADVANTAGES TO BE GAINED FROM THE 'DOUBLE AGENT' SYSTEM

(1) For Counter-Espionage

During 1914-1918 the Censorship and the British Intelligence Service abroad provided the bulk of the information for counter-espionage work. Postal communication has now ceased to play quite so important a part in espionage work, whilst, since the German conquest of the Continent, the British Secret Service operates under grave difficulties. In these circumstances the 'double agent' system has acquired a new and greater importance in counter-espionage work. It enables us to gain an insight into the personnel, methods, and means of communication of the German espionage organization in this country, while we are also led to the discovery of other agents supplied to the 'double agent' as contacts. These at a chosen moment can be eliminated or brought under our control.

By building up a 'double agent' organization and establishing the enemy's confidence in it, we limit other enemy espionage activities. Incidentally, as the enemy is forced to run the system on a cash basis, funds are diverted which might otherwise be expended on enterprises not under our control.

APPENDICES

(2) <u>For Cypher Work</u>

When 'double agents' carry out wireless transmission in cipher the enemy is encouraged to believe in the security of his Secret Service ciphers. It is particularly important at the present time, when we are far advanced in the understanding of certain German cyphers, to retain these cyphers in use. Messages from a whole network of German Secret Service wireless stations (used both for espionage and operations) have become comprehensible in the course of the last few months and M.I.5. and M.I.6. have in consequence been enabled to build up a picture of the enemy organization on the Continent and to gain advanced information of intended enterprises against this country.

It is also possible that new German cyphers may be broken if we are able through our 'double agents' to 'plant' information which comes back to us in cypher through the German Secret Service wireless.

(3) <u>For Operations</u>

From the questionnaires, some of which are supplied in great detail to 'double agents', Service experts can sometimes comprehend how much information is already at the disposal of the enemy, and can sometime make accurate guesses at his intended objectives.

More important still is the fact that if, and only if, confidence on the enemy's side has been established in a particular 'double agent', it will be possible at the appropriate moment to mislead the enemy as to large scale military operations. When such a moment arrives M.I.5. and M.I.6. will not hesitate to sacrifice their 'double agent' or group of 'double agents' if important operational results are to be expected from the sacrifice.

THE PRESENT PROBLEM

M.I.5. and M.I.6. must emphasize that only by constant planning in advance and by the maintenance of an adequate flow of consistent and plausible reports to the enemy can the 'double agent' system be kept in being and made available for effective use. This policy, no doubt, involves the taking of certain risks, but we submit that the advantages, actual and prospective, which may be gained are sufficient justification for taking these risks.

We have at the moment two main groups of 'double agents' working from this country. The first and more important is in wireless communication with the German Secret Service abroad. The second communicates by personal contact and by secret writing by air mail, mainly to the German organization in Lisbon. There are also other agents working abroad.

From our experience of these two systems we can say that most of the information required by the German Secret Service relates to air matters. Latterly, and doubtlessly in view of German air attacks and the projected invasion of this country, the German Secret Service has been asking specific questions about the location of factories, military movements, air-raid damage and the like. Such questions raise the issue of risk to life and property versus Intelligence value in its most direct form. Are we really securing sufficient advantages to compensate for the information which we give to the enemy? The present problem is, in fact, to find a suitable plan which will ensure that we gain more (or with good fortune much more) on the swings than we lose on the roundabouts.

POSSIBLE FUTURE LINES OF DEVELOPMENT

1. The 'double agents' could be graded and developed in accordance with the importance attached to them. Subsidiary and less important agents could then be used on a short term basis with the expectation of their early eclipse and for the deliberate and immediate misleading of the enemy in matters of detail. The very few really important agents – especially those who have been in the confidence of the German Secret Service for some time – should be the ones entrusted with the handling over of such accurate information as can, after due consideration by the Service Departments, be released. These agents should be held in readiness and at the disposal of the Service Departments for a large scale deception which would at a critical moment be of paramount operational importance.

2. In order to build up the important agents into positions whence at a given moment they can mislead the enemy with the greatest effect, it is necessary to have some idea of the form which this deception will have to take. If, for example, the handing over of false battle positions or large-scale troop movements is contemplated, our most important 'double agents' must gradually be provided with suitable military contacts from whom they could derive important military information; if a political deception is contemplated they would have to be provided with political contacts. In any case a condition of success would be that all such contacts were made gradually and over a fairly long period.

3. Information relating to factory sites, military defence positions and bombing targets of all kinds, would mainly be entrusted to Grade 2 'double agents'. It should then be possible to apply several kinds of devices to mislead the enemy. For example apparently accurate information could be given which would in fact refer to dummy targets in the vicinity of a site, whose exact position had been asked for by the German Secret Service. For this purpose the co-operation of Colonel Turner's department would be essential. Alternatively really accurate information about a site might be provided, and a hot reception prepared for the expected German raiders. In any case it is suggested that dummy sites which are prepared to attract German raiders should be pin-pricked on the maps which the German Secret Service has provided to certain 'double agents'.

Up to the present the chief function of M.I.5. and M.I.6. in this matter has been to provide the machinery with which to mislead the enemy and to invite the Service Departments to plan for its use. But there is a real danger that the 'double agent' system which has been built up may be allowed to collapse

because no adequate use is made of it. The present committee are
to co-ordinate suggestions from its members for making full use
of the machinery provided; to construct plans developed from
these suggestions and, if necessary, to press for the putting of
these plans into operation.

M.I.5. (B.2a)
27th December, 1940

(KV 4/63 Formation and minutes of meetings of the Twenty Committee
in connection with traffic for special agents.)

APPENDIX B

The *Garbo* Network February 1944

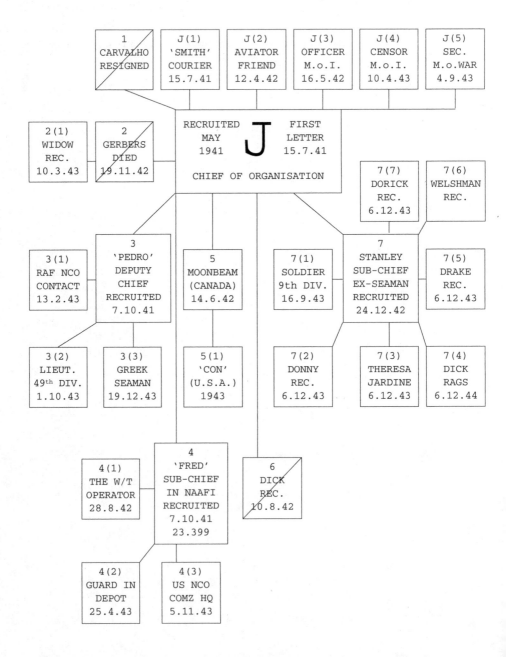

APPENDICES

APPENDIX C – SPY CODENAMES

Albert
The radio operator in *Gilbert's Atlas* team. He never knew he was really working for the Allies.

Alert
A notional agent run by the Thirty-One Committee in Beirut, who provided information by letter to the Abwehr via *Crude*, a British double agent who was supposedly an Abwehr informant in Istanbul. See *Crude*.

Artist
The Abwehr's Johann 'Johnny' Jebsen; never a committed Nazi, he agreed to work for the British and came under SIS control in September 1943.

Balloon
Dickie Metcalfe, an MI5 agent purporting to work as a sub-agent of *Tricycle*.

Benedict network
A notional network serving *Garbo* by 1944, consisting of an RAF NCO, a lieutenant in the 49th Infantry Division, and a Greek communist who believed that *Garbo* was working for the Russians.

Biscuit
Sam McCarthy, a conman who worked for MI5 as a spy and became a double agent on his acceptance by the Abwehr in 1940. *Biscuit* provided the Germans with his identity card and a traveller ration book, which had been altered by MI5 to contain a flaw. By this means British police were able to identify subsequent German spies, whose papers had been forged based on *Biscuit's* documents.

Bronx
Elvira Chaudoir, the daughter of the Peruvian chargé d'affaire in Vichy France, who had lived in England since the beginning of the war. A socialite, she was first recruited by MI6, who sent her to visit her parents in Vichy France where she was accepted as a German spy; on her return to the UK in 1943 she was enrolled as a double agent.

Brutus
Roman Czerniawski, a Polish air officer who had headed a resistance network in France before being captured. Recruited by the Germans to come to Britain to foster discontent in the Free Polish contingent there, *Brutus* arrived in England in October 1942 and after an initial period of distrust began active deception work for the British in early 1944. He played a key part in Operation *Fortitude*.

Careless   A Polish airman shot down in 1939, who managed to escape to Spain in April 1941, where he allowed himself to be recruited by the Abwehr under the name Clark Korab. Having revealed his contact with the Abwehr to the ship's captain on the way to England, he was retained by MI5 as a double agent, focusing on anti-aircraft defences, although after a number of indiscretions he was interned in Camp 020.

Celery   Walter Dicketts, a former air intelligence officer from World War I, who had been cashiered for dishonesty and had served several jail sentences for financial fraud. After meeting with *Snow*, he tried to report him to the intelligence services as a German spy, and found himself recruited by MI5 and working with *Snow* on a mission to Lisbon in 1941.

Charlie   A Manchester businessman of German–English parentage who had, with one of his younger brothers, been forced into working for the Abwehr by the threat of reprisals against the third brother in Germany. Identified only as Eschborn, he was betrayed to MI5 by *Snow* in October 1939.

Cheese   This was initially the codename of a single agent, Renato Levi, an Italian Jew who was approached by the Abwehr in December 1939 and reported this to the British in Genoa. Having worked during the invasion of France he was sent to Egypt by the Italian SIM in 1940. Reporting there to SIME, he was set up as the head of what was to be a key radio network in the Middle East. The name *Cheese* became an umbrella term for this network, which was one of the most successful of all the Allied double cross operations in the war. See *Lambert*.

Chinois   Chouali ben Larbi, one of three double agents placed at the disposal of A Force by the French Deuxième Bureau in 1943, to address the task of breaking the resistance of the Afrika Korps in Tunisia.

Chopin   *Brutus's* radio operator. In the clandestine world of European resistance movements in which Brutus had been involved, radio operators were often known as 'pianists' and spy networks 'orchestras', hence the musical connection.

Claudius   Mrs Mathilde Krafft, a naturalized British citizen, who was a payment channel for *Snow*. She was caught and interned in 1939.

APPENDICES

Cobweb and *Beetle*   A team of double agents working in Iceland.

Crude   A British double agent, supposedly an Abwehr informant working as a janitor in the British consulate in Istanbul. See *Alert*.

Dagobert network   A notional network serving *Garbo* by 1944, whose fictional agents comprised *Stanley* and his seven colleagues in the in the Welsh Nationalist movement 'Brothers in the Aryan World Order'. See *Benedict* network.

Dragonfly   Hans George, born to German parents and recruited by the Abwehr in 1940, of which he informed the British authorities. Working for MI5 he transmitted meteorological reports to the Germans, and facilitated their communications with *Father*. His case was closed in January 1944 after the Germans failed to pay him.

Dreadnought   *Tricycle*'s brother Ivo Popov. Throughout 1943 he selected potential sub-agents for his brother in Yugoslavia. He initially passed them to the Abwehr's 'Johnny' Jebsen (*Artist*) for German spy training, after which they arrived in Britain to begin their careers as German agents under MI5's control. Such agents included *Meteor*, the *Worm* and *Freak*.

Le Duc   *Gilbert*'s second-in-command in the *Atlas* team. Unlike his colleagues he supported *Gilbert* in his work for the Allies.

Duteil   The *Atlas* team's expert in sabotage. He was unaware that his boss *Gilbert* was working for the Allies, and was arrested to avoid his discovering this.

Falcon   The radio mechanic on *Gilbert*'s *Atlas* team. Like his colleagues *Albert* and *Duteil*, he was unaware that his team leader was a double agent.

Father   Henri Arents, a distinguished Belgian air force pilot, who arrived from Lisbon in 1941 on an Abwehr mission to steal an RAF plane. Having contacted the Belgian authorities in Lisbon, Arents was received by MI5 and was quickly 'turned' to double cross work. His case was active until June 1943.

Freak   A Yugoslav who arrived in Britain in 1943; he became the radio operator for *Tricycle*'s network.

Gander   Karl Goose, a member of the Brandenburg Regiment, who was parachuted into Britain in October 1940 after completing three weeks' intensive training by the Abwehr in espionage and radio transmission. Arrested immediately after his arrival following a tip-off by *Snow*, he willingly joined the growing number of double agents. His case was closed in November 1940 after failing to establish contact with Germany.

Garbo   Juan Pujol García, one of the most important figures in the war of deception. Initially rejected by the British authorities in Madrid, he embarked on a complicated series of fabrications which enabled him to be recruited, first by the Abwehr with the codename *Arabel*, and, after a period in which he was known to SIS as *Bovril*, eventually by MI5, who arranged for his transport to England in April 1942. He became one of their greatest double agents, preserving his cover beyond the end of the war.

Gelatine   Friedl Gartner, an Austrian socialite to whom Dusko Popov (*Tricycle*) became romantically linked, and who started to work as his sub-agent, along with *Balloon*, in 1941. She supplied the Germans with political information that she was supposed to have picked up from society gossip. Remained active until the end of hostilities in Europe.

Gilbert   Originally the head of the Abwehr's best agent network in North Africa, *Gilbert* offered his network of four sub-agents, who were responsible for the Germans' *Atlas* mission in Tunis, to the French Deuxième Bureau in 1943. Of the four, only one was aware that his leader was working as a double agent for the British. See *Albert*, *Le Duc*, *Duteil* and *Falcon*.

Guinea   James Ponsonby, an English commercial attaché and member of SOE. Recruited by A Force in July 1943, he was based in Tangiers as a channel for passing deception.

GW   Gwilym Williams, a Welshman working as a spy for the British security services, who was introduced to the Abwehr by *Snow* in September 1938. His case was shut down in February 1942 after the arrest of his Spanish contact.

Hamlet, Mullet   A trio of businessmen recruited in 1943. The
and *Puppet*   instigator of this network was *Hamlet*, a half-Jewish Austrian who reluctantly agreed to work for the Abwehr. In Lisbon he became friends with an Englishman who acted as his business representative in England and was codenamed *Mullet* by the British. Another friend of *Hamlet*'s acted as

APPENDICES

	his link to General von Falkenhausen, the military governor of Belgium, and was recruited by the SIS as *Puppet*. Case closed in May 1944 after the collapse of *Tricycle*.
Hektor/Josephine	Codenames used by Karl Heinz Krämer, a freelance spy for the Abwehr based in Sweden. He had a network of contacts in the Finnish, Hungarian and Japanese secret services, and claimed sources in France, Britain, Portugal and the United States. In his reports to Berlin he used the codename *Hektor* for all air-related intelligence and *Josephine* for naval matters.
Humble	A notional agent run by the Thirty-One Committee in Beirut, who provided information that was passed to the Axis through a Turkish customs official known as *Smooth*.
Jeff	Tor Glad, a Norwegian who arrived in Banffshire, Scotland, in April 1941 with John Moe and enlisted as a double agent codenamed *Jeff*. He was judged unreliable and interned in August 1941, after which his case was continued by a substitute. See *Mutt*.
Kondor network	Run by Count Laszlo Almasy, or *Salam*, this network consisted of German agents *Max* and *Moritz* in Egypt.
Lambert	Sergeant Ellis from the Royal Corps of Signals, assigned as *Cheese*'s radio operator in Egypt and given the notional identity of a Syrian national of Russian descent called Paul Nicossof, an anti-Soviet White Russian. *Lambert* headed up the *Cheese* network from 1942, and became one of the Abwehr's most trusted operators. See *Misanthrope*.
the *Lemons*	*Little Lemon* was a Greek sailor run by the Thirty-Three Committee in Cyprus, along with his companion *Big Lemon*.
Meteor	A Croat officer who arrived in April 1943 as a late recruit to *Tricycle*'s network.
Misanthrope	This was the notional Greek girlfriend assigned to *Lambert*. Her part was played by an actual Greek girl recruited and trained by SIME, known as the *BGM* (Blond Gun Moll).
Le Moco	A German spy parachuted in near Tunis in July 1944 to help *Gilbert*. He was only too happy to work with *Gilbert* on behalf of the Allies.
Mullet	An Englishman who acted as *Hamlet*'s representative in England.

Mutt	John Moe, a Norwegian who landed in Banffshire, Scotland, in April 1941 with Tor Glad and immediately gave himself up to the authorities. After detailed interrogation he was set up as a double agent with the codename *Mutt*. See *Jeff*.
Ostro	Paul Fidrmuc, a Czech businessman and 'bogus' spy operating in Lisbon, outside the control of MI5. By 1944 he was inventing information and selling it to the Abwehr.
Peppermint	José Brugada, the Spanish press attaché in London, recruited in early 1942 after MI5 discovered his involvement in a Spanish espionage set up. His case expired in April 1943 due to a breakdown in communications.
the *Pessimists*	The *Pessimists* were three Greeks who were intercepted in northern Syria having landed by boat in summer 1942. The chief, codenamed *Pessimist C* and known to the Germans as *Mimi*, was probably bringing money to *Lambert*; he had previously been in contact with MI6 in Athens. His two companions, Costa and Basile (*Pessimists B* and *Z* respectively) were jailed, though given a notional existence to supply their chief with information to send back to Sofia by wireless. *Pessimist C* became a leading double cross agent.
Pogo	The Spaniard identified as del Pozo came to Britain in 1940 as a press correspondent for the Spanish Institute of Political Studies. Shortly after his arrival in Britain he arranged to meet *GW* to supply him with a cash payment from the Abwehr. MI5 contemplated interning him, but before they could do so the Ministry of Information arranged to have him sent back to Spain in February 1941.
Puppet	A friend of *Hamlet*'s, who acted as his link with General von Falkenhausen.
Quicksilver	A Greek air force officer who accepted an offer to spy for the Abwehr as a chance to get over to the British. He had two assistants, *Rio* and *Gala*. While his subordinates were locked up and allowed only a notional existence, *Quicksilver* was turned to double cross work in Beirut.
Rainbow	Bernie Kiener. Born in Britain to a German mother, Kiener had grown up in Germany but returned to England in 1938. When approached by a friend with what he rightly surmised would lead to an invitation to become a spy for the Abwehr, Kiener contacted MI5. On their instructions

he went to Germany and was recruited into the Abwehr, formally becoming a British double agent upon his return to the United Kingdom. Reported on aviation and air defences before his case was closed in June 1943 after a lack of German interest.

Rover   A young Polish sailor who had been captured by the Nazis, and joined the German secret service, agreeing to go to Britain as a spy. He arrived in England in May 1944 and was put to work as a double cross agent; however, by the time the Germans returned his calls, his services had been dispensed with, and a substitute was used instead. His case was maintained until May 1945.

the *Savages*   An Abwehr team of three intercepted on its arrival in Cyprus in July 1943 and run by the Thirty-Three Committee in Cyprus. *Savage I* reported to his German controllers that he had moved to Cairo with his wireless transmitter and had obtained employment in the Allied Liaison Branch of GHQ. His companions were jailed.

Silver   Bhagat Ram Talwar, a Hindu and communist activist, who fed the Abwehr's station in Kabul with deceptive information from 1943.

Skoot   See *Tricycle*.

Snow   Arthur George Owens, a Welshman and Welsh Nationalist who during his business travels abroad passed technical secrets to the British intelligence services under the codename *Snow*. In 1936 he offered his services to the Abwehr, who gave him the codename *Johnny*. Continuing to pass intelligence to British, *Snow* was the first of the double agents, and his work was the origin of the entire double cross system. His case was shut down in April 1941 after he claimed to have revealed his association with the British secret services to the Abwehr.

Summer   Gösta Caroli, a Swede with a German mother, who was a mechanic by trade. He was trained by the Abwehr along with his partner, the Dane Wulf Schmidt, and was parachuted into Britain in September 1940, where he was captured and 'turned' by MI5. However, his state of mind was fragile, and after he tried to escape in January 1941 his case was wound up.

Tate   Wulf Schmidt, a Dane who worked for the Abwehr under
                  the codename *Leonhart*. He arrived in Britain by parachute
                  in September 1940, shortly after his partner, the Swede
                  Gösta Caroli. After some effort he was persuaded to work
                  as a double agent for the British. He was one of the most
                  successful double cross spies during the war and remained
                  in contact with the Germans until May 1945.

Treasure   Nathalie 'Lily' Sergueiev, born in Russia but raised in
                  Paris, was recruited by the Abwehr in 1940 when working
                  as a journalist. She arrived in Britain in 1943, having
                  stipulated that she would work for the Allies if they
                  arranged for her and her pet terrier Frisson to travel to the
                  United Kingdom. The difficulties involved in arranging the
                  dog's passage to Britain nearly wrecked the British security
                  services' operations in 1944. The case was wound down
                  in December 1944.

Tricycle/Skoot The Yugoslav, Dusko Popov. A rich lawyer with a playboy
                  lifestyle, he was recruited by *Artist* ('Johnny' Jebsen)
                  in 1940 as *Ivan* to mix with British high society, report on
                  possible opposition to Churchill and identify people who
                  might be willing to negotiate with Germany. Having revealed
                  this to the British secret services, Popov came to London at
                  their arrangement, and began his career as a double agent with
                  the initial codename *Skoot*. When joined by sub-agents *Balloon*
                  and *Gelatine*, as head of a network of three agents he was re-
                  named *Tricycle*. Throughout 1943 he expanded his network to
                  include sub-agents recruited by his brother, *Dreadnought*, in
                  Yugoslavia and trained by the Abwehr before transferring to
                  Britain – these agents included *Meteor*, the *Worm* and *Freak*.

the *Worm*   One of *Tricycle*'s later recruits, who came to Britain in
                  September 1943.

Zigzag   Edward Arnold Chapman, who was parachuted into
                  Britain as a German agent in December 1942, charged
                  with blowing up the de Havilland works in Hatfield. His
                  German codename was *Fritzchen* (Little Fritz). He willingly
                  became a double agent. His case was finally closed down in
                  November 1944 due to security concerns.

APPENDICES

APPENDIX D – OPERATIONS AND PLANS

1940

Operation *Compass* The Allied counter-offensive to recapture Sidi Barrani from Mussolini's forces, launched on 9 December.

Operation *Lena* An espionage offensive against Great Britain in the prelude to the planned invasion. German spies were trained as forward scouts for the invasion troops, locating potential invasion beaches and landing sites for parachutists and gliders. If the invasion took place they were to make contact with the invading forces and act as guides through the countryside.

Operation *Seelöwe* (*Sealion*) The German codename for Hitler's proposed invasion of the British Isles scheduled for September, but postponed indefinitely after failure to win the air battle over Britain.

1941

Operation *Camilla* A British cover plan to disguise the offensive against the Italian army in Eritrea and Abyssinia. This plan hinted the British would attack through Somaliland.

Operation *Crusader* General Auchinleck's counter-offensive against Rommel in North Africa, launched on 17 November.

Plan *IV* A largely unsuccessful plan devised by Ewen Montagu to pass bogus naval intelligence to the Abwehr through Dusko Popov (*Skoot / Tricycle*).

Plan *Midas* A British plan to facilitate payments to German spies in UK to maintain interest in them. The money actually went into British secret service coffers.

1942

Operation *Bertram* The tactical counterpart to *Treatment*, a plan devised and implemented by Lieutenant Colonel Charles Richardson. This involved the use of dummy equipment and the 'laying' of a bogus pipeline to convince the Germans the British would attack from the south of the

Alamein line, rather than along the northern coastal road as was actually planned.

Operation *Cascade* — An operation masterminded by Dudley Clarke in March 1942 to build up and plant a fake order of battle on the Germans, showing the British to be much stronger than was actually the case. It was a long-running operation and is credited as the cornerstone of Allied success in deceiving Hitler.

Operation *Hardboiled* — A notional Allied assault against Stavanger in Norway.

Plan *Kennecott* — Part of the cover plan for the *Torch* landings. See *Overthrow*.

Operation *Nightcap* — The operation put in place to capture *Fritzchen* (Little Fritz), later *Zigzag*, on his arrival into England by parachute in December 1942.

Operation *Overthrow* — A bogus cross-channel invasion plan to divert attention and troops from Churchill's planned attack on the Mediterranean. It was a continuation of the discarded *Sledgehammer* plan.

Operation *Sentinel* — An operation planned by General Auchinleck's Director of Camouflage, Major Geoffrey Barkas, following Rommel's drive towards Egypt. It involved the construction of dummy camps and equipment around the Alamein area to suggest to Rommel that Auchinleck's forces were much larger than they actually were.

Operation *Sledgehammer* — A plan favoured by the United States for an early and direct assault across the English Channel into north-west Europe. It was discarded in favour of *Torch* after lobbying by Churchill.

Operation *Solo* — A bogus threat against Norway to prevent Germany sending troops to the Mediterranean. *Solo I* suggested that Trondheim and Narvik were the target of the troops mustering on the Clyde, but who were really earmarked for Operation *Torch*. *Solo II* gave the impression that the troops en route for *Torch* were actually sailing to Dakar. See Operation *Hardboiled*.

Operation *Torch* — The planned Allied landings in French North Africa, set for November 1942.

Plan *Townsman* — Part of the *Torch* cover plan, suggesting the British were going to relieve Malta.

Operation *Treatment* A ruse by which A Force were to use intelligence channels to make the Germans believe that the British offensive at El Alamein would commence on 6 November.

1943

Operation *Avalanche* Actual American landings at Salerno with the objective of capturing the port of Naples.

Plan *Barclay* A cover plan for Operation *Husky*, the plan for the invasion of Sicily in 1943.

Operation *Baytown* Actual British landings in Calabria on 3 September 1943 aimed at drawing German troops away from the Naples area.

Plan *Boardman* A cover plan for operations *Baytown* and *Avalanche* developed by A Force, which aimed at weakening German forces in the south and centre of the Italian peninsula while pinning down Axis reserves in the Balkans and mainland Greece.

Operation *Boothby* Part of Plan *Boardman*, suggesting an attack on Apulia on the heel of Italy by the British III Corps, as well as feints against Gofore on the south Italian peninsula.

Operation *Brimstone* Part of Operation *Mincemeat* and the cover plan for *Husky*, this was the codename for a bogus attack on Sardinia.

Plan *Cockade* An umbrella name for a series of plans to deter the Germans from detaching troops either to the Mediterranean or to the Russian front, by simulating threats to northern France and Norway. Expanding on what had already been attempted, *Cockade* was supposed to culminate in an ambitious mock invasion of the Pas de Calais. This was aimed at tying down German troops and also drawing the Luftwaffe into a pitched battle over the English Channel. On balance it was a failure.

Operation *Husky* Genuine Allied plan for the invasion of Sicily in 1943.

Plan *Jael* A cover plan for Operation *Neptune* drafted in August 1943. It claimed the Allies had given up on making a cross-Channel attack and would continue to concentrate on the Mediterranean theatre through the course of 1944.

Operation *Mincemeat* An operation of April 1943, linked to Operation *Husky*, which involved planting false documents on a dead body washed up in Spain. The documents suggested preparations for Sicily were a cover for an invasion of Sardinia, and that the Allies were planning an operation in the eastern Mediterranean.

Mulberry	A codename for a set of prefabricated port installations the Allies would tow to Normandy in lieu of capturing a French port intact. The fact German intelligence did not ask its spies to investigate the mulberries was an indication that surprise at Normandy would be achieved.
Plan *Pointblank*	Actual codename for air bombardment of Germany, running alongside Plan *Jael*.
Plan *Starkey*	Part of the *Cockade* plan, this was a false plan for an Allied attack on the Pas de Calais between 8 and 14 September. According to the deception plan, after the bridgehead was established by *Starkey*, a second attack would follow, codenamed *Wadham*.
Plan *Tindall*	Part of *Cockade*, this was a continuation of the threat to Norway by bogus Allied forces.
Operation *Torrent*	Known as 'Appendix Y' of the *Overlord* plan, this replaced Plan *Jael* in September 1943. Its aims were threefold: (i) to make the German High Command believe that the Pas de Calais was the target for the 1944 invasion of France rather than Normandy; (ii) to cause the Germans to think that D-Day would be later than was the case; and (iii) once the assault began, to try to pin down as many land and air forces to the east of the Pas de Calais as possible for at least a fortnight, by indicating that the Normandy landings were a feint. See *Overlord* (1944).
Plan *Wadham*	Part of *Cockade*, this was a bogus invasion of Brittany planned to follow Plan *Starkey* on 22 September.
Plan *Withstand*	Part of Plan *Barclay*, a notional move against Turkey to divert attention from the invasion of Sicily in 1943. See Operation *Husky*.

1944

Operation *Anvil*	The codename for the actual landing in the south of France in August 1944. Renamed *Dragoon* in August 1944 after *Anvil* codename was compromised.

APPENDICES

Operation *Bodyguard* A cover plan for the invasion of France in 1944, drawn up after the final details of *Overlord* were agreed in November/December 1943; the name was given to the overall deception policy for the war against Germany in 1944, and provided a framework for a number of subsidiary plans, such as *Graffham*, *Rankin*, *Royal Flush* and *Zeppelin*.

Operation *Chettyford* A Force's deception plan for the Anzio landings. This plan indicated that a pincer move was about to be mounted by the Seventh United States Army under Patton against Pisa on the west coast and Rimini on the east coast, with the objective of containing German reserves to the north of the country. When it came to providing cover for *Anvil* a similar tactic was used.

Operation *Copperhead* A 1944 ruse using an actor to pose as 'Monty' in a series of publicized events close to the date of the invasion of France.

Plan *Ferdinand* A false operation in the Mediterranean, devised as a cover for *Anvil*. It suggested that all the military preparations for *Anvil* were geared for a direct assault on Genoa. See Operation *Ironside* and Plan *Vendetta*.

Operation *Fortitude* A cover plan for Operation *Neptune*. It had two parts: *Fortitude South* supposed that at D+45 an assault would be carried out on the Pas de Calais, with the aim of securing a bridgehead, capturing Antwerp, and thrusting deep into Germany. *Fortitude North* was a plan to liberate Norway and thus pin down German troops in Scandinavia, rather than France.

Operation *Foxley* An unrealized SOE plan to assassinate Hitler.

Plan *Graffham* A plan devised by the LCS as part of Operation *Bodyguard*, which complemented *Fortitude North* and consisted of a series of diplomatic deceptions designed to suggest that the Allies were trying to bring Sweden into the war.

Operation *Ironside* Part of the cover plan for *Overlord*, *Ironside* suggested a landing in the Bay of Biscay by Allied troops sailing directly from the United States. See also Plans *Ferdinand* and *Vendetta*.

Operation *Market Garden* Actual airborne operation to seize a crossing point over the Rhine at Arnhem.

Operation *Neptune* The cross-Channel attack phase of Operation *Overlord*.

Operation *Overlord* Plan for the invasion of western Europe planned by the Allies for spring 1944. See also Plans *Jael* and *Pointblank*, *Mulberry* and Operation *Torrent* (all 1943).

Plan *Premium* An attempt in 1944 to draw German attention towards the Pas de Calais, using the *Mullet*, *Puppet*, *Hamlet* network though a series of investigations into insurance policies for industrial sites in the region. It was cancelled when the arrest of *Artist* threatened to blow the whole double agent network.

Plan *Quicksilver* Devised by Colonel David Strangeways, this plan was part of *Fortitude South*. It had six parts, entitled *Quicksilver I – Quicksilver VI*, and provided a detailed description of how *Neptune* would be disguised.

Plan *Rankin* An actual plan to exploit any dramatic weakening of German forces or a withdrawal from western Europe. Part of Operation *Bodyguard*.

Plan *Royal Flush* Part of *Bodyguard*, this plan saw diplomatic approaches made to neutral countries to attempt to gain concessions for bogus Allied operations.

Plan *Skye* A radio deception plan drawn up to implement *Fortitude North*, communicating details of the largely notional 4th Army.

Operation *Titanic* An SAS plan to deceive the Germans about the extent of the Normandy airborne landings by creating dummy parachutists that simulated grenade and rifle fire. There were four versions of this plan, *Titanic I–IV*.

Plan *Vendetta* A cover plan for *Neptune* suggesting a threat to southern France to deter German troops from being redeployed to Normandy while the beachhead was being established. See Plan *Ferdinand* and Operation *Ironside*.

Plan *Wantage* The replacement for Plan *Cascade* in February 1944, creating 26 bogus divisions in the run-up to the *Neptune* attack.

Plan *Zeppelin* The part of *Bodyguard* covering the eastern Mediterranean. Its aim was to retain as many German troops in the Balkans and Greece before and after *Neptune* as possible.

APPENDICES

APPENDIX E – ACRONYMS

ATS	Auxiliary Territorial Service.
B1a	Section of MI5 responsible for running double agents.
BEF	British Expeditionary Force.
BUF	British Union of Fascists.
CIGS	Chief of the Imperial General Staff: the commander of the British Army.
COSSAC	Chief of Staff to the Supreme Allied Commander.
CSDIC	Combined Services Detailed Interrogation Centre.
CSS	Chief of the Secret Service (head of SIS).
CTD	Colonel Turner's department.
DMI	Director of Military Intelligence.
DNB	Deutsche Nachrichtenburo (Goebbels' news agency)
DNI	Director of Naval Intelligence.
DSO	Defence Security Officer.
FBI	Federal Bureau of Investigation.
FOPS	Future Operations Planning Section.
FUSAG	First United States Army Group.
GC&CS	Government Code and Cypher School.
GHQ	General Headquarters.
GOC	General Officer Commanding.
HDE	Home Defence Executive.
ISK	Intelligence Service Knox (deciphered Abwehr 'Engima' messages).
ISOS	Intelligence Section, Oliver Strachley, referring to the decrypts of German coded messages intercepted

by the RSS and deciphered by Strachley's group from the codes given by the Germans to *Snow*.

ISSB	Inter-Services Security Branch, an offshoot of the JIC.
JIC	Joint Intelligence Committee. Body responsible for coordinating and making intelligence assessments to the Chiefs of Staff.
JPS	Joint Planning Staff.
LCS	London Controlling Section.
LDV	Local Defence Volunteers, the forerunner of the Home Guard.
LVF	Légion des Volontaires Français, French volunteers recruited to fight against the Soviet Union.
MEIC	Middle East Intelligence Centre.
MEW	Ministry of Economic Warfare.
MI5	British Security Service responsible for combating all counter-espionage in the UK and throughout the Empire. With no powers of arrest, MI5 worked closely with police Special Branch during the war.
MI6	British Secret Intelligence Service (SIS). Responsible for gathering secret intelligence gathering and also for counter-espionage outside the UK and Imperial territorial limits. As there was a crossover with MI5 in this area, Section V was created in order to pass relevant intelligence on to the Security Service. The head of Section V, Felix Cowgill, was widely accused of extreme subjectivity in deciding what was relevant, and for not passing important information to MI5 at key moments in the war.
MI11	The War Office.
MPI	Mean Point of Impact.
MSS	Most Secret Source.
NAAFI	Navy, Army and Air Force Institutes: recreational centres for servicemen and women.

NBBS	New British Broadcasting Station, a German propaganda service.
NID	Naval Intelligence Division.
OSS	Office of Strategic Services.
POW	Prisoner of War.
PPF	Parti Populaire Français, the French fascist party.
PWE	Political Warfare Executive.
RHSA	Reichssicherheitshauptamt (Main Security Office of the Reich); the Nazi security service.
RN	Royal Navy.
RSLO	Regional Security Liaison Officer.
RSS	Radio Security Service.
SCIU	Special Counter-Intelligence Unit.
SHAEF	Supreme Headquarters Allied Expeditionary Force.
SIM	Servizio Informazioni Militare (the Italian intelligence service).
SIME	Security Intelligence Middle East.
SIS	See MI6.
SOE	Special Operations Executive.
TR	Travaux Ruraux, French works programme used as a front for counter-espionage organization.
USAAF	United States Army Air Force.
W Board	Wireless Board, senior approving body for deception material.
XX Committee	Approving body for deception material given to double agents, also known as the Twenty Commitee.
Y Service	Generic name for radio intercept services.

SOURCES AND FURTHER READING

MANUSCRIPT SOURCES

NATIONAL ARCHIVES, KEW

KV 4/63 – KV 4/69, Formation and minutes of the Twenty Committee in connection with Double Cross agents; KV 4/185 – KV 4/196, Liddell Diaries from 1939 Aug 01 to 1945 Jun 30; CAB 154/6, A Force permanent record file Narrative War diary (see also: CN 26/1); CAB 154/100 – CAB 154/101, Historical record of deception in the war against Germany and Italy (the Wingate narrative); WO 106/5921, Operation MINCEMEAT: copies of documents made available to press; WO 169/24898, case history of agent GILBERT; KV 2/39 – KV 2/42, GARBO case files; KV 2/445 – KV 2/453, Selected Historical Papers from the SNOW case; KV 2/674, Selected Historical Papers from the CELERY Case; KV 2/845 – KV 2/866, TRICYCLE case files; KV 2/1067, MUTT & JEFF case file; KV 2/1070 – KV 2/1083, BALLOON case files; KV 2/1133, CHEESE case file; KV 2/1275 – KV 2/1280, GELATINE case files; KV 2/455 – KV 2/463, *ZIGZAG* case files; KV 2/464 – KV 2/466, TREASURE case file.

CHURCHILL ARCHIVES CENTRE, CHURCHILL COLLEGE, CAMBRIDGE
CHAR 20/25 CIGs to Prime Minister 31.10.41.

LIDDELL HART CENTRE FOR MILITARY ARCHIVES
GB99 KCLMA Robertson T. A.

PUBLISHED SOURCES

Alexander of Tunis, Earl, *The Alexander Memoirs 1940–1945* (London: Cassell, 1962)

Al-Sadat, Anwar (trans. Thomas Graham), *Revolt on the Nile* (London: Allan Wingate, 1957)

Baker White, John, *The Big Lie* (London: Evans, 1955)

Barkas, Geoffrey, *The Camouflage Story* (London: Cassell, 1952)

Behrendt, Hans-Otto, *Rommel's Intelligence in the Desert Campaign: 1941–1943* (London: Kimber, 1985)

Bower, Tom, *The Perfect English Spy* (London: Heinemann, 1995)

SOURCES AND FURTHER READING

Brown, Anthony Cave, *Bodyguard of Lies* (London: W. H. Allen, 1975)

Brown, Anthony Cave, *The Secret Servant* (London: Joseph, 1988)

Carlson, John Roy, *Cairo to Damascus* (New York: Alfred A. Knopf, 1951)

Casey, William, *The Secret War against Hitler* (London: Simon and Schuster, 1989)

Churchill, Winston S., *The Second World War*, 6 vols (London: Cassell and Co Ltd, 1949)

Clarke, Dudley, *Seven Assignments* (London: Jonathan Cape, 1948)

Clifton James, M. E., *I Was Monty's Double* (London: Rider and Co., 1954)

Cruickshank, Charles G., *Deception in World War II* (Oxford: Oxford University Press, 1979)

Czerniawski, Roman Garby, *The Big Network* (London: George Ronald, 1961)

Delmer, Denis Sefton, *The Counterfeit Spy* (London: Hutchinson, 1971)

Delmer, Denis Sefton, *Black Boomerang* (London: Secker and Warburg, 1962)

D'Este, Carlo, *Patton: A Genius for War* (London: HarperCollins, 1995)

Dobinson, Collin, *Fields of Deception* (London: Methuen, 2000)

Eisenhower, Dwight D., *Crusade in Europe* (London: William Heinemann Ltd, 1948)

Eppler, John (trans. S. Seago), *Operation Condor: Rommel's Spy* (London: Macdonald and Jane's, 1977)

Fairbanks Jr, Douglas, *Hell of a War* (London: Robson Books, 1995)

Farago, Ladislas, *The Game of the Foxes* (London: Hodder and Stoughton, 1971)

Fisher, David, *The War Magician* (New York: Coward-McCann, 1983)

Foot, M. R. D. and Langley, J. M., *MI9 Escape and Evasion 1939–1945* (London: Bodley Head, 1979)

Foot, M. R. D., *Resistance* (London: Eyre Methuen, 1976)

Garnett, David, *The Secret History of PWE: The Political Warfare Executive 1939–1945* (London: St Ermin's, 2002)

Gerard, Philip, *Secret Soldiers: The Story of World War II's Heroic Army of Deception* (New York: Dutton, 2002)

Handel, Michael I., *Strategic and Operational Deception in the Second World War* (London: Frank Cass, 1987)

Harris, Tomás (intro. by Mark Seaman), *Garbo – The Spy Who Saved D-Day* (Richmond: Public Record Office, 2000)

Hart-Davis, Duff, *Peter Fleming* (London: Cape, 1974)

Hesketh, Roger, *Fortitude: The D-Day Deception Campaign* (London: St Ermin's, 1999)

Hinsley, F. H. et al., *British Intelligence in the Second World War*, 5 vols (London: HMSO, 1979–90)

Holt, Thaddeus, *The Deceivers: Allied Military Deception in the Second World War* (London and New York: Scribners/Simon and Schuster, 2004)

Howard, Michael, *British Intelligence in the Second World War*, vol. 5, *Strategic Deception* (London: HMSO, 1990)

Jones, R. V., *Most Secret War* (London: Hamilton, 1978)

Kahn, David, *Hitler's Spies* (London: Hodder and Stoughton, 1978)

Lewin, Ronald, *The Chief: Field Marshal Lord Wavell: Commander-in-Chief and Viceroy 1939–1947* (London: Hutchinson, 1980)

Lewin, Ronald, *Life and Death of the Afrika Corps* (London: Batsford, 1977)

Lewin, Ronald, *Ultra Goes to War* (London: Hutchinson, 1978)

Lochner, Louis (ed. & trans.), *The Goebbels Diaries* (London: Hamish Hamilton, 1948)

Macintyre, Ben, *Agent Zigzag: The True Wartime Story of Eddie Chapman: lover, betrayer, hero, spy* (London: Bloomsbury, 2007)

Maskelyne, Jasper, *Magic – Top Secret* (London and New York: Stanley Paul, 1949)

Masterman, J. C., *The Double-Cross System in the War of 1939–1945* (New Haven and London: Yale University Press, 1972)

Masterman, J. C., *On the Chariot Wheel* (London: Oxford University Press, 1975)

Miller, Joan, *One Girl's War* (Brandon: Dingle, 1986)

Miller, Russell, *Codename Tricycle: The True Story of the Second World War's Most Extraordinary Double Agent* (London: Secker and Warburg, 2004)

Moen, Jan, *John Moe: Double Agent* (Edinburgh: Mainstream, 1986)

Montagu, Ewen, *Beyond Top Secret U* (London: P. Davies, 1977)

Montagu, Ewen, *The Man Who Never Was* (London: Evans Bros. 1953)

Montgomery of Alamein, *Memoirs* (London: Collins, 1958)

Morgan, Sir Frederick, *Overture to Overlord* (London: Hodder and Stoughton Ltd, 1950)

Mure, David, *Practise to Deceive* (London: Kimber, 1977)

Mure, David, *Master of Deception* (London: Kimber, 1980)

The New Yorker Book of War Pieces – London 1939 to Hiroshima 1945 (New York: Reynal & Hitchcock, 1947)

Niven, David, *The Moon's a Balloon* (London: Hamilton, 1971)

Paillole, Paul, *Fighting the Nazis* (New York: Enigma Books, 2003)

Philby, Kim, *My Silent War* (London: MacGibbon and Kee Ltd., 1968)

Popov, Dusko, *Spy Counter Spy* (London: Weidenfeld and Nicolson, 1974)

Pujol, Juan, (with Nigel West), *Garbo* (London: Weidenfeld and Nicolson, 1985)

Ramsey, Winston G. (ed.), *German Spies in Britain* (After the Battle, Number 11, 1976)

Reit, Seymour, *Masquerade: The Amazing Camouflage Deceptions of World War II* (London: Hale, 1979)

Ritter, Nikolaus, *Deckname Dr. Rantzau: Die Aufzeichnungen des Nikolaus Ritter, Offizier im Geheimen Nachrichtendienst* (Hamburg: Hoffmann and Campe, 1972)

Scotland, Alexander, *The London Cage* (London: Evans Bros, 1957)

Sergueiev, Lily, *Secret Service Rendered* (London: Kimber, 1968)

Shirer, William, *The Rise and Fall of the Third Reich* (London: Secker and Warburg, 1960)

Simpson, A. W. B., *In the Highest Degree Odious* (Oxford: Clarendon Press, 1994)

Stephens, Robin (edited by Oliver Hoare), *Camp 020: MI5 and the Nazi Spies: The Official History of MI5's Wartime Interrogation Centre* (Richmond: Public Record Office, 2000)

Strong, Sir Kenneth, *Intelligence at the Top* (London: Cassell, 1968)

Sykes, Steven, *Deceivers Ever: Memoirs of a Camouflage Officer* (Speldhurst: Spellmount, 1990)

Talwar, Bhagat Ram, *The Talwars of Pathan Land and Subhas Chandra's Great Escape* (New Delhi: People's Pub. House, 1976)

Trevelyan, Julian, *Indigo Days* (London: MacGibbon and Kee, 1957)

West, Nigel, *The Crown Jewels: The British Secrets at the Heart of the KGB Archives* (London: HarperCollins, 1998)

West, Nigel (ed.), *The Liddell Diaries*, 2 vols (London: Routledge, 2005)

West, Nigel, *MI5: British Security Service Operations 1909–1945* (London: Bodley Head, 1981)

Wheatley, Dennis, *The Deception Planners* (London: Hutchinson, 1980)

Wheatley, Dennis, *Stranger than Fiction* (London: Hutchinson, 1959)

White, John Baker, *The Big Lie* (London: Evans, 1955)

Wighton, Charles and Peis, Gunter, *They Spied on England: Based on the German Secret Service War Diary of General Lahousen* (London: Odhams, 1958)

Wingate, Ronald, *Not in the Limelight* (London: Hutchinson, 1959)

Winterbotham, F. W., *The Ultra Secret* (London: Weidenfeld and Nicolson, 1974)

Wintle, Alfred Daniel, *The Last Englishman* (London: Michael Joseph, 1968)

Young, Martin and Stamp, Robbie, *Trojan Horses: Deception Operations in the Second World War* (London: Bodley Head, 1989)

ENDNOTES

PREFACE

1. Carl von Clausewitz, *On War* (Harmondsworth: Penguin Books Ltd, 1968), p.274.

CHAPTER 1: *SNOW*

1. *Snow*'s physical characteristics are known from KV 2/444.
2. As we will see, there is often something apposite in the codenames assigned to individuals by the security services. Owens was codenamed *Snow* because it was a part anagram of his name.
3. Ladislas Farago, *The Game of the Foxes* (London: Hodder and Stoughton, 1971), p.153.
4. Ibid, p.40.
5. Charles Wighton and Gunter Peis, *They Spied on England: Based on the German Secret Service War Diary of General Lahousen* (London: Odhams, 1958), p.104.
6. J. C. Masterman, *The Double-Cross System in the War of 1939–1945* (New Haven and London: Yale University Press, 1972), p.37.
7. Wighton and Peis, *They Spied on England*, p.105.
8. F. H. Hinsley et al., *British Intelligence in the Second World War* (London: HMSO, 1979–90), vol.4, p.41.
9. Nikolaus Ritter, *Deckname Dr. Rantzau: Die Aufzeichnungen des Nikolaus Ritter, Offizier im Geheimen Nachrichtendienst* (Hamburg: Hoffmann and Campe, 1972), p.150.
10. Nigel West, *MI5: British Security Service Operations 1909–1945* (London: Bodley Head, 1981), pp.137–40.
11. For a full study of 18(b) see A. W. B. Simpson's *In the Highest Degree Odious* (Oxford: Clarendon Press, 1994).
12. Ben Macintyre, *Agent Zigzag* (London: Bloomsbury, 2007), p.68.
13. Tom Bower, *The Perfect English Spy* (London: Heinemann, 1995), p.33. Bower reports the pub as being in Jermyn St, but Robertson's brother-in-law through his second marriage gives the location as the Brompton Road. There are in fact a number of pubs by that name in London.
14. The triple agent theme is put forward in Ladislas Farago's *The Game of the Foxes*. He asserts that by giving himself up to the British authorities, Owens in effect gambled possession of his transmitter in order to win his freedom and allow him to carry on working for the Germans. Although his subsequent actions do lend themselves to the hypothesis that Owens was a loyal German spy, there is still a lingering possibility that Owens worked only for himself in order to realize financial rewards – which were considerable. J. C. Masterman described Owens as having 'an enormous salary – a salary that would make a cabinet minister's salary look stupid' (N/A file: KV 2/450).
15. In his book *The Double-Cross System*, Masterman describes the first message sent by *Snow* as the true beginning of the double cross system. He calls the Welshman

the *fons et origo* (source and origin) of all MI5's double agent activities for the war (p.36).

16. Hinsley, *British Intelligence*, vol.1, p.311. Both Farago and Masterman describe this man as a Voluntary Interceptor (VI) – a radio ham monitoring the airwaves for enemy transmissions.

17. Farago, *The Game of the Foxes*, p.180.

18. Nigel West, *The Liddell Diaries*, vol.1 (London: Routledge, 2005), p.39. In terms of purchasing power, £470 in 1939 would be worth slightly under £20,000 today.

19. West, *MI5*, p.142; Lily's detention order is found in KV 2/446.

20. West, *The Liddell Diaries*, vol.1, p.39.

21. Ibid, p.58.

22. See KV 2/706.

23. See KV 2/454.

24. West, *The Liddell Diaries*, vol.1, p.40.

25. Hinsley, *British Intelligence*, vol.4, p.44 and pp.311–12; Ewen Montagu, *Beyond Top Secret U* (London: P. Davies, 1977), p.34.

26. KV 4/444–53.

27. Masterman, *The Double-Cross System*, pp.46–47. The name Bernie Kiener is given by Guy Liddell (West, *The Liddell Diaries*, vol.1, p.75). Previously *Rainbow* was identified by Nigel West as a Portuguese named Pierce.

28. West, *The Liddell Diaries*, vol.1, p.80.

29. Hinsley, *British Intelligence*, vol.4, p.88.

30. West, *The Liddell Diaries*, vol.1, pp.80–81.

31. Joan Miller, *One Girl's War* (Brandon: Dingle, 1986), p.82.

32. West, *MI5,* pp.224–25, and West, *The Liddell Diaries*, vol.1, p.77.

33. *The New Yorker Book of War Pieces – London 1939 to Hiroshima 1945* (New York: Reynal & Hitchcock, 1947), p.36.

34. Kim Philby, *My Silent War* (London: Macgibbon and Kee Ltd, 1968), p.51; Joan Miller, *One Girl's War*, p.107.

CHAPTER 2: THE INVASION SPIES

1. William Shirer, *The Rise and Fall of the Third Reich* (London: Secker and Warburg, 1960), p.755.

2. Denis Sefton Delmer, *Black Boomerang* (London: Secker and Warburg, 1962), pp.10–11.

3. Winston S. Churchill, *The Second World War*, vol.2 (London: Cassell and Co Ltd, 1949), p.230.

4. For the rest of this and other of Churchill's speeches visit www.churchill-society-london.org.uk.

5. Ladislas Farago, *The Game of the Foxes* (London: Hodder and Stoughton, 1971), p.235.

6. F. H. Hinsley et al., *British Intelligence in the Second World War* (London: HMSO, 1979–90), vol.4, p.321.

7. Farago, *The Game of the Foxes*, p.240.

8. Robin Stephens (edited by Oliver Hoare), *Camp 020: MI5 and the Nazi Spies: the Official History of MI5's Wartime Interrogation Centre* (Richmond: Public Record Office, 2000), p.134. Stephens' case history says the man was an air raid warden; Nigel West's *MI5: British Security Service Operations 1909–1945* (London: Bodley Head, 1981) says the man was an RAF officer living nearby.

9. Coded messages from Winston G. Ramsey (ed.), *German Spies in Britain* (After the Battle, number 11, 1976), p.15.

10. Stephens, *Camp 020*, p.15.

11. 'Alarming' description by Joan Miller, *One Girl's War* (Brandon: Dingle, 1986), p.82. Second quote from Kim Philby, *My Silent War* (London: Macgibbon and Kee Ltd, 1968), p.35.

12. Stephens, *Camp 020*, p.109.

13. Ibid, p.118.

14. In David Kahn, *Hitler's Spies* (London: Hodder and Stoughton, 1978), and other accounts of the Abwehr, Schmidt was known to the Abwehr as Hans Hansen. To avoid confusion we have used the name familiar to the British security services. Equally, Caroli is sometimes given to be a Finn – he was known to be a Swede by MI5. Caroli is also sometimes known as Jorgen Bjoernson or Axel Hilberg in other works.

15. J. C. Masterman, *The Double-Cross System in the War of 1939–1945* (New Haven and London: Yale University Press, 1972), p.49.

16. Nigel West, *The Liddell Diaries*, vol.1 (London: Routledge, 2005), pp.92–93.

17. Ibid, p.98.

18. See entry of 13 September, KV 4/186 Liddell Diary March–October 1940.

19. Stephens, *Camp 020*, p.140 and West, *The Liddell Diaries*, vol.1, p.122. It is often believed that Schmidt took a long time to break down and only agreed to work as a double cross agent after almost two weeks' interrogation. However, the Liddell diaries and Stephen's 020 report clearly indicate the chronology suggested here.

20. Stephens, *Camp 020*, p.140 and West, *The Liddell Diaries*, vol.1, p.98.

21. Ian Cobain, 'The Secrets of the London Cage', (*The Guardian*, 12 November 2005). Scotland had served in the German Army in Africa before World War I, and had then been an interrogator during that conflict. He caused mayhem when he submitted his memoirs to be censored by the War Office in June 1950. Officials told Scotland to lock the manuscript away and threatened him with prosecution under the Official Secrets Act if he did not. A censored version of the book was released in 1957.

22. 24 September KV 4/186 Liddell Diary March–October 1940.

23. Stephens, *Camp 020*, pp.149–50.

CHAPTER 3: BURNING LIES

1. F. H. Hinsley et al., *British Intelligence in the Second World War* (London: HMSO, 1979–90), vol.4, p.67.

2. 23 September, KV 4/186 Liddell Diary March–October 1940.

3. Ewen Montagu, *Beyond Top Secret U* (London: P. Davies, 1977), p.40.

4. Dennis Wheatley, *The Deception Planners* (London: Hutchinson, 1980), p.18.

5. 1 October 1940, KV 4/186 Liddell Diary March–October 1940.

6. The speed of eight knots was suggested by an SIS report. 23 September 1940, KV 4/186 Liddell Diary March–October 1940. In fact it was probably half that at best.

7. Charles G. Cruickshank, *Deception in World War II* (New York: Oxford University Press, 1979), p.15.

8. David Garnett, *The Secret History of PWE: The Political Warfare Executive 1939–1945* (London: St Ermin's, 2002), pp.214–15.

9. John Baker White, *The Big Lie* (London: Evans, 1955), p.15.

10. Winston S. Churchill, *The Second World War,* vol.2 (London: Cassell and Co Ltd, 1949), p.275.

11. Ibid, p.275.

12. Denis Sefton Delmer, *Black Boomerang* (London: Secker and Warburg, 1962), pp.15–16.

13. Unless marked otherwise, for this section see Colin Dobinson, *Fields of Deception* (London: Methuen, 2000).

14. Seymour Reit, *Masquerade: The Amazing Camouflage Deceptions of World War II* (London: Hale, 1979), p.56.

15. Ibid, p.54.

CHAPTER 4: THE SYSTEM

1. Joan Miller, *One Girl's War* (Brandon: Dingle, 1986), pp.86–88.

2. Michael Howard, *British Intelligence in the Second World War,* vol.5, *Strategic Deception* (London: HMSO, 1990), p.17.

3. KV/4/187 Liddell Diary.

4. J.C. Masterman, *On the Chariot Wheel* (London: Oxford University Press, 1975), p.209 and the Liddell Diary (2 December 1940) KV/4/187.

5. Tom Bower, *The Perfect English Spy* (London: Heinemann, 1995), p.20.

6. Ibid, p.27.

7. Masterman, *On the Chariot Wheel*, p.221.

8. Kim Philby was less kind, describing White as 'a nice and modest man' but who had 'a tendency to agree with the last person he spoke to'. To MI5's Joan Miller, Dick White came across as a weak individual, although she wondered if that was not a deliberate ruse to look ineffectual on his part. (Philby, *My Silent War* (London: MacGibbon and Kee Ltd, 1968), p.51; Joan Miller, *One Girl's War*, p.107).

9. Bower, *The Perfect English Spy*, p.37.

10. Masterman, *The Double-Cross System in the War of 1939–1945* (New Haven and London: Yale University Press, 1972), p.36.

11. Mure had a problem with what he called 'private armies' and with Masterman in particular for publishing his book *The Double-Cross System* although it was against the government's wishes. David Mure, *Master of Deception* (London: Kimber, 1980), pp.181–82.

12. Bower, *The Perfect English Spy*, p.44.

13. Ewen Montagu, *Beyond Top Secret U* (London: P. Davies, 1977), p.48.

14. Masterman, *On the Chariot Wheel*, p.223.

15. Montagu, *Beyond Top Secret U*, pp.48–49.

16. The filmmaker Ivor Montagu had set up the International Table Tennis Federation in 1926 and served as its first president until 1967. He also became a member of the Central Committee of the Communist Party in 1938 and maintained a close link with the Soviet embassy. During the war he was a journalist on the *Daily Worker* newspaper.

17. See Howard, *Strategic Deception*, p.9.

18. KV/47/187. Liddell was sorry to see Beaumont-Nesbitt go as he had always been very helpful to MI5.

19. F. H. Hinsley et al., *British Intelligence in the Second World War* (London: HMSO, 1979–90), vol.4, p.100.

20. Hinsley, *British Intelligence in the Second World War*, vol.4, p.100.

21. Ibid, pp.96–97.

22. Stephens, *Camp 020*, p.46.

23. Howard, *Strategic Deception*, p.16; Liddell Diary 3 February 1941 (KV/4/187); also see Philby, *My Silent War*, for a good account of the inter-departmental wrangling over decrypts.

CHAPTER 5: *SNOW* FALLS

1. J. C. Masterman, *The Double-Cross System in the War of 1939–1945* (New Haven and London: Yale University Press, 1972), p.3.

2. Ladislas Farago, *The Game of the Foxes* (London: Hodder and Stoughton, 1971), p.266. His identity was not recorded.

3. Meems' file at the National Archives is KV 2/2428.

4. Liddell quotes Paulton's report in his diary entry for 13 January 1941 (KV/4/187).

5. Masterman, *The Double-Cross System*, p.52 and Joan Miller, *One Girl's War* (Brandon: Dingle, 1986), p.91.

6. *Celery* KV 2/674.

7. Ibid.

8. Ibid.

9. Sir Ronald Wingate, *Not in the Limelight* (London: Hutchinson & Co., 1959).

10. Remarkably this photo and note survived and are still in *Celery*'s case file at the National Archives, KV 2/674.

11. Liddell Diary, April 10 (KV/4/187).

12. KV 2/451.

13. Charles Wighton and Gunter Peis, *They Spied on England: Based on the German Secret Service War Diary of General Lahousen* (London: Odhams, 1958), pp.101–02.

14. Ibid, pp.108–09.

15. Nikolaus Ritter, *Deckname Dr. Rantzau: Die Aufzeichnungen des Nikolaus Ritter, Offizier*

im Geheimen Nachrichtendienst (Hamburg: Hoffmann and Campe, 1972), p.254.

16.   Ibid, p.212.

17.   Ibid, p.259.

18.   Ibid, p.290.

19.   Ibid, p.320.

CHAPTER 6: THE 'DICKY' PERIOD

1   Jan Moen, *John Moe: Double Agent* (Edinburgh: Mainstream, 1986), p.163–66.

2.   Ibid, p.186.

3.   Ibid, p.188.

4.   Robin Stephens (edited by Oliver Hoare), *Camp 020: MI5 and the Nazi Spies: the Official History of MI5's Wartime Interrogation Centre* (Richmond: Public Record Office, 2000), p.162.

5.   Liddell Diary, 10 April (KV/4/187).

6.   Ladislas Farago, *The Game of the Foxes* (London: Hodder and Stoughton, 1971), p.260.

7.   Ibid, p.265.

8.   KV 4/64.

9.   Farago, *The Game of the Foxes*, p.265.

10.   Ewen Montagu, *Beyond Top Secret U* (London: P. Davies, 1977), pp.58–59.

11.   Russell Miller, *Codename Tricycle: The True Story of the Second World War's Most Extraordinary Double Agent* (London: Secker and Warburg, 2004), p.75.

12.   Joan Miller, *One Girl's War* (Brandon: Dingle, 1986), p.89.

13.   Miller, *Codename Tricycle*, p.88.

14.   If the Twenty Committee was privy to the information that Japan was planning to attack Pearl Harbor one might expect to find mention of this in the committee's minutes after the attack. The minutes for that period make no mention of this; however, some of the original pages had been substituted for re-typed ones prior to their public release.

15.   See KV 4/190.

16.   Miller, *Codename Tricycle*, p.138.

CHAPTER 7: SPANISH INTRIGUES

1.   Robin Stephens (edited by Oliver Hoare), *Camp 020: MI5 and the Nazi Spies: the Official History of MI5's Wartime Interrogation Centre* (Richmond: Public Record Office, 2000), pp.178–79; Michael Howard, *British Intelligence in the Second World War,* vol.5, *Strategic Deception* (London: HMSO, 1990), p.104.

2.   Nigel West, *The Liddell Diaries*, vol.1 (London: Routledge, 2005), p.189.

3.   Kim Philby, *My Silent War* (London: Macgibbon and Kee Ltd, 1968), pp.37–38.

4.   Ibid, p.35.

5.   West, *The Liddell Diaries*, vol.1, p.223.

6.   Stephens, *Camp 020*, pp.179–80.

7.   J. C. Masterman, *The Double-Cross System in the War of 1939–1945* (New Haven

8. KV 4/64.

9. Juan Pujol (with Nigel West), *Garbo* (London: Weidenfeld and Nicolson, 1985), p.39.

10. In Pujol's account he says he went to the embassy himself. This account opts for the version written at the end of the war by Tomás Harris, Pujol's case officer.

11. Ewen Montagu, *Beyond Top Secret U* (London: P. Davies, 1977), p.114.

12. Tomás Harris (intro. by Mark Seaman), *Garbo – the Spy Who Saved D-Day* (Richmond: Public Record Office, 2000), pp.58–59.

13. West, *The Liddell Diaries*, vol.1, p.228.

14. Ibid, p.229.

15. KV 4/64.

16. Cyril Mills was the son of Bertram Mills, the premier circus owner in Britain.

17. Harris had a Spanish mother and a British father. He was a gifted artist and art dealer and was introduced into secret service by his friendship with the notorious 'Cambridge spies' Kim Philby, Guy Burgess and Anthony Blunt.

CHAPTER 8: 'A' FORCE

1. John Roy Carlson (pen name of the Armenian-American Arthur A. Derounian), *Cairo to Damascus* (New York: Alfred A. Knopf, 1951), p.114.

2. F. H. Hinsley et al., *British Intelligence in the Second World War* (London: HMSO, 1979–90), vol.1, pp.191–95.

3. Hinsley, *British Intelligence in the Second World War*, vol.4, p.150.

4. Ibid, p.162.

5. Ronald Lewin, *The Chief: Field Marshal Lord Wavell: Commander-in-Chief and Viceroy 1939–1947* (London: Hutchinson, 1980), p.53.

6   Michael Howard, *British Intelligence in the Second World War,* vol.5, *Strategic Deception* (London: HMSO, 1990), p.33.

7. Dudley Clarke, *Seven Assignments* (London: Jonathan Cape, 1948), p.7.

8. Ibid, p.219.

9. David Mure, *Practise to Deceive* (London: Kimber, 1977), pp.21–22.

10. Howard, *Strategic Deception*, p.35.

11. David Mure says one of A Force's first operations was to support an attack by the Long Range Desert Group on elite Italian Blackshirts at the Siwa Oasis. He says that dummy parachutists were dropped by aircraft with fire crackers round their waists to simulate Tommy-gun fire. Mure says this operation took place before the Sidi Barrani operation, which makes it before A Force's formation. However, it is possible this operation was undertaken by individuals that went on to serve A Force (Mure, *Practise to Deceive*, pp.21–22).

12. Howard, *Strategic Deception*, p.35.

13. Mure gives *Cheese* the Abwehr codename *Orlando* in *Practise to Deceive* and then refers to him as *Moses* in *Master of Deception*.

14. CAB 154/100 Wingate report, vol.1, p.30.

15. Mure initially stated that Levi used a secret Jewish network to facilitate his passage to Egypt. In *Master of Deception* he corrected himself, and attributed that link to another agent.

16. Howard, *Strategic Deception*, p.36.

17. Mure, *Master of Deception* (London: Kimber, 1980), p.67.

18. Ibid, p.70.

19. Hinsley, *British Intelligence in the Second World War*, vol.4, p.166.

20. CAB 154/100 Wingate report, vol.1, p.45.

21. Nigel West, *The Liddell Diaries*, vol.1 (London: Routledge, 2005), pp.180–81.

22. Ewen Montagu, *Beyond Top Secret U* (London: P. Davies, 1977), pp.110–11.

23. West, *The Liddell Diaries*, vol.1, p.181.

24. Liddell Diary, 11 November 1941 (KV 4/88).

25. CHAR 20/25 CIGS to Prime Minister 31.10.41 (Churchill Archives Centre, Churchill College, Cambridge).

26. See the Churchill Papers: CHAR 20/25 (Churchill Archives Centre, Churchill College, Cambridge).

27. West, *The Liddell Diaries*, vol.1, p.185.

28. Nigel West, *The Crown Jewels: The British Secrets at the Heart of the KGB Archives* (London: HarperCollins, 1998), p.307–09.

CHAPTER 9: THE CONTROLLING OFFICER

1. These papers were published after the war in Dennis Wheatley's book *Stranger than Fiction* (London: Hutchinson, 1959).

2. Dennis Wheatley, *The Deception Planners* (London: Hutchinson, 1980), p.12.

3. Duff Hart-Davis, *Peter Fleming* (London: Jonathan Cape Ltd, 1974), pp.241–42.

4. Ronald Lewin, *The Chief: Field Marshall Lord Wavell: Commander-in-Chief and Viceroy 1939–1947* (London: Hutchinson, 1980), pp.196–97.

5. J. C. Masterman, *The Double-Cross System in the War of 1939–1945* (New Haven and London: Yale University Press, 1972), p.107.

6. Quoted by Wheatley, *The Deception Planners*, p.80.

7. Michael Howard, *British Intelligence in the Second World War*, vol.5, *Strategic Deception* (London: HMSO, 1990), p.243.

8. 'Unreal' was the description used by Masterman, *The Double-Cross System*, p.106.

9. Howard, *Strategic Deception*, pp.28–29.

10. Nigel West, *The Liddell Diaries*, vol.1 (London: Routledge, 2005), pp.307–08.

11. F. H. Hinsley et al., *British Intelligence in the Second World War* (London: HMSO, 1979–90), vol.4, p.129.

12. Ewen Montagu, *Beyond Top Secret U* (London: P. Davies, 1977), p.138.

13. Martin Young and Robbie Stamp, *Trojan Horses: Deception Operations in the Second World War* (London: Bodley Head, 1989), p.177.

14. Tomás Harris (intro. by Mark Seaman), *Garbo – The Spy Who Saved D-Day* (Richmond: Public Record Office, 2000), p.90.

15. Howard, *Strategic Deception,* p.54–58.
16. Harris, *Garbo,* p.103.
17. Ibid, p.102.
18. Ronald Wingate, *Not in the Limelight* (London: Hutchinson, 1959), pp.198–99.

CHAPTER 10: EL ALAMEIN

1. Roy R. Behrens, 'Art, culture and camouflage', from *Tate etc: Visiting and Revisiting Art, etcetera* (Issue 4, Summer 2005).
2. See www.maskelynemagic.com for a fuller examination of the magician's role.
3. Julian Trevelyan, *Indigo Days* (London: MacGibbon and Kee, 1957), p.152.
4. Geoffrey Barkas, *The Camouflage Story* (London: Cassell, 1952) pp.181–82.
5. CAB 154/100, Wingate narrative, vol.1, p.63.
6. Anthony Cave Brown, *Bodyguard of Lies* (London: W. H. Allen, 1975), p.101.
7. See Hans-Otto Behrendt, *Rommel's Intelligence in the Desert Campaign: 1941–1943* (London: Kimber, 1985).
8. John Roy Carlson, *Cairo to Damascus* (New York: Alfred A. Knopf, 1951), p.113.
9. F. H. Hinsley et al., *British Intelligence in the Second World War* (London: HMSO, 1979–90), vol.4, p.166.
10. David Mure, *Master of Deception* (London: Kimber, 1980), p.107.
11. Earl Alexander of Tunis, *The Alexander Memoirs 1940–1945* (London: Cassell, 1962), p.10.
12. Martin Young and Robbie Stamp, *Trojan Horses: Deception Operations in the Second World War* (London: Bodley Head, 1989), p.61.
13. Alexander's despatch 'The African Campaign from El Alamein To Tunis' was printed as a supplement to *The London Gazette* on 5 February 1948 (London: Stationery Office, 1948).
14. For doubts see also Hinsley, *British Intelligence in the Second World War*, vol.2, p.416.
15. Mure, *Master of Deception*, p.91.
16. Michael Howard, *British Intelligence in the Second World War,* vol.5, *Strategic Deception* (London: HMSO, 1990), pp.65–66.
17. Montgomery of Alamein, *Memoirs* (London: Collins, 1958), p.121.
18. Young and Stamp, *Trojan Horses*, p.71.
19. Barkas, *The Camouflage Story*, p.191.
20. Letter to Sykes of 7 November 1942, in Steven Sykes, *Deceivers Ever* (Speldhurst: Spellmount, 1990), p.95.
21. Montgomery, *Memoirs*, p.122.

CHAPTER 11: THE DEVELOPMENT OF AGENT CASES

1. David Mure, *Practise to Deceive* (London: Kimber, 1977), p.31 and Michael Howard, *British Intelligence in the Second World War,* vol.5, *Strategic Deception* (London: HMSO, 1990), p.68.
2. Mure, *Practise to Deceive*, p.70. Mure's version of this phrase was coarser.
3. Ibid, p.101.

4. F. H. Hinsley et al., *British Intelligence in the Second World War* (London: HMSO, 1979–90), vol. 4, pp.229–30.
5. Nigel West, *The Liddell Diaries*, vol.2 (London: Routledge, 2005), p.103 (19 August 1943).
6. Duff Hart-Davis, *Peter Fleming* (London: Jonathan Cape Ltd, 1974), p.280.
7. Paul Paillole, *Fighting the Nazis* (New York: Enigma Books, 2003), p.113.
8. Ibid, p.391.
9. Anon, 'Les Services Spéciaux de la Défense Nationale pendant la guerre 1939–1945: Le T.R. africain participe à la victoire de Tunisie' (see the Amicale des Anciens des Services Spéciaux de la Défense Nationale (France), www.aassdn.org).
10. KV 2/458.
11. KV 2/458.
12. See Ben Macintyre, *Agent Zigzag* (London: Bloomsbury, 2007).
13. KV 4/191.

CHAPTER 12: *MINCEMEAT*

1. Ewen Montagu, *Beyond Top Secret U* (London: P. Davies, 1977), p.143.
2. F. H. Hinsley et al., *British Intelligence in the Second World War* (London: HMSO, 1979–90), vol.3, p.77.
3. Paul Paillole, *Fighting the Nazis* (New York: Enigma Books, 2003), p.393.
4. CAB 154/100, Wingate report, vol.1, p.32, and *Gilbert* dossier WO 169/24898.
5. Ewen Montagu, *The Man Who Never Was* (London, Evans Bros., 1953), p.22.
6. Montagu, *Beyond Top Secret U*, p.146.
7. J. C. Masterman, *The Double-Cross System in the War of 1939–1945* (New Haven and London: Yale University Press, 1972), p.137.
8. Some believe the corpse was exchanged with a 'fresher' one at the last minute. John Melville, aged 37, had been a coder on the aircraft carrier HMS *Dasher* and had been killed when it blew up in the Clyde Estuary on 27 March 1943. See Ben Fenton, 'Tracking down a most unlikely hero' (*Daily Telegraph*, 28 October 1996).
9. Michael Howard, *British Intelligence in the Second World War,* vol.5, *Strategic Deception* (London: HMSO, 1990), p.91.
10. Hinsley, *British Intelligence in the Second World War*, vol.3, p.78.
11. Louis Lochner (ed. & trans.), *The Goebbels Diaries* (London: Hamish Hamilton, 1948), p.312.

CHAPTER 13: LONDON CALLING

1. See Michael Howard, *British Intelligence in the Second World War,* vol.5, *Strategic Deception* (London: HMSO, 1990) and CAB 154/100, Wingate report, pp.37–38.
2. Nigel West, *The Liddell Diaries*, vol.2 (London: Routledge, 2005), p.269.
3. Paul Paillole, *Fighting the Nazis* (New York: Enigma Books, 2003), pp.396–97.
4. David Garnett, *The Secret History of PWE: The Political Warfare Executive 1939–1945* (London: St Ermin's, 2002), pp.196–97.
5. Unless specified otherwise, this account relies on Denis Sefton Delmer's excellent autobiography *Black Boomerang* (London: Secker and Warburg, 1962).

6.   Garnett, *The Secret History of PWE*, p.41.
7.   Report quoted by Garnett, *The Secret History of PWE*, p.45.
8.   Ibid, pp.44–45.
9.   Lee Richards, 'Sir Stafford Cripps and the German Admiral's Orgy – The Gustav Siegfried Eins Controversy' (article for Psywar.org). Much more information on PWE propaganda and subversion campaigns can be found on this excellent website.
10. R.V. Jones, *Most Secret War* (London: Hamilton, 1978), p.387.
11. Jones knew 'George' was heavily involved with *Mincemeat* and rules out Ewen Montagu by naming the latter in the same piece. Also, coincidentally or not, in Montagu's *The Man Who Never Was* (London: Evan Bros, 1953), Cholmondeley's character was named 'George'.
12. Jones, *Most Secret War*, pp.215–22.

CHAPTER 14: THE *FORTITUDE* PLAN

1.   Roger Hesketh, *Fortitude: The D-Day Deception Campaign* (London: St Ermin's, 1999), p.24.
2.   Sir Frederick Morgan, *Overture to Overlord* (Hodder and Stoughton Ltd, 1950), p.91.
3.   Ibid, p.104.
4.   Michael Howard, *British Intelligence in the Second World War*, vol.5, *Strategic Deception* (London: HMSO, 1990), p.80.
5.   For these factors see Morgan, *Overture to Overlord*, pp.139–40.
6.   Ronald Wingate, *Not in the Limelight* (London: Hutchinson, 1959), p.209.
7.   Hesketh, *Fortitude*, p.11n.
8.   David Mure, *Master of Deception* (London: Kimber, 1980), pp.9–10 and p.242.
9.   Dennis Wheatley, *The Deception Planners* (London: Hutchinson, 1980), p.220.
10. Ibid, p.177.
11. Charles G. Cruickshank, *Deception in World War II* (New York: Oxford University Press, 1979), p.112.
12. When Montgomery came back from Italy the deception planners advised him to keep a low profile, not to be seen in uniform and to take a house at the edge of town. Instead he booked a suite at Claridges and on his first night back turned up at the Palladium theatre in full uniform, whereupon he received a five-minute ovation from his admiring public (Dennis Wheatley, *Stranger than Fiction* London: Hutchinson, 1959), p.174).

CHAPTER 15: BY SPECIAL MEANS

1.   F. H. Hinsley et al., *British Intelligence in the Second World War* (London: HMSO, 1979–90), vol.4, p.237.
2.   J. C. Masterman, *The Double-Cross System in the War of 1939–1945* (New Haven and London: Yale University Press, 1972), p.128.
3.   Nigel West, *The Liddell Diaries*, vol.2 (London: Routledge, 2005), p.206.
4.   Hinsley, *British Intelligence in the Second World War*, vol.4, p.278; Roger Hesketh, *Fortitude: The D-Day Deception Campaign* (London: St Ermin's, 1999), p.206; Robin Stephens (edited by Oliver Hoare), *Camp 020: MI5 and the Nazi Spies: the*

ENDNOTES

Official History of MI5's Wartime Interrogation Centre (Richmond: Public Record Office, 2000), p.354.

5. West, *The Liddell Diaries*, vol.2, p.161.
6. Lily Sergueiev, *Secret Service Rendered* (London: Kimber, 1968), p.141. In the English translation of the book, Frisson is called 'Babs'.
7. Masterman, *The Double-Cross System*, pp.159–60.
8. Hinsley, *British Intelligence in the Second World War*, vol.4, p.239.
9. Hesketh, *Fortitude,* pp.95–96.
10. Ibid, pp.126–30.

CHAPTER 16: VINDICATION

1. F. H. Hinsley et al, *British Intelligence in the Second World War* (London: HMSO, 1979–90), vol.3, p.80.
2. Nigel West, *The Liddell Diaries*, vol.2 (London: Routledge, 2005), pp.204–05.
3. As Hesketh was in charge of the sub-section for Special Means in Ops.B that points to himself. However, he elsewhere writes that he only once met *Garbo* during the war and that was by accidentally bumping into him with Tommy Harris in Jermyn Street.
4. Martin Young and Robbie Stamp, *Trojan Horses: Deception Operations in the Second World War* (London: Bodley Head, 1989), pp.78–81.
5. David Garnett, *The Secret History of PWE: The Political Warfare Executive 1939–1945* (London: St Ermin's, 2002), p.410.
6. Roger Hesketh, *Fortitude: The D-Day Deception Campaign* (London: St Ermin's, 1999), p.102.
7. Tomás Harris (intro. by Mark Seaman), *Garbo – The Spy Who Saved D-Day* (Richmond: Public Record Office, 2000), p.183.
8. Denis Sefton Delmer, *The Counterfeit Spy* (London: Hutchinson, 1971), p.164.
9. Harris, *Garbo*, p.204.
10. Delmer, *The Counterfeit Spy*, p.182.
11. Hesketh, *Fortitude*, p.207.
12. Ibid, p.210.
13. Sir Kenneth Strong, *Intelligence at the Top* (London: Cassell, 1968), pp.141–42.
14. Dwight D. Eisenhower, *Crusade in Europe* (London: William Heinemann Ltd, 1948), p.316.
15. Dennis Wheatley, *The Deception Planners* (London: Hutchinson, 1980), p.212.
16. J. C. Masterman, *The Double-Cross System in the War of 1939–1945* (New Haven and London: Yale University Press, 1972), p.179.
17. Harris, *Garbo*, pp.250–51.
18. Michael Howard, *British Intelligence in the Second World War,* vol.5, *Strategic Deception* (London: HMSO, 1990), pp.169–72.
19. Howard, *Strategic Deception*, p.178.
20. R.V. Jones, *Most Secret War* (London: Hamilton, 1978), p.422.
21. Ibid, p.423.

CHAPTER 17: MEDITERRANEAN SWANSONG

1. Charles G. Cruickshank, *Deception in World War II* (New York: Oxford University Press, 1979), p.147.
2. David Mure, *Practise to Deceive* (London: Kimber, 1977), p.236.
3. Michael Howard, *British Intelligence in the Second World War,* vol.5, *Strategic Deception* (London: HMSO, 1990), pp.137–38.
4. J. C. Masterman, *The Double-Cross System in the War of 1939–1945* (New Haven and London: Yale University Press, 1972), p.161.
5. Roger Hesketh, *Fortitude: The D-Day Deception Campaign* (London: St Ermin's, 1999), p.105.
6. Masterman, *The Double-Cross System*, p.162.
7. Nigel West, *The Liddell Diaries*, vol.2 (London: Routledge, 2005), p.208.
8. Dennis Wheatley, *The Deception Planners* (London: Hutchinson, 1980), p.190.
9. West, *The Liddell Diaries*, vol.2, p.202.
10. David Mure, *Master of Deception* (London: Kimber, 1980), p.252.
11. West, *The Liddell Diaries*, vol.2, p.202.
12. Hesketh, *Fortitude*, p.189.
13. Wheatley, *The Deception Planners*, p.168.
14. Denis Sefton Delmer, *The Counterfeit Spy* (London: Hutchinson, 1971), p.126.
15. Howard, *British Intelligence in the Second World War*, p.112.
16. Paul Paillole, *Fighting the Nazis* (New York: Enigma Books, 2003), p.396.
17. West, *The Liddell Diaries*, vol.2, p.225.
18. It has long been believed that Churchill was behind this change of name. His opposition to the landing in the south of France is well documented, as was Eisenhower's insistence that it went ahead. When Churchill backed down, it is said he changed the name of the operation to *Dragoon*, implying he had been 'dragooned' into agreeing to it.

CHAPTER 18: THE FINAL DECEITS

1. Michael Howard, *British Intelligence in the Second World War,* vol.5, *Strategic Deception* (London: HMSO, 1990), p.192.
2. Howard, *Strategic Deception,* p.192.
3. Nigel West, *The Liddell Diaries*, vol.2 (London: Routledge, 2005), p.166.
4. Ibid, p.222.
5. Ewen Montagu, *Beyond Top Secret U* (London: P. Davies, 1977), p.160.
6. J. C. Masterman, *The Double-Cross System in the War of 1939–1945* (New Haven and London: Yale University Press, 1972), p.161.
7. Ibid, p.181.
8. Howard, *Strategic Deception*, p.183.
9. Montagu, *Beyond Top Secret U*, p.176.

EPILOGUE

1. J. C. Masterman, *The Double-Cross System in the War of 1939–1945* (New Haven and London: Yale University Press, 1972), pp.162–63.
2. Tomás Harris (intro. by Mark Seaman), *Garbo – The Spy Who Saved D-Day* (Richmond: Public Record Office, 2000), p.288.

INDEX

Figures in **bold** refer to illustrations.

INDEX

INDEX